高等院校双语示范教材·法学系列

金融法（双语版）

Financial Law

袁达松　编著

对外经济贸易大学出版社
中国·北京

图书在版编目（CIP）数据

金融法：双语版 / 袁达松编著. —北京：对外经济贸易大学出版社，2012
高等院校双语示范教材. 法学系列
ISBN 978-7-5663-0302-8

Ⅰ. ①金… Ⅱ. ①袁… Ⅲ. ①金融法－双语教学－高等学校－教材 Ⅳ. ①D912.28

中国版本图书馆 CIP 数据核字（2012）第 043905 号

金融法（双语版）

Financial Law

袁达松 **编著**

责任编辑：汪友年

对外经济贸易大学出版社
北京市朝阳区惠新东街 10 号 邮政编码：100029
邮购电话：010－64492338 发行部电话：010－64492342
网址：http://www.uibep.com E-mail：uibep@126.com

唐山市润丰印务有限公司印装 新华书店北京发行所发行
成品尺寸：185mm×230mm 25 印张 502 千字
2012 年 2 月北京第 1 版 2012 年 2 月第 1 次印刷

ISBN 978-7-5663-0302-8
印数：0 001－3 000 册 定价：46.00 元

金融法的双语教学

（代序*）

一、开课

在大学法学院开新课，是要进行论证的，大致的内容是开课的必要性、可行性分析，主要是介绍申请开课的教师本人的教学科研背景和经验、教学内容和课时、教材和参考资料的选用、教学方法和教学对象等。关于教学科研背景方面，在中国人民大学做博士后和在中山大学攻读博士学位期间，我分别给本科生开了“公司法”和“经济法”课程（博士后阶段），给硕士研究生开了“比较经济法”和“金融法专题研究”（读博士期间），再加上在清华大学和美国天普大学参加清华/天普 TSINGHUA/TEMPLE LL.M. 项目学习相关课程的经历，还算可以胜任。关于教学内容方面，用课题论证原话就是：“以中国法为基础”、“介绍外国法以美国法为主”和“以相关国际法为补充”，属于“公共平台课程”，课时是每周 2 小时，共进行 16 周的教学，时间很紧；北京师范大学不统一给本科生订购教材，学生按照任课老师列举的书单自行购买，双语教学的教材建设还不完善，暂时只有法律出版社“高等学校法学双语教材”系列，但可能是一般大学多数主要在国际法相关课程开课的原因，现有已经出版了的教材都集中在国际法方面，还没有“金融法”的双语教材版本出来，我的方案是同时使用中文教材和英文教材，教材列举大致是国内通行的中文教材如《金融法概论》等，英文教材如 Tomson West 的 ST. PAUL，MINN.的 Regulations of Financial Institutions，参考资料除中文相关法律、法规和案例以外，就是英文的 Starting off Right in Law School, Introductions to the Law and Legal System of the United States, Black's Law Dictionary 和元照中英文法律词典等。关于教学方式，我是以讲授法（lecturing）和案例分析法（case briefing）相结合的方式进行讲解。关于教学对象，本课程针对的对象是法学本科二年级和三年级学生，教学时间是下学期。

二、授课

开课第一节，照例是老师和学生的自我介绍，大致讲一下课程安排，重复一下“培养方案”的内容和教材的要求，以及全学期的学习进度（syllabus）、平时考核和期末考

---

* 本代序节选自：袁达松. 在法学院双语教学公司法和金融法——兼谈天普项目学习在中国法学教学中的应用//王正志. 当代热点法律问题研究——天普校友论文集. 北京：对外经济贸易大学出版社，2009：167-171. 部分内容有调整。

试方式等；然后，选定课代表。由于第一节课，学生都没有准备学习资料，就大致讲解了学科的背景、基本知识结构和中英文内容的学习安排，顺带征询一下学生对中英文学习比重的要求。学校对于双语教学的要求是总体上英文的比例要大于中文，但具体如何安排，还是由任课老师灵活掌握的。学生们普遍要求中英文兼顾并重，一方面这两门课都是比较重要而实用的课程，他们希望在掌握好中国法的同时也能学好外国法。所以，我最后会告诉大家，每门课每周的两节课，基本上是在第一节课先讲授学科基础知识和相关中国法，然后在第二节课进行相关的外国法案例分析，课堂发言、课外作业和期末论文使用英文进行，以达到总体上的英文比例占多数的要求。

第一周上课还有一些时间，我介绍了自己在天普学习美国法的认识，着重讲解了美国案例的内容构成、阅读方法和分析方法（briefing），并把本人做的两个 brief 对比评述，其中之一比较简单，另外一个做得相对深入全面，试图让学生对初步了解如何着手阅读和分析美国案例。

课后，安排课代表和班级班干部协助复印部分学习资料，由于学校不统一订购教材，学生选课也不能尽早确定，难以统一预订外国法教材，只能圈定部分案例进行复印，所以外国法部分基本上是一个重新进行的教材、案例和资料汇编，尽管是学习用途，学校基于尊重知识产权要求我们不能整本复印，但客观上我们也不可能及时通过中国图书进出口公司提前预订购买原版教材，学生的经济负担能力也是个问题，这些问题都要逐步协调解决。

从第二周到第三周，主要训练学生学会阅读美国案例和做分析摘要，主要使用 Starting off Right in Law School 中的案例，可喜的是通过为期三周的训练，学生已经基本掌握美国案例阅读和分析了。从第四周开始，正式开始相关学科的讲授，按照方案，第一节课先用中文讲授中国法基本知识，第二节课用英文讲授美国法案例，两方面内容尽量相衔接。中国学生被动接受的学习习惯仍然很大，加上语言上的障碍使他们不大敢于放开喉咙用英文来回答提问，所以开始时，美国法案例还是要讲授，帮助学生进行摘要分析。于是乎，我进一步提出平时考核方法，要求他们按宿舍分成学习小组，每周推选一个同学作代表在课堂上用英文发言，对相关案例进行摘要分析，然后由其他同学用英文提问，发言的同学用英文作答。这个方法效果不错，因为开始时，他们都会推选英文水平较高且学习相对积极的同学先行发言，后来，其他同学也慢慢上手了，开口讲英文的勇气也因为课堂气氛而酝酿出来了。另外，我还要求他们每人提交一篇书面的英文案例分析摘要，逼迫他们掌握分析方法和相关案例知识。就这样，为期十六周的授课很快就过去了，在第十六周，我给他们讲解了英文论文的写作方法（IRAC 模式），要求他们结合上课所学习的中国法内容和其所分析的美国法案例，进行比较研究，用英文写一篇中美比较法论文。经过十六周的学习，学生们基本上都掌握了相关的中国法和美国法知识，用两周时间撰写好并提交了相应的学期论文。

三、成效

由于我以在天普项目学习所得“现学现教”进行双语教学，学生普遍反映我的教学与其他没有使用案例教学法的双语教学有所不同。没有使用案例教学法的双语教学，难以掌握英美普通法的基本知识，容易变成法律英语学习，而不是真正的专业法律知识学习。

通过案例摘要分析，学生们基本学会了相关美国法案例的裁判原理，使他们开拓了思维方式，而不仅仅是传统中国法的成文法逻辑三段论推理，也培养了他们进一步比较中美法律的兴趣。

一些申请到美国留学的学生，把他们在双语学习的经历和体会写到了申请手续中的个人陈述（personal statement）当中去，也有一些学生让我给他写推荐信。结果，当年共有三名学生被录取到美国的大学法学院攻读 LL.M.。

还有一些学生参加国内的法学院硕士研究生入学考试，也认为我教的双语课帮他们在法学英语的笔试或面试打下了基础，考上了理想的法学院。

四、致谢

本书得以与读者见面，与对外经济贸易大学出版社各位编辑的敬业精神分不开，也离不开笔者在清华大学法学院和美国天普大学法学院学习时打下的基础，以及在金融法双语课程中与笔者教学相长的学生们，在此一并感谢！

袁达松

2012 年 2 月

目　　录

Contents

第一章 金融法基础理论

第一节　金融法的渊源和体系

金融法是调整金融关系的法律规范的总称。金融法是由众多金融法律规范组成的法律体系，而不是一部单一的法典。金融法律规范的来源有多种：在判例法国家，有判例法和制定法；在大陆法国家，有立法机关制定的金融法律、法规等；此外，还包括相关国家之间签订的国际条约以及国际社会公认的国际惯例。按照调整金融关系类型的不同，可以将金融法律规范分为不同的金融法律制度，它们共同构成统一的金融法律体系。

一、中国金融法的渊源和体系

中国是成文法国家，中国金融法的渊源为相关机构制定的有关金融组织及其活动的规范性法律文件。这其中既包括立法机关——中国全国人民代表大会及其常务委员会以及省、自治区或经法律授权的其他地方人民代表大会及其常务委员会制定的金融法律、地方性和区域自治的金融法规，又包括国务院、中国人民银行等行政机关为具体实施相关金融法律而制定的金融法规、规章及规范性文件，也包括司法机关——中国最高人民法院和最高人民检察院为适用相关金融法律、法规而制定的司法解释。此外，中国缔结或参加的与金融相关的国际条约、协定也是中国金融法的一个渊源。而一些影响广泛、为国际社会公认的国际惯例，则是中国金融法的非正式渊源。

按照金融部门的不同，中国金融法大体上可以分为中央银行及商业银行法律制度、证券法律制度、保险法律制度、信托法律制度、证券投资基金法律制度及金融衍生品法律制度等。对此，中国已经颁布了以《中国人民银行法》、《中华人民共和国商业银行法》、

《中华人民共和国银行业监督管理法》、《中华人民共和国证券法》、《中华人民共和国保险法》、《中华人民共和国信托法》、《中华人民共和国证券投资基金法》、《期货交易管理条例》以及《银行业金融机构衍生产品交易业务管理办法》等为中心的一系列法律、法规，由此构成一个完整的中国金融法律体系。

鉴于中国法的“一国两制三法域”现状，广义的中国金融法也包括台港澳地区颁布和施行的金融法律、法规。

二、美国金融法的渊源和体系

美国是判例法国家，其法律渊源包括由相关立法部门颁布的制定法以及由法院判例构成的判例法。制定法和判例法构成美国金融法的主要渊源。其中，制定法既包括相关立法机关制定的金融法律，同时也包括获得授权的金融监管机关制定的金融监管规则（包括监管规定、监管政策、业务指南及法规解释等）。不同于其他法律部门，在金融法领域，制定法为执法和行政的主要依据，构成美国金融法的首要渊源。

由于美国是联邦制国家，因此其法律体系呈现出联邦和州两层法律并行的特点。在金融法领域，联邦层面的金融法律与各州的金融法律并驾齐驱，在各自管辖的范围内分别适用。美国金融法律大多是在特定历史时期为解决特定问题而制定或修改的，因此并不十分成体系。按照具体金融部门的不同，美国主要的金融法律概述如下：

在银行业领域，除各州的法律外，主要的联邦法律有《1863 年国民银行法》、《1913 年联邦储备法》、《1933 年银行法》（其中包含《格拉斯—斯蒂格尔法案》（Glass-Steagall Banking Act））、《1956 年银行控股公司法》、《1980 年存款机构放松管制与货币控制法》、《1982 年甘恩—圣哲曼储蓄机构法》、《1989 年金融机构改革、恢复与强制执行法》、《1991 年联邦存款保险公司改进法》、《1994 年里格尔—尼尔州际银行及分行效率法》、《1999 年金融服务现代化法》。

在证券、期货领域，除各州关于证券监管的蓝天法（Blue Sky Laws）以外，主要的联邦法律有《商品交易法》（CEA）、《2000 年商品期货现代化法》（CFMA）、《1933 年证券法》（Securities Act of 1933）、《1934 年证券交易法》（Securities Exchange Act of 1934）、《1940 年投资公司法》、《1940 年投资顾问法》、《2002 年萨班斯—奥克斯利法》（the Sarbanes-Oxley Act of 2002）等。

在保险领域，各州制定的保险法律、法规构成保险领域法律的主要部分。联邦层面的保险法律较少，最重要的法律为《麦卡伦—弗格森法案》，该法确定了各州对保险业监管的权力。

2010 年 7 月 21 日，美国总统奥巴马签署《多德—弗兰克华尔街改革和消费者保护法案》（The Dodd-Frank Wall Street Reform and Consumer Protection Act），这是一部

涉及整个金融业监管改革的法案，覆盖范围涉及银行、证券、保险及金融衍生品等各个领域。

第二节 金融监管制度

金融业作为市场经济的重要部门，同样存在着市场失灵的问题。由于金融业具有极强的社会性，其所产生的市场失灵无疑具有更加严重的破坏力。因此，建立和完善健全的金融监管制度，具有十分重要的意义。

金融监管是指有关政府部门根据法律、行政法规的授权，对金融机构和金融业务活动进行监督管理的行为。实行金融监管，在金融机构的市场准入、退出以及业务经营方面设置相关的要求，对于保证金融机构依法经营、促进金融机构之间的公平竞争、维护金融消费者的合法权益、确保金融市场乃至整个国民经济的安全与稳定，都起着至关重要的作用。各国无不重视金融监管，纷纷以立法的方式将其有关金融监管的制度确立下来。不同的国家，其金融监管制度呈现出不同的特点。

一、中国“一行三会”监管体制

中国已经建立了相对完善的金融监管体制，即“一行三会”的监管体制。“一行”指中国人民银行，是中国的中央银行，负责制定和执行货币政策，防范和化解金融风险，维护金融稳定；“三会”指中国银行业监督管理委员会（下称“中国银监会”）、中国证券监督管理委员会（下称“中国证监会”）以及中国保险监督管理委员会（下称“中国保监会”），三者各司其职，分别负责对不同的金融部门进行行业监管。

中国金融监管体制，是自20世纪80年代中国金融业的发展而建立和完善起来的。在此之前，囿于计划经济体制的限制，中国并未建立现代意义上的金融业，采取的是中国人民银行集金融监管、货币政策、商业银行等职能于一身的经营管理体制。

20世纪80年代之后，一些国有商业银行从中国人民银行中分离出来，计划经济体制被打破。随着金融产品的不断增加、资本市场和保险业的迅速发展，跨行业经营的竞争局面开始在中国商业银行中出现，很多商业银行设有自己的信托、投资和证券公司。这一时期，中国形成了综合经营、统一监管的格局。中国人民银行作为单一的金融监管机构，不仅负责对银行业务的监管，而且还充当国家证券主管机关，管理股票和债券，负责证券发行、上市的审批；同时，保险监管职能也由中国人民银行承担。

20世纪90年代以后，中国证监会、中国保监会相继于1992年和1998年设立。至此，中国人民银行分离了证券及保险监管职能，中国金融分业监管体制初步形成。2003年3月，中国十届全国人大一次会议通过了关于国务院机构改革方案的决定，将中国人民银行对银行、资产管理公司、信托投资公司及其他存款类金融机构的监管职能分离出来，成立了中国银行业监督管理委员会，标志着中国金融业分业监管制度的最终确立。

"三会"分设之后，中国形成了中国银监会、中国证监会和中国保监会共同负责金融微观监管，中国人民银行负责宏观金融稳定的监管体制。为弥补分业监管的不足，中国银监会、中国证监会和中国保监会在明确分工的同时，也积极展开部门间的合作。2004年6月，三家监管机构共同签署了《在金融监管方面分工合作的备忘录》，明确了相互之间的职责分工、信息收集与交流以及协调合作的工作机制（包括三家监管机构之间的"监管联席会议机制"和"经常联系机制"），加强了三家监管机构之间的监管交流与合作。

二、美国"双重多头"监管体制

美国金融监管体制的形成始于20世纪30年代。1929—1933年经济危机后，美国颁布了一系列法律（尤其是1933年的《格拉斯—斯蒂格尔法案》），开始采取金融分业经营及监管的体制。经过几十年的发展变化，美国形成了当今世界上最为复杂的金融监管模式——"双重多头"金融监管模式。所谓"双重"是指联邦和州均设有金融监管机构行使监管职权；"多头"则是指联邦设立多种监管机构，并主要采用"机构监管"，按照银行、证券和期货业、保险业分别设立专门的监管部门。目前，美国政府在联邦一级的金融监管机构主要有联邦储备系统（Federal Reserve System，FRS）、货币监理署（Office of the Comptroller of the Currency，OCC）、联邦存款保险公司（Federal Deposit Insurance Corporation，FDIC）、储蓄机构管理局（Office of Thrift Supervision，OTS）[①]、国家信用合作社管理局（National Credit Union Administration，NCUA）、证券交易委员会（Securities and Exchange Commission，SEC）、商品期货交易委员会（Commodity Futures Trading Commission，CFTC）等，分别对各类金融机构实施专业的交叉监管。

在对银行业的监管中，双重多头的监管表现得最为明显。双重表现为联邦政府机构管理在联邦注册的"国民银行"，而州政府监管机构管理在州注册的商业银行。另外，任何一家银行都要受到多个监管机构的监管。如果是国民银行，在成立时，首先要到隶属于美国财政部的货币监理署办理注册登记手续，得到其审查批准后方能营业，国民银行的运营还要受其制定的有关资本运营、贷款结构、存款安全等业务经营方面的条例的监管；作为国民银行，还必须加入联邦储备系统，成为联邦储备系统的会员，接受美联储的监管；同时，国民银行必须向联邦存款保险公司投保，因此需接受联邦存款保险公司的监管。对于州立的商业银行而言，首先要受到州银行监管机构的监管；因向联邦存款

① 随着美国2010年《华尔街改革与消费者保护法》的颁布，OTS已于2011年7月21日并入OCC，原先由OTS行使的职能由合并后的OCC行使。

保险公司投保，则需接受联邦存款保险公司的监管；如果其加入美国联邦储备系统，相应地要受到美联储的监管。

就金融业的其他部门而言，监管相对单一。对证券期货机构及证券期货市场的监管主要由证券交易委员会、商品期货交易委员会和证券投资者保护公司（Securities Investor Protection Corporation，SIPC）共同负责；对信用合作社的监管主要由国家信用合作社管理局负责；对储贷会的监管主要由储蓄机构管理局负责；而保险行业则主要由州一级进行监管，各州及华盛顿特区和美国属地的保险监管者组成美国保险监理官协会（National Association of Insurance Commissioners，NAIC）作为一个自律组织协调各地保险监管。

1999 年，美国通过了《1999 年金融服务现代化法》，该法打破了美国金融业分业经营的壁垒，允许金融控股公司通过设立子公司的形式经营多种金融业务，但是金融控股公司本身并不开展业务，其主要职责是申领执照，对集团公司和子公司进行行政管理。对于伴随金融控股公司而来的混业经营的金融业，美国监管当局设计了一种“伞形”的监管体制。美联储被赋予伞形监管职能，成为金融控股公司的基本监管者，负责对金融控股公司的法人主体进行监管，而金融控股公司中的子公司则仍大体沿用分业监管模式。对金融控股公司的伞形监管，其实质还是一种“混业经营下的分业监管模式”。

美国这种纵横交错的立体监管模式，可以发挥监管专业化分工优势，还可产生监管竞争优势。但在实践中也暴露出其诸多缺陷，尤其在 2008 年金融危机爆发后，美国随即对这种监管体制进行了大规模改革。

三、案例资料

美国“双重多头”的金融监管体制曾是美国金融业发展繁荣的坚实基础，也一直被视为全球的典范。但是，这种监管体制也有其内在的诸多缺陷，这些缺陷导致监管的有效性大打折扣。2008 年金融危机的爆发，将美国金融监管体制存在的缺陷暴露无遗。金融危机爆发后，美国开始对其现有的金融监管体制进行反思，随之而来的是大规模的金融监管改革。

作为美国国会下属的独立机构，美国政府问责署（Government Accountability Office，GAO）致力于推动美国政府全面履行其职责。2008 年金融危机爆发前后，GAO 发布了一些报告，对美国金融监管体制存在的不足进行分析，提出改革建议，为国会立法改革提供参考。其中，2009 年 9 月，GAO 发布了题为《金融监管：近期的危机再次确认改革美国监管体制的必要》的报告。在报告中，GAO 指出：在过去几十年里，金融市场以及金融产品发生的一些重大变化，对美国当前的金融监管体制形成重大的挑战，而美国现行监管体制未能应对这些挑战。GAO 提到美国金融监管体制的几个重大缺陷，包括多头监管导致监管标准的不统一、对金融衍生产品缺乏监管、在对重要的金融市场参与者的监管上存在漏洞、缺少对金融系统性风险的关注等。GAO 的分析并非全面，但是 GAO 的一系列报告推动了美国金融监管改革的进程。

Financial Regulation: Recent Crisis Reaffirms the Need to Overhaul the U.S. Regulatory System

...

U.S. Financial Regulatory System's Failure to Keep Pace with Market Developments Underscores the Need for Reforms

As a result of 150 years of changes to financial regulation in the United States, the regulatory system has become complex and fragmented. Today, responsibilities for overseeing the financial services industry are shared among almost a dozen federal banking, securities, futures, and other regulatory agencies, numerous self-regulatory organizations, and hundreds of state financial regulatory agencies. For example:

- Insured depository institutions are overseen by five federal agencies—the Federal Deposit Insurance Corporation (FDIC), the Board of Governors of the Federal Reserve System (Federal Reserve), the Office of the Comptroller of the Currency (OCC), the Office of Thrift Supervision (OTS), and the National Credit Union Administration (NCUA)—and states supervise state-chartered depository and certain other institutions.
- Securities activities and markets are overseen by the Securities and Exchange Commission (SEC) and state government entities, and private sector organizations performing self-regulatory functions.
- Commodity futures markets and activities are overseen by the Commodity Futures Trading Commission (CFTC) and also by industry self-regulatory organizations.
- Insurance activities are primarily regulated at the state level with little federal involvement.

Other federal regulators also play important roles in the financial regulatory system, such as the Federal Trade Commission, which acts as the primary federal agency responsible for enforcing compliance with federal consumer protection laws for financial institutions such as finance companies that are not overseen by another financial regulator.

Much of this structure has developed as the result of statutory and regulatory measures taken in response to financial crises or significant developments in the financial services sector. For example, the Federal Reserve was created in 1913 in response to financial panics and instability around the turn of the century, and much of the remaining structure for bank and securities regulation was created as the result of the Great Depression turmoil of the 1920s and 1930s. Changes in the types of financial activities permitted for financial institutions and their affiliates have also shaped the financial regulatory system over time. For example, under the Glass-Steagall provisions of the Banking Act of 1933, financial institutions were prohibited from simultaneously offering commercial and investment banking services, but with the passage of the Gramm-Leach-Bliley Act of 1999, Congress permitted financial institutions to fully engage in both types of activities, under certain conditions.

Various Market Developments Have Revealed Limitations in the Existing Regulatory Structure

Several key developments in financial markets and products in the past few decades have significantly challenged the existing financial regulatory structure….

Regulators have struggled, and often failed, to identify the systemic risks posed by large and interconnected financial conglomerates, as well as new and complex products, and to adequately manage these risks. These firms' operations increasingly cross financial sectors, but no single regulator is tasked with assessing the risks such an institution might pose across the entire financial system. In addition, regulators have had to address problems in financial markets resulting from the activities of sometimes less-regulated and large market participants—such as nonbank mortgage lenders, hedge funds, and credit rating agencies—some of which play significant roles in today's financial markets. Further, the increasing prevalence of new and more complex financial products has challenged regulators and investors, and consumers have faced difficulty understanding new and increasingly complex retail mortgage and credit products. Standard setters for accounting and financial regulators have also faced growing challenges in ensuring that accounting and audit standards appropriately respond to financial market developments. And despite the increasingly global aspects of financial markets, the current fragmented U.S. regulatory structure has complicated some efforts to coordinate internationally with other regulators.

Because of this hearing's focus on prudential regulation of the banking industry, I would like to reinforce that our prior work has repeatedly identified limitations of the fragmented banking regulatory structure. For example:

● In 1996, we reported that the division of responsibilities among the four federal bank oversight agencies in the United States was not based on specific areas of expertise, functions or activities, either of the regulator or the banks for which they are responsible, but based on institution type and whether the banks were members of the Federal Reserve System. Despite their efforts to coordinate, this multiplicity of regulators was cited as resulting in inconsistent treatment of banking institutions in examinations, enforcement actions, and regulatory decisions.

- In a 2007 report, we noted that having bank holding company affiliates supervised by multiple banking regulators increased the potential for conflicting information to be provided to the institution, such as when a large, complex banking organization initially received conflicting information from the Federal Reserve, its consolidated supervisor, and OCC, its primary bank supervisor, about the firm's business continuity provisions.

- In 2005, we reported that a difference in authority across the banking regulators could lead to problems in oversight. For example, FDIC's authority over the holding companies and affiliates of industrial loan corporations was not as extensive as the authority that the other supervisors have over the holding companies and affiliates of banks and thrifts. For example, FDIC's authority to examine an affiliate of an insured depository institution exists only to disclose the relationship between the depository institution and the affiliate and the effect of that relationship on the depository institution. Therefore, any reputation or other risk from an affiliate that has no relationship with the industrial loan corporation could go undetected.

- In a 2004 report, we noted cases in which interagency cooperation between bank regulators has been hindered when two or more agencies share responsibility for supervising a bank. For example, in the failure of Superior Bank of West Virginia problems between OTS, Superior's primary supervisor, and FDIC hindered a coordinated supervisory approach, including OTS refusing to let FDIC participate in at least one examination. Similarly, disagreements between OCC and FDIC contributed to the 1999 failure of Keystone Bank.

- In a 2007 report, we expressed concerns over the appropriateness of having OTS oversee diverse global financial firms given the size of the agency relative to the institutions for which it was responsible.

Our recent work has further revealed limitations in the current regulatory system, reinforcing the need for change and the need for an entity responsible for identifying existing and emerging systemic risks. In January 2009, we designated modernizing the outdated U.S. financial regulatory system as a new high-risk area to bring focus to the need for a broad-based systemwide transformation to address major economy, efficiency, and effectiveness challenges. We have found that:

- Having multiple regulators results in inconsistent oversight. Our February 2009 report on the Bank Secrecy Act found that multiple regulators are examining for compliance with the same laws across industries and, for some larger holding companies, within the same institution. However, these regulators lack a mechanism for promoting greater consistency, reducing unnecessary regulatory burden, and identifying concerns across industries. In July 2009, we reported many violations by independent mortgage lenders of the fair lending laws intended to prevent lending discrimination could go undetected because of less comprehensive oversight provided by various regulators.

- Lack of oversight exists for derivatives products. In March 2009, we reported that the lack of a regulator with authority over all participants in the market for credit default swaps (CDS) has made it difficult to monitor and manage the potential systemic risk that these products can create.

- Gaps in the oversight of significant market participants. We reported in May 2009 on the issues and concerns related to hedge funds, which have grown into significant market participants with limited regulatory oversight. For example, under the existing regulatory structure, SEC's ability to directly oversee hedge fund advisers is limited to those that are required to register or voluntarily register with the SEC as an investment advisor. Further, multiple regulators (SEC, CFTC, and federal banking regulators) each oversee certain hedge fund-related activities and advisers. We concluded that given the recent experience with the financial crisis, regulators should have the information to monitor the activities of market participants that play a prominent role in the financial system, such as hedge funds, to protect investors and manage systemic risk.

- Lack of appropriate resolution authorities for financial market institutions. We recently reported that one of the reasons that federal authorities provided financial assistance to at least one troubled institution—the insurance conglomerate AIG—in the crisis stemmed from concerns that a disorderly failure by this institution would have contributed to higher borrowing costs and additional failures, further destabilizing fragile financial markets. According to Federal Reserve officials, the lack of a centralized and orderly resolution mechanism presented the Federal Reserve and Treasury with few alternatives in this case. The lack of an appropriate resolution mechanism for non-banking institutions has resulted in the federal government providing assistance and having significant ongoing exposure to AIG.

- Lack of a focus on systemwide risk. In March 2009 we also reported on the results of work we conducted at some large, complex financial institutions that indicated that no existing U.S. financial regulator systematically looks across institutions to identify factors that could affect the overall financial system. While regulators periodically conducted horizontal examinations on stress testing, credit risk practices, and risk management, they did not consistently use the results to identify potential systemic risks and have only a limited view of institutions' risk management or their responsibilities. Our July 2009 report on approaches regulators used to restrict the use of financial leveraging—the use of debt or other products to purchase assets or create other financial exposures—by financial institutions also found that regulatory capital measures did not always fully capture certain risks and that none of the multiple regulators responsible for individual markets or institutions had clear responsibility to assess the potential effects of the buildup of systemwide leverage.

Recognition of the need for regulatory reform extends beyond U.S. borders. Various international organizations such as the G20, G30, Bank for International Settlements, and Committee on Capital Markets Regulation have all reported that weaknesses in regulation contributed to the financial crisis. Specifically, among other things, these reports pointed to the fragmented regulatory system, the lack of a systemwide view of risks, and the lack of transparency or oversight of all market participants as contributing to the crisis. Further, the reports noted that sound regulation and a systemwide focus were needed to prevent instability in the financial system, and that recent events have clearly demonstrated that regulatory failures had contributed to the current crisis.

…

资料来源：*GAO: "Financial Regulation: Recent Crisis Reaffirms the Need to Overhaul the U.S. Regulatory System", GAO-09-1049T, September 29, 2009, available at http://www.gao.gov/new.items/d091049t.pdf.*

第三节 金融危机以来金融法的发展

2008年，发端于美国的金融危机肆虐全球，使全球金融业遭受重创。金融危机发生的一个重要原因在于全球金融监管体系存在问题，原有的金融监管体系未能阻止危机的爆发。危机发生后，各主要经济体纷纷进行反思，加强对金融监管体制的改革。各国金融监管改革的深入推进，促进了金融法的发展。

一、国际金融监管改革的目标和方向

2008年金融危机以来，二十国集团（G20）成为国际经济金融治理最重要的平台。G20领导人系列峰会明确了国际金融监管的目标和时间表，并定期审议国际金融监管改

革进展，确定国际金融改革的最终方案。

按照二十国集团领导人确定的金融监管改革目标和时间表，在国际金融监管组织和各国监管当局的积极参与下，各国在金融监管改革上达成了更多的共识：在宏观系统层面，将系统性风险纳入金融监管框架，建立宏观审慎监管制度；在中观市场层面，强化金融市场基础设施建设，矫正金融市场失灵；在微观机构层面，提升单家金融机构的稳健性，强化金融体系稳定的微观基础。

宏观系统层面的改革措施包括：建立与宏观经济金融环境和经济周期挂钩的监管制度，弱化金融体系与实体经济之间的正反馈效应；扩大金融监管范围，将“影子银行”体系纳入金融监管框架；强化对系统重要性金融机构（Systemically Important Financial Institutions，SIFIs）的监管，降低机构“大而不倒”导致的道德风险；加强母国和东道国监管当局之间的协调，降低风险跨境传递等。

中观市场层面的改革措施包括：推进建立单一的、高质量的国际会计准则；改进风险定价模式，避免过于依赖脱离现实的模型假设；加强外部评级机构的监管，降低金融机构对外部评级的依赖程度等。

微观机构层面的改革措施包括：资本监管改革，引入杠杆率监管制度，建立流动性监管标准、动态拨备制度，改革公司治理监管规则，推动金融机构实施稳健的薪酬机制，强化并表监管和对表外业务的监管等。

二、中美金融改革措施

（一）中国

尽管中国在本次金融危机中所受冲击相对较小，但这很大程度上是因为中国金融市场尚不够发达，没有完全开放。事实上，中国的金融监管体系也面临着诸多风险和挑战。尤其是，随着中国经济的不断发展，中国金融结构也变得日益复杂，一些新的金融工具如银证合作、银信合作、信证合作、银行与基金合作、投资连接保险产品等在中国不断涌现，混业经营初见端倪，这对中国现行分业监管的有效性提出了严峻的挑战。

在金融危机爆发后，中国密切关注各国金融监管改革的动向，从中吸取经验教训，并结合本国金融业发展的实际情况，采取了相关的改革措施。

首先，金融危机中所出现的危机跨境传导现象，令各国认识到加强全球金融监管的重要性。为此，中国积极推进国际监管合作，参与制定和严格遵守全球共同的交易规则和监管规则。金融危机后，中国分别加入金融稳定理事会（FSB）和巴塞尔委员会，成为其正式成员，全面参与该组织框架下的金融监管政策对话；中国银监会还引入巴塞尔委员会改革建议中的新监管指标，并在其基础上积极推进资本充足率、动态拨备率、杠杆率和流动性比率四项监管工具的建设；中国银监会还发布新的银行业监管标准，进一步推动“巴塞尔Ⅱ”、“巴塞尔Ⅲ”的同步实施。

其次，中国更加重视系统新风险问题。在2012年1月召开的全国金融工作会议上，中国国务院总理温家宝对今后一个时期金融改革发展作出部署时提到，要加强和改进金融监管，切实防范系统性金融风险。银行业要建立全面审慎的风险监管体系。证券业要完善市场制度，强化行为监管，保护投资者合法权益。保险业要加强偿付能力监管，完善分类监管制度。此外，中国还从机构改革的角度出发，考虑并讨论了在中国银监会、中国证监会、中国保监会之上设立更高级别的跨部门的金融监管机构，以更好地监管和协调国内现有的银行、证券和保险监管部门，应对综合监管、系统性风险监管等诸多问题。

再次，在全球金融危机后，加强投资者保护已经成为国际趋势。为顺应这种趋势，中国已决定在金融监管机构系统“一行三会”（中国人民银行、中国银监会、中国证监会及中国保监会）统一增设新的投资者保护机构。中国保监会增设的保险消费者权益保护局、中国证监会增设的投资者保护局已相继挂牌成立。这是中国在后金融危机时代金融监管改革发展的具体举措之一。

最后，为适应国内形势的变化，中国人民银行、中国银监会、中国证监会以及中国保监会等金融监管部门协调加强，推进了合作的步伐。不同金融监管部门之间的协调监管，对于维护金融稳定起到了非常重要的作用。目前中国监管部门之间已经实现部分信息联动，相互之间可以通过内部网络，实现数据和相关信息的查询，确保第一时间有效地实现相互联动。①

（二）美国

面对金融危机中暴露出的金融监管制度缺陷，美国朝野从政府到国会、从法律界到学术界展开了全面反思和讨论，各种改革的建议不断涌现。

2008年3月31日，美国财政部公布了《现代金融监管构架改革蓝图》（Blueprint for a Modernized Financial Regulatory Structure），提出对美国金融监管体制进行重建，建立以目标为基础监管模式。改革蓝图提出了一个长期的监管框架，但其牵涉的监管机构编制的重新整合成本巨大，改革方案的推行阻力重重。

2009年6月17日，美国总统奥巴马在白宫公布了名为《金融监管改革：新基础：重建金融监管》（Financial Regulatory Reform: A New Foundation: Rebuilding Financial Supervision and Regulation）的改革方案，拉开了美国金融监管改革的大幕。改革方案经过国会的讨价还价，最终形成《多德—弗兰克华尔街改革和消费者保护法案》，并于2010年7月获得通过。该法案号称自“大萧条”以来改革力度最大、影响最深远的金融监管

① 王来华，李乃燕. 中国金融监管协调机制存在的问题及对策分析. 海南金融，2010（1）.

改革议案，反映了美国对2008年金融危机的全面反思。

美国金融监管改革的首要任务在于，加强对系统性金融风险的防范，防止所谓“大而不倒”(Too-Big-To-Fail)的超级金融机构经营失败而引发新的系统性危机；同时，保护消费者免受金融欺诈、保证充分的信息披露。美国的金融监管改革围绕监管系统性风险和消费者金融保护两大核心展开，在“多德—弗兰克法案”中着重推进了以下几个方面的改革措施：

一是更新监管体系框架，以改变多头监管下的“监管重叠”和“监管空白”痼疾。成立金融稳定监管委员会（Financial Stability Oversight Council，FSOC），应对系统性风险；强化对美联储的授权与制衡；将现有的货币监理署和储蓄机构监理署合并，以监管全国性的银行机构；成立消费者金融保护局（Consumer Financial Protection Bureau，CFPB），加强对金融消费者的保护；在财政部下设联邦保险办公室（Office of National Insurance，ONI），强化联邦对保险业的监管。

二是加强对金融机构的微观监管。限制“大而不倒”机构的过度扩张；引入“沃尔克规则”(Volcker Rule)，限制银行进行自营交易；增加公司治理中薪酬的透明度。

三是建立有序的破产处置和自救机制，对系统重要性金融机构提出更高的资本充足率、杠杆限制、流动性和风险管理要求；将所有具有系统重要性的银行和非银行机构纳入美联储的监管之下；授予联邦存款保险公司破产清算授权（Resolution Authority），在超大金融机构经营失败时，对其采取安全有序的破产清算程序等。

四是健全金融市场监管体系。加强对对冲基金等“影子银行”体系的监管；确立信用证券化产品的风险留存要求，限制金融衍生品投机交易；强化对评级机构的监管，注重保护投资者利益。

三、案例资料

2008年金融危机爆发后，金融稳定理事会在促进全球金融监管改革方面发挥着重要作用。危机以来，金融稳定理事会积极协调各国金融当局以及国际组织的工作，寻求建立有效的监管政策并在跨区域、跨行业的范围内加以实施，以加强全球金融系统的稳定性。

金融稳定理事会，前身为金融稳定论坛（FSF），是根据2009年4月G20伦敦峰会宣言正式组建，成员包括G20成员国和相关经济体及有关国际组织，是G20领导人倚重和国际公认的推动全球金融标准制定与执行的核心机构。根据G20伦敦峰会公报，金融稳定理事会有权监督该集团达成的改革方案的执行情况。金融稳定理事会的工作，有力地推动了金融法制的发展。

2010年11月9日，金融稳定理事会向G20首尔峰会领导人提交了一封信函，阐述了金融监管改革在如下几个方面的进展：银行资本及流动性标准、对系统重要性金融机构（SIFIs）道德风险的处理、金融监管的强度和有效性、场外衍生品市场的改革、降低对信用评级机构评级依赖的原则。以上几个方面，是对2008年金融危机的部分回应，也是各国金融监管当局下一阶段需着重予以解决的问题。金融法下一步的发展，必然会围绕以上问题的解决而不断深入推进。

Progress of Financial Regulatory Reforms

November 9, 2010

To G20 Leaders:

The Seoul Summit will mark the delivery of two central elements of the reform programme launched in Washington to create a sounder financial system and reduce systemic risk globally: a materially strengthened global framework for bank capital and liquidity, and a comprehensive policy framework to address the moral hazard risks associated with institutions that are too big (or complex) to fail.

The reform programme launched at the Washington Summit was necessarily ambitious and the timetable demanding. Propelled by your support and determination, and reflecting an unprecedented intensity of international co-operation, the core policy reforms have been delivered on time.

Full and internationally consistent implementation of the agreed reforms will be essential if they are to have the impact on global financial stability that you intend. The process of implementation is well underway at national and regional levels, as detailed in the reports submitted to you. But much still lies ahead of us and your continued strong support will be needed to see through the changes in laws and regulations required.

Bank capital and liquidity standards

The new capital and liquidity standards developed by the Basel Committee on Banking Supervision will reduce the likelihood and severity of future financial crises and create a less procyclical banking system that is better able to support long-term economic growth. They have been designed to substantially raise the quality, quantity and international consistency of bank capital and liquidity; constrain the buildup of leverage and maturity mismatches; and introduce capital buffers above the minimum requirements that can be drawn upon in bad times.

The FSB and the Basel Committee, in close collaboration with the BIS and IMF, have assessed the macroeconomic impact of the transition to the new Basel III standards. The resulting transition arrangements have been designed to ensure that implementation does not harm the economic recovery. National implementation of the risk-based capital requirements will begin on 1 January 2013. Member countries will translate the capital rules into national laws and regulations before that date. From that point forward, the capital requirements rise each year, with the transition to the newly agreed levels fully completed on 1 January 2019.

Addressing the moral hazard risk associated with SIFIs

Systemically important financial institutions (SIFIs) are firms whose disorderly failure, because of their size, complexity and systemic interconnectedness, would cause significant disruption to the wider financial system and economic activity. Too often, because we have lacked the tools and the capacity to co-ordinate resolution across borders, we have answered the threatened failure of such firms by bailing them out using taxpayer funds.

We have agreed a policy framework, work processes and timelines for addressing the systemic and moral hazard risks associated with SIFIs.

The framework calls for action in five areas:

- First, and foremost, improvements on resolution regimes to ensure that any financial institutions can be resolved without disruptions to the financial system and without taxpayer support.
- Second, a requirement that SIFIs and initially in particular global SIFIs (G-SIFIs) have additional loss absorption capacity beyond the Basel III standards to reflect the greater risks that these institutions pose to the global financial system.
- Third, more intensive supervisory oversight for financial institutions which may pose systemic risk.
- Fourth, stronger robustness standards for core financial infrastructure to reduce contagion risks from the failure of individual institutions.
- Fifth, peer review by an FSB Peer Review Council of the effectiveness and consistency of national policy measures for G-SIFIs, beginning by end-2012.

With your endorsement, we will implement this framework. It will require legal reforms in many of our countries to make feasible the resolution of any financial institution without taxpayer exposure to loss while protecting vital economic functions through mechanisms which make it possible for shareholders and unsecured and uninsured creditors to absorb losses in their order of seniority.

In improving our resolution regimes, we will need to achieve the legal preconditions and degree of legal harmonisation that permit rapid and efficient resolution of the global operations of a SIFI. This will require clear mandates and capacity in law for national resolution authorities to cooperate and to share the information needed for effective recovery and resolution, and the elimination of provisions in national laws that hamper fair cross-border resolution.

G-SIFIs will be subject to a sustained process of mandatory recovery and resolution planning that will assess their resolvability under applicable resolution regimes. Where resolvability not assured, authorities should have the powers, exercisable under clear criteria, to require financial institutions to make the changes to their legal and operational structure that ensure there resolvability.

Supervisory intensity and effectiveness

As you stressed at the Toronto Summit, improved rules-such as Basel III and those described above for addressing SIFIs-on their own are not enough. Every country must have a supervisory system that is up to the task of ensuring that the new regulations are backed up by effective risk assessments and enforcement. Moreover, supervisors must have the powers to be able to detect problems proactively and intervene early to reduce the impact of potential stresses on individual firms and therefore on the financial system as a whole.

The actions and implementation processes we have proposed, which have been developed in consultation with the IMF, focus on the following elements necessary to deliver more effective and intense supervision:

- Ensuring that supervisors have unambiguous mandates, sufficient independence and appropriate resources;
- Providing supervisors with the full suite of powers necessary for effective early intervention;
- Improving supervisory standards to reflect the complexity of financial institutions and the system as a whole; and
- Increasing the frequency of assessments of supervisory regimes.

We have set ambitious timelines for national authorities and standard setters to follow up on the recommended actions. FSB thematic peer reviews and IMF/World Bank FSAP assessments will monitor national implementation.

OTC derivatives reforms

At the Toronto Summit, you called for acceleration of the implementation of the G20 commitments for reform of the OTC derivatives market. In response, international standard setters and national authorities working through the FSB have agreed approaches to implement these reforms in an internationally consistent and non-discriminatory way. The report submitted to you sets out recommendations for addressing the G20 commitments concerning standardisation, central clearing, organised platform trading, and reporting to trade repositories.

This report is only the first step toward consistent implementation of the G20 commitments, and highlights the amount of work that remains going forward. Authorities will need to coordinate closely to minimise the potential for regulatory arbitrage. The FSB will review regular reports on progress in implementing the necessary reforms as from March 2011.

Principles for reducing reliance on CRA ratings

In Toronto, you asked us to develop Principles for reducing reliance on external ratings in rules and regulations. The goal is to reduce the cliff effects and herding associated with CRA ratings changes. These arise in large measure because we—as authorities—have "hard wired" CRA ratings into rules and regulations, which produces a mechanistic market response to rating changes. Accordingly, the principles call on standard setters and national regulatory authorities to assess references to CRA ratings in laws and regulations and, wherever possible, remove them or replace them by suitable alternative standards of creditworthiness.

The principles address the use of ratings in prudential standards; policies of investment managers and institutional investors; central bank operations; private sector margin arrangements; and disclosures by issuers of securities. Change in this area will not and cannot happen overnight, since alternative creditworthiness standards need to be developed. But the direction in which we want to move is clear.

Reform programme going forward

Under your leadership, the G20 have delivered on an ambitious financial reform agenda. This has been essential to maintain public and political support for an open and integrated global financial system.

The FSB will monitor and regularly report on the progress of consistent international implementation of these reforms. In doing so, we will draw on the FSB peer review process, and where needed, along with our international member bodies, set up subject specific monitoring processes. We evaluated the implementation by all members of compensation standards in early 2010 and will do so again in 2011. Other key areas will be implementation of the new capital and liquidity rules, and the national implementation of G-SIFI policy measures…

资料来源：金融稳定理事会网站 *http://www.financialstabilityboard.org/publications/r_101109.pdf,* 访问日期 2011/11/12.

第二章 中央银行法律制度

第一节 中央银行的组织机构

一、中国人民银行

中国的中央银行是中国人民银行，对此《中国人民银行法》已有明确的规定。中国人民银行具有如下几个特点：首先，中国人民银行是政府机构，是国务院下属的，为实现国家在货币、金融方面的相关职能而设立的部门；其次，中国人民银行是独立的政府机构，依法独立执行货币政策，履行职责，开展业务，不受地方政府、各级政府部门、社会团体和个人的干涉；最后，中国人民银行须对中国的立法机构——全国人民代表大会负责，应当向全国人民代表大会常务委员会提出有关货币政策情况和金融业运行情况的工作报告。

根据《中国人民银行法》的规定，中国人民银行的组织机构包括：

（1）领导机构。中国人民银行的领导机构是其决策机构和执行机构，包括行长一人，副行长若干人。行长根据国务院总理提名，由全国人大决定；全国人大闭会期间，由全国人常委会决定，由国家主席任免；副行长由国务院总理任免。中国人民银行实行行长负责制，行长领导中国人民银行工作，副行长协助行长工作。

（2）咨询机构。中国人民银行设立货币政策委员会，是中国人民银行内设的制定货币政策的咨询议事机构。其职责是在综合分析宏观经济形势的基础上，依据国家的宏观经济调控目标，讨论以下有关内容并提出建议：货币政策的制定、调整；一定时期内的货币政策控制目标；货币政策工具的运用；有关货币政策的重要措施；货币政策与其他宏观经济政策的协调。

（3）总行其他内设机构。中国人民银行出于职能分工的需要，内设多个职能司（厅），包括：办公厅（党委办公室）、条法司、货币政策司、金融市场司、金融稳定局、调查统计司、会计财务司、支付科技司、科技司、货币金银局、国库局、国际司、内审司、人事司（党委组织部）、研究局、征信管理局、反洗钱局（保卫局）、党委宣传部。

（4）分支机构。中国人民银行根据履行职责的需要设立分支机构，作为中国人民银行的派出机构。中国人民银行对分支机构实行垂直的统一领导和管理。中国人民银行的分支机构根据中国人民银行的授权，维护本辖区的金融稳定，承办有关业务，不受地方政府的干涉。

（5）其他机构，包括驻外机构和直属单位。中国人民银行在世界各地设有几个代表处，分别代表中国人民银行行使相关职权。此外，中国人民银行还有多个直属单位（如中国反洗钱监测分析中心、中国人民银行征信中心、中国外汇交易中心（全国银行间同业拆借中心）、中国金融出版社、中国人民银行清算总中心和中国印钞造币总公司等），这些单位直属中国人民银行领导，但其财务与业务活动都是独立的。

二、美国联邦储备系统

美国最早具有中央银行职能的机构是历史上的美国第一银行和美国第二银行。但是，直到《1913 年联邦储备法》的出台，美国建立了美国联邦储备系统，由该系统履行中央银行的相关职能，由此才建立正式的中央银行。

经过多年的发展，一个由联邦储备理事会和 12 家联邦储备银行及数千家会员银行组成的较为完整的中央银行体系已在美国形成。

（1）联邦储备理事会（The Board of Governors of The Federal Reserve System，下称美联储），设在华盛顿，是联邦政府机构，是整个联邦系统负责全面政策的最高决策机关。该理事会由 7 名理事组成，均须由美国总统提名，经参议院批准后方可上任，任期为 14 年。联邦储备理事会直接对国会负责，每年向国会呈交两次书面报告，汇报整个国民经济情况、货币政策的执行过程以及第二年的货币政策计划。国会可以随时召集联邦储备理事会主席和其他成员就书面报告的有关问题进行讨论。

（2）联邦公开市场委员会（Federal Open Market Committee，FOMC），是联邦储备系统中专门负责制定和执行公开市场运用政策的决策机构。联邦公开市场委员会由 12 名委员组成，其中 7 名是联邦储备理事会的理事，联邦储备理事会主席也是联邦公开市场委员会主席。

（3）联邦储备银行与会员银行。联邦储备银行（Federal Reserve Bank），既是美国联邦储备系统中的政策执行部门，也是具体办理中央银行业务的业务部门。根据《1913 年联邦储备法》的规定，美国全境被划分成 12 个联邦储备区，在每个储备区分别设立一家联邦储备银行。储备银行在各自的储备区内又可设立分行。从所有制来说，联邦储备银行不是国家所有，其股本是其所在区会员银行认购的。但由于它执行发行货币、代理国库、制定货币政策、管理金融等职能，所以它是中央银行——12家联邦储备银行的每一家都是其所在地区的中央银行。根据美国法律的规定，凡根据联邦法律在联邦注册的国民银行必须参加联邦储备系统成为会员银行，根据各州法律在各州注册的州银行可自愿申请加入联邦储备系统。

（4）消费者金融保护局，根据2010年《多德—弗兰克华尔街改革和消费者保护法案》新设的机构。该机构设立在美国联邦储备系统内，但保持独立的监管权力，局长由总统直接任命。由于消费者金融涉及面很广，该机构可以监管各类银行和非银行机构，包括所有资产规模在100亿美元以上的信贷机构和各类金融中介，而且可以独立制定监管条例并监督实施，从而保证美国消费者在选择使用住房按揭、信用卡和其他金融产品时，得到清晰、准确的信息，同时杜绝隐藏费用、掠夺性条款和欺骗性的做法。①

美国联邦储备系统的特点在于：首先，联储体系不是由联邦政府控制，而是由12个地区联储银行和联储委员会共同执行中央银行职能；其次，联储体系由成员银行共同拥有，而不是由联邦政府所有，其性质是私有的，具有很强的独立性。

三、案例资料

美国建国之初，主张加强中央集权的人士曾主张设立中央银行，但却遭到强烈主张个人自由的人士的反对。在19世纪大部分时间，美国是“自由银行业”（free banking）时代，没有中央银行。直到20世纪初，美国发生了几场金融大恐慌，致使公众、国会议员要求政府干预私人银行业。经过激烈的讨论，美国参众两院最终作出妥协，通过了《1913年联邦储备法》，从而揭开了美国金融银行发展的新篇章。

美国《1913年联邦储备法》的通过，是美国金融业发展史上的一个里程碑。《1913年联邦储备法》初步确立起较为完备中央银行体系，确保了中央银行的独立性，增强了支付效率，稳定了金融经济，从而在国民经济中发挥了不可替代的作用。

以下节选了《1913年联邦储备法》中联邦储备区、联邦储备银行以及联邦储备理事会三节的内容，这三节的内容勾勒出了美国中央银行成立之初的基本架构。

① 郭东. 金融危机后美国投资者保护制度的变化. 中国金融，2010（18）.

Federal Reserve Act

…

Section 2. Federal Reserve Districts

1. Establishment of Reserve Cities and Districts

As soon as practicable, the Secretary of the Treasury, the Secretary of Agriculture and the Comptroller of the Currency, acting as "The Reserve Bank Organization Committee," shall designate not less than eight nor more than twelve cities to be known as Federal reserve cities, and shall divide the continental United States, excluding Alaska, into districts, each district to contain only one of such Federal reserve cities. The determination of said organization committee shall not be subject to review except by the Board of Governors of the Federal Reserve System when organized: Provided that the districts shall be apportioned with due regard to the convenience and customary course of business and shall not necessarily be coterminous with any State or States. The districts thus created may be readjusted and new districts may from time to time be created by the Board of Governors of the Federal Reserve System, not to exceed twelve in all. Such districts shall be known as Federal reserve districts and may be designated by number. When the State of Alaska or Hawaii is hereafter admitted to the Union the Federal Reserve districts shall be readjusted by the Board of Governors of the Federal Reserve System in such manner as to include such State. Every national bank in any State shall, upon commencing business or within ninety days after admission into the Union of the State in which it is located, become a member bank of the Federal Reserve System by subscribing and paying for stock in the Federal Reserve bank of its district in accordance with the provisions of this Act and shall thereupon be an insured bank under the Federal Deposit Insurance Act, and failure to do so shall subject such bank to the penalty provided by the sixth paragraph of this section.

[Partly incorporated in 12 USC 222 and 223. As amended by acts of July 7, 1958 (72 Stat. 350); March 18, 1959 (73 Stat. 12).]

2. Powers of Organization Committee

Said organization committee shall be authorized to employ counsel and expert aid, to take testimony, to send for persons and papers, to administer oaths, and to make such investigation as may be deemed necessary by the said committee in determining the reserve districts and in designating the cities within such districts where such Federal reserve banks shall be severally located. The said committee shall supervise the organization in each of the cities designated of a Federal reserve bank, which shall include in its title the name of the city in which it is situated, as "Federal Reserve Bank of Chicago."

[Omitted from U.S. Code except part of last sentence, which is incorporated in 12 USC 225. Part of original Federal Reserve Act; not amended.]

3. Subscription to Stock by National Banks

Under regulations to be prescribed by the organization committee, every national banking association in the United States is hereby required, and every eligible bank in the United States and every trust company within the District of Columbia, is hereby authorized to signify in writing, within sixty days after the passage of this Act, its acceptance of the terms and provisions hereof. When the organization committee shall have designated the cities in which Federal reserve banks are to be organized, and fixed the geographical limits of the Federal reserve districts, every national banking association within that district shall be required within thirty days after notice from the organization committee, to subscribe to the capital stock of such Federal reserve bank in a sum equal to six per centum of the paid-up capital stock and surplus of such bank, one-sixth of the subscription to be payable on call of the organization committee or of the Board of Governors of the Federal Reserve System, one-sixth within three months and one-sixth within six months thereafter, and the remainder of the subscription, or any part thereof, shall be subject to call when deemed necessary by the Board of Governors of the Federal Reserve System, said payments to be in gold or gold certificates.

[Partly incorporated in 12 USC 282. Part of original Federal Reserve Act; not amended. For provisions concerning stock subscriptions by state banks and trust companies, see section 9.]

4. Liability of Shareholders of Reserve Banks

The shareholders of every Federal reserve bank shall be held individually responsible, equally and ratably, and not one for another, for all contracts, debts, and engagements of such bank to the extent of the amount of their subscriptions to such stock at the par value thereof in addition to the amount subscribed, whether such subscriptions have been paid up in whole or in part, under the provisions of this Act.

[12 USC 502. Part of original Federal Reserve Act; not amended.]

…

8. Stock Offered to Public

Should the subscriptions by banks to the stock of said Federal reserve banks or any one or more of them be, in the judgment of the organization committee, insufficient to provide the amount of capital required therefor, then and in that event the said organization committee may, under conditions and regulations to be prescribed by it, offer to public subscription at par such an amount of stock in said Federal reserve banks, or any one or more of them, as said committee shall determine, subject to the same conditions as to payment and stock liability as provided for member banks.

[Omitted from U.S. Code. Part of original Federal Reserve Act; not amended.]

…

Section 4. Federal Reserve Banks

1. Organization of Reserve Banks

When the organization committee shall have established Federal reserve districts as provided in section two of this Act, a certificate shall be filed with the Comptroller of the Currency showing the geographical limits of such districts and the Federal reserve city designated in each of such districts. The Comptroller of the Currency shall thereupon cause to be forwarded to each national bank located in each district, and to such other banks declared to be eligible by the organization committee which may apply therefor, an application blank in form to be approved by the organization committee, which blank shall contain a resolution to be adopted by the board of directors of each bank executing such application, authorizing a subscription to the capital stock of the Federal reserve bank organizing in that district in accordance with the provisions of this Act.

[Omitted from U.S. Code. Part of original Federal Reserve Act; not amended.]

…

4. General Corporate Powers

Upon the filing of such certificate with the Comptroller of the Currency as aforesaid, the said Federal reserve bank shall become a body corporate and as such, and in the name designated in such organization certificate, shall have power—First. To adopt and use a corporate seal.

Second. To have succession after the approval of this Act until dissolved by Act of Congress or until forfeiture of franchise for violation of law.

Third. To make contracts.

Fourth. To sue and be sued, complain and defend, in any court of law or equity.

Fifth. To appoint by its board of directors a president, vice presidents, and such officers and employees as are not otherwise provided for in this Act, to define their duties, require bonds for them and fix the penalty thereof, and to dismiss at pleasure such officers or employees. The president shall be the chief executive officer of the bank and shall be appointed by the Class B and Class C directors of the bank, with the approval of the Board of Governors of the Federal Reserve System, for a term of 5 years; and all other executive officers and all employees of the bank shall be directly responsible to the president. The first vice president of the bank shall be appointed in the same manner and for the same term as the president, and shall, in the absence or disability of the president or during a vacancy in the office of the president, serve as chief executive officer of the bank. Whenever a vacancy shall occur in the office of the president or the first vice president, it shall be filled in the manner provided for original appointments; and the person so appointed shall hold office until the expiration of the term of his predecessor.

Sixth. To prescribe by its board of directors, by-laws not inconsistent with law, regulating the manner in which its general business may be conducted, and the privileges granted to it by law may be exercised and enjoyed.

Seventh. To exercise by its board of directors, or duly authorized officers or agents, all powers specifically granted by the provisions of this Act and such incidental powers as shall be necessary to carry on the business of banking within the limitations prescribed by this Act.

Eighth. Upon deposit with the Treasurer of the United States of any bonds of the United States in the manner provided by existing law relating to national banks, to receive from the Secretary of the Treasury circulating notes in blank, registered and countersigned as provided by law, equal in amount to the par value of the bonds so deposited, such notes to be issued under the same conditions and provisions of law as relate to the issue of circulating notes of national banks secured by bonds of the United States bearing the circulating privilege, except that the issue of such notes shall not be limited to the capital stock of such Federal reserve bank.

[12 USC 341. As amended by act of Feb. 25, 1927 (44 Stat. 1234), which amended subparagraph "Second;" by act of Aug. 23, 1935 (49 Stat. 703), which amended subparagraph "Fifth" effective March 1, 1936; by act of Sept. 23, 1994 (108 Stat. 2293), which amended subparagraph "Eighth;" and by act of July 21, 2010 (124 Stat. 2126), which amended subparagraph "Fifth." As to issuance of Federal Reserve bank notes and redemption of bonds securing such notes, see section 18, and note to the first paragraph of that section.]

5. Authority to Commence Business

But no Federal reserve bank shall transact any business except such as is incidental and necessarily preliminary to its organization until it has been authorized by the Comptroller of the Currency to commence business under the provisions of this Act.

[12 USC 341. Part of original Federal Reserve Act; not amended.]

…

Section 10. Board of Governors of the Federal Reserve System

1. Appointment and Qualification of Members

The Board of Governors of the Federal Reserve System (hereinafter referred to as the "Board") shall be composed of seven members, to be appointed by the President, by and with the advice and consent of the Senate, after the date of enactment of the Banking Act of 1935, for terms of fourteen years except as hereinafter provided, but each appointive member of the Federal Reserve Board in office on such date shall continue to serve as a member of the Board until February 1, 1936, and the Secretary of the Treasury and the Comptroller of the Currency shall continue to serve as members of the Board until February 1, 1936. In selecting the members of the Board, not more than one of whom shall be selected from any one Federal Reserve district, the President shall have due regard to a fair representation of the financial, agricultural, industrial, and commercial interests, and geographical divisions of the country. The members of the Board shall devote their entire time to the business of the Board and shall each receive an annual salary of $15 000, payable monthly, together with actual necessary traveling expenses.

[12 USC 241. As amended by acts of June 3, 1922 (42 Stat. 620); Aug. 23, 1935 (49 Stat. 704). Prior to the enactment of the Banking Act of 1935, approved Aug. 23, 1935, the Board of Governors of the Federal Reserve System was known as the Federal Reserve Board. See note to the third paragraph of section 1. The portion of this paragraph dealing with salaries of Board members has in effect been amended numerous times, most recently by Executive Order. Prior to the act of December 27, 2000, section 1002 of which revised the executive schedule, the salary of the chairman of the Board was set at executive schedule level 2 and the salary of other members at level 3. The salary of the chairman of the Board is now set at executive schedule level I, and the salary of other members at level II (see 2 USC 358 and 5 USC 5313 and 5314).]

…

3. Assessments on Federal Reserve Banks

The Board of Governors of the Federal Reserve System shall have power to levy semiannually upon the Federal reserve banks, in proportion to their capital stock and surplus, an assessment sufficient to pay its estimated expenses and the salaries of its members and employees for the half year succeeding the levying of such assessments, together with any deficit carried forward from the preceding half year, and such assessments may include amounts sufficient to provide for the acquisition by the Board in its own name of such site or building in the District of Columbia as in its judgment alone shall be necessary for the purpose of providing suitable and adequate quarters for the performance of its functions. After September 1, 2000, the Board may also use such assessments to acquire, in its own name, a site or building (in addition to the facilities existing on such date) to provide for the performance of the functions of the Board. After approving such plans, estimates, and specifications as it shall have caused to be prepared, the Board may, notwithstanding any other provision of law, cause to be constructed on any site so acquired by it a building or buildings suitable and adequate in its judgment for its purposes and proceed to take all such steps as it may deem necessary or appropriate in connection with the construction, equipment, and furnishing of such building or buildings. The Board may maintain, enlarge, or remodel any building or buildings so acquired or constructed and shall have sole control of such building or buildings and space therein.

[12 USC 243. As reenacted without change by act of June 3, 1922 (42 Stat. 621); and amended by acts of June 19, 1934 (48 Stat. 1108) and Dec. 27, 2000 (114 Stat. 3027). By act approved June 27, 1935 (49 Stat. 425), provision was made for the furnishing of steam from the central heating plant to the Federal Reserve Board, now the Board of Governors of the Federal Reserve System.]

4. Principal Offices; Expenses; Deposit of Funds; Members Not to Be Officers or Stockholders of Banks

The principal offices of the Board shall be in the District of Columbia. At meetings of the Board the chairman shall preside, and, in his absence, the vice chairman shall preside. In the absence of the chairman and the vice chairman, the board shall elect a member to act as chairman pro tempore. The Board shall determine and prescribe the manner in which its obligations shall bc incurred and its disbursements and expenses allowed and paid, and may leave on deposit in the Federal Reserve banks the proceeds of assessments levied upon them to defray its estimated expenses and the salaries of its members and employees, whose employment, compensation, leave, and expenses shall be governed solely by the provisions of this Act, specific amendments thereof, and rules and regulations of the Board not inconsistent therewith; and funds derived from such assessments shall not be construed to be Government funds or appropriated moneys. No member of the Board of Governors of the Federal Reserve

System shall be an officer or director of any bank, banking institution, trust company, or Federal Reserve bank or hold stock in any bank, banking institution, or trust company; and before entering upon his duties as a member of the Board of Governors of the Federal Reserve System he shall certify under oath that he has complied with this requirement, and such certification shall be filed with the secretary of the Board. Whenever a vacancy shall occur, other than by expiration of term, among the six members of the Board of Governors of the Federal Reserve System appointed by the President as above provided, a successor shall be appointed by the President, by and with the advice and consent of the Senate, to fill such vacancy, and when appointed he shall hold office for the unexpired term of his predecessor.

[12 USC 244. As amended by acts of June 3, 1922 (42 Stat. 621); June 16, 1933 (48 Stat. 167); Aug. 23, 1935 (49 Stat. 705). The reference to "the six members" of the Board of Governors is an apparent error in the law and should read "the seven members." See section 10, first paragraph.]

…

8. Issuance of National Currency and Federal Reserve Notes

Section three hundred and twenty-four of the Revised Statutes of the United States shall be amended so as to read as follows:

Sec. 324. There shall be in the Department of the Treasury a bureau charged with the execution of all laws passed by Congress relating to the issue and regulation of national currency secured by United States bonds, and under the general supervision of the Board of Governors of the Federal Reserve System, of all Federal Reserve notes, except for the cancellation and destruction, and accounting with respect to such cancellation and destruction, of Federal Reserve notes unfit for circulation, the chief officer of which bureau shall be called the Comptroller of the Currency and shall perform his duties under the general directions of the Secretary of the Treasury. The Comptroller of the Currency shall have the same authority over matters within the jurisdiction of the Comptroller as the Director of the Office of Thrift Supervision has over matters within the Director's jurisdiction under section 3(b)(3) of the Home Owners' Loan Act. The Secretary of the Treasury may not delay or prevent the issuance of any rule or the promulgation of any regulation by the Comptroller of the Currency.

[12 USC 1. As reenacted without change by act of June 3, 1922 (42 Stat. 621); and amended by acts of May 20, 1966 (80 Stat. 161) and Sept. 23, 1994 (108 Stat. 2232).]

…

第二节　中央银行的业务

中央银行处于一国银行体系的中心环节，是一国货币金融的最高权力机构。为实现其固有的银行职能，中央银行必须依法从事一定的活动，开展一定的业务。中央银行的作用也是通过它的日常业务活动体现出来。

一、中国人民银行的业务

根据《中国人民银行法》的规定，中国人民银行出于执行货币政策和管理金融的需要，可以开展一系列的业务。中国人民银行在开展相关业务时，应当严格按照法律、行政法规的规定进行，并贯彻国家的方针政策；同时，应当遵循市场经济活动的规则，不得享有业务经营的特权。

依照《中国人民银行法》的规定，中国人民银行可经营的业务，既包括贷款、再贴现、证券买卖、保管金银及外汇储备等资产业务，也包括货币发行、代理国库、集中存款准备金、占用清算资金等负债业务，还包括代理发行和兑付国债、清算业务、金银管理业务等既不形成资金来源，也不运用自己的资产但属于职责范围内的服务性业务。

中国人民银行的业务活动具有如下几个特点：（1）以有利于履行职责为原则，业务活动开展不以营利为目的，而是通过提供业务服务来稳定货币、稳定金融，调节宏观经济的发展；（2）业务对象特定，主要是商业银行和其他金融机构，不经营一般商业银行业务，不直接对一般企业和个人开展业务。

根据《中国人民银行法》的规定，中国人民银行禁止从事以下业务：（1）不得对政府财政透支，不得直接认购、包销国债和其他政府债券；（2）不得向地方政府、各级政府部门提供贷款；（3）不得向非银行金融机构以及其他单位和个人提供贷款，但国务院决定中国人民银行可以向特定的非银行金融机构提供贷款的除外；（4）不得向任何单位和个人提供担保。

二、美国联邦储备系统的业务

美国联邦储备系统的一项重要职能是，向美国政府、公众、金融机构以及外国机构等提供可靠的金融服务。联邦储备系统在履行此项职能时，既作为政府的银行，也作为银行的银行发挥作用。作为政府的银行，它管理着政府的资金，为政府各部门的收支提供服务，协助政府发行债务凭证；作为银行的银行，它接受各银行的准备金存款，办理各银行间的清算业务，向银行发放短期贷款。美国联邦储备系统提供的服务大多数同银行支付体系有关，其余则涉及与美联储地位相称的其他服务。

第一，货币供应。联储体系的一个重要作用，就是保证经济有足够的货币来满足公众需要。货币在联储体系的循环投入和退出，是以存款机构为分配渠道的。存款机构扩充或缩减货币时，要从联储银行或分支机构取得现金或向联储归还现金，并相应地借记或贷记在其联储账户上。

第二，支票处理。在美国，支票主要用于支付数额较大的交易。在电子支付方式出现以前，支票一直是美国最受欢迎的非现金支付方式。联储在全国设立了多个票据清算中心进行支票处理服务。

第三，电子资金转账。联储直接介入两类电子资金转账服务，即资金电子转账和自动交换所。电子资金转账由所谓的“联储电传”（Federal wire）执行，该电传与联储分理处、存款机构、美国财政部和其他政府机构相联结。联储电传主要用于大额美元支付，通常数分钟内完成。自动交换所是20世纪70年代初期建立的，现已发展成一个全国范围内的清算机制，提供一系列借贷和转账程序。联储经营的自动交换所，向所有的存款机构提供自动转账服务。

第四，清算、托收等业务。联储对私营支票清算所、自动交换协会和资金电子转账等支付机制提供的服务，称为“纯清算”。纯清算一般涉及私营机构在联储账户上发生的净借贷项目。每个营业日结束时，汇总各机构在联储发生的所有交易，清算出参与机构的净会计头寸。联储还向存款机构提供其他服务：存款机构可凭其在联储存放的政府证券，获得抵押贷款；联储还接受非现金托收业务，包括快到期或已到期的政府息票和证券，银行承兑、提单、跟单汇票和支票等。

第五，财政代理。联邦储备系统作为美国政府的财政代理，为美国财政部、其他政府机构、政府资助的企业、部分国际组织提供多种银行业务。它所提供的财政代理业务包括：维护财政部的银行账户，操作支付系统，发行、保管、转让证券等，这些财政代理业务与向银行系统提供的业务大致相同或相近。

第六，国际业务。联储向外国中央银行、国际货币基金等国际金融机构提供服务。联储提供的最重要的服务是每日收付外国官方账户的美元交易。外国官方机构的美元收支相当大的比例是通过纽约联储银行处理。纽约联储银行为这些机构买卖外汇，并代为借记或贷记其美元账户。联储从许多的投资和管理服务中收取费用。

三、案例资料

支票清算，是法律授予联邦储备系统经营的重要业务之一。但是，联邦储备系统提供高效的支票清算服务，却有可能对一些小的银行构成威胁。下面的 American Bank & Trust Co. v. Federal Reserve Bank of Atlanta 案就涉及这一问题。

在该案中，一些乡村银行从支票的偿付过程中赚取利润。后来，联邦储备银行参与支票清算。乡村银行声称，联邦储备银行参与支票清算，是为了迫使乡村银行加入联储系统或通过在联邦储备银行开立清算账户而提高资本储备率。为了达到这一目的，联邦储备银行意图累积乡村银行应予支付的支票直到其达到较大的数额，然后向乡村银行提示付款并要求乡村银行支付现金。联邦储备银行参与支票清算的行为，致使这些乡村银行无法再赚取到利润，严重地影响到它们的生存。因此，针对联邦储备银行的诉讼被提交到法院，要求禁止联邦储备银行累积支票然后大规模提示要求现金付现的行为。联邦地区法院和上诉法院均驳回了原告的起诉。案件最终被上诉至美国联邦最高法院。

美国联邦最高法院对此案分别于1921年和1923年作出了判决。在1921年的判决中，最高法院认为，联邦储备银行提示支票要求付现，是其权利，但是若以损害他人的利益为目的，则不被允许，因此将案件发回重审。后联邦储备银行答复说，其提示支票时，付款行可以以汇票付款而并非必须支付现金，且其并未意图损害乡村银行的利益。联邦地区法院在重审过程中也认定，联邦储备银行并不存在损害或胁迫乡村银行的意图，因此驳回了原告的诉讼请求。联邦上诉法院维持原判。在1923年的判决中，联邦最高法院认定：国会授权联邦储备银行提供支票清算服务，尽管这在客观上确实导致乡村银行遭受损失，但这种损失是基于合法竞争所导致的，是当他人引进先进设备或一个更为有效的竞争者进入市场时，经营者通常要面对的，这是法律不予以救济的损害。

American Bank & Trust Co. v. Federal Reserve Bank of Atlanta

256 U.S. 350 (1921)

MR. JUSTICE HOLMES delivered the opinion of the Court.

This is a bill in equity brought by country banks incorporated by the State of Georgia against the Federal Reserve Bank of Atlanta, incorporated under the laws of the United States, and its officers. It was brought in a state court but removed to the district court of the United States on the petition of the defendants. A motion to remand was made by the plaintiffs, but was overruled. The allegations of the bill may be summed up in comparatively few words. The plaintiffs are not members of the Federal Reserve System, and many of them have too small a capital to permit their joining it—a capital that could not be increased to the required amount in the thinly populated sections of the country where they operate. An important part of the income of these small institutions is a charge for the services rendered by them in paying checks drawn upon them at a distance and forwarded, generally by other banks, through the mail. The charge covers the expense incurred by the paying bank and a small profit. The banks in the Federal Reserve System are forbidden to make such charges to other banks in the System. Federal Reserve Act of December 23, 1913, c. 6, § 13; 38 Stat. 263; amended March 3, 1915, c. 93; 38 Stat. 958; September 7, 1916, c. 461; 39 Stat. 752, and June 21, 1917, c. 32, §§ 4, 5; 40 Stat. 234, 235. It is alleged that, in pursuance of a policy accepted by the Federal Reserve Board, the defendant bank has determined to use its power to compel the plaintiffs and others in like situation to become members of the defendant, or at least to open a nonmember clearing account with defendant, and thereby, under the defendant's requirements, to make it necessary for the plaintiffs to maintain a much larger reserve than in their present condition they need. This diminution of their lending power, coupled with the loss of the profit caused by the above mentioned clearing of bank checks and drafts at par, will drive some of the plaintiffs out of business and diminish the income of all. To accomplish the defendants' wish, they intend to accumulate checks upon the country banks until they reach a large amount, and then to cause them to be presented for payment over the counter or by other devices detailed to require payment in cash in such wise as to compel the plaintiffs to maintain so much cash in their vaults as to drive them out of business or force them, if able, to submit to the defendant's scheme. It is alleged that the proposed conduct will deprive the plaintiffs or their property without due process of law, contrary to the Fifth Amendment of the Constitution, and that it is ultra vires. The bill seeks an injunction against the defendants' collecting checks except in the usual way. The district court dismissed the bill for want of equity, and its decree was affirmed by the circuit court of appeals. 269 F. 4. The plaintiffs appealed, setting up want of jurisdiction in the district court and error in the final decree.

We agree with the court below that the removal was proper. The principal dependant was incorporated under the laws of the United States, and that has been established as a ground of jurisdiction since Osborn v. Bank of the United States, 9 Wheat. 738; Pacific Railroad Removal Cases, 115 U. S. 1; Matter of Dunn, 212 U. S. 374. We shall say but a word in answer to the appellants' argument that a suit against such a corporation is not a suit arising under those laws within § 24 of the Judicial Code of March 3, 1911, c. 231, 36 Stat. 1087. The contrary is established, and the accepted doctrine is intelligible, at least since it is part of the plaintiffs' case that the defendant bank existed and exists as an entity capable of committing the wrong alleged and of being sued. These facts depend upon the laws of the United States. Bankers' Trust Co. v. Texas & Pacific Ry. Co., 241 U. S. 295, 241 U. S. 306-307; Texas & Pacific Ry. Co. v. Cody, 166 U. S. 606. See further Smith v. Kansas City Title & Trust Co., 255

U. S. 180. A more plausible objection is that, by the Judicial Code, § 24, sixteenth, except as therein excepted, national banking associations, for the purposes of suits against them, are to be deemed citizens of the states in which they are respectively located. But we agree with the court below that the reasons for localizing ordinary commercial banks do not apply to the federal reserve banks created after the Judicial Code was enacted, and that the phrase "national banking associations" does not reach forward and include them. That phrase is used to describe the ordinary commercial banks, whereas the others are systematically called "federal reserve banks." We see no sufficient ground for supposing that Congress meant to open the questions that the other construction would raise.

On the merits, we are of opinion that the courts below went too far. The question at this stage is not what the plaintiffs may be able to prove, or what may be the reasonable interpretation of the defendants' acts, but whether the plaintiffs have shown a ground for relief if they can prove what they allege. We lay on one side as not necessary to our decision the question of the defendants' powers, and, assuming that they act within them, consider only whether the use that, according to the bill, they intend to make of them will infringe the plaintiffs' rights. The defendants say that the holder of a check has a right to present it to the bank upon which it was drawn for payment over the counter, and that, however many checks he may hold, he has the same right as to all of them, and may present them all at once, whatever his motive or intent. They ask whether a mortgagee would be prevented from foreclosing because he acted from disinterested malevolence, and not from a desire to get his money. But the word "right" is one of the most deceptive of pitfalls; it is so easy to slip from a qualified meaning in the premise to an unqualified one in the conclusion. Most rights are qualified. A man has at least as absolute a right to give his own money as he has to demand money from a party that has made no promise to him; yet if he gives it to induce another to steal or murder, the purpose of the act makes it a crime.

A bank that receives deposits to be drawn upon by check, of course, authorizes its depositors to draw checks against their accounts, and holders of such checks to present them for payment. When we think of the ordinary case, the right of the holder is so unimpeded that it seems to us absolute. But, looked at from either side, it cannot be so. The interests of business also are recognized as rights, protected against injury to a greater or less extent, and in case of conflict between the claims of business, on the one side, and of third persons, on the other, lines have to be drawn that limit both. A man has a right to give advice, but advice given for the sole purpose of injuring another's business and effective on a large scale might create a cause of action. Banks as we know them could not exist if they could not rely upon averages and lend a large part of the money that they receive from their depositors on the assumption that not more than a certain fraction of it will be demanded on any one day. If, without a word of falsehood, but acting from what we have called disinterested malevolence, a man by persuasion should organize and carry into effect a run upon a bank and ruin it, we cannot doubt that an action would lie. A similar result, even if less complete in its effect, is to be expected from the course that the defendants are alleged to intend, and to determine whether they are authorized to follow that course, it is not enough to refer to the general right of a holder of checks to present them, but it is necessary to consider whether the collection of checks and presenting them in a body for the purpose of breaking down the petitioner's business as now conducted is justified by the ulterior purpose in view.

If this were a case of competition in private business, it would be hard to admit the justification of self-interest, considering the now current opinion as to public policy expressed in statutes and decisions. But this is not a private business. The policy of the federal reserve banks is governed by the policy of the United States with regard to them, and to these relatively feeble competitors. We do not need aid from the debates upon the statute under which the Reserve Banks exist to assume that the United States did not intend by that statute to sanction this sort of warfare upon legitimate creations of the states.

Decree reversed.

American Bank & Trust Co. v. Federal Reserve Bank of Atlanta

262 U.S. 643,43 S.Ct. 649,67 L.Ed. 1153 (1923)

Mr. Justice BRANDEIS delivered the opinion of the Court.

After the decision in this case reported in 256 U. S. 350, 41 Sup. Ct. 499, 65 L. Ed. 983, an answer was filed which denied, in large part, the allegations of the bill. Then, by an amended answer, the Federal Reserve Bank disclaimed any intention of demanding payment in cash, when presenting checks at the banks, and averred its willingness to accept payment in drafts, either on the drawee's Atlanta correspondent or on any other solvent bank, if collectible at par. The District Court heard the case upon the evidence. It found that the Federal Reserve

Bank was not inspired by any ulterior purpose to coerce or to injure any nonmember bank which refused to remit at par. It found that the evidence was insufficient to sustain any charge that the Federal Reserve Bank was exercising its rights so as to injure or oppress plaintiff banks. And it found, specifically, that the evidence did not sustain the charge that the Federal Reserve Bank accumulated checks upon nonmember country banks until they reached a large amount and then caused the checks to be presented for payment over the counter, in order to compel plaintiff banks to keep in their vaults so much cash that they would be obliged either to agree to remit at par or to go out of business. With regard to publication on the par list of the names of nonassenting banks, the District Court held that the evidence did not justify a finding that such publication was made in order to injure or oppress plaintiff banks. But it was of opinion that insertion of their names might lead to the belief that the plaintiff banks had agreed to remit at par. An injunction was, therefore, granted against inclusion of their names on the par list. The relief sought was in all other respects denied. The decree left the Federal Reserve Bank free to publish that it would make collection at par of checks upon any bank in any town, thus including those in which plaintiffs had their respective places of business. 280 Fed. 940. These findings were approved by the Circuit Court of Appeals, and the decree was affirmed. 284 Fed. 424.

The case is here on an appeal taken by the plaintiffs. The evidence was conflicting. No adequate reason is shown why the concurrent findings of fact made by the two lower courts should not be accepted by us. Luckenbach v. W. J. McCahan Sugar Refining Co., 248 U. S. 139, 145, 39 Sup. Ct. 53, 63 L. Ed. 170, 1 A. L. R. 1522. Whether on the undisputed facts plaintiffs were entitled to additional relief is the main question for decision. In order to decide that question it is necessary to consider the course of business formerly prevailing and the changes wrought by the attempt to introduce universal par clearance and collection of checks through the Federal Reserve Banks.

A large part of the checks drawn on country banks are sent to payees who reside in places other than that in which thc drawee bank is located. Payment of such a check is ordinarily secured through the payee's depositing it in his local bank for collection. This bank ordinarily used, as the means for presenting the check to the drawee, a clearing house and/or correspondent banks. Formerly when he check was so presented, the drawee ordinarily paid, not in cash, but by a remittance drawn on his balance in some reserve city or by a credit with some correspondent. This process of collection yielded to the country bank a twofold profit. It earned some profit by the small service charge called exchange, which it made for the remittance or the credit. And it earned some profit by using the depositor's money during the period (sometimes weeks) in which the check was traveling the often circuitous route, with many stops, from the payee's bank to its own, and also while the exchange draft was being collected. These avenues to profit are, in large measure, closed by the Federal Reserve Banks' course of action. These banks do not pay any exchange charges to the drawee. And their superior facilities so shorten the time required to collect checks that the drawee bank's balances available for loans are much reduced. Largely because of the fact that the reserve banks thus make the collection without any deduction for exchange, most checks on country banks are now routed through the reserve banks. Although there is, as the District Court found, no intentional accumulation or holding of checks in order to embarrass, the advantages offered by the Federal Reserve Banks have created a steady flow in increased volume of checks on country banks so routed. That the action contemplated by the Federal Reserve Bank will subject the country banks to certain losses is clear. In order to protect them from the resulting loss it would be necessary to prevent the Federal Reserve Banks from accepting the checks for collection. For these banks cannot be compelled to pay exchange charges or to abandon superior facilities.

The contention is that the injunction should issue, because it is ultra vires the Federal Reserve Banks to collect checks on banks which are not members of the system or affiliated with it, through establishing an exchange balance, and which have definitely refused to assent to clearance at par. It is true that Congress has created in the reserve banks institutions special in character, with limited functions and with duties and powers carefully prescribed. Those in respect to the collection of checks are clearly defined. The original act (Act Dec. 23, 1913, c. 6, § 13, 38 Stat. 251, 263) authorized the reserve banks to—

> "receive from any of its member banks, and from the United States, deposits of * * * checks * * * upon solvent member banks, payable upon presentation; or, solely for exchange purposes, may receive from other Federal Reserve Banks deposits of * * * checks * * * upon solvent member or other Federal Reserve Banks, payable upon presentation."

By the amendment to section 13 by Act Sept. 7, 1916, c. 461, 39 Stat. 752, the class of checks receivable was extended to "checks payable upon presentation within the district." By the amendment to section 13 by Act June 21, 1917, c. 32, § 4, 40 Stat. 232, 235, the class of banks from which checks might be received "solely * * * for collection" was extended. Comp. St. 1918, Comp. St. Ann. Supp. 1919, § 9796. By the latter amendment the facilities offered by the Federal Reserve Banks were made available also to such nonmembers as became affiliated with the Federal Reserve system by establishing the required balance "to offset items in transit." It is true, also, that in practice this amendment might result in excluding checks on particular banks from the class collectible through the Federal Reserve Banks. For it enacted the clause which prohibits payment of exchange charges by Federal Reserve Banks. And as this prohibition would prevent Reserve Banks from using the usual channels in making collection of checks drawn on those country banks which insist upon exchange charges, the Reserve Bank might find it impossible or unwise, as a matter of banking practice, to collect such checks at all. But the class of checks to which the Reserve Bank's collection service might legally be applied, was le t by the amendment as those "payable upon presentation within its district." Wherever collection can be made by the Federal Reserve Bank, without paying exchange, neither the common law, nor the Federal Reserve Act precludes their undertaking it, if it can be done consistently with the rights of the country banks already determined in this case. 256 U. S. 350, 41 Sup. Ct. 499, 65 L. Ed. 983.

Federal Reserve Banks are, thus, authorized by Congress to collect for other Reserve Banks, for members, and for affiliated nonmembers, checks on any bank within their respective districts, if the check is payable on presentation and can in fact be collected consistently with the legal rights of the drawee without paying an exchange charge. Within these limits Federal Reserve Banks have ordinarily the same right to present a check to the drawee bank for payment over the counter, as any other bank, state or national, would have. For section 4 (38 Stat. 251, 254 [Comp. st. § 9788]) provides that the Federal Reserve Banks shall have power:

> "Seventh. To exercise by its board of directors, or duly authorized officers or agents, all powers specifically granted by the provisions of this act and such incidental powers as shall be necessary to carry on the business of banking within the limitations prescribed by this act."

The findings of fact negative the charges of wrongful intent and of coercion. The Federal Reserve Bank has formally declared that it is willing, when presenting checks, to accept in payment a draft of the drawee bank upon its Atlanta correspondent or a draft upon any other solvent bank—if collectible at par. Country banks are not entitled to protection against legitimate competition. Their loss here shown is of the kind to which business concerns are commonly subjected when improved facilities are introduced by others, or a more efficient competitor enters the field. It is damnum absque injuria. As the course of action contemplated by the Federal Reserve Bank is not ultra vires, we need not consider whether lack of power, if it had existed, would have entitled plaintiffs to relief. Compare National Bank v. Matthews, 98 U. S. 621, 25 L. Ed. 188; Blair v. Chicago, 201 U. S. 400, 450, 26 Sup. Ct. 427, 50 L. Ed. 801.

Some minor objections are urged. The Federal Reserve Bank of Atlanta serves, directly, only the Sixth Reserve District, which includes Georgia. It is contended that the decree should be reversed because the District Court refused to allow the intervention as plaintiffs of banks located outside of that district; because that court refused to admit evidence of the activities engaged in by other Federal Reserve Banks in other districts under the approval of the Federal Reserve Board; and because the court admitted certain joint answers to interrogatories propounded under equity rule 58 (33 Sup. Ct. xxxiv). We cannot say that the trial court abused the discretion vested in it, or erred, in so ruling.

Affirmed.

第三节　中央银行的货币政策

一、中国人民银行的货币政策

根据《中国人民银行法》的规定，在中国，国家货币政策的制定和执行均由中国人民银行负责。中国人民银行货币政策目标是保持货币币值的稳定，并以此促进经济增长。中国在中国人民银行内特设货币政策委员会，作为中国人民银行制定货币政策的咨询议事机构。根据《中国人民银行货币政策委员会条例》的相关规定，货币政策委员会的职责是，在综合分析宏观经济形势的基础上，依据国家的宏观经济调控目标，讨论以下货币政策事项并提出建议：货币政策的制定、调整；一定时期内的货币政策控制目标；货币政策工具的运用；有关货币政策的重要措施；货币政策与其他宏观经济政策的协调。

为实现既定的货币政策目标，中央银行一般需要通过货币政策工具的运作，调节货币供应量。货币政策工具，指中央银行为实现货币政策目标所运用的策略手段。根据《中国人民银行法》的规定，中国人民银行为执行货币政策，可以运用下列货币政策工具：

第一，要求银行业金融机构按照规定的比例交存存款准备金。在中国，所有吸收一般存款（相对财政性存款而言的存款）的金融机构，都有按规定比例和期限缴存存款准备金的义务。存款准备金率由中国人民银行规定、调整、公布，并组织其分支机构具体实施。

第二，确定中央银行基准利率。基准利率是一国利率体系中起主导作用的基础利率，它的水平和变动决定其他各种利率的水平和变化。

第三，为在中国人民银行开立账户的银行业金融机构办理再贴现。再贴现政策，是中央银行通过调整其对金融机构办理票据再贴现的再贴现率，来扩大或缩小金融机构的信贷量，从而促使信用扩张或收缩的政策措施。

第四，向商业银行提供贷款，即再贷款。再贷款主要以发行货币、财政性存款、存款准备金为资金来源。中国人民银行通过再贷款控制和调节商业银行的信贷活动，从而控制和调节货币供应量和信用总量。

第五，在公开市场上买卖国债、其他政府债券和金融债券及外汇，即公开市场业务。中国人民银行通过公开市场业务，以吞吐基础货币，从而控制和调节货币供应量的业务活动。

第六，国务院确定的其他货币政策工具。这是法律规定的有关选择性、补充性货币政策工具的兜底条款。在中国，目前这些政策工具主要有：特种存款、证券市场信用控制、消费信用控制、不动产信用控制及窗口指导、道义劝告等。

二、美国联邦储备系统的货币政策

美国联邦储备系统最重要的职能之一便是制定和执行货币政策，以实现充分就业和稳定物价、实现经济稳定增长的目标。美国联邦储备系统实施货币政策有三大法宝：调整法定准备金比率、调整贴现率、公开市场业务。

（一）调整法定准备金比率

在美国，商业银行等接受存款的机构在接受存款以后，必须要按联邦储备系统的要求保留一定比例的准备金以应付客户提取存款。这部分准备金需要存在联邦储备系统，并且没有利息收益。由联邦储备系统规定的准备金比率称为法定准备金比率。由于联邦储备系统有权在一定的范围内调整法定储备金比率，它可以利用这个手段去影响美国的货币供给量。调整法定准备金比率是一项威力巨大的货币手段，是否调整法定准备金比率由联邦储备理事会作出决定。

在通货膨胀时期，联邦储备系统可以提高法定准备金比率。为了补充准备金，商业银行不得不收缩贷款，减少存款和投资，从而带来信贷规模和货币供给量的缩小。而在经济萧条时期，为了刺激经济的复苏，联邦储备系统可以降低法定准备金比率。法定准备金比率的下降使商业银行出现了多余的储备，它们在追求利润的动机的支配下将增加贷款，从而使信贷规模和货币供给量扩大。

（二）调整贴现率

当商业银行出现准备金不足或短期流动资金不足时，它们可以通过联邦储备银行的贴现专柜借入短期流动资金，联邦储备系统也可以利用调整贴现率的方法来调节银行的借款数量，从而达到影响货币供给量的目的。调整贴现率一般先由联邦储备银行提出，在征得联邦储备理事会批准后实施。

当联邦储备系统降低贴现率时，银行可以按较低的成本取得短期贷款，这样银行一方面可以减少它所保留的流动资产，另一方面因成本下降也可以降低贷款利率。因此，货币供给量会在一定程度上扩大。相反，当联邦储备系统提高贴现率时，银行需要按较高的成本取得短期贷款，这样银行一方面不得不保留较多的流动资产，另一方面因成本上升也会提高贷款利率。因此，货币供给量会在一定程度上收缩。

（三）公开市场业务

公开市场业务是指联邦储备系统在市场上买卖有价证券，主要是国库券、其他联邦政府债券、联邦机构债券和银行承兑汇票。如果联邦储备系统认为需要增加货币供给，其会向会员银行购买有价证券，货币供应量增加，随后的效应就是市场利率下降、投资增加、经济增长。相反，如果美联储认为需要减少货币供给，便会出售有价证券，从而减少银行体系的准备金，减少货币供应量。

公开市场业务由公开市场委员会负责。在公开市场委员会召开例会前，工作人员向各个成员递交经济形势的分析报告。在会议上，每一个委员都要陈述自己的意见。在会议形成买卖政府或其他债券的决议以后，交由联邦储备银行实施。

除了上述常规货币政策手段之外，美联储还进行了一系列的货币政策创新，相继推出了多种新的流动性管理工具，以增加市场的流动性供给，放松银根，恢复市场信心。这种货币政策创新包括：定期拍卖融资便利（Term Auction Facility）、一级交易商信贷便利（Primary Dealer Credit Facility）以及定期证券借贷工具（Term Securities Lending Facility）。此外，美联储还通过资产支持商业票据货币市场共同基金融资工具（Asset-Backed Commercial Paper Money Market Mutual Fund Liquidity Facility）、商业票据融资工具（Commercial Paper Funding Facility）及货币市场投资者融资工具（Money Market Investor Funding Facility，）等金融创新工具，以及与多国央行达成互换协议的形式，向市场注入大量资金，以提高市场的流动性。

三、案例资料

通过提高或降低存款准备金要求以调节货币供应量，是各国央行实施货币政策的重要手段。在美国，调整存款准备金率也是美联储惯用的控制货币供给的手段。但是，美联储主要对国民银行实施监管，因此其实施的存款准备金政策只能影响到国民银行，诸多州银行则游离于美联储的货币控制范围之外。

为此，美国国会在1980年通过了《货币控制法案》(Money Control Act，MCA)，要求美国所有银行均遵守美联储的存款准备金要求，而不再施行之前的双轨制。MCA的通过，引发了州银行的不满。下面的First Bank and Trust Co. v. Board of Governors of Federal Reserve System案即因MCA的通过而导致的争议。

该案中，原告在1980年以前是一家国民银行。由于作为联储会员行所提取的准备金额度更高，原告决定退出联储体系转而申请州特许状成为州银行，并于1980年3月3日获得州特许状。同日，原告即将其准备金余额从地区联邦储备银行中取出。

退出联邦储备系统的银行并非原告一家，在当时社会上掀起了“银行大逃亡”的浪潮，由此造成美联储日益失去对货币供给的控制的状况。1980年，美国国会通过MCA，要求所有银行，无论其是否是联储会员，都强制性地遵守统一的存款准备金要求。但是，对于非会员银行，其被允许在8年时间内逐渐转入适用强制性存款准备金的要求，而会员行则须一直根据联邦规章提取准备金。

1980年6月13日，原告请求联储理事会作出其已于1979年7月1日前退出联储体系的决定，以使自己可于8年内逐渐适用准备金要求或可由于立即适用准备金要求存在困难而申请“困难豁免”。但联储理事会拒绝了其请求，原告遂向法院提起诉讼，质疑MCA的效力。

联邦地区法院判决认为，从MCA的立法史来看，其主要目的之一就是要平衡非会员行与会员行间存款准备金的差别。对强制性准备金要求的规定，目的在于遏制银行逃离联储体系现象的进一步恶化，试图通过规定非会员行逐步适用期的方式来减少退出联储体系对会员行的吸引力，使退出联储并转而申请州特许状的方式不再具有明显的优势。退出联储体系银行数的减少，使得联储理事会对国家货币供给的控制能力得以保障。根据这一立法意图，国会选择MCA通过前的某个时间，作为确定一家银行是否是联储会员从而是否适用该法案中过渡条款的时间点，这一做法是合理的。因此，法院判决原告败诉。

First Bank and Trust Co. v. Board of Governors of Federal Reserve System

605 F. Supp. 555 (E.D. Ky. 1984)

WILHOIT, District Judge.

This action is before the Court on objections to the Magistrate's Report and Recommendation (the "Report") that declared portions of the Monetary Control Act of 1980

(MCA), as originally enacted, to be unconstitutional by virtue of the Fifth Amendment's due process clause, although the Report upheld the constitutionality of the MCA as it was amended in 1982. The Board of Governors of the Federal Reserve (the "Board") filed objections to the Report, to which First Bank & Trust Company ("First Bank"), the plaintiff herein, responded. The Board has replied to bank's response, and the matter is, therefore, fully submitted to this Court.

I. FACTS

This action concerns the validity of the MCA of 1980, and as amended in 1982. In its pertinent parts, the MCA extended reserve requirements to all banks in the United States whether the bank was a *558 member of the Federal Reserve System or not. Prior to 1980, a dual system of reserve requirements for banks was in existence. Banks that were members of the Federal Reserve were required to post reserves in accordance with the regulations of the Board. Banks not a member of the Federal Reserve could keep reserves in accordance with state banking laws. All nationally chartered banks are required to be members of the Federal Reserve and comply with its reserve requirements. State-chartered banks could be members of the Federal Reserve, but if they were not, they did not have to comply with the Board's reserve requirements.

This dual system has been in existence for some time. In recent years it began to be unprofitable for many banks to maintain membership in the Federal Reserve System because of the relatively high cost of services provided by the Federal Reserve, and more importantly, because of the growing loss of profits occasioned by Federal Reserve's relatively high percentage of required reserves, many banks began to leave the System.

Prior to 1980, First Bank was a nationally chartered bank. Because of the greater amount of idle reserves it had to hold being a member of the Federal Reserve, First Bank's Board of Directors in 1979, decided to withdraw from the System and seek a state charter. The bank's shareholders approved the Board of Director's decision on February 26, 1980. A state charter was obtained March 3, 1980, and on the same day, the Bank withdrew its reserve balances from the Federal Reserve Bank of Cleveland, relinquishing its stock in the system.

The rising tide of "bank flight" from the Federal Reserve System did not escape Congress' attention. Indeed, in 1979, at least five bills appeared in Congress aimed at correcting the Federal Reserve's growing lack of control over the money supply.

Many of the proposed bills imposed mandatory reserve requirements for all banks including non-member banks. On November 1, 1979, however, the Senate passed S. 1347 with an amendment removing mandatory reserve requirements. The House had already approved legislation that did not require mandatory reserves for non-member banks. Therefore as of November 1, 1979, it appeared Congress would not pass legislation mandating reserves requirements for all banks.

Newsletters in the banking industry were circulated assuring bankers that Congress would not legislate mandatory reserve requirements because both houses had approved legislation without such a requirement. The news that Congress would not impose mandatory reserves reached the Board of Directors of First Bank and was one of the precipitating factors in its decision to withdraw from the Federal Reserve System.

The Conference Committee Report of the MCA, which was rendered on March 21, 1980, and which includes the provisions under dispute in this lawsuit, re-imposed mandatory reserve requirements. The Conference Report was approved by both houses of Congress and signed into law by President Carter on March 31, 1980.

The pertinent provisions of the MCA, as finally passed and signed by the President, provide that non-member banks shall be allowed an eight-year phase-in of the mandatory reserve requirements. Member banks, however, were not given any phase-in period and had to maintain reserves in accordance with federal regulations as always.

Under regulations promulgated by the Board shortly after the MCA was passed, a bank that was formerly a member but had withdrawn, must have taken some unambiguous, irrevocable action toward withdrawal before July 1, 1979 to be eligible for the eight-year phase-in program. The regulations further provided that the Board may extend the time for posting reserves in "hardship" cases. These regulations, however, were promulgated without notice or comment as laid out in the procedures, of 5 U.S.C. § 553(b).

On June 13, 1980, First Bank petitioned the Board for a determination that it had *559 withdrawn from membership prior to July 1, 1979. On July 19th, the bank petitioned a second time seeking in the alternative a determination that the financial hardship exception as laid out in the regulations was applicable to it. Both petitions were denied on September 26, 1980: the first, for the reasons that the bank had not taken unambiguous, irrevocable steps to withdraw before July 1, 1979; and the second, for the reason that the bank's financial condition as of June 30, 1980 did not warrant application of the hardship exception. After the Board denied reconsideration of its decision, the bank posted its required reserve deposits in October 1980. In February 1981, First Bank brought this action seeking judicial review of the Board's decision under 5 U.S.C. §§ 701-06 and 12 U.S.C. § 632.

In October 1982, Congress passed the Garn-St. Germain Act amending the MCA. Congress recognized that the lack of any phase-in period for banks that had recently withdrawn from the Federal Reserve System could work an extreme hardship. The Garn-St. Germain amendments granted banks that had withdrawn between July 1, 1979 and March 31, 1980 a limited phase-in period.

This matter was referred to the United States Magistrate for a Report and Recommendation, see 28 U.S.C. § 636(b)(1)(B), after the defendants moved to dismiss or in the alternative for summary judgment and the plaintiff responded and cross-moved for summary judgment. The Court agrees with most of the Magistrate's Report and adopts portions of the Report herein as and for its own opinion.

...

In its complaint plaintiff seeks a declaration that 12 U.S.C. § 461(b)(8)(D)(i) violates its substantive due process rights as guaranteed by the Fifth Amendment of the Constitution. Plaintiff contends that the MCA's original provisions violated its rights by providing no phase-in period for banks which had withdrawn from the Federal Reserve System after July 1, 1979; of particular concern was the fact that the date selected was almost nine months before the enactment of the original provision in the MCA. Additionally, at issue are the provisions as modified by the Garn-St. Germain Act.

[18] [19] It is well established that legislative acts adjusting the burden and benefits of economic life come to the court with a presumption of constitutionality. Hodel v. Indiana, 452 U.S. 314, 323, 101 S.Ct. 2376, 2382, 69 L.Ed.2d 40 (1981); Richardson v. Secretary of Labor, 689 F.2d 632, 633 (6th Cir. 1981), cert. denied, 461 U.S. 928, 103 S.Ct. 2088, 77 L.Ed.2d 299. In areas of economic regulation, the courts have consistently deferred to legislative determinations as to the desirability of particular statutory discriminations. Id. Unless the classification trammels fundamental personal rights or is drawn on an inherently suspect classification, its constitutionality is presumed and the challenged classification need only be rationally related to a legitimate governmental interest. Id.

[20] [21] This rational relationship test means that the court must defer to congressional judgment unless it is demonstrably arbitrary or irrational. Duke Power Co. v. Carolina Environmental Study Group, Inc., 438 U.S. 59, 83-84, 98 S.Ct. 2620, 2635-36, 57 L.Ed.2d 595 (1977). Underinclusiveness alone does not make a legislative classification invalid. Richardson, 689 F.2d at 634.

[22] However, this case involves not merely the questions of whether Congress could

pass legislation concerning the reserve requirements in the Federal Reserve system or whether it could extend those requirements to non-member banks. Clearly, it has that authority consistent with the Constitution.

At issue are the constitutional problems occasioned by the retroactive application of the statute in question. As the Supreme Court in Usery v. Turner Elkhorn Mining Co., 428 U.S. 1, 16-17, 96 S.Ct. 2882, 2892-93, 49 L.Ed.2d 752 (1976), pointed out, it is not necessarily true that "what Congress can legislate prospectively, it can legislate *565 retrospectively;" the retrospective aspects of legislation must also meet the due process test and what may justify law prospective in application may not suffice with a retroactive statute. The Magistrate's Report recommended the MCA, as passed in its original form, be found unconstitutional because of its retroactive effect. The Court does not agree.

In reaching his conclusion, the Magistrate relied on several cases which have been recently disapproved by the United States Supreme Court. See Pension Benefit Guaranty Corp. v. R.A. Gray & Co., 467 U.S. 717, 104 S.Ct. 2709, 81 L.Ed.2d 601 (1984). The Magistrate relied and the parties focused their arguments on Nachman Corp. v. Pension Benefit Guaranty Corp., 592 F.2d 947 (7th Cir.1979), *aff'd* on other grounds, 446 U.S. 359, 100 S.Ct. 1723, 64 L.Ed.2d 354. The four-pronged analysis of the constitutionality of retroactive legislation as laid out in the Nachman case was rejected in Pension Benefit Guaranty Corp. v. R.A. Gray & Co., supra 467 U.S. at—n. 6, 104 S.Ct. at 2717 n. 6. Instead, the Supreme Court stated that the rational basis test is what should be applied to legislation that bears on the economic benefits and burdens of retroactive federal legislation. See id. 467 U.S. at—, 104 S.Ct. at 2718.

The Court assumes *arguendo* that the MCA, as originally enacted and amended, was retroactive in application although the Court realizes a substantial question is posed whether it is in fact retroactive. The Court finds, however, that even if it were said to be retroactive, there is a rational basis for its retrospective effect. This is all that is required for upholding the legislation under the Fifth Amendment's Due Process clause. See id.

It is clear from the legislative history behind the MCA that one of the principle purposes of the Act was to equalize the inequities between the amount of reserves required to be kept by non-member banks vis-a-vis member banks. In attempting to equalize these inequities, by establishing mandatory reserve requirements for all banks, Congress intended to curb the rising tide of bank flight from the Reserve System. Bank flight created what many, including Congress, perceived to be an alarming decrease in the amount of the nation's money supply directly controllable by the Federal Reserve Board. The equalization brought about by the

MCA, albeit accomplished through a phase-in for non-member banks, has the effect of reducing the attractiveness for member banks to withdraw from the System. There is no longer any significant competitive advantage to be gained by forfeiting Reserve membership in favor of a state charter. With fewer banks, therefore, "fleeing" from the Reserve System, the Board is assured of not losing any more control over the nation's money supply via its member banks.

Pursuant to the intent behind the MCA, it is clear Congress had a rational purpose in picking a date prior in time to the Act's enactment for determining which banks would be deemed member or non-member banks for purposes of the Act's phase-in provision. First of all, Congress wanted to curb bank flight and therefore was not going to reward banks that had recently withdrawn from the System in anticipation of Congress' imposing mandatory reserve requirements. More importantly, Congress wanted to equalize the inequitable differences in the amount of reserves required of member and non-member banks. Congress no longer wanted member banks to be at a competitive disadvantage with their non-member counterparts. At the same time, Congress did not want to impose mandatory reserves on non-member banks effective immediately without some transitional, phase-in provisions to ease the financial hardship that might be occasioned on non-member banks having to increase their required reserves. The phase-in provisions of the Act allow non-member banks the opportunity to gradually post the increased reserves required of them by the federal government.

Transitional, phase-in provisions are, of course, short term, anti-equalization measures. Moreover, equalization of the differing *566 amounts of reserves required by federal and state regulations was one of the primary purposes of the Act. Consequently, Congress did not want to extend the transitional, phase-in provisions to any banks that did not need the benefit of the phase-in provisions. Indeed, within the overall intent of the Act, the phase-in provisions were tolerated *only* to ease the hardship that might otherwise be created for non-member banks that have never been subjected to federal reserve requirements.

Recently withdrawn banks—i.e. banks that have withdrawn from the Reserve within the past nine months—would not be significantly oppressed by immediately posting the mandatory reserves required of all banks under the Act. These banks, having recently been members of the Reserve, would not be as financially oppressed in posting reserves in amounts which they were required to keep when they were member banks. Certainly for them, putting up the reserves would not be as much of a hardship as it would be for banks that had never been required to keep such a level of reserves. Congress could, therefore, rationally conclude that banks which had been members of the Reserve as of July 1, 1979, approximately nine months before the MCA's enactment, should not benefit from the transitional, phase-in provisions.

Given this rationale for the legislative scheme, First Bank simply cannot point to any lack of a rational basis for the way in which the MCA, as originally enacted and/or as amended in 1982, attempts to impose mandatory reserve requirements on non-member banks. Congress rationally discriminated between recently withdrawn non-member banks and all other non-member banks. The rationale is, simply put, that recently withdrawn banks do not *need* the benefit of a phase-in while other non-member banks do. At the same time, Congress rationally chose to make the operative date in the Act nine months prior to its enactment. The rational basis for this is simply that it avoids extending the transitional, phase-in provisions to banks that really do not need it, at least they do not need it to the extent other banks that had never been members may need it. Cf. Pension Benefit Guaranty Corp. v. R.A. Gray & Co., 467 U.S. at—, 104 S.Ct. at 2717-19.

There is, therefore, no equal protection or retroactive (due process) problems with the MCA, either as originally enacted or amended. Although the Bank's complaint—that it has been inequitably treated vis-a-vis other state banks because it was not permitted a phase-in period for posting reserves while other state banks were permitted such a phase-in—is a compelling and logical argument the Court does not believe the argument raises a substantial constitutional question. There being a rational basis for requiring the Bank to post its reserves without a phase-in, the Court believes the argument is a matter best settled in the political arena. Indeed, it is for this reason the Court believes that the Board adopted the "hardship exception" in its regulations and that Congress later enacted the limited, phase-in provisions of the Garn-St. Germain Amendments of 1982.

Consequently, the Court refuses to adopt the Magistrate's report in this respect and agrees with the Board with regard to the validity of the MCA and the regulatory scheme promulgated pursuant thereto….

第四节 中央银行的监管职能

一、中国人民银行的监管职能

中国现代金融业自改革开放开始不断发展。改革开放之初，中国人民银行作为中国的金融业监管机构，履行对包括银行、信托、证券和保险等行业的全面监管职能。随着证券、保险、银行和信托业的监管职能先后从中国人民银行分离出来，中国人民银行成为了只负责宏观金融稳定监管的中央银行。根据《中国人民银行法》的规定，中国人民银行在国务院领导下，制定和执行货币政策，防范和化解金融风险，维护金融稳定。

根据《中国人民银行法》的规定，中国人民银行的宏观金融监管职能包括履行以下几个方面的职责：（1）发布与履行与其职责有关的命令和规章；（2）依法制定和执行货币政策；（3）发行人民币，管理人民币流通；（4）监督管理银行间同业拆借市场和银行间债券市场；（5）实施外汇管理，监督管理银行间外汇市场；（6）监督管理黄金市场；（7）持有、管理、经营国家外汇储备、黄金储备；（8）经理国库；（9）维护支付、清算系统的正常运行；（10）指导、部署金融业反洗钱工作，负责反洗钱的资金监测；（11）负责金融业的统计、调查、分析和预测；（12）作为国家的中央银行，从事有关的国际金融活动；（13）国务院规定的其他职责。

为履行其宏观金融监管职能，中国人民银行享有如下的金融监管权力：

第一，对金融市场的监测、调控权。中国人民银行依法监测金融市场的运行情况，对金融市场实施宏观调控，促进其协调发展。

第二，直接检查监督权。中国人民银行有权对金融机构以及其他单位和个人的下列行为进行检查监督：执行有关存款准备金管理规定的行为；与中国人民银行特种贷款有关的行为；执行有关人民币管理规定的行为；执行有关银行间同业拆借市场、银行间债券市场管理规定的行为；执行有关外汇管理规定的行为；执行有关黄金管理规定的行为；代理中国人民银行经理国库的行为；执行有关清算管理规定的行为；以及执行有关反洗钱规定的行为。

第三，建议检查监督权。中国人民银行根据执行货币政策和维护金融稳定的需要，可以建议中国银监会对银行业金融机构进行检查监督。中国银监会应当自收到建议之日起三十日内予以回复。

第四，特定情况下的全面检查监督权。当银行业金融机构出现支付困难，可能引发金融风险时，为了维护金融稳定，中国人民银行经国务院批准，有权对银行业金融机构进行检查监督。

第五，获取有关报表、资料权。中国人民银行根据履行职责的需要，有权要求银行业金融机构报送必要的资产负债表、利润表以及其他财务会计、统计报表和资料。

第六，编制和公布全国金融统计数据权。中国人民银行负责统一编制全国金融统计数据、报表，并按照国家有关规定予以公布。

第七，相关处罚权。在宣传品、出版物或者其他商品上非法使用人民币图样的，印制、发售代币票券，以代替人民币在市场上流通的，以及违反上述中国人民银行享有直接检查监督权的相关行为且有关法律、行政法规未作处罚规定的，中国人民银行均有权进行处罚。

二、美国联邦储备系统的监管职能

在美国，联邦储备系统作为中央银行，具有制定货币政策和金融监管的双重职能，但在日常工作中，其任务重心体现在执行金融监管的职能上。联邦储备系统的金融监管职能，主要由联邦储备理事会（美联储）负责。美联储通过联邦储备银行对会员银行的监督管理来履行其监管职能。

在美国，外资银行、国民银行以及加入联邦储备系统的州立银行均受到美联储的监管，美联储负责审批和监督它们的业务种类、内容和范围。此外，美联储还负责制定全国统一的金融规章。美国所有银行，不论其是否是联邦储备系统的成员行，都必须遵守美联储制定的金融管理规章，并接受联邦储备银行的检查。《1999 年金融服务现代化法》颁布以后，美国改进原有的分业监管体制，形成一种“伞形监管模式”。在这种模式下，金融控股公司的各子公司根据业务的不同接受不同行业监管机构的监管，而美联储为金融控股公司伞状监管者，负责评估和监控混业经营的金融控股公司整体资本充足性、风险管理的内控措施以及集团风险对存款子公司潜在影响等。因此，美联储还负责对金融控股公司进行监管。

2008 年以来，美国遭遇了自“大萧条”以来最严重的金融与经济危机。为此，美国对其金融监管体系实施改革，并于 2010 年 7 月通过了《多德—弗兰克华尔街改革与消费者保护法案》。法案对美国金融监管体系进行了大幅调整和加强，大幅扩充了美联储的监管职权，确立了美联储在美国系统性风险管理和金融监管框架中的核心地位。改革之后的美联储地位空前提高，职权空前扩大①：

首先，法案第一章设立了以财政部长为首、美联储及其他联邦金融监管机构组成的“金融稳定监管委员会”，以应对美国金融稳定的风险。该委员会可以建议美联储对系统重要性金融机构实施更严格的审慎监管；可以以 2/3 多数将对美国金融稳定构成威胁的非银行金融机构交由美联储监管。美联储可以自行或根据委员会的要求，对大型复杂金融机构制定并实施与其潜在风险相适应的更严格的审慎监管标准（包括更严格的资本、杠杆率、流动性、风险管理、信用敞口等要求），并定期举行压力测试。美联储对所有系统重要性机构（包括非银行金融机构）及其子公司拥有检查权和执行权，并对这些机构的重大收购活动行使批准权。

其次，法案第三章废除了储蓄机构管理局，将其职能分别并入三家机构，其中美联储接收对储贷控股公司（savings and loan holding companies）的监管。改革后，美联储对

① 刘向民. 美联储监管之责缘何扩大. 中国改革，2011（3）.

金融机构的并表监管权力得以空前扩大，其监管对象包括：资产规模500亿美元以上的银行控股公司、金融控股公司、非银行金融机构、外国银行；原本就受美联储监管的州成员银行、外国银行、500 亿美元以下的银行控股公司和金融控股公司；以及新接收的储贷控股公司。同时，法案还要求美联储对受其监管的、总资产大于500亿美元的银行控股公司、储贷控股公司、外国银行以及非银行金融机构收取监管费。

再次，法案第八章规定系统重要性的支付、清算、结算活动以及相应的金融基础设施（financial market utilities，FMUs），即支付结算系统等，由美联储监管。美联储将针对这些活动和FMUs制定相应的风险管理标准，包括：资本金、保证金和抵押品要求；参与方与对手方违约风险控制；清算和结算的时间要求等。美联储单独或由相应金融监管机构负责这些风险管理标准的检查和执行。

最后，法案第十章规定在美联储之下设立相对独立的消费者金融保护局，统一行使目前由不同金融监管机构分散行使的金融消费者权益保护职责。消费者金融保护局监管整个消费金融服务市场，有权根据联邦法律制定金融消费者保护规则，并负责检查和实施。

三、案例资料

在美国，按照《国际银行法》及《1991 年外国银行监管实施法》的规定，外国银行要在美国设立分支机构，必须获得美联储的批准。在审核外国银行设立分支机构的申请时，美联储主要考虑的因素包括：该外国银行是否（1）直接在美国境外从事银行业；（2）向美联储提供了供其充分评估申请所必需的信息；（3）受到母国监管机构全面的综合监管。

上述考量因素，实际上给予了美联储巨大的自由裁量权。尤其是其中第（3）点，申请银行是否受到母国监管机构全面的综合监管，并没有一个统一的标准，完全由美联储自己评定。《国际银行法》同时规定了全面综合监管的例外条款，即如果美联储无法认定提交申请的银行受到母国监管部门的全面综合监管，那么在同时具备以下条件的情况下，美联储亦可批准申请：（1）外国银行的母国监管机构在积极地建立对银行的综合监管安排；（2）所有其他的因素（其中很重要的一个方面为申请银行及其母国监管机构采取的反洗钱措施）与美联储的批准相符。这一例外条款，实际上还是属于美联储酌情裁量的范围。

对于中资银行提出的在美设立分支机构的申请，美联储往往以不理解中国对银行的监管体制为由，不承认中国目前建立起了对银行的全面综合监管，由此拒绝或者延缓对中资银行申请的批准。2011 年 4 月 8 日，美联储批准中国交通银行在旧金山设立分支机构的申请，此时距离提交申请之日已近两年。在美联储发布的批准令中，着重讨论的同样是中国银行业监管部门对交通银行是否建立起综合监管体制的问题。

FEDERAL RESERVE SYSTEM

Order Approving Establishment of a Branch

Bank of Communications Co., Ltd. ("BOCOM"), Shanghai, People's Republic of China, a foreign bank within the meaning of the International Banking Act ("IBA"), has applied under section 7(d) of the IBA to establish a limited federal branch in San Francisco, California. The Foreign Bank Supervision Enhancement Act of 1991, which amended the IBA, provides that a foreign bank must obtain the approval of the Board to establish a branch in the United States.

Notice of the application, affording interested persons an opportunity to comment, has been published in a newspaper of general circulation in San Francisco, California (The Recorder, March 9, 2009). The time for filing comments has expired, and the Board has considered all comments received.

BOCOM, with total assets of approximately $599 billion, is the fifth largest bank in China. The government of China owns approximately 43.8 percent of BOCOM's shares. The Hongkong and Shanghai Banking Corporation Limited, Hong Kong, People's Republic of China, a subsidiary of HSBC Holdings plc, London, England, owns 19 percent of the shares of BOCOM. No other shareholder owns more than 5 percent of the shares of BOCOM.

BOCOM engages primarily in corporate and retail banking and treasury operations throughout China, including Hong Kong and Macau. Outside China, BOCOM operates branches in Japan, Singapore, South Korea, and Germany and a representative office in the United Kingdom. In the United States, BOCOM operates a federal branch in New York. BOCOM would meet the requirements for a qualifying foreign banking organization under Regulation K.

The proposed San Francisco branch would engage in wholesale deposit-taking, lending, trade finance, and other banking services. As a limited branch, it would be prohibited from accepting deposits from sources other than those permitted by section 5 of the IBA and section 25A of the Federal Reserve Act.

Under the IBA and Regulation K, in acting on an application by a foreign bank to establish a branch, the Board must consider whether the foreign bank (1) engages directly in the business of banking outside the United States; (2) has furnished the Board with the information it needs to assess the application adequately; and (3) is subject to comprehensive supervision on a consolidated basis by its home country supervisors. The Board also considers additional standards as set forth in the IBA and Regulation K.

The IBA includes a limited exception to the general standard relating to comprehensive, consolidated supervision. This exception provides that, if the Board is unable to find that a foreign bank seeking to establish a branch, agency, or commercial lending company is subject to comprehensive supervision or regulation on a consolidated basis by the appropriate authorities in its home country, the Board may nevertheless approve the application provided that: (i) the appropriate authorities in the home country of the foreign bank are actively working to establish arrangements for the consolidated supervision of such bank; and (ii) all other factors are consistent with approval. In deciding whether to exercise its discretion to approve an application under authority of this exception, the Board must also consider whether the foreign bank has adopted and implemented procedures to combat money laundering. The Board also may take into account whether the home country of the foreign bank is developing a legal regime to address money laundering or is participating in multilateral efforts to combat money laundering. That is the standard applied by the Board in this case.

As noted above, BOCOM engages directly in the business of banking outside the United States. BOCOM also has provided the Board with information necessary to assess the application through submissions that address the relevant issues.

The Board is continuing to work actively with the appropriate supervisory authorities in China to understand their system for the consolidated supervision of BOCOM and other major Chinese banks. Those discussions are constructive and ongoing. Based on all the facts of record, the Board has determined that BOCOM's home country supervisory authority is, at a minimum, actively working to establish arrangements for the consolidated supervision of BOCOM and that considerations relating to the steps taken by BOCOM and its home jurisdiction to combat money laundering are consistent with approval under this standard. The Board has approved applications from other Chinese banks to establish U.S. branches under this standard.

The China Banking Regulatory Commission ("CBRC") is the principal supervisory authority of BOCOM, including its foreign subsidiaries and affiliates. The CBRC has the authority to license banks, regulate their activities, and approve expansion, both domestically and abroad. The CBRC has no objection to BOCOM's establishment of the proposed branch. It supervises and regulates BOCOM, including its subsidiaries and foreign operations, through a combination of targeted on-site examinations and continuous consolidated off-site monitoring. Since its establishment in 2003, the CBRC has enhanced existing supervisory programs and developed new policies and procedures designed to create a framework for the consolidated supervision of banks in China.

On-site examinations by the CBRC cover, among other things, the major areas of operations: corporate governance and senior management responsibilities; capital adequacy; asset structure and asset quality (including structure and quality of loans); off-balance-sheet activities; earnings; liquidity; liability structure and funding sources; expansionary plans; internal controls (including accounting controls and administrative systems); legal compliance; accounting supervision and internal auditing (including accounting controls and administrative systems); and any other areas deemed necessary by the CBRC.

Off-site monitoring is conducted through the review of required annual, semiannual, quarterly, or monthly reports on, among other things, asset quality, capital adequacy, liquidity, risk management, corporate governance, affiliate transactions, and internal controls.

BOCOM is required to be audited annually by an accounting firm approved by the PBOC, and the results are shared with the CBRC and the PBOC. The scope of the required audit includes a review of BOCOM's financial statements, asset quality, and internal controls. The CBRC may order a special audit at any time. In addition, in connection with its listing on the Shanghai and Hong Kong stock exchanges, BOCOM is required to have external audits conducted under both International Financial Reporting Standards and generally accepted accounting practices under Chinese law. BOCOM is required to publish its financial statements annually. BOCOM conducts internal audits of its offices and operations, including its overseas operations, generally on an annual schedule. The internal audit results are shared with the CBRC, the PBOC, and BOCOM's external auditors. The proposed branch would be subject to internal audits.

Chinese laws impose various prudential limitations on banks, including limits on transactions with affiliates and on large exposures. The CBRC is authorized to require any bank to provide information and to impose sanctions for failure to comply with such requests. The CBRC also has authority to impose administrative penalties, including warnings, fines, and removal from office, for violations of applicable laws and rules. Criminal violations are transferred to the judicial authorities for investigation and prosecution.

In recent years, the Chinese government has enhanced its anti-money laundering regime. In 2005, it took initial steps to adopt an anti-money laundering law, the PRC Anti-Money

Laundering Law ("AML Law"). The AML Law and two related rules, the Rules for Anti-Money Laundering by Financial Institutions ("AML Rules") and the Administrative Rules for the Reporting of Large-Value and Suspicious Transactions by Financial Institutions ("LVT/STR Rules") were enacted in October 2006 and December 2006, respectively. The AML Law and AML Rules became effective on January 1, 2007, and the LVT/STR Rules became effective on March 1, 2007. Together, the law and two related rules establish a regulatory infrastructure to assist China's anti-money laundering efforts.

An Anti-Money Laundering Bureau ("AML Bureau") was established within the PBOC in 2003 to coordinate anti-money laundering efforts at the PBOC and among other agencies. The AML Bureau also supervised the creation of the China Anti-Money Laundering Monitoring and Analysis Center ("AML Center") in September 2004. The AML Center collects, monitors, analyzes, and disseminates suspicious transaction reports and large-value transaction reports. The AML Center sends suspicious transaction reports to the AML Bureau for further investigation. The PBOC issued additional rules in 2007 and 2008 providing clarification of, or further strengthening the implementation of, operating procedures, customer due diligence and risk classification, recordkeeping, AML monitoring and reporting of suspicious transactions to the AML Center, and the international remittance agency business. China improved its AML regime in 2009 by amending its criminal law to further criminalize money laundering activities and other financial crimes.

China participates in international fora that address the prevention of money laundering and terrorist financing. China is a member of the Financial Action Task Force ("FATF") and is a party to the 1988 U.N. Convention Against the Illicit Traffic of Narcotics and Psychotropic Substances, the U.N. Convention Against Transnational Organized Crime, the U.N. Convention Against Corruption, and the U.N. International Convention for the Suppression of the Financing of Terrorism.

As noted, the PBOC is China's primary supervisor for anti-money laundering matters. Like the CBRC, the PBOC supervises and regulates BOCOM through a combination of on-site examinations and off-site monitoring. On-site examinations focus on BOCOM's compliance with anti-money laundering laws and rules, including the AML Law, AML Rules, and LVT/STR Rules. Off-site monitoring is conducted through the review of periodic reports. In performing its responsibilities, the PBOC may require any bank to provide information and can impose administrative penalties for violations of applicable laws and rules.

The PBOC over time has increased requirements for its supervised institutions. In 2008, the PBOC promulgated a notice requiring the designation of a chief AML compliance officer as a high-level manager to ensure the provision of adequate AML resources and timely flow of information to employees with AML responsibility throughout the institution. The same notice also required the risk rating of customers, among other improvements in AML controls. The PBOC requires the filing of reports on suspicious activities and certain other transactions, and it recently has developed a policy of encouraging its supervised institutions to move from prescriptive criteria towards a more risk-based and subjective method of suspicious activity detection and reporting. In addition, banks are required to establish a customer identification system in accordance with applicable rules jointly promulgated by the PBOC and the three functional financial services regulators, to record the identities of customers and information relating to each transaction, and to retain retail transaction documents and books. BOCOM has policies and procedures to comply with Chinese laws and rules regarding anti-money laundering. BOCOM represents that it has taken additional steps on its own initiative to combat money laundering and other illegal activities. BOCOM states that it has implemented measures consistent with the recommendations of the FATF and that it has put in place policies, procedures, and controls to ensure ongoing compliance with all statutory and regulatory requirements, including designating anti-money laundering compliance personnel and conducting routine employee training at all BOCOM branches. BOCOM's compliance with anti-money laundering requirements is monitored by the PBOC and by BOCOM's internal and external auditors.

The Board has also considered carefully the financial and managerial factors in this case. China has adopted risk-based capital standards that are consistent with those established by the Basel Capital Accord ("Accord"). BOCOM's capital is in excess of the minimum levels that would be required by the Accord and is considered equivalent to capital that would be required of a U.S. banking organization. Managerial and other financial resources of BOCOM are consistent with approval, and BOCOM appears to have the experience and capacity to support the proposed branch. In addition, BOCOM has established controls and procedures for the proposed branch to ensure compliance with U.S. law. In particular, BOCOM has stated that it will apply strict anti-money laundering policies and procedures at the branch consistent with U.S. law and regulation and will establish an internal control system at the branch consistent with U.S. requirements to ensure compliance with those policies and procedures.

With respect to access to information about BOCOM's operations, the Board has reviewed the restrictions on disclosure in relevant jurisdictions in which BOCOM operates and has communicated with relevant government authorities regarding access to information. BOCOM has committed to make available to the Board such information on the operations of BOCOM and any of its affiliates that the Board deems necessary to determine and enforce compliance with the IBA, the Bank Holding Company Act, and other applicable federal law. To the extent that the provision of such information to the Board may be prohibited by law or otherwise, BOCOM has committed to cooperate with the Board to obtain any necessary consents or waivers that might be required from third parties for disclosure of such information. In light of these commitments and other facts of record, and subject to the condition described below, the Board has determined that BOCOM has provided adequate assurances of access to any necessary information that the Board may request.

China has made progress toward adopting a system of financial regulation for its financial system to mitigate the risk to financial stability from its banks. The PBOC, CBRC, other financial supervisory agencies, and other agencies in China have taken joint measures to strengthen and improve macroeconomic management, promote financial reform, and maintain financial stability. China has established a system of preliminary indicators for monitoring financial stability, developed methodology and operational frameworks for monitoring financial risks, and published an annual China Financial Stability Report since 2005. The CBRC has established mechanisms to cooperate with supervisory authorities in at least 25 other countries for the supervision of cross-border banking. In addition, the PBOC and CBRC officially joined the Basel Committee on Banking Supervision on behalf of China and since their accession, have actively participated in the revision of Basel II and in working groups. China also is active in the ongoing work of the Financial Stability Board.

On the basis of all the facts of record, and subject to the commitments made by BOCOM, as well as the terms and conditions set forth in this order, BOCOM's application to establish a branch is hereby approved. Should any restrictions on access to information on the operations or activities of BOCOM and its affiliates subsequently interfere with the Board's ability to obtain information to determine and enforce compliance by BOCOM or its affiliates with applicable federal statutes, the Board may require termination of any of BOCOM's direct or indirect activities in the United States, or in the case of any such operation licensed by the Office of the Comptroller of the Currency ("OCC"), recommend termination of such operation.

Approval of this application also is specifically conditioned on compliance by BOCOM with the commitments made in connection with this application and with the conditions in this order. The commitments and conditions referred to above are conditions imposed in writing by the Board in connection with this decision and may be enforced in proceedings under 12 U.S.C. § 1818 against BOCOM and its affiliates.

By order of the Board of Governors, effective April 8, 2011.

(Footnote omitted)

资料来源：美联储网站 *http：//www.federalreserve.gov/newsevents/press/orders/order20110408.pdf*，访问日期 2011/11/15.

第三章

商业银行法律制度

第一节　商业银行的历史

商业银行是历史发展最悠久、业务开展最为广泛、对社会经济生活影响最重要的金融机构，是各国金融体系的主体。开展活期存款、为工商企业提供短期贷款是早期商业银行的主要业务，也是商业银行的滥觞。现代意义上的商业银行是以工商企业和居民家庭为主要服务对象，通过开展广泛的金融业务来实现盈利最大化目标的金融企业，是商品经济不断发展的产物。①

一、中国商业银行的历史

中国现代商业银行的发展开始于 20 世纪 70 年代末。从 1979 年初开始，在改革开放方针的指引下，中国恢复了中国农业银行负责农村金融业务，从中国人民银行中分设出了中国银行负责外贸信贷和外汇业务，从财政部中分设出了中国人民建设银行（1996 年 3 月更名为中国建设银行）负责长期投资和贷款业务。1983 年 9 月，中国国务院发布《关于中国人民银行专门行使中央银行职能的决定》，明确规定中国人民银行专门行使中央银行的职能，同时决定成立中国工商银行，接办中国人民银行原有的信贷和储蓄等商业银行业务。至此，中国基本形成了以四大国家专业银行为骨干所组成的银行体系。

当然，改革开放之初的国家专业银行，在从事商业性信贷业务的同时又从事政策性信贷业务，并非完全意义上的商业银行。20 世纪 90 年代，中国相继成立了专门办理政策性信贷业务的国家开发银行、中国进出口银行及中国农业发展银行，并完成了国家专

① 李树生，冯瑞河. 金融学概论. 北京：中国金融出版社，2005：122.

业银行向国有独资商业银行的改造。

除了国有商业银行之外，在改革开放的推动之下，其他类型的银行也迅速发展。在交通银行于1986年7月重组成以公有制为主的股份制全国性综合银行之后，中国境内相继成立了中信实业银行、招商银行、中国光大银行、华夏银行、上海浦东发展银行、民生银行等12家股份制银行。此外，中国于1986年通过《中华人民共和国邮政法》，将邮政储蓄业务法定为邮政企业的业务之一，从而使邮政储蓄遍布全国，形成了一个“准银行”系统。同时，中国人民银行于1995年开始在全国16个城市进行在城市信用社的基础上组建城市合作银行的试点。同年2月，中国第一家城市商业银行——深圳城市商业银行成立。

除了中资商业银行以外，外资商业银行在中国也迅速发展。早在1985年，中国就颁布了《中华人民共和国经济特区外资银行、中外合资银行管理条例》，允许外国金融机构在中国经济特区设立营业性分支机构。随后，中国陆续允许在其他几个城市设立营业性外资金融机构。1994年2月，中国颁布了《中华人民共和国外资金融机构管理条例》，对包括外资商业银行在内的外资金融机构在中国经营进行了全面的规定。

1995年5月，中国通过了《中华人民共和国商业银行法》（下称《商业银行法》）。这部法律总结了中国改革开放以来商业银行改革的实践经验，创造性地借鉴并吸收了各国商业银行立法的成功经验和做法。该法不仅适用于中资的商业银行，还适用于外资商业银行、中外合资商业银行、外国商业银行分行（当然，2006年通过的《外资银行管理条例》在适用上具有优先性）；同时，对于城市信用合作社、农村信用合作社办理存款、贷款和结算等业务以及邮政企业办理商业银行的有关业务，也适用该法有关规定。《商业银行法》的颁布和实施，对于保护商业银行、存款人和其他客户的合法权益，规范商业银行行为，维护商业银行经营自主权，提高商业银行信贷资产质量，加强金融监管，维护金融秩序，推动商业银行改革的逐步深入，都具有重要的意义。随着《商业银行法》的颁布，中国商业银行的发展开始走向法制化、规范化的轨道。

2001年12月，中国加入世界贸易组织。根据中国入世的承诺，中国将逐步取消外资银行进入中国的限制，全面开放商业银行业。在金融业开放及外资进入的威胁下，中国商业银行的发展面临着严峻的挑战。为此，中国决定进一步加强对商业银行的监管，推进商业银行的改革。

2003年3月，中国十届全国人大一次会议通过了《关于国务院机构改革方案的决定》。根据该决定，中国银行业监督管理委员会（即中国银监会）于2003年4月28日正式挂牌成立，行使原由中国人民银行行使的银行业监督管理职权。2003年12月，中国第十届全国人大常委会第六次会议通过了《中华人民共和国银行业监督管理法》、《全国人大常委会关于修改〈中国人民银行法〉的决定》以及《全国人大常委会关于修改〈商业银行法〉的决定》，明确规定了中国银监会的监管职能，使其对银行业的监督有法可依，同时也对中国人民银行的职能重新进行了定位，强化了其与制定和执行货币政策有关的职能。在立法的基础之上，中国逐步建立了相对完善的银行业监管体制。

二、美国商业银行的历史

美国自建国之初，商业银行就有着快速的发展。早期的商业银行都是州立银行，从各州政府获取特许状并向州政府纳税，联邦银行尚不存在。这时银行活动的范围和权力通常限制于州的授权范围之内。州特许银行的建立作为一个标志，从此拉开了延续至今的州对银行实施监管传统的序幕。

在 19 世纪早期，美国联邦政府尝试过建立联邦层面的银行，并分别以国会特许的方式组建了第一合众国银行和第二合众国银行，但这两家联邦银行在特许状到期后未能续期，建立联邦银行的努力以失败告终。直到《1863 年国民银行法》获得通过，美国建立了一个由联邦授权的、货币监理署特许和监管的国民银行体系。依据《1863 年国民银行法》设立的联邦特许的商业银行开始同州特许银行展开竞争，美国进入到一个双重银行体系（dual banking system）时代。

从 19 世纪中期到 20 世纪初期，美国发生过多次危及银行体系的金融恐慌。最终，美国国会通过了《1913 年联邦储备法》，建立了联邦储备系统，作为美国的中央银行。但是，联储的建立并未终结州银行和国民银行体系间的竞争。在国民银行必须加入新联储系统的同时，州银行也可以同等条件申请加入。此后，美国商业银行进入平稳发展时期。

1929—1933 年的经济危机给美国银行业带来重创，大量商业银行纷纷破产倒闭，美国银行体系几乎崩溃。这场危机引发了美国银行业的多项重大改革，其中最为重要的是 1933 年银行法（即《格拉斯—斯蒂格尔法案》）出台。该法案规定：任何以吸收存款业务为主要资金来源的商业银行，不得同时经营证券投资等长期性资产业务；任何经营证券业务的银行，也不能经营吸收存款等商业银行业务；商业银行不准经营代理证券发行、证券包销、证券零售、证券经纪等业务；商业银行的员工不得在各种投资银行机构兼职；商业银行不得设立从事证券业务的分支银行或附属机构。该法案令美国金融业形成了银行、证券分业经营的模式。此外，在该法案的基础之上，美国还成立了联邦存款保险公司，推行联邦存款保险制度。

《格拉斯—斯蒂格尔法案》出台后，美国商业银行进入了一段繁荣发展的时期。但是，20 世纪 80 年代，随着金融自由化趋势席卷全球，外资银行大举进入美国。由于分业经营的限制，美国商业银行的竞争力日益下降。美国金融监管当局被迫进行了一系列改革。最终，美国总统克林顿签署了《1999 年金融服务现代化法》。该法的颁布，标志着自 1933

年来《格拉斯—斯蒂格尔法案》中对美国的商业银行、证券和保险业间跨业经营所设限制的解除，彻底为商业银行全面从事金融业务敞开了大门。

《1999 年金融服务现代化法》开启了美国商业银行混业经营的时代，但是美国分业监管体制并没有调整，造成了监管的错位与滞后。2008 年，美国爆发了一场严重的金融危机，其对美国包括商业银行业在内的金融业造成巨大冲击。危机之后，美国开始反思其金融监管体制，并于 2010 年颁布了《多德—弗兰克华尔街改革和消费者保护法案》，对其金融监管体制进行全面改革。《多德—弗兰克华尔街改革和消费者保护法案》从系统性风险的防范、消费者和投资者保护、衍生品市场监管、住宅抵押市场监管、银行监管、对冲基金监管、信用评级公司行为、美联储救市行为透明度、华尔街薪酬体系等方面进行了调整和改革。

三、案例资料

美国《1999 年金融服务现代化法》，是美国商业银行发展历史上具有巨大意义的一部法律。该法的核心内容是废止 1933 年通过的《格拉斯—斯蒂格尔法案》以及其他一些相关的法律中有关限制商业银行、证券公司和保险公司三者跨界经营的条款。美国总统克林顿在签署该法律时，发表了一篇热情洋溢的讲话，对该法的主要内容及其对美国消费者、社区以及各种规模的经营者的意义进行了阐述。通过阅读克林顿的讲话，可以看出《1999 年金融服务现代化法》对促进美国包括商业银行在内的金融业发展将起到巨大的促进作用。

事实上，《1999 年金融服务现代化法》通过后的几年时间里，美国商业银行的确获得了飞速发展，在国际上的竞争力也大大加强。但是，这场繁荣的背后，掩藏着巨大的风险，并最终于 2008 年演化成一场席卷美国乃至全球的金融危机。

Statement on Signing the Gramm-Leach-Bliley Act

November 12, 1999

Today I am pleased to sign into law S. 900, the Gramm-Leach-Bliley Act. This historic legislation will modernize our financial services laws, stimulating greater innovation and competition in the financial services industry. America's consumers, our communities, and the economy will reap the benefits of this Act.

Beginning with the introduction of an Administration-sponsored bill in 1997, my Administration has worked vigorously to produce financial services legislation that would not only spur greater competition, but also protect the rights of consumers and guarantee that expanded financial services firms would meet the needs of America's underserved communities. Passage of this legislation by an overwhelming, bipartisan majority of the Congress suggests that we have met that goal.

The Gramm-Leach-Bliley Act makes the most important legislative changes to the structure of the U.S. financial system since the 1930s. Financial services firms will be authorized to conduct a wide range of financial activities, allowing them freedom to innovate in the new economy. The Act repeals provisions of the Glass-Steagall Act that, since the Great Depression, have restricted affiliations between banks and securities firms. It also amends the Bank Holding Company Act to remove restrictions on affiliations between banks and insurance companies. It grants banks significant new authority to conduct most newly authorized activities through financial subsidiaries.

Removal of barriers to competition will enhance the stability of our financial services system. Financial services firms will be able to diversify their product offerings and thus their sources of revenue. They will also be better equipped to compete in global financial markets.

Although the Act grants financial services firms greater latitude to innovate, it also contains important safety and soundness protections. While the Act allows common ownership of banking, securities, and insurance firms, it still requires those activities to be conducted separately within an organization, subject to functional regulation and funding limitations.

Both the Vice President and I have insisted that any financial services modernization legislation must benefit American communities by preserving and strengthening community reinvestment. I am very pleased that the Act accomplishes this goal. The Act establishes an important prospective principle: banking organizations seeking to conduct new nonbanking activities must first demonstrate a satisfactory record of meeting the credit needs of all the communities they serve, including low-and moderate-income communities. Thus, the law will for the first time prohibit expansion into activities such as securities and insurance underwriting unless all of the organization's banks and thrifts maintain a "satisfactory" or better rating under the Community Reinvestment Act (CRA). The CRA will continue to apply to all banks and thrifts, and any application to acquire or merge with a bank or thrift will continue to be reviewed under CRA, with full opportunity for public comment. The bill offers further support for community development in the form of a new Program for Investment in Microentrepreneurs (PRIME), to provide technical help to low-and moderate-income microentrepreneurs.

The Act includes a limited extension of the CRA examination cycle for small banks and thrifts with outstanding or satisfactory CRA records, but expressly preserves the ability of regulators to examine these institutions at any time for reasonable cause, and does not affect regulators' authority in connection with an application. The bill also includes a requirement for disclosure and reporting of CRA agreements. The Act and its legislative history have been crafted to alleviate burdens on banks and thrifts and those working to stimulate investment in underserved communities. It is critical that depository institutions and their community partners continue efforts that have led to the highest home ownership rate in our history, including a particularly dramatic increase in recent years in minority and low-income home ownership. My Administration remains committed to ensuring that implementation of these provisions does not in any way diminish community reinvestment, and stands ready to remedy any problems that may arise.

Last May, I proposed strong and enforceable Federal privacy protections for consumers' financial information. I am very pleased that the Act provides a number of the new protections that I proposed.

Under the Act, financial institutions must clearly disclose their privacy policies to customers up front and annually, allowing consumers to make truly informed choices about privacy protection. For the first time, consumers will have an absolute right to know if their financial institution intends to share or sell their personal financial data, either within the corporate family or with an unaffiliated third-party. Consumers will have the right to "opt out" of such information sharing with unaffiliated third parties. These protections constitute a significant change from existing law, under which information on everything from account balances to credit card transactions can be shared or sold by a financial institution without a customer's knowledge or consent, including the sale of information to telemarketers and other nonfinancial firms.

Of equal importance, these restrictions have teeth. For the first time, the Act allows privacy protection to be included in regular bank examinations. The Act grants regulators full authority to issue privacy rules and to use the full range of their enforcement powers in case of violations. The Act grants new, and needed, rulemaking authority under the existing Fair Credit Reporting Act. In addition, it establishes new penalties to prevent pretext calling, by which unscrupulous persons use deceptive practices to determine the financial assets of consumers. The Act will specifically allow the States to provide stronger privacy protections if they choose to do so.

Although these are significant steps forward, we will continue to press for even greater privacy protections—especially choice about whether personal financial information can be shared within a corporate family. Privacy is fundamental to Americans, and to my Administration.

The Act also streamlines supervision of bank holding companies and preserves financial regulation along functional lines. Activities generally will be overseen by those regulators who are most knowledgeable about a given financial activity, including the Securities and Exchange Commission for securities activities and State regulators for insurance activities. Given the broad new affiliations permissible under this legislation, I fully expect our regulators to work together to protect the integrity of our financial system. The bill also promotes the safety and soundness of our financial system by enhancing the traditional separation of banking and commerce. The bill limits the ability of thrift institutions to affiliate with commercial companies.

There are provisions of the Act that concern me. The Act's redomestication provisions could allow mutual insurance companies to avoid State law protecting policyholders, enriching insiders at the expense of consumers. We intend to monitor any redomestications and State law changes closely, returning to the Congress if necessary. The Act's Federal Home Loan Bank (FHLB) provisions fail to focus the FHLB System more on lending to community banks and less on arbitrage activities and short-term lending that do not advance its public purpose.

The Act raises certain constitutional issues with respect to the insurance privacy provisions in title V. The Act might be construed as contrary to Supreme Court decisions that hold that the Congress may not compel States to enact or administer a Federal regulatory program. I interpret section 505(c) of the Act, however, as providing States with a constitutionally permissible choice of whether to participate in such a program. States that choose to participate will gain the powers listed in section 505(c); States that decline will not. I believe that the Congress, in giving States a choice (in section 505(c)) whether to "adopt regulations to carry out this subtitle," intended to allow States to accept or decline all of the rulemaking and enforcement obligations assigned to State authorities under sections 501-505 of the Act. This interpretation is consistent with the explanation in the conference report that both the rulemaking and enforcement roles of State insurance authorities are voluntary not mandatory.

Section 332(b) of S. 900 provides for Presidential appointment of the board of directors of the National Association of Registered Agents and Brokers (NARAB), established by the bill in the event that certain stated conditions occur. Because members of the NARAB board would exercise significant Federal governmental authority under those conditions, they must be appointed as Officers pursuant to the Appointments Clause of the Constitution. Under section 332(b)(1) of the bill, the President would be required to make such appointments from lists of candidates recommended by the National Association of Insurance Commissioners. The Appointments Clause, however, does not permit such restrictions to be imposed upon the President's power of appointment. I therefore do not interpret the restrictions of section 332(b)(1) as binding and will regard any such lists of recommended candidates as advisory only.

The Gramm-Leach-Bliley Act is a major achievement that will benefit American consumers, communities, and businesses of all sizes. I thank all of those individuals who played a role in the development and passage of this historic legislation.

WILLIAM J. CLINTON

The White House, November 12, 1999.

资料来源：*William J. Clinton: "Statement on Signing the Gramm-Leach-Bliley Act", November 12, 1999. Online by Gerhard Peters and John T. Woolley, The American Presidency Project, available at http://www.presidency.ucsb.edu/ws/?pid=56922.*

第二节　商业银行的组织机构

一、中国商业银行的组织机构

根据中国《商业银行法》的规定，商业银行是指依照该法和《中华人民共和国公司法》设立的吸收公众存款、发放贷款、办理结算等业务的企业法人。商业银行以其全部法人财产独立承担民事责任。

在中国，商业银行的设立实行核准制，即设立商业银行应当经中国银监会审查批准。设立商业银行，应当具备一定的条件，尤其是注册资本必须达到法律规定的最低限额。此外，申请人应当向中国银监会提交包括申请书、可行性研究报告等在内的文件、资料。未经中国银监会批准，任何单位和个人不得从事吸收公众存款等商业银行业务，任何单位不得在名称中使用“银行”字样。经批准设立的商业银行，由中国银监会颁发经营许可证，并凭该许可证向工商行政管理部门办理登记，领取营业执照。

在中国，商业银行的经营范围由其章程规定，报中国银监会批准。商业银行可以经营下列部分或者全部业务：吸收公众存款；发放短期、中期和长期贷款；办理国内外结算；办理票据承兑与贴现；发行金融债券；代理发行、代理兑付、承销政府债券；买卖政府债券、金融债券；从事同业拆借；买卖、代理买卖外汇；从事银行卡业务；提供信用证服务及担保；代理收付款项及代理保险业务；提供保管箱服务；以及经中国银监会批准的其他业务。经中国人民银行批准，商业银行还可以经营结汇、售汇业务。

根据中国《商业银行法》的规定，商业银行的具体组织形式、组织机构适用《中华人民共和国公司法》的规定，即商业银行的组织形式为公司，其包括有限责任公司形式和股份有限公司形式。当然，考虑到中国商业银行发展的实际状况，中国《商业银行法》还规定，在该法施行前设立的商业银行，其组织形式、组织机构不完全符合《中华人民共和国公司法》规定的，可以继续沿用原有的规定，适用《中华人民共和国公司法》的日期由国务院规定。

商业银行根据业务需要可以在中国境内外设立分支机构。设立分支机构必须经中国银监会审查批准。在中国境内的分支机构，不按行政区划设立。商业银行在中国境内设立分支机构，应当按照规定拨付与其经营规模相适应的营运资金额。拨付各分支机构营运资金额的总和，不得超过总行资本金总额的60%。经批准设立的商业银行分支机构，由中国银监会颁发经营许可证，并凭该许可证向工商行政管理部门办理登记，领取营业执照。商业银行分支机构不具有法人资格，在总行授权范围内依法开展业务，其民事责任由总行承担。

在中国，商业银行以安全性、流动性、效益性为经营原则，实行自主经营，自担风险，自负盈亏，自我约束。商业银行依法开展业务，不受任何单位和个人的干涉，但是却要受到中国银监会的监管。商业银行的名称、章程及注册资本等重大事项的变更，应当经中国银监会批准；商业银行的分立、合并，在适用《中华人民共和国公司法》规定的同时，还应当经中国银监会审查批准。此外，任何单位和个人购买商业银行股份总额5%以上的，应当事先经中国银监会批准。

除典型的商业银行外，在中国，一些办理存款、贷款和结算等商业银行业务的企业，如城市信用合作社、农村信用合作社以及邮政企业等，虽然其银行业务的经营适用《商业银行法》，但是其设立和组织机构适用其他专门的法律。此外，中国在商业银行以外还存在一些从事货币信用业务和金融服务业务的金融机构，即非银行金融机构，包括经中国银监会批准设立的信托公司、企业集团财务公司、金融租赁公司、汽车金融公司、货币经纪公司、境外非银行金融机构驻华代表处等机构。非银行金融机构主要的职能是开拓直接融资业务，补充银行服务的不足，从而促进金融业的发展。中国已于 2007 年 8 月颁布《非银行金融机构行政许可事项实施办法》，对非银行金融机构的设立、变更、终止、业务范围调整和业务品种增加以及董事和高级管理人员任职资格等都作了详细规定。

二、美国商业银行的组织机构

商业银行是美国金融体系的中坚力量，在金融业领域占有举足轻重的地位。美国商业银行有国民银行及州立银行之分，即商业银行可以在联邦和州两个级别的政府进行注册及获得特许状，是双轨银行制模式。

国民银行是根据《1863年国民银行法》向联邦政府注册的商业银行，此类银行一般规模较大，资金实力雄厚。国民银行从货币监理署获得特许状，并且在其公司名称中必须含有“国民”（national）的字样。

设立联邦特许的国民银行，需要向唯一的联邦银行特许机构——货币监理署提交申请，货币监理署对每一份申请展开详细的审查，在申请符合所有法律及监管标准时，货币监理署将授予特许状。设立国民银行，申请人除了必须获得货币监理署的批准之外，还必须分别获得联邦储备系统和联邦存款保险公司的批准。货币监理署作为国民银行的主要监管机构，对国民银行进行监管与检查。在美国，所有国民银行都必须获取联邦存款保险，这使得它们受到联邦存款保险公司的检查与监管。此外，所有的国民银行都必须加入联邦储备系统，成为联储会员。由此，国民银行还受到美联储的监管。

州立银行是根据各州的银行立法向各州政府注册的商业银行，此类银行的规模相对比较小。在美国，多数商业银行都是从其所在州的相关政府部门获取特许状，因此受到州银行监管机构的监管。

由于州立银行是分属于不同的州管辖，因此成立州银行的法律及审批的标准因州而异，但是各州的规定基本相似。州特许的商业银行可以选择是否加入联邦储备系统，而非像国民银行那样必须加入。加入联邦储备系统，使得它们可以使用联邦储备系统的支付与流动性工具及设施，但同时它们要受到美联储的监管和检查，并且还应当获取联邦存款保险，这也就意味着还要受到联邦存款保险公司的监管。

国民银行成立后可以向州银行转换，并且不需要货币监理署批准，只需要将其转换的意向书面通知其所在区货币监理署分局，以便取得关于终止国民银行身份的具体指示。国民银行身份终止后，该银行可向州银行主管机构提出成立州银行的申请。此外，州银行也可以向国民银行转换，只要州银行具备成立国民银行的注册资本，同时符合《1863年国民银行法》的相关规定且并不与州银行法相冲突，经货币监理署批准，即可转为国民银行。

除了商业银行之外，在美国，还有几类非银行金融机构能够经营商业银行的业务。

首先，银行控股公司及金融控股公司。银行控股公司法将银行控股公司定义为拥有或控制一个或一个以上的美国商业银行的实体。所有的银行控股公司都必须在美联储注册，并受到美联储的严格监管及检查。银行控股公司法禁止银行控股公司从事任何除银行业、控制或管理银行以及与银行业“紧密相关”的活动之外的经营活动。如果银行控股公司符合特定的资本及管理标准，并向美联储提交申请，那么其可以变成金融控股公司。《1999年金融服务现代化法》对银行控股公司法进行了修改，以允许金融控股公司从事广泛的属于金融性质的活动，包括保险、证券承销及交易以及商业银行业。作为银行控股公司的特殊一员，所有金融控股公司仍旧受到美联储的监管与检查。

其次，储贷机构（thrifts）。历史上，储贷机构是向住房消费者提供抵押贷款的存款机构。多年以来，储贷机构不断扩大其业务范围，尽管最核心的业务仍旧是住房贷款。美国国会在 1987 年的银行公平竞争法中确立了一项合格储贷机构借款人（Qualified Thrifts Lender）测试，以便确保储贷机构关注于向美国消费者提供住房抵押贷款：要获得储贷机构特有的诸多利益和优惠，必须首先成为合格的储贷机构借款人，这要求申请人至少 65%的组合资产符合储贷机构的投资要求，即主要进行住房抵押及相关投资。

再次，信用合作社（credit union）。它是由其存款人所有的免税的金融机构，其通常经营商业银行提供的一系列服务，但是范围较为有限。信用合作社通常向存款人提供储蓄及支票账户、网上银行以及信用卡服务。一般而言，信用合作社只能接受该社所明确的范围内（如在相同职业工作或生活在同一社区）的个人作为存款人。

最后，工商业贷款公司（industrial loan companies，ILCs），是指由商业企业拥有的金融机构。工商业贷款公司的经营与商业银行十分相似，但是它们可以通过以下任意一种方式能够避免受到如同银行控股公司一样的监管，不受商业——银行业分业经营的障碍限制：总资产少于 1 亿美元；不接受活期存款；或者自 1987 年以来不存在控制权的变更。工商业贷款公司通常享有与州商业银行相同的权力，它必须向联邦存款保险公司投保并受其监管。此外，工商业贷款公司还受到所在州的监管机构监管。

三、案例资料

美国《1933 年银行法》的通过使得银行的扩张受到限制。随后，银行业掀起了成立银行控股公司的浪潮。通过成立银行控股公司，再由控股公司分别控制多家银行及与银行业务无关的商业企业，由此实现扩张和多元化经营。银行控股公司的出现，造成资源过度集中以及反竞争的经济后果，同时使得相关银行业务逃避了监管部门的监管。为了回应这一现实，美国国会于 1956 年制定了《银行控股公司法》，并于 1970 年进行修订，以将银行控股公司置于美联储的监管之下。

在 1956 年《银行控股公司法》及其 1970 年的修正案中，均有“祖父条款”（grandfather clause）的规定，即在法律规定的日期之前银行控股公司直接或通过下属子公司间接合法从事的业务，在法案颁布后可继续从事该等业务而无须再获得美联储的批准。这一祖父条款，合理地兼顾了银行控股公司的既有利益，减少了法案推行的阻力。但是，这一条款也时常会引发纠纷。下面的 Cameron Financial Corp. v. Board of Governors of the Federal Reserve System 案即是因“祖父条款”而起。

在该案中，原告是一家成立于 1968 年 5 月 4 日的银行控股公司，其控制着一家国民银行，该国民银行同时经营着快递业务。随后，原告全资收购了一家快递公司，并将国民银行的快递业务转移至快递公司。1970年《银行控股公司法》的修正案通过后，原告面临着能否继续通过下属子公司从事快递业务的问题。原告援引修正案中的“祖父条款”，为其控制的快递公司（非银行子公司）经营的快递业务主张祖父权利，但是美联储拒绝了原告要求。原告随即起诉，要求法院审查美联储的决定。

原告与美联储争议的核心在于，“祖父条款”中的“下属子公司”（subsidiary）是何含义。原告认为，该“下属子公司”包括银行子公司和非银行子公司（banking and nonbanking subsidiary）；美联储则认为，“下属子公司”只指非银行子公司，不包括银行子公司，因此原告在法律规定的日期之前不存在经营快递业务的非银行子公司，无权援引“祖父条款”。

原告和美联储的观点针锋相对。法院认为，鉴于1970年法案中使用的“子公司”的用语本身并不明确，因此有必要从法案制定的大背景以及促使该法案出台的考量因素出发，来界定“子公司”的含义。在回顾了1970年法案的立法意图和背景之后，法院认为：相关立法的目的是为了实现对银行控股公司全方位的监管。原告如果将快递业务保留由下属的国民银行经营，那么还存在OCC对此进行监管；现在原告已经把快递业务全部转移至快递公司，如果仍能主张祖父权利的话，就不存在任何监管部门的监管了。

法院认为，防止原先受到监管的业务（通过将该等业务转移至非银行子公司的方式）逃避监管，似乎是拒绝给予祖父权利的有说服力的理由。因此，将模糊的“子公司”解释为仅指非银行子公司，与1970年修正案的目的完全相符。法院由此支持了美联储的决定。可见，在美国，尽管商业银行组织形式多样，但无论采取何种变通的形式，意图逃避监管将是非常困难的。

Cameron Financial Corp. v. Board of Governors of the Federal Reserve System

497 F.2d 841 (4th Cir. 1974)

ADAMS, Circuit Judge.

This appeal presents a formidably complicated question of statutory construction. Specifically, we must decide whether section 4(a)(2) of the Bank Holding Company Act extends so-called “grandfather” privileges to a bank holding company which controlled, prior to June 30, 1968, a bank subsidiary that also engaged in limited courier activities, but which “spun-off” the courier activities to a nonbanking subsidiary subsequent to June 30, 1968.

The Factual Background

There exists no disagreement concerning the factual background prompting this litigation. Cameron Financial Corporation, a bank holding company, was established on May 4, 1968. It controlled, among other things, one bank, First Union National Bank of North Carolina. First Union operated courier services at the time of Cameron's organization. Several months after Cameron was organized, on July 29, 1968, Courier Express Corporation was incorporated and Cameron shortly thereafter acquired all of Courier's common stock. Courier Express proceeded to purchase all of the equipment used by First Union in its courier activities. The net result of this reorganization was to remove the courier activities from the regulatory authority of the Comptroller of the Currency and to leave them largely unregulated. Courier Express is presently authorized to transport a variety of materials intrastate in North Carolina and Virginia and interstate between North Carolina and South Carolina, Virginia and Tennessee.

Prior to December 31, 1970, the Bank Holding Company Act did not cover one-bank holding companies. However, on that date, Congress amended the Act primarily to bring within the Act's regulatory scope one-bank holding companies like Cameron. The Board of Governors of the Federal Reserve, pursuant to section 4(a)(2) of the Act, notified Cameron that it may be entitled to grandfather privileges under that section, which had been added in 1970, and requested Cameron to furnish information relating to its courier operations. Cameron complied with the Board's request by furnishing such information and, in addition, claimed grandfather rights for the courier services operated by its nonbanking subsidiary, Courier Express. The Board, however, advised Cameron that only activities conducted by a nonbanking subsidiary prior to June 30, 1968 were entitled to grandfather privileges under section 4(a)(2). Since Cameron had effected the transfer of the assets and, hence, the courier operations from First Union to Courier Express after June 30, 1968, no nonbanking subsidiary of Cameron was engaged, prior to the critical date, in the activities sought to be grandfathered. The Board, therefore, concluded that "no indefinite grandfather benefits accrue(d) to Cameron Financial with respect to the activities carried on by the Courier Express Corporation." Cameron thereupon filed a petition for review of the Board's determination.

Section 4(a)(2) of the Bank Holding Company Act

Although the Bank Holding Company Act provides for the imposition of significant limitations on the conduct of nonbanking activities by bank holding companies, section 4(a)(2), nonetheless, permits a bank holding company to "engage in those activities in which directly or through a subsidiary... it was lawfully engaged on June 30, 1968... and it has been continuously engaged since June 30, 1968...."

The Board may require a holding company to cease activities falling within the parameters of the grandfather proviso if, after an opportunity for a hearing has been afforded, "it determines, having due regard to the purposes of this chapter that such action is necessary to prevent undue competition, conflicts of interest, or unsound bank practices...." Otherwise, activities within the proviso's terms may continue indefinitely.

…

Both Cameron and the Board offer plausible syntactical arguments supporting their competing views of the reach of the term "subsidiary" in section 4(a)(2). This antiphony, by itself, strongly suggests that the bare words of the statute cannot conclusively answer the question posed by this appeal. With the process of statutory construction in this posture, it is necessary to examine the statutory scheme more broadly and to acquire an appreciation of the general considerations motivating its enactment. These two inquiries are inextricably intertwined and it would seem, therefore, unobjectionable first to attempt to reach an informed conclusion regarding the considerations underlying the enactment of the Bank Holding Company Act generally and the 1970 Amendments in particular.

Prior to 1956, a bank holding company, then completely unregulated, was utilized to achieve geographical expansion and service diversification unattainable by its banking subsidiary along because by its banking subsidiary alone because to national or state regulation. Misgivings were developing among Congressmen that proliferation of the bank holding device was having anticompetitive effects in the economy. Banking resources were becoming increasingly concentrated and the combination in one enterprise of a major creditor in a locality, a bank, and another service business created a condition ripe for exploitation through tying relationships. In response to these concerns, Congress enacted the Bank Holding Company Act of 1956.

In essence, the Act brought multibank holding companies under the regulatory authority of the Federal Reserve Board. It limited the acquisition of banking subsidiaries and restricted the scope of allowable diversification. But the 1956 Act did not extend to one-bank holding companies. Since concentration of banking resources was facilitated by the acquisition of several banking subsidiaries, the bank holding company that controlled only one bank did not represent as significant a threat to competition as the multi-bank holding company. Further, the general small size, at the time, of one-bank holding companies and the absence of evidence of competitive abuse of the one-bank holding company device provided support in terms of the Act's objectives for exempting from the reach of the Act the holding companies that controlled only one bank.

But several large banks responded to the promise of stricter regulation as the result of court rulings limiting the authority of the Comptroller of the Currency to permit national banks wide-ranging entrepreneurial discretion by turning to the one-bank holding company device. "The nations largest banks," including the six largest, "rushed to form one-bank holding companies, many of which engaged in commercial and industrial enterprises not even arguably within banking powers, such as TV broadcasting, furniture manufacturing, and pizza parlors." In view of the large growth of the assets held by the one-bank holding company industry, and in view of the theoretical freedom of a one-bank holding company to engage in any business, or acquire anything it desires..., Congress amended the Act to include within its regulatory scheme one-bank holding companies as well as the multi-bank holding companies already covered.

The 1970 Amendments were directed primarily at the portent of serious anticompetitive consequences presented by the trend of unregulated one-bank holding company proliferation and expansion. Congress was not, therefore, eager to effect a dramatic alteration of the existing organizational structure of the banking industry. Furthermore, Congress "felt that the one-bank holding companies existing at the time set in the clause, most of which were quite small, had not caused great problems and was thus reluctant to require them to undergo the hardships of divestiture, which would be particularly harsh for small banks."

Turning to an examination of how these considerations are reflected in the statutory scheme, we note that one-bank holding companies that seek to engage in nonbanking activities or to continue to engage in such activities initiated subsequent to the grandfather date of June 30, 1968, must seek Board approval pursuant to section 4(c)(8), which provides:

> Such prohibitions shall not, with respect to any other bank holding company, apply to—shares of any company the activities of which the Board after due notice and opportunity for hearing has determined (by order or regulation) to be so closely related to banking or managing or controlling banks as to be a proper incident thereto. In determining whether a particular activity is a proper incident to banking or managing or controlling banks the Board shall consider whether its performance by an affiliate of a holding company can reasonably be expected to produce benefits to the public, such as greater convenience, increased competition, or gains in efficiency, that outweigh possible adverse effects, such as undue concentration of resources, decreased or unfair competition, conflicts of interest, or unsound banking practices. In orders and regulations under this subsection, the Board may differentiate between activities commenced de novo and

activities commenced by the acquisition, in whole or in part, of a going concern;....

Thus, "under section 4(c)(8), an application may not be approved without an affirmative showing that public benefits exceed harms...."

If, however, the activity of the one-bank holding company falls within the scope of the grandfather proviso of section 4(a)(2), the Board may order the bank holding company to disassociate itself from the activity "if it determines, having due regard to the purposes (of the Act), that such action is necessary to prevent undue concentration of resources, decreased or unfair competition, conflicts of interest, or unsound banking practices...." Although section 4(a)(2) dispenses with the requirement that the Board consider possible beneficial consequences resulting from allowing the bank holding company to participate in a given activity, the bank holding company need not establish that the particular activity is "closely related to banking" as it must under section 4(c)(8).

Even after the Board has ordered a one-bank holding company to terminate an activity, the holding company may retain control of the subsidiary for a period of ten years. In contrast, a denial of approval under section 4(c)(8) apparently requires termination of the activity forthwith. Hence, even though both sections—4(a)(2) and 4(c)(8)—possess features that tend to facilitate the Board's efforts to accomplish the statutory objectives, the Board may well prefer remitting a bank holding company to proceedings pursuant to section 4(c)(8) because this latter section makes available immediate termination and places the burden on the bank holding company to show that the activity is closely related to banking.

Cameron's Claim for Grandfather Privileges and the Statutory Objectives and Scheme

The geographic scope of the courier services conducted by Cameron has broadened since the post-June 30, 1968 transfer of these activities from Cameron's banking to its nonbanking subsidiary. It also appears that Cameron now offers a wider variety of courier services than it did when all courier operations were conducted by its banking subsidiary. So long as the courier services were conducted by the banking subsidiary, the Board lacked regulatory authority over them. Indeed, so long as banking authorities such as the Comptroller of the Currency were overseeing the courier activities when they were conducted by the bank itself, it would appear that the danger of anti-competitive consequences was substantially mitigated. However, when Cameron transferred these courier activities to its nonbanking subsidiary, there existed no regulatory authority guarding against potential competitive abuse unless, of course, the transfer occurred after June 30, 1968, which in this case it did, and the term "subsidiary" in section 4(a)(2), as the bank contends, is interpreted to refer solely to nonbanking subsidiaries.

To prevent the formerly regulated activities of a banking subsidiary to escape regulation through transfer of such activities to a nonbanking subsidiary seems a persuasive reason for declining to extend grandfather privileges to the activities conducted prior to June 30, 1968 by a banking subsidiary. To construe the ambiguous term "subsidiary" to relate to a nonbanking subsidiary only, and thus to achieve this result, seems entirely consistent with the objectives of the 1970 Amendments.

Deciding that Cameron's courier activities do not qualify under section 4(a)(2) does not necessarily mean that Cameron must divest itself of its courier business. It still may show that its courier services are closely related to banking under section 4(c)(8). Certainly, Cameron's case before the Board in a section 4(c)(8) proceeding would be substantially strengthened by the recent addition to Regulation Y that includes certain courier services among the activities regarded as closely related to banking. Cameron would, of course, have to establish that its own services do come within the ambit of the addition to Regulation Y. At the same time, it would be able to press the argument made here that Cameron's participation in courier activities has pro-competitive effects.

On balance, it would seem more consistent to require Cameron to seek approval of its expended courier activities in a section 4(c)(8) proceeding than to permit such activities to continue on a perhaps unregulated basis by virtue of section 4(a)(2).

Conclusion

In sum, since we agree with the Board that "subsidiary" in section 4(a)(2) does not refer to a banking subsidiary, Cameron's courier activities are not entitled to grandfather privileges under that section. Accordingly, Cameron's petition for review will be denied.

第三节 存款法律制度

存款是商业银行等具有存款业务经营资格的金融机构接受客户存入资金，并在存款人支取存款时支付存款本息的一种信用业务。吸收存款是商业银行最主要、最基本的负债业务，是商业银行组织资金来源的业务，对商业银行资产业务的开展具有基础性作用。各国均制定了相关的法律对商业银行的存款业务予以规范。

一、中国商业银行的存款业务

中国并未制定一部统一的存款管理法来对商业银行的存款业务予以规范，有关存款的管理规定散见于《宪法》、《民法通则》、《中国人民银行法》、《商业银行法》、《储蓄管理条例》、《人民币利率管理规定》、《人民币单位存款管理办法》等法律、法规中。这些法律、法规构成了中国存款法律制度。

在中国，存款业务经营实行许可制。只有经过中国银监会的许可方可从事吸收公众存款的业务。当然，具备吸收公众存款资格的机构，除了商业银行之外，还包括经批准城乡信用合作社以及邮政储蓄机构。

在中国，按照存款来源的不同，存款业务可被分为个人储蓄存款业务和单位存款业务。按照《储蓄管理条例》的规定，储蓄是指个人将属于其所有的人民币或者外币存入储蓄机构，储蓄机构开具存折或者存单作为凭证，个人凭存折或者存单可以支取存款本金和利息，储蓄机构依照规定支付存款本金和利息的活动。按照《人民币单位存款管理办法》的规定，（人民币）单位存款是指企业、事业、机关、部队和社会团体等单位在金融机构办理的人民币存款，包括定期存款、活期存款、通知存款、协定存款及经中国人民银行批准的其他存款。在中国商业银行业务中，习惯上称其为对公存款。商业银行开展个人储蓄存款业务和单位存款业务，均需要遵守相关的业务规则，对此《储蓄管理条例》和《人民币单位存款管理办法》等法律、法规已有详细的规定。

根据中国《商业银行法》的规定，商业银行应当保障存款人的合法权益不受任何单位和个人的侵犯。保护存款人利益，是中国关于商业银行存款法律制度最核心的内容。存款人的法律保护体现在方方面面，具体而言主要包括：

第一，对个人存款人的保护。商业银行办理个人储蓄存款业务，应当遵循存款自愿、取款自由、存款有息、为存款人保密的原则；对个人储蓄存款，除非法律另有规定，商业银行有权拒绝任何单位或者个人查询、冻结、扣划。此外，商业银行破产清算时，在支付清算费用、所欠职工工资和劳动保险费用后，应当优先支付个人储蓄存款的本金和利息。

第二，对单位存款人的保护。对单位存款，除非法律另有规定，商业银行有权拒绝任何单位或者个人查询、冻结、扣划。

第三，利率管制。商业银行应当按照中国人民银行规定的存款利率的上下限，确定存款利率，并予以公告，不得违反规定提高或者降低利率。

第四，商业银行应当按照中国人民银行的规定，向中国人民银行交存存款准备金，留足备付金。存款准备金是商业银行依据法律的规定，按吸收存款的一定比例缴存于中央银行的存款。备付金，或称“支付准备金”，是指商业银行为保证存款支付和资金清算而保留的清偿资金，包括商业银行的库存现金、在中央银行的存款以及购买国债及政策性银行债券。存款准备金和备付金，是对存款人利益保护的重要措施之一。

第五，商业银行应当保证存款本金和利息的支付，不得拖延、拒绝支付存款本金和利息。

第六，商业银行已经或者可能发生信用危机，严重影响存款人的利益时，中国银监会可以对该银行实行接管。接管的目的是对被接管的商业银行采取必要措施，以保护存款人的利益，恢复商业银行的正常经营能力。

第七，商业银行如有以下行为，对存款人造成财产损害的，应当承担支付迟延履行的利息以及其他民事责任：无故拖延、拒绝支付存款本金和利息的；非法查询、冻结、扣划个人储蓄存款或者单位存款的；违反法律规定对存款人造成损害的其他行为。

二、美国商业银行的存款业务

商业银行的运营资金，主要来自于其负债和资本。商业银行的负债中，最主要的就是存款人的存款。美国相关法律对商业银行的存款业务进行了相关的规管。

在美国，商业银行往往收取与存款相关的费用，以此获得收入。一些银行对某些类型的账户收取账户维持费，多数银行对诸如止付通知、透支支票或拒付存款支票等特殊情况收取费用。此外，商业银行往往还对银行客户使用其他银行的 ATM 机收取附加费用。关于商业银行对存款的收费，一些州政府试图对此予以限制和规管，但是联邦银行监管机构（如货币监理署）则坚持应当允许商业银行根据自身的市场战略及维持金融机构安全和稳健的要求，自行设定合理的非利息收费和费用。

关于商业银行的存款利率，20 世纪 30 年代的经济危机之后，美国国会试图制止银行间在向存户支付的利息率上展开的具有潜在破坏性的竞争。《1933 年银行法》中，国会禁止向活期存款支付利息，并且制定了储蓄账户的利率上限，由此利率竞争和活期货币市场的行为得到了规制。[①]为了提高商业银行的竞争力，美国国会最终于 20 世纪 80 年代废除了利率上限的限制。由此，美国形成了商业银行利率自由化的格局。但是，关于禁止向活期存款支付利息的法律规定，得到保留。

在美国，关于商业银行存款最具特色的是其存款保险制度。美国的存款保险制度于 20 世纪 30 年代确立。为了挽救在经济危机的冲击下已濒临崩溃的银行体系，美国国会在 1933 年通过《格拉斯—斯蒂格尔法案》，在该法的基础之上，联邦存款保险公司作为一家为银行存款保险的政府机构于 1934 年成立并开始实行存款保险，以避免挤兑，保障银行体系的稳定。1950 年，美国国会通过《联邦存款保险法》，在美国完全确立了存款保险制度。

在美国，国民银行和加入联储的州成员银行必须向联邦存款保险公司投存款保险，其他州银行可以选择是否投保，但实际上几乎所有的美国商业银行都向联邦存款保险投

---

① [美] 莉莎·布鲁姆，杰里·马卡姆. 银行金融服务业务的管制：案例与资料. 李杏杏，等，译. 2 版. 北京：法律出版社，2006：337.

保。联邦存款保险公司并非对所有存款都实行保险，只负责对活期存款账户、定期存款账务、储蓄存款账务等提供存款保险，对银行同业存款、境外金融中心存款等不实行保险。当投保银行破产倒闭时，联邦存款保险公司对存款人存款的最高清偿额是 10 万美元，如果一个存款人在同一银行有多个账户，受到联邦存款保险的保额也不能超过 10 万美元；如果同一存款人在好几个银行开有账户，那么他在每个银行账户的存款都会得到最高达 10 万美元的保护。超过限额的存款待破产机构财产清理完毕后，作为破产债权获取清偿。联邦存款保险公司对投保银行具有监管权。除了日常的检查之外，联邦存款保险公司负责对有问题银行进行处理。处理主要有三种方式：一是让健康的银行将其吸收或合并；二是通过贷款方式进行资金救援；三是宣告该银行破产，并具体负责破产财产的清算和债务清偿，同时对其保险的存款负责支付。

三、案例资料

在美国，商业银行通常会收取与存款有关的费用，并且对这一收入来源的依赖性日益增加。其中，大多数银行都会对透支支票的行为收取费用。银行的存款客户往往基于各种理由反对这种收费。下面的 Video Trax，Inc. v. NationsBank，N.A. 案就涉及银行对支票账户收取透支项目费用的争议。

该案中，原告声称，被告收取透支费的行为，实质上是对原告违反银行法而收取的高利贷性质的利息，是非法的。被告则主张，透支费的收取，是用于满足处理透支支票账户所需的费用，是一项管理费用，并非高利贷利息。

原告试图从各个角度去论证，被告收取透支费实质上就是以透支的数额向原告放贷从而收取利息的行为，但是法院否定了原告的主张。法院认为，对透支的支票账户收费的唯一理由是，存款人没有遵守存款协议中的条款，该等条款要求存款人在账户中维持足够的存款数额，以应付一切情形下的支票的提示。

当然，尽管商业银行有权对存款收取相关的费用，但是其必须尽到充分的披露义务。

Video Trax, Inc. v. NationsBank, N.A.

33 F.Supp.2d 1041 (S.D.Fla., 1998),

aff'd, 205 F. 3d 1358 (11th Cir.), *cert. denied*, 531 U.S. 822(2000)

GOLD, District Judge.

THIS CAUSE is before the Court upon cross motions for summary judgment by Plaintiff, Video Trax, Inc. ("Plaintiff"), and Defendant NationsBank, N.A. ("Defendant"). Plaintiff brought this class action pursuant to the National Bank Act, 12 U.S.C. §§ 85 and 86 (the "Bank Act"). Plaintiff alleges that the Overdraft Item Fee (the "OD fee") on checking accounts charged by Defendant, a national banking association, was actually a subterfuge to exact a usurious rate of interest in violation of the Bank Act. Defendant avers that the OD fee was an administrative cost to cover the processing of checks drawn in excess of the collected balance in a depositor's account, and was not interest as contemplated by the Bank Act and Florida's usury statute, §§ 687.01, *et seq.,* Fla.Stat. Therefore, according to Defendant, since the OD fee is not "interest," it is not usurious.

The parties request the Court to determine, as a matter of law, whether the OD fee is really interest, based on an extension of credit to cover checks in excess of Plaintiff's uncollected balance in its business checking account. Jurisdiction of the Court is invoked pursuant to 28 U.S.C. § 1331, as arising under federal law. After careful consideration of the parties' arguments, the relevant case law and the record as a whole, and being otherwise advised in the premises, the Court concludes that the contested charges do not constitute interest, and thus, the transaction was not usurious.

I. Factual and Procedural Background

The parties concede that no disputed issues of fact exist to preclude judgment as a matter of law. The undisputed facts in the record reveal that Defendant is a nationally chartered banking institution, organized and existing under the laws of the United States. At all relevant times, Defendant was authorized to transact, and was transacting, business in branch offices located in the State of Florida.

Plaintiff is a corporation organized under the laws of the State of Florida. At all times relevant to this cause, Plaintiff was authorized to do business, and was conducting business, in Dade County, Florida.

On June 10, 1992, Plaintiff opened a Simple Analysis Business Checking account at NCNB National Bank of Florida, N.A., Defendant's predecessor. The obligations of the parties were governed by the signature cards, deposit agreements, and schedules of fees in effect from the inception of the account until the account was terminated on February 18, 1997.

[1] As evidenced by the account agreement, Plaintiff agreed in writing to pay a flat fee when a check presented to Defendant for payment exceeded the collected balance in Plaintiff's account. In addition, Defendant *1045 charged interest on overdraft sums to the extent those sums exceeded collected balances in Plaintiff's account. The rate of interest charged was Defendant's prime rate plus 3%, and was subject to the maximum rate permissible by law.

Throughout the history of the parties' banking relationship, several checks were presented for payment against Plaintiff's account when the account contained insufficient funds to cover the checks. Pursuant to the deposit agreements and the bank's policies, which policies were incorporated into the deposit agreement between the parties, Defendant exercised its option to either honor or dishonor the checks. If a check was honored, an overdraft was permitted to exist in Plaintiff's account. If Defendant chose not to honor the check, it was returned unpaid. Plaintiff's account history reflects that, pursuant to this practice, out of a total of 212 checks presented when insufficient funds existed in Plaintiff's account, ninety-two checks were honored, while 120 checks were returned.

According to Defendant's schedule of fees, a flat, per item fee was charged against Plaintiff's account whether the check was honored or returned. From January 1, 1995 through June 31, 1995, checking account customers, including Plaintiff, were charged a flat fee of $25 for all overdrafts or checks returned for insufficient funds. That fee increased to $27 from July 1, 1995 through the duration of Plaintiff's relationship at Defendant's institution. There was no relation between the flat fee charged and the amount of the check, overdraft, or period of time the overdraft existed in the account. The interest charged against the account for overdrafts was calculated on the basis of the average daily overdrawn account balance.

Plaintiff alleges that the periodic charges for interest, when aggregated with the overdraft fees, constitute "interest" in excess of the lawful amount allowed under the Bank Act. According to Plaintiff, Defendant assessed "interest" in excess of $18 000 on an average annual overdraft balance of approximately $6 000, a total of over 300% in interest.

Upon Plaintiff's demand for the "excess interest," Defendant refused to refund any monies, on the basis that the "not sufficient fund fee" (the "NSF fee") and the OD fee were administrative charges, commonly utilized in the banking industry to cover processing charges and to deter depositors from overdrawing their accounts. Defendant contends that NSF and OD fees do not constitute "interest" within the meaning of the usury provisions of the Bank Act, and therefore, Plaintiff cannot avoid its contractual obligations by claiming protection under the usury laws.

…

III. Analysis and Discussion

The Amended Complaint, although not delineated as such, consists of a single count alleging that Defendant's practice of charging OD fees, in addition to assessing interest against the average daily overdrawn account balance, constituted usury. The parties agree that the sole issue for determination is whether the OD fee was really "interest" that, when aggregated with the interest charged on the average daily overdrawn balance, was usurious.

…

B. The Meaning of "Interest" As Contemplated in the Usury Prohibitions

Plaintiff alleges that the OD fees are "interest" under the Bank Act, and that the "interest" charged by Defendant, in the form of OD fees, exceeds that allowed by Florida law. Thus, Plaintiff alleges that Defendant's practices are usurious.

[11] [12] The Bank Act does not expressly define "interest rate" or "rates of interest" as used in § 85. Moreover, there is nothing in the legislative history of the Bank Act from which to glean a possible congressional intent to include the OD fees at issue within the definition of "interest." In the absence of an express definition or clear congressional intent, it is incumbent upon the Court to "begin with the language employed by Congress," and assume that the ordinary meaning of "interest" accurately expresses legislative purpose. Morales, 504 U.S. at 382, 112 S.Ct. at 2036; see also CSX Transportation, 507 U.S. at 664, 113 S.Ct. at 1737; FMC Corp., 498 U.S. at 57, 111 S.Ct. at 407. "[W]here words are employed in a statute which had at the time a well-known meaning at common law or in the law of this country[,] they are presumed to have been used in that sense unless the context compels to the contrary." Lorillard v. Pons, 434 U.S. 575, 583, 98 S.Ct. 866, 871, 55 L.Ed.2d 40 (1978). Courts interpreting the meaning of "interest" must apply a "strict, that is literal construction" to avoid subjecting banks to double interest penalties under the Bank Act. See Tiffany v. National Bank of Missouri, 85 U.S. (18 Wall.) 409, 410, 21 L.Ed. 862 (1873).

Interest has been understood to include any compensation allowed by law or fixed by the parties for the use or forbearance of *1050 money, or the price which is fixed for the use of money. See Deputy v. DuPont, 308 U.S. 488, 498, 60 S.Ct. 363, 368, 84 L.Ed. 416 (1940). The common definition of "interest rate" has been held to be the "percentage of an amount of money which is paid for its use for a specified time." *Black's Law Dictionary* 730 (5th ed.1979). Similarly, "interest" has been defined as "a charge for borrowed money[,] generally *a percentage of the amount borrowed.*" *Webster's Ninth New Collegiate Dictionary* 630 (1989) (emphasis added). The plain and ordinary meaning of "interest" or "interest rate" does not include OD fees, NSF fees, and similar contingent or default charges. See, e.g., United States v. Philadelphia Nat'l Bank, 374 U.S. 321, 328, 83 S.Ct. 1715, 1722, 10 L.Ed.2d 915 (1963) (charges for banking services, "such as service charges for checking privileges, are free of governmental regulation, state or federal"); see also Lloyd v. Scott, 29 U.S. (4 Pet.) 205, 226, 7

L.Ed. 833 (1830).

The determination of the maximum amount of interest which may be charged for the use of money loaned has always been within the police power of the state, and the details of and exceptions to the legislation have rested within the discretion of the state legislature. See Griffith v. Connecticut, 218 U.S. 563, 568-69, 31 S.Ct. 132, 133, 54 L.Ed. 1151 (1910). In § 85 of the Bank Act, Congress expressly and unambiguously stated that a national bank was subject to the interest provision of the laws of the state in which the bank was located. Accordingly, Congress may look to the laws of the states to define the term "interest," as well as to set the allowable rate of interest. See Tikkanen v. Citibank (South Dakota) N.A., 801 F.Supp. 270, 278 (D.Minn.1992).

1. *Overdraft Fees on Demand Deposit Checking Accounts Are Not "Interest"*

[13] Even assuming that the Bank Act preempts state law regarding the characterization of interest considered usurious, which the Court does not concede is appropriate, Plaintiff's claim that the OD fees are interest and therefore are subjected to usury laws must fail. As a threshold matter, except as the term "interest" relates to credit transactions, such as loans or credit card services, no provision of federal law discusses bank charges for NFS checks, or, for that matter, bank charges for any service performed for depositors of checking accounts.

"Interest" as used in the Bank Act includes:

> any payment compensating a creditor or prospective creditor for an extension of credit, making available of a line of credit, or any default or breach by a borrower of a condition upon which credit was extended. It includes, among other things, the following fees connected with credit extension or availability: numerical periodic rates, late fees, not sufficient funds (NSF) fees, overlimit fees, annual fees, cash advance fees, and membership fees....

12 C.F.R. § 7.4001(a) (1997). Because the OD fees were not imposed in connection with a credit transaction, the fees are not interest as defined by the Bank Act. Rather, the fee arises from the terms of the deposit agreements, which incorporate the schedule of fees. These types of charges are addressed by 12 C.F.R. § 7.4002, which provides:

> (a) *Customer charges and fees.* A national bank may charge its customers non-interest charges and fees, including deposit account service charges....

(b) *Considerations.* The establishment of non-interest charges and fees, and the amounts thereof, *is a business decision to be made by each bank, in its discretion, according to sound banking judgment and safe and sound banking principles.* A bank reasonably establishes non-interest charges and fees if the bank considers the following factors, among others:

(1) The cost incurred by the bank, plus a profit margin, in providing the service;

(2) The deterrence of misuse by customers of banking services;

*1051 (3) The enhancement of the competitive position of the bank in accordance with the bank's marketing strategy; and

(4) The maintenance of the safety and soundness of the institution.

(c) *Interest.* Charges and fees that are "interest" within the meaning of 12 U.S.C. § 85 are governed by § 7.4001 and not by this section.

The OD fees charged by Defendant are precisely those described in § 7.4002.

[14] Moreover, the fees at issue substantially satisfy the reasonableness factors set forth in 12 C.F.R. § 7.4002(b). Defendant's "Noninterest Income Project" report states that the bank's primary concern "is the extensive daily aggregate work effort by the branches and officers expended in the processing of NSF/OD transactions... [which] requires substantial review and intervention by the branches and officers." Defendant determined that the decision to pay or return a check "sends a distinct message to the customer as to whether their behavior is to be encouraged or discouraged."

[15] Analyzing the pattern of customer behavior and recognizing the additional financial risk to the bank, Defendant concluded that, since the majority of the potential overdraft checks are eventually honored, and the fact that the bank receives no additional fees when the item is presented a second time, honoring the check the first time provides little additional risk. Nevertheless, Plaintiff challenges Defendant's application of the considerations prescribed in § 7.4002(b), claiming that the fees are excessive for the services rendered. Plaintiff alleges that the cost analysis, based on the amount of the OD fee and the actual expense incurred by Defendant for processing an overdrawn check, does not justify the amount of the fee imposed. However, Plaintiff has presented no evidence to substantiate its accusation that the OD fees were unconscionable and were imposed in contravention of the considerations required for analyzing and assessing the propriety of the fees.

Even if Plaintiff proffered competent evidence of profit percentages, such evidence does not automatically prove that the fees were unreasonable. In fact, the Code of Federal Regulations permit nationally chartered banks to recover the "cost incurred" for processing bad cheeks, "plus a profit margin." 12 C.F.R. § 7.4002(b)(1).

Additionally, national banks are required to set non-interest charges and fees based on the "maintenance of the safety and soundness of the institution." 12 C.F.R. § 7.4002(b)(4). Defendant's OD fees are a fair and efficient method of allocating the administrative costs consequent to processing checks presented against insufficient funds. Depositors who maintain insufficient balances create operational costs directly attributable to their failure to comply with the terms of their agreement. Banks must adopt systems to track such behavior and respond to it appropriately. Since banks must refrain from engaging in unsafe and unsound practices, see 12 U.S.C. § 1818(e), it is more than conceivable that a charge for overdrawn checks which is low enough to avoid attack as unreasonable would fail to discourage the writing of such checks.

2. *Defendant's OD Fees Are Not Interest Under Florida Law*

The Office of the Comptroller of the Currency has declared that the federal definition *1052 of "interest" does not take precedence over the manner in which states define the term. See 12 C.F.R. § 7.4001(c) ("The Federal definition of the term 'interest' does not change how interest is defined by the individual states (nor how the state definition of interest is used) solely for purposes of state law."). Therefore, if certain fees are not considered interest "for purposes of evaluating compliance with state usury limitations... when calculating the maximum interest that lending institutions may charge under those limitations," such fees are not deemed to be interest under federal law. Id.

[16] Applying Florida law, the OD fee charged by Defendant for the presentment of checks against an overdrawn account is not interest for the purpose of determining whether a transaction is usurious. Although the terms "fee" and "charge," in their legal acception, have a very broad meaning, as used generally, they refer to a price demanded for services rendered, "to fix or demand such a price, or any act by which the charging party manifests his purpose to demand the amount fixed or allowed for the [service]." Benson v. First Trust & Savings Bank, 105 Fla. 135, 142 So. 887, 891 (Fla.1932).

Contrary to Plaintiff's assertion, Florida's formula for calculating interest on loans and credit advances belies the fact that Defendant's OD fees are a subterfuge for excessive interest. The rate of interest on Florida transactions is:

calculated by first computing the advance or forbearance *as a percentage of the total stated amount of such loan....* This percentage shall then be divided by the number of years, and fractions thereof, of the loan... *according to its stated maturity date, without regard to* early maturity in the *event of default.* The resulting annual percentage rate shall then be added to the stated annual percentage rate of interest to produce the effective rate of interest for purposes of this chapter.

§ 687.03(3), Fla.Stat. (emphasis added).

The clear language of § 687.03(3) refers to the particular term stated on the face of a loan document. The statute explicitly states that the calculation of unlawful rates of interest "shall apply only to loans and advances of credit." § 687.03(2)(b), Fla.Stat. Thus, Plaintiff's usury claim cannot stand unless Defendant's OD fees were a charge for receiving a loan or were incident to or a condition for the extension of credit.

C. Honoring Checks on Overdrawn Accounts Is Not an Extension of Credit

Plaintiff argues that, by honoring checks for which insufficient funds exist in a checking account, Defendant was actually extending credit to Plaintiff. This extension of credit, according to Plaintiff, is synonymous with a loan. Therefore, the OD fee assessed on these "loans" constitutes interest. Accordingly, since the OD fee charged by Defendant exceeded the lawful rate of interest permitted in Florida, it was usurious.

Plaintiff relies heavily on Smiley v. Citibank (S.D.), N.A., 517 U.S. 735, 116 S.Ct. 1730, 135 L.Ed.2d 25 (1996), to support its contention that a loan was extended in connection with its checking account. The Court finds Plaintiff's reliance on Smiley is misplaced.

The Smiley Court unanimously held that the word "interest" in § 85 was ambiguous and that the Comptroller's judgment as to its meaning was entitled to deference under the principles set forth in Chevron U.S.A. Inc. v. Natural Resources Defense Council, Inc., 467 U.S. 837, 104 S.Ct. 2778, 81 L.Ed.2d 694 (1984). See Smiley, 116 S.Ct. at 1732-33; Doe v. Norwest Bank Minnesota, N.A., 107 F.3d 1297, 1301-02 (8th Cir.1997). The Court then concluded that the OCC's inclusion of credit card late fees within the meaning of "interest" was a reasonable interpretation of the statute. Smiley, 116 S.Ct. at 1735. Because the law of South Dakota, Citibank's home state, permitted banks to charge late fees, the determination that late fees are interest for purposes of the Bank Act led to the dismissal of the state-law claims of Smiley, a California resident. See id. at 1732.

Here, the Court faces a different issue. The late fees at issue in Smiley arose from that plaintiff's relationship with the bank as a *credit card holder,* an arrangement which *1053 unambiguously is based on "an extension of credit, making available of a line of credit, or any default or breach by a borrower of a condition upon which credit was extended." 12 C.F.R. § 7.4001(a). A credit card holder fits neatly into the debtor role in a creditor/debtor relationship, which is essential to invoke § 85 of the Bank Act. In the instant case, Defendant's OD fees stem from a deposit agreement between a bank and one or more of its depositors. Although a creditor/debtor relationship exists, the roles are reversed: the bank is the debtor and the depositor is the creditor. MJZ Corp. v. Gulfstream First Bank & Trust, N.A., 420 So.2d 396, 397 (Fla. 4th DCA 1982). Thus, the threshold question is whether the OD fees in this case are "connected with credit extension or availability," 12 C.F.R. § 7.4001(a), and accordingly, whether the usury laws apply at all.

Significantly, the Smiley Court approved the definition of "interest" found in 12 C.F.R. § 7.4001, which includes a reference to NSF charges. However, § 7.4001 clearly provides that NSF fees are interest if, and only if, the fee is a "payment compensating a creditor... for an extension of credit." 12 C.F.R. § 7.4001(a). In the present case, the NSF and OD fees charged to Plaintiff were not compensating Defendant for an extension of credit. The fees were charged for the processing of bad checks. Thus, the holding and reasoning of the Supreme Court in Smiley is inapplicable.

This Court is without benefit of binding law to resolve this unique issue in Plaintiff's favor. Indeed, the federal cases which analyze the usurious nature of interest, and charges which can be incorporated into the calculation of interest, deal with loans and similarly structured transactions. These transactions unambiguously entail the extension of credit. This, alone, raises suspicions about Plaintiff's novel argument. However, by analogy, case law exists which distinguishes loans from check transactions, and compels a determination that the payment of checks against an overdrawn account is not an extension of credit, and that the OD fee charged for such services is not interest.

1. *Loan Transactions Versus Checking Account Relationships*

[17] Plaintiff would argue that the word "loan" is intentionally broad, and covers all circumstances in which there has been a *de facto* loan. Plaintiff urges that even Defendant considers the honoring of checks drawn against overdrawn accounts an "unsecured extension of credit." Such a broad interpretation of this term places form over substance, in contravention of the intent and purpose behind the usury laws.

[18] Although a loan may exist regardless of the form of the transaction, "whether or not

[a] transaction constitutes a loan, is to be determined from the surrounding facts in the particular case." Calcasieu-Marine Nat'l Bank of Lake Charles v. American Employers' Ins. Co., 533 F.2d 290, 297 (5th Cir.1976) (quoting source omitted). Courts should not interpret the transaction in a manner which would defeat the probable intentions of the parties. See id. at 296.

The classic definition of a loan is "a contract by which one delivers a sum of money to another and the latter agrees to return at a future time a sum equivalent to that which he borrows." In re Grand Union Co., 219 F. 353, 356 (2d Cir.1914). Moreover, "to constitute a loan, there must be a contract whereby, in substance one party transfers to the other a sum of money which that other agrees to pay absolutely, *together with such *1054 additional sums as may be agreed upon for its use.*" Id. (emphasis added). Essentially, it is a contractual arrangement between two parties.

[19] In contrast, a check "is a contract in writing by which the drawer contracts with the payee that the bank will pay to the payee therein the amount designated on presentation." Sawgrass Builders, Inc. v. Realty Coop., Inc., 172 Ga.App. 324, 323 S.E.2d 243, 244 (Ga.Ct.App.1984) (quoting source omitted). Unlike a loan note, which is a promise by the maker to pay a specified sum and described as a two-party instrument—the parties being the maker and a payee—a check constitutes an order on a third party, a bank, to pay a specified sum and is a three-party instrument—the parties being a drawer, a drawee or payor bank, and a payee. The differences between these types of instruments and underlying transactions are apparent in the respective definitions promulgated in the Uniform Commercial Code. *Compare* UCC § 3-104(f) (1990) (definition of check) *with* UCC § 3-104(e) (1990) (definition of note).

The Supreme Court has noted the dichotomy between loan documentation and checks. See Don E. Williams Co. v. Commissioner of Internal Revenue, 429 U.S. 569, 97 S.Ct. 850, 51 L.Ed.2d 48 (1977). In that case, the Court declared that:

> The promissory note, even when payable on demand and fully secured, is still, as its name implies, only a promise to pay, and does not represent the paying out or reduction of assets. A check, on the other hand, is a direction to the bank for immediate payment, is a medium of exchange, and has come to be treated for federal tax purposes as a conditional payment of cash.

Id. at 582-83, 97 S.Ct. at 858.

When a bank honors a check, it reasonably expects the check to be paid in the normal course of business. See Pioneer Valley Sav. Bank v. Indemnity Ins. Co., 225 F.Supp. 404, 411 (N.D.Iowa 1964), *aff'd,* 343 F.2d 634 (8th Cir.1965). Checks, as the most common items handled by banks, are handled in bulk as cash items on the assumption that they will be honored in most cases; provisional credits are entered immediately at all stages of the collection process, and become final without further action upon payment by the drawee bank. See Calcasieu-Marine Nat'l Bank, 533 F.2d at 300 (citation omitted).

The Court cannot agree with Plaintiffs argument that the deposit agreement relative to Plaintiff's checking account treats an overdraft as an application for advance credit. The implementation of OD and NSF fees was based on the banking industry's awareness that a depositor often writes checks under the mistaken belief that he has, or will have, sufficient funds to cover the check, without any intent to apply for credit. The imposition of the fee is solely contingent upon the depositor's failure to comply with the terms of the deposit agreement, which require the maintenance of sufficient funds to cover all checks presented.

2. *Contingent Default Fees Are Not Interest*

There is a significant body of law establishing that fees imposed as a result of a contingency are not considered interest in divining a violation of the usury laws. Prior to the passage of the Bank Act in 1864, the U.S. Supreme Court examined the dichotomy between "interest rates" and "contingent default charges," and determined that the latter are not interest for purposes of § 85. See Lloyd v. Scott, 29 U.S. at 226. In addressing whether late fees constituted interest, the Court held that:

> If a party agree[s] to pay a specific sum exceeding the lawful interest, provided he do[es] not pay the principal by a day certain, it is not usury. By a punctual payment of the principal, he may avoid the payment of the sum stated, which is considered a penalty.

Id. Accordingly, a fee, even when calculated according to a percentage of the amount owed, is not rendered usurious by a depositor's agreement to pay the fee contingent upon his delinquency, because the payment or non-payment of that fee is completely within the depositor's control.

One year prior to the enactment of the Bank Act, the Supreme Court once again spoke to the dissimilarities between interest *1055 rates and contingent default charges, and stated that when "[t]he payment of anything additional depends also upon a contingency, and not upon any happenings of a certain event, [such is] insufficient to make a loan usurious." Spain v.

Hamilton's Administrator, 68 U.S. (1 Wall.) 604, 626, 17 L.Ed. 619 (1863).

These cases stand for the proposition that only where the charge is required for a loan, and not where it is contingent on the happening of an uncertain event, will the charge be considered "interest." Because Congress is presumed to have adopted the federal common law meaning of "interest" in enacting § 85, see Perrin v. United States, 444 U.S. 37, 42, 100 S.Ct. 311, 314, 62 L.Ed.2d 199 (1979); Burns v. Alcala, 420 U.S. 575, 580-81, 95 S.Ct. 1180, 1184, 43 L.Ed.2d 469 (1975), the statute cannot be interpreted to include contingent default charges within the depositor's control, such as the OD fees imposed by Defendant in this case.

The logic behind this distinction is clear. If charges and fees within the depositors control, such as the OD fees in dispute, are deemed "interest," banks could not possibly know whether the ultimate rate on any given account would exceed the interest ceiling provided by law. The depositor could, therefore, render his account usurious, and hence unlawful, by simply maintaining insufficient funds in the account, thereby incurring an amount of fees equal to a usurious rate.

[20] In the absence of clear congressional intent to the contrary, the Court finds that the term "interest rates" or "rates of interest" as used in § 85 of the Bank Act ought to be construed in compliance with the term's plain and ordinary meaning, and its well entrenched federal common law meaning, so as not to include contingent default fees. See Cipollone v. Liggett Group, Inc., 505 U.S. 504, 521-22, 112 S.Ct. 2608, 2620, 120 L.Ed.2d 407 (1992).

3. *Florida Is in Accord Regarding the Assessment of Contingent Default Fees*

[21] Florida courts adhere to Supreme Court precedent, and do not characterize fees received for participating in uncertain transactions as interest for purposes of usury determinations. See, e.g., Kraft v. Mason, 668 So.2d 679, 684 (Fla. 4th DCA 1996). Repeatedly, those courts have found that an agreement to pay fees is not usurious when payment depends upon a contingency. See, e.g., Bailey v. Harrington, 462 So.2d 861 (Fla. 3d DCA), *review denied*, 472 So.2d 1180 (Fla.1985).

Plaintiff admits that "[t]he charging of the 'Overdraft Item Fee' was *a condition* of the extension of credit when the Bank allowed a customer to overdraw their account." Plaintiff's Motion for Summary Judgment, at page 10 (emphasis added). It was within Plaintiff's control to avoid the OD fees. Reviewing the record before the Court, it is clear that no part of the deposit agreement contains a promise to pay anything absolutely in addition to the amount of the check presented against Plaintiff's account. The payment of anything additional depends entirely on a contingency, and not upon any happening of a certain event, which of itself is insufficient to make Defendant's OD fee usurious. Accordingly, Plaintiff's contention that Defendant's OD fee is a subterfuge for charging a usurious rate of interest must fail.

…

Based on the foregoing, NationsBank's Motion for Final Summary Judgment is granted. Plaintiff, Video Trax, Inc.'s Motion for Summary Judgment is denied. As this Order disposes of all issues raised in this action, all pending motions are denied as moot.

第四节　贷款法律制度

贷款是商业银行等金融机构的资产业务，是商业银行资金收益的最主要来源，因而是商业银行的业务核心。商业银行的贷款业务，也是各国金融法律、法规规范的重点。

一、中国商业银行的贷款业务

贷款是商业银行的资产业务之一，也是商业银行的核心业务。在中国，商业银行开展贷款业务，除了适用最基本的交易法律（如《民法通则》、《合同法》以及《担保法》等）之外，还应当适用《商业银行法》以及中国人民银行和中国银监会根据《商业银行法》颁布的相关监管规定（如《贷款通则》、《固定资产贷款管理暂行办法》以及《流动资金贷款管理暂行办法》等）。

根据《贷款通则》的规定，贷款业务可作如下分类：

按照商业银行是否承担风险可分为自营贷款（商业银行以合法方式筹集的资金自主发放的贷款，其风险由商业银行承担，并由商业银行收回本金和利息）、委托贷款（由政府部门、企事业单位及个人等委托人提供资金，由商业银行即受托人根据委托人确定的贷款对象、用途、金额期限、利率等代为发放、监督使用并协助收回的贷款。商业银行只收取手续费，不承担贷款风险）以及特定贷款（经国务院批准并对贷款可能造成的损失采取相应的补救措施后责成国有独资商业银行发放的贷款）。

按照贷款期限的长短可分为短期贷款（贷款期限在一年以内（含一年）的贷款）、中期贷款（贷款期限在一年以上（不含一年）五年以下（含五年）的贷款）以及长期贷款（贷款期限在五年（不含五年）以上的贷款）。

按照贷款有无担保可分为信用贷款（借款人不提供任何担保，完全凭借其商业信用而发放的贷款）、担保贷款（包括保证贷款、抵押贷款以及质押贷款）和票据贴现（商业银行以购买借款人未到期商业票据的方式发放的贷款）。

根据《商业银行法》及其他相关的监管规定，商业银行开展贷款业务，应当遵守如下的要求：

第一，商业银行根据国民经济和社会发展的需要，在国家产业政策指导下开展贷款业务。贷款业务的开展，应当以安全性、流动性、效益性为经营原则。

第二，商业银行应当实行审贷分离、分级审批的制度。商业银行应当建立贷款管理岗位责任制度，实行审贷分离、相互约束的机制；同时贷款发放、延期偿还、贷款呆账处理和实行贷款制裁等，都要实行审批，同一商业银行系统间应当合理确定各级行的审批贷款的权限。

第三，商业银行贷款，借款人应当提供担保。商业银行应当对保证人的偿还能力，抵押物、质物的权属和价值以及实现抵押权、质权的可行性进行严格审查。经商业银行审查、评估，确认借款人资信良好，确能偿还贷款的，可以不提供担保。

第四，在贷款利率的确定方面，商业银行应当按照中国人民银行规定的贷款利率的上下限，确定贷款利率。

第五，对关系人发放贷款的限制。商业银行不得向关系人发放信用贷款；向关系人发放担保贷款的条件不得优于其他借款人同类贷款的条件。在中国，关系人是指商业银行的董事、监事、管理人员、信贷业务人员及其近亲属，以及前述人员投资或者担任高级管理职务的公司、企业和其他经济组织。

第六，资产负债比例的管理。在中国，商业银行贷款，应当遵守下列资产负债比例管理的规定：资本充足率不得低于 8%；贷款余额与存款余额的比例不得超过 75%；流动性资产余额与流动性负债余额的比例不得低于 25%；对同一借款人的贷款余额与商业银行资本余额的比例不得超过 10%；中国银监会对资产负债比例管理的其他规定。

第七，商业银行享有发放贷款的自主权。任何单位和个人不得强令商业银行发放贷款或者提供担保。商业银行有权拒绝任何单位和个人强令要求其发放贷款或者提供担保。同时，借款人到期不归还担保贷款的，商业银行依法享有要求保证人归还贷款本金和利息或者就该担保物优先受偿的权利。商业银行因行使抵押权、质权而取得的不动产或者股权，应当自取得之日起二年内予以处分。

为促进商业银行完善信贷管理，科学评估信贷资产质量，中国银监会制定了《贷款风险分类指引》。根据该指引的要求，商业银行应当至少将贷款划分为正常、关注、次级、可疑和损失五类，后三类合称为不良贷款。商业银行应在贷款分类的基础上，根据有关规定及时足额计提贷款损失准备，核销贷款损失。同时，商业银行应依据有关信息披露的规定，披露贷款分类方法、程序、结果及贷款损失计提、贷款损失核销等信息。

二、美国商业银行的贷款业务

在美国，商业银行可以向企业和个人发放贷款，发放的贷款形成商业银行的资产。在发放贷款的过程中，商业银行必须遵守相关的监管规定。对商业银行的贷款，美国相关的法律、法规主要关注如下几个方面的内容：

首先是贷款限额。对商业银行向某一个借款人贷款额度的限制是保证银行安全和良好运作的重要和常见措施。根据美国法律的规定，向一个借款人提供的贷款所受的基本限额是不得超过银行未减损股本和未减损盈余的15%。商业银行的董事会通过其贷款委员会对贷款限额进行监控。如果出现违反贷款限额的情况，董事会成员可能需要对商业银行在这些贷款中所受到的损失进行赔偿。在美国，如果一笔潜在的贷款数额巨大，以至于超过一家银行的贷款限额，这家银行可能会出卖这笔贷款的参与权或是联合其他银行进行银团贷款，以避免违反贷款限额的规定。①

其次是内部人贷款（insider loans）。在美国，商业银行可以向其内部人提供贷款，但是这种贷款受到相关的监管和限制。这样设计的初衷在于，既不希望商业银行因为内部人的压力而作出不稳健的信贷决定，又不希望商业银行因失去了内部人这一客户群体而减少收入。内部人通常被界定为包括商业银行的高管、董事及主要股东。根据美国相关法律的要求，向内部人贷款的条件不能比向其他借款人贷款的条件更为优惠且此类贷款通常需要获得董事会的事先批准。同时，法律还限定了内部贷款的限额。

最后是贷款人责任问题。贷款人的责任，包括两个方面的内容：第一，基于贷款合同而产生的责任。即贷款人根据贷款合同采取了相关行动（既包括积极行动，如行使担保权占有担保物，也包括消极行动，如未能按时发放贷款），但是借款人对此存在异议因而提起诉讼。第二，基于法律规定的特殊责任。在美国，相关的环境保护法律对贷款人的责任提出了要求。相关主体可援引联邦环境法律（例如美国国会通过的《环境反应赔偿和责任综合法案》）要求贷款人对清理环境废物的费用承担责任。除了联邦法律外，某些州可能也制定有类似的法律规定这种责任。

在美国，比起商业性贷款，消费者贷款业务受到更为严格的限制。美国国会和各州均颁布了相关的法律、法规，对消费者贷款进行管制。这种管制通常包括：第一，对高利贷（usury）的管制，包括要求贷款人详尽披露贷款利率信息或者对贷款利率进行限制两种手段；第二，贷款人向消费者披露贷款所需的真实费用，从而使得消费者掌握信息，对不同的贷款选择进行比较；第三，对贷款人发放贷款的公平性进行监管（如1974年制定的《信贷机会平等法案》（Equal Credit Opportunity Act）），禁止种族、肤色、宗教、出生地、年龄或是政府援助收入等因素，实行贷款歧视；第四，禁止“划红线拒贷”（redlining）的行为，划红线拒贷是指商业银行在地图上的某一个区域划上红圈，并且无论贷款申请人的信誉如何，都拒绝以位于这一区域内的财产为担保发放贷款的行为的形象称呼；第

---

① ［美］莉莎·布鲁姆，杰里·马卡姆. 银行金融服务业务的管制：案例与资料. 李杏杏，等，译. 2版. 北京：法律出版社，2006：214.

五，禁止掠夺性放贷（Predatory Lending），掠夺性放贷是指贷款人（lender)的放贷条件和利率与其所承担的风险不一致，存在欺骗借款人、收取不合理的费用、安排不合理的贷款方式等行为的放贷行为。

三、案例资料

在美国，商业银行提供信贷必须遵守一些强制性法律的要求。其中，1974 年生效的《信贷机会平等法案》要求商业银行在发放贷款时，不基于性别或是婚姻状态实行歧视。该法案随后被扩张适用，要求商业银行不得以种族、肤色、宗教、出生地、年龄等原因实行歧视。

下面的 Latimore v. Citibank Fed. Sav. Bank 案涉及商业银行发放贷款时的种族歧视问题。与雇佣案件中的种族歧视不同，在商业银行信贷歧视的案件中，往往不存在相应的不同种族的申请者之间的竞争问题。此时，自认为受到歧视的贷款申请者，应当提交多少证据才能确立种族歧视的存在？

Latimore v. Citibank Fed. Sav. Bank 案中，法院向我们揭示了相关的证据要求：如果同时存在情况近似的白人和黑人申请者，基于二者之间的竞争关系，发放贷款的商业银行就有责任合理地解释为什么给白人更好的待遇；如果不存在这样的情形，那么所谓的歧视受害者就必须以传统的方式表明，有足够的直接或间接证据证明存在种族歧视，从而确立一个可供裁判的问题。

Latimore v. Citibank Fed. Sav. Bank

151 F.3d 712 (7th Cir. 1998)

POSNER, Chief Judge.

Helen Latimore, a black woman, brought a suit charging racial discrimination in real estate lending by Citibank and two of its employees, in violation of an assortment of federal civil rights laws including the Equal Credit Opportunity Act, 15 U.S.C. § 1691(a)(1), and the Fair Housing Act, 42 U.S.C. §§ 3605(a), (b). The district court granted summary judgment for the defendants. Latimore's appeal requires us to consider what the prima facie case of credit discrimination is, that is, how much evidence a plaintiff must submit in order to withstand a motion for summary judgment. There is no reason to think that the answer will be different depending on the particular civil rights statute sued under.

Owner of a home in a largely black neighborhood on the south side of Chicago, Latimore applied to Citibank for a $51 000 loan secured by the home. She satisfied Citibank's standards for creditworthiness, but the bank's rules also required that the ratio of the appraised value of the security (Latimore's home) to the amount of the loan not exceed 75 percent. The bank's appraiser, defendant Kernbauer, appraised the property at only $45 000, yielding a loan-to-value ratio of 113 percent. When defendant Lundberg, the account executive handling Latimore's application, informed her that the appraised value of the home was too low to support a loan in the amount sought, Latimore told Lundberg that the house had been appraised less than a year earlier for $82 000. Lundberg asked Latimore for the appraisal report, and when Lundberg received it she sent it together with Kernbauer's report to the bank's appraisal review department. The department declined to overrule Kernbauer's appraisal, on the ground that the comparable sales on which the $82 000 appraisal had been based weren't really comparable, because they involved property more than six blocks from Latimore's home. And so Latimore did not receive the loan. Some months later she applied for a loan from another bank, which appraised her home at $79 000 and made her the loan, though for a smaller amount than she had sought from Citibank ($46 000 instead of $51 000) and at a one percent higher interest rate. The damages sought are the additional interest plus certain consequential damages.

[1] In most discrimination cases, the plaintiff can establish a prima facie case either by presenting evidence of having been actually discriminated against on some forbidden ground such as race or by satisfying the *McDonnell Douglas* standard. See, e.g., McDonnell Douglas Corp. v. Green, 411 U.S. 792, 93 S.Ct. 1817, 36 L.Ed.2d 668 (1973); Furnco Construction Corp. v. Waters, 438 U.S. 567, 98 S.Ct. 2943, 57 L.Ed.2d 957 (1978). Under that standard, in a typical case of employment discrimination, involving say the denial of a promotion to a black employee, the plaintiff would have to show only that he was qualified for the promotion and that a white got it instead, and the burden would then be on the employer to come forth with a noninvidious reason for why the white rather than the black got the promotion. Although the *McDonnell Douglas* standard originated and evolved in cases involving racial discrimination in employment, it has been extended to all sorts of other discrimination not even limited to the employment setting. See, e.g., Coco v. Elmwood Care, Inc., 128 F.3d 1177 (7th Cir. 1997); Leffel v. Valley Financial Services, 113 F.3d 787, 792 (7th Cir. 1997); Hornick v. Noyes, 708 F.2d 321, 325 n. 8 (7th Cir. 1983); Teahan v. Metro-North Commuter R. Co., 951 F.2d 511, 514 (2d Cir. 1991); Lipsett v. University of Puerto Rico, 864 F.2d 881, 896-97, 899 (1st Cir. 1988). So numerous are these extensions that we were not surprised when the bank's counsel

invited us to use *McDonnell Douglas* as a template in credit discrimination cases as well.

*714 The propriety of such use was assumed in Simms v. First Gibraltar Bank, 83 F.3d 1546, 1558 (5th Cir. 1996); Moore v. U.S. Dept. of Agriculture, 55 F.3d 991, 995 (5th Cir. 1995), and Ring v. First Interstate Mortgage, Inc., 984 F.2d 924, 926 (8th Cir. 1993). But it was not discussed and wholesale transposition of the *McDonnell Douglas* standard to the credit discrimination context would display insensitivity to the thinking behind the standard. Normally the burden of producing evidence of each element of the plaintiff's claim is on the plaintiff. There has to be a reason for shifting the burden to the defendant. It is not reason enough that essential evidence is in the defendant's possession and would be difficult for the plaintiff, even with the aid of modern pretrial discovery, to dig out of the defendant. Before the defendant may be put to the burden of producing evidence, the plaintiff has to show that there is some ground for suspecting that the defendant has indeed violated the plaintiff's rights. Otherwise we would have a regime of pre-complaint discovery. Anyone could put anyone else to the burden of producing evidence without having anything better than a hope and a prayer that the evidence would establish a violation. Cf. Bruce L. Hay, "Allocating the Burden of Proof," 72 *Ind. L.J.* 651 (1997).

The fact that a qualified black is passed over for promotion in favor of a white has been thought sufficiently suspicious to place on the defendant the minimum burden of presenting a non-invidious reason why the black lost out. But it is the competitive situation-the black facing off as it were against the white-that creates the (minimal) suspicion, and there is no comparable competitive situation in the usual allegation of credit discrimination. Latimore was not competing with a white person for a $51 000 loan. A bank does not announce, "We are making a $51 000 real estate loan today; please submit your applications, and we'll choose the application that we like best and give that applicant the loan." If a bank did that, and a black and a white each submitted an application, and the black's application satisfied the bank's criteria of creditworthiness and value-to-loan ratio yet the white received the loan, we would have a situation roughly parallel to that of a *McDonnell Douglas* case. And when we have an approximation to such a situation, a variant of the *McDonnell Douglas* standard may apply, as we shall see. But such cases are rare, and this is not one of them. The Supreme Court has reminded us that *McDonnell Douglas* was not intended to be a straitjacket into which every discrimination case must be forced kicking and screaming. See, e.g., McDonnell Douglas Corp. v. Green, supra, 411 U.S. at 802 n. 13, 93 S.Ct. 1817; U.S. Postal Service Bd. of Governors v. Aikens, 460 U.S. 711, 715, 103 S.Ct. 1478, 75 L.Ed.2d 403 (1983). In Diaz v. Fort Wayne

Foundry Corp., 131 F.3d 711, 712-13 (7th Cir. 1997), we pointed out the unsuitability of the McDonnell Douglas framework when there is no basis for comparing the defendant's treatment of the plaintiff with the defendant's treatment of other, similarly situated persons.

The reason the bank-the (principal) defendant-urges adoption of the standard is that it construes it to require that Latimore show not only that she was creditworthy by the bank's standards, which she was, but also that she satisfied the bank's appraiser, which she did not, about the value of her house. There is no question that to be a qualified borrower-the counterpart to a worker who is performing to his employer's satisfaction in the employment discrimination context (an element of the prima facie case that we emphasized in Coco v. Elmwood Care, Inc., supra, 128 F.3d at 1179-80)-the plaintiff has to meet the lender's requirements for collateral as well as to establish personal creditworthiness. But Citibank does not require that the borrower satisfy *its* appraiser; it requires only that the appraised value bear a specified relation to the amount of the loan sought, and the opinion of its own appraiser is not conclusive evidence of that value. The bank is willing to consider evidence from other sources and to overrule its own appraiser. The bank's appraisal review department could have overruled Kernbauer; that's why the bank has an appraisal *review* department.

Latimore argues, in her own variant of *McDonnell Douglas* (so strong is the magnetic *715 field of that opinion), that all she had to show in order to withstand summary judgment was that her house was in a minority neighborhood, an appraisal (but not necessarily the defendant's) estimated the value of the house to be at least as great as the loan, the plaintiff was creditworthy, yet the loan was rejected. This cannot be right either, and not only because creditors rarely lend up to the value of the collateral and because there is nothing remotely suspicious about the bank's 75 percent rule. Appraisals are fallible, and if banks reposed automatic, unthinking trust in all third-party appraisals they would not employ their own appraisers, as Citibank does. No reasonable suspicion of racial discrimination can arise from the mere fact of a discrepancy between an appraisal conducted by another bank and the appraisal made by Citibank's employee.

Latimore's proposed prima facie case, like the bank's, lacks any comparison between the treatment of blacks and the treatment of whites. At the heart of *McDonnell Douglas* is the idea that if the black is treated worse than the white in a situation in which there is no *obvious* reason for the difference in treatment (such as that the black lacks an essential qualification for the promotion), there is *something* for the employer to explain; and although the competitive situation which invites and facilitates comparison is usually missing from credit discrimination cases, sometimes there will be another basis for comparison. Suppose, for example, that Latimore and Eromital (who is white), apply at roughly the same time for roughly the same-sized loan from the same Citibank office. The two prospective borrowers are equally creditworthy and the collateral they offer to put up is appraised at the same amount. Both applications are forwarded to Ms. Lundberg and she turns down Latimore's application and approves Eromital's. The similarity in the situations of the white and the black would be sufficient to impose on Citibank a duty of explaining why the white was treated better. No effort at making such a comparison was attempted here.

[2] [3] So neither *McDonnell Douglas* nor the kind of *McDonnell Douglas* knock off which we have just sketched (and for which support can be found in Simms v. First Gibraltar Bank, supra, 83 F.3d at 1558) is available here. But that does not end the case. It is always open to a plaintiff in a discrimination case to try to show in a conventional way, without relying on any special doctrines of burden-shifting, that there is enough evidence, direct or circumstantial, of discrimination to create a triable issue. See, e.g., Trans World Airlines, Inc. v. Thurston, 469 U.S. 111, 121, 105 S.Ct. 613, 83 L.Ed.2d 523 (1985); Wallace v. SMC Pneumatics, Inc., 103 F.3d 1394, 1399 (7th Cir. 1997); Hill v. Metropolitan Atlanta Rapid Transit Authority, 841 F.2d 1533, 1539 (11th Cir. 1988). And Latimore has tried to do that. She hired an expert to conduct a retrospective appraisal, that is, an appraisal of the value of her home at the time that Citibank appraised it. The expert came in with an appraisal of $62 000. But this gets her nowhere. Under the bank's 75 percent rule, which Latimore doesn't claim to be racially discriminatory, a $62 000 appraisal would not support a $51 000 loan; 75 percent of $62 000 is $46 500 (almost exactly what she got from the other bank, but at a higher interest rate). Real estate appraisal is not an exact science, moreover, and so the fact that Citibank's appraisal was lower than someone else's does not create an inference of discrimination. For all that appears, Citibank uses conservative appraisal methods-perhaps in order to keep interest rates low, for remember that while Latimore did succeed eventually in obtaining a loan on her house, she had to pay a higher interest rate and on a smaller loan than she wanted.

Latimore argues that Citibank exhibited favoritism toward white would-be borrowers. The specific contention is that these white borrowers were similarly situated to Latimore in the sense of wanting loans of the same amount secured by property having the same appraised value, but that Lundberg went out of her way to help them raise the appraised value of their property and she didn't go out of her way to help Latimore. Specifically, when she reported to a white borrower that the appraised value of his property was too low to support the loan he was seeking, she would encourage him to find additional "comparables" (comparable sales) of which the bank's appraiser might not have *716 known, in order to justify an increase in the appraised value. But remember that when Lundberg informed Latimore of the results of Kernbauer's appraisal, Latimore told her about the other appraisal, and Lundberg urged her to send that in. The fact that Latimore had gotten a higher appraisal implied additional comparables, since appraisals of residential real estate are based on comparable sales. By asking for the higher appraisal, Lundberg was in effect encouraging Latimore to submit additional comparables. It was not Lundberg's fault that they turned out not to satisfy the bank's definition of comparability. She did for Latimore what she did for white people in Latimore's position.

[4] [5] One last bit of "evidence" must be considered. It concerns the notes on which Kernbauer based his appraisal. Kernbauer stored them in a filing cabinet in his office. Later the branch in which he worked was closed, and according to Citibank the notes were lost in the turmoil of the closing. The bank retained the report containing the appraisal and produced the report to the plaintiff in the course of discovery proceedings. The notes, along with the report itself, were required to be retained for 25 months after the denial of Latimore's application, 12 C.F.R. § 202.12(b)(1)(i), and the loss of the notes occurred within that period. The violation of a record retention regulation creates a presumption that the missing record contained evidence adverse to the violator. Hicks v. Gates Rubber Co., 833 F.2d 1406, 1418-19 (10th Cir. 1987); Favors v. Fisher, 13 F.3d 1235, 1239 (8th Cir. 1994). But Citibank's explanation, which was not controverted, showed that the disappearance of Kernbauer's notes was inadvertent, and an inadvertent failure to comply with the regulation is not a violation of it. 12 C.F.R. § 202.14(c). So the presumption did not attach. Cf. S.C. Johnson & Son, Inc. v. Louisville & Nashville R. Co., 695 F.2d 253, 258-59 (7th Cir. 1982).

Taking all the evidence as favorably to the plaintiff as the record permits, no reasonable jury could find that she was turned down because of her race; and so the grant of summary judgment to the defendants must be affirmed. Anderson v. Liberty Lobby, Inc., 477 U.S. 242, 248, 106 S.Ct. 2505, 91 L.Ed.2d 202 (1986); Seshadri v. Kasraian, 130 F.3d 798, 804 (7th Cir. 1997); Halperin v. Abacus Technology Corp., 128 F.3d 191, 200 (4th Cir. 1997).

[6] We conclude by registering our displeasure with the plaintiff's decision to join Kernbauer, the appraiser, as a defendant. It is true that the Fair Housing Act imposes liability on "any person" who discriminates. 42 U.S.C. § 3605(a); cf. Patterson v. P.H.P. Healthcare Corp., 90 F.3d 927, 944 (5th Cir. 1996). It is also true that while the Equal Credit Opportunity

Act imposes liability only on "creditors" the term may be broad enough to encompass an appraiser, 12 C.F.R. § 202.2(1) (a creditor is "a person who, in the ordinary course of business, regularly participates in the decision of whether or not to extend credit"), though this we need not decide. There is, however, no ground for even a suspicion that Kernbauer's appraisal of Latimore's home was racially motivated. In 1993, the year in which Latimore's application was turned down, Kernbauer appraised the property of 69 blacks, and only two of their applications (besides Latimore's) were turned down, which hardly suggests that Kernbauer is trying to discourage blacks from obtaining Citibank loans. But as the bank's lawyers (representing Kernbauer and Lundberg as well) do not ask for sanctions for the filing of a frivolous claim against Kernbauer, we shall let the matter drop with a warning that this court does not look with favor on the promiscuous joinder of minor employees as defendants in cases against their employers. Cf. Flip Side Productions, Inc. v. Jam Productions, Ltd., 843 F.2d 1024, 1036 (7th Cir. 1988).

AFFIRMED.

第五节　中间业务法律制度

商业银行的中间业务或称表外业务，是指商业银行在资产与负债的基础上，利用其技术、信息、机构、信誉等优势，不运用或较少运用其资金，以中间人或代理人的身份替客户办理收付、咨询、代理、担保和其他委托事项，提供各类金融服务而收取一定费用的业务。商业银行的中间业务已经成为与银行传统的资产业务和负债业务并驾齐驱的三大业务之一。

一、中国商业银行的中间业务

根据中国《商业银行法》的规定，除吸收存款及发放贷款外，商业银行还可以经营下列部分或者全部业务：办理票据承兑与贴现；代理发行、代理兑付、承销政府债券；代理买卖外汇；从事银行卡业务；提供信用证服务及担保；代理收付款项及代理保险业务；提供保管箱服务；以及经中国银监会批准的其他业务。上述业务均属于商业银行的中间业务。

在中国，商业银行经营中间业务，必须在其章程中明确相关的经营范围，并报中国银监会批准。中间业务大多属于银行和非银行金融机构交叉经营的领域。由于中国实行严格的“分业经营、分业管理”的体制，因此商业银行不得经营信托业、证券业及保险业。这使得商业银行中间业务领域的拓展受到一定限制，尤其是许多与资本市场相结合的中间业务品种无法开办，并由此限制了银行与信托、保险、证券业的合作空间，中间业务品种和服务手段的创新也受到一定束缚。

从20世纪90年代中期开始，中国境内的商业银行开始逐渐开拓中间业务，但是直到2001年和2002年，中国人民银行才先后颁布《商业银行中间业务暂行规定》以及《关于落实〈商业银行中间业务暂行规定〉有关问题的通知》，对商业银行开办中间业务的市场准入、中间业务的清理和分类以及中间业务的监管等，进行了规定。目前，上述两个规定均已被废止。中国关于商业银行中间业务的法律规定散见于各类法律、法规、部门规章之中，办理不同类型的中间业务受到不同的法律规定的约束。

在中国，商业银行开办中间业务，受到中国银监会的监管，具体是由中国银监会内设的创新监管部负责监管的。在创新监管部的主导之下，诸多管理商业银行中间业务（包括银行卡业务、理财业务、衍生品交易业务以及代理保险业务等）的部门规章和规范性文件予以发布，对商业银行办理中间业务予以规范。

商业银行开展中间业务所收取的费用，是其重要的利润来源，也是监管部门重点监管的对象。根据中国《商业银行法》的规定，商业银行办理业务，提供服务，按照规定收取手续费。收费项目和标准由中国银监会、中国人民银行根据职责分工，分别会同国务院价格主管部门制定。2003年，中国银监会会同中国国家发展和改革委员会颁布了《商业银行服务价格管理暂行办法》。根据该暂行办法的规定，商业银行服务价格分别实行政府指导价和市场调节价。商业银行依据该暂行办法制定服务价格，应至少于执行前 15个工作日向中国银监会报告，同时应抄送中国银行业协会，并应至少于执行前10个工作日在相关营业场所公告。此外，根据中国银监会的要求，商业银行服务收费要严格遵守合法、合规原则；商业银行制定和调整服务收费要坚持定价测算原则；商业银行服务收费要坚持履行社会责任；商业银行服务收费要坚持风险可控原则。

二、美国商业银行的中间业务

20世纪30年代大萧条之前，美国商业银行处于自由发展时期，经营所受管制较少。当时，全能银行制下的商业银行允许以混业经营的形式从事投资银行等中间业务，中间业务一度繁荣。20世纪30年代之后，美国通过立法逐渐确立了商业银行严格分业经营的体制，并对利率进行管制，使得商业银行中间业务的发展几乎处于停滞状态。

自20世纪80年代以来，美国逐步放松利率管制，美国商业银行业务多元化有了较大的发展，银行收入中来自中间业务的收入有了较大的增长。进入90年代，随着银行业竞争的加剧，美国各大银行更是着力于发展中间业务来扩大利润来源，增强竞争力。

美国通过了《1999年金融服务现代化法》，以促进银行、证券公司和保险公司之间的联合经营，建立一个金融机构之间联合经营、审慎管理的金融体系，从而加强金融服务业的竞争，提高其效率。《1999年金融服务现代化法》的颁布，宣告美国商业银行混业经营时代的到来。在这一背景之下，美国的商业银行拥有更大的中间业务发展自主权。为满足客户各种需求，商业银行的中间业务产品日新月异、层出不穷，中间业务范围日益广泛、种类不断增多，中间业务逐渐成为商业银行的主要业务品种和收入来源。

在美国，在商业银行非利息收入构成要素中，托管业务收入、传统的银行手续费收入、投资银行业务收入、证券交易收入、保险收入以及信用卡业务收入等所占比重较大，构成美国商业银行中间业务收入的重要来源。

美国建立了一整套完整的法律体系，对商业银行中间业务作了详细而全面的规定。关于商业银行经营中间业务的法律，不仅体现在银行业法律之中，在信托、保险及证券业等的法律中，也有相关规定。例如，《1934年证券交易法》就对银行参与证券承销业务进行了特别的规定。在这一背景之下，中间业务中银行与客户关系的调整、当事人权利义务有明确的规范，使得中间业务法律关系具有稳定性、可预期性和确定性，避免因法律真空导致银行与客户之间的纠纷，为商业银行中间业务的健康发展提供了法律保障。

三、案例资料

支付结算业务是指由商业银行为客户办理因债权债务关系引起的与货币支付、资金划拨有关的收费业务。支付结算业务，是商业银行非常重要的中间业务之一。在提供支付结算业务过程中，如果因商业银行的行为而导致第三人损失，第三人能否对商业银行提起侵权之诉？下面的 Eisenberg v. Wachovia Bank，N.A.案对此问题进行了回答。

该案的基本案情是：一名叫做 Douglas Walter Reid（下称 Douglas）的人实施了一起欺诈性投资，原告 Eisenberg 是该欺诈投资的受害人。Douglas 欺骗原告，声称自己是 Bear Stearns 公司的高级副总裁，并说服原告进行一笔虚假的投资。原告依照 Douglas 的指示，通过电子网络向被告 Wachovia 银行转入 100 万美元的资金，以存入一个名为“Douglas Walter Reid dba Bear Stearns”的账户，最终支付给“Bear Stearns”。Wachovia 银行接受了该笔转账资金，并将其存入由 Douglas 开立并控制的特定账户的贷项之下。Douglas 提取了全部资金，并挪为己用。在这一过程中，Wachovia 银行的职员并未对 Douglas 以 Bear Stearns 公司的名义行事是否获得了授权进行确认。事实上，Douglas 没有获得授权，也与 Bear Stearns 公司没有任何关系。

原告遂起诉 Wachovia 银行，主张 Wachovia 银行对与其客户进行交易的人负有注意义务，Wachovia 银行违反了这种注意义务，没有察觉也没有防止他人对 Wachovia 银行账户的欺诈性使用，导致原告遭受损失。该案中，法院要解决的主要问题是：非银行客户受到银行客户利用银行服务所进行的欺诈损害，银行是否对该非银行客户负有注意义务并承担赔偿责任。

法院最终认定：银行对与其没有直接关系的非客户，不负有注意义务。因此，该案中 Wachovia 银行对原告不负有注意义务，原告关于被告疏忽的诉讼请求应予以驳回。

商业银行在提供支付结算业务时，作为金融中介，通常对当事人的交易只进行形式性审查，相关的交易风险，主要由交易的当事方自己去判断。因此，如果一方当事人利用其银行账户实施欺诈行为，通常银行是无须对与其无关联的另一方当事人的损失承担责任的。

Eisenberg v. Wachovia Bank, N.A.

301 F.3d 220 (4th Cir. 2002)

BEEZER, Senior Circuit Judge.

Eric Eisenberg ("Eisenberg") appeals the district court's dismissal of his complaint alleging two claims of negligence against Wachovia Bank, N.A. ("Wachovia"). We affirm.

I

The district court dismissed Eisenberg's complaint pursuant to Federal Rule of Civil Procedure 12(b)(6). We state the relevant facts as alleged by the complaint. See Harrison v. Westinghouse Savannah River Co., 176 F.3d 776, 783 (4th Cir. 1999) ("In its review of Rule 12(b)(6) dismissals, this Court must accept as true all of the Appellant's allegations and must construe factual allegations in the light most favorable to the plaintiff.").

Eisenberg was the victim of a fraudulent investment scheme perpetrated by Douglas Walter Reid ("Reid"). Reid falsely represented to Eisenberg that he was a senior vice president of Bear Stearns Companies, a large financial securities firm, and convinced Eisenberg to make a putative investment. At Reid's direction, Eisenberg transferred $1 000 000 via electronic wire to a Wachovia branch bank in North Carolina for deposit in an account bearing the name "Douglas Walter Reid dba Bear Stearns," "For Further Credit to BEAR STEARNS." The electronic transfer was made through the "Fedwire" wire service operated by the Federal Reserve Bank. Wachovia accepted the transfer and deposited the funds to the credit of the specified account, which had been opened by and was under the control of Reid. Reid withdrew almost all of Eisenberg's funds and converted them to his own use.

Wachovia's customer agreements do not restrict the name under which a new customer may open a bank account. The Wachovia employee who opened Reid's account did not verify that Reid was authorized to operate under the name Bear Stearns. Reid possessed no such authority and was not in any way affiliated with Bear Stearns.

Eisenberg filed a complaint against Wachovia in federal court on the basis of diversity jurisdiction, see 28 U.S.C. § 1332, asserting two claims of negligence. The first claim alleged that Wachovia negligently allowed Reid to establish and operate a fraudulent bank account and negligently failed to train its employees to detect fraud. The second claim alleged that Wachovia was vicariously liable for its employee's negligence in allowing Reid to open the bank account without proper verification. Both claims include the allegation that Wachovia breached a duty of care owed to people like Eisenberg, who transact with Wachovia customers, to detect and prevent the fraudulent use of its bank accounts.

Wachovia moved to dismiss the complaint pursuant to Federal Rule of Civil Procedure 12(b)(6). Wachovia argued that both negligence claims are preempted by Federal Reserve Board Regulation J ("Regulation J"), Subpart B, 12 C.F.R. §§ 210.25-210.32 (2002). Wachovia also argued, in the alternative, that the claims fail as a matter of law because Wachovia does not owe Eisenberg a duty of care. Agreeing that the claims are preempted, the district court granted Wachovia's motion and dismissed the complaint with prejudice. The court did not address Wachovia's alternative argument for dismissal based on the absence of a duty of care.

We review de novo the district court's dismissal of the complaint and can affirm on any basis fairly supported by the record. Korb v. Lehman, 919 F.2d 243, 246 (4th Cir. 1990). We hold that Regulation J does not preempt Eisenberg's negligence claims but the claims still fail because Wachovia does not owe Eisenberg a duty of care under the facts of this case.

…

Wachovia reasserts on appeal an alternative argument for dismissal, not decided by the district court, that Eisenberg fails to allege one essential element in a negligence claim. Wachovia contends that it does not owe Eisenberg a duty of care and therefore cannot be held liable in negligence for Eisenberg's injury.

Under North Carolina law, "[n]egligence is the failure to exercise proper care in the performance of a legal duty owed by a defendant to a plaintiff under the circumstances." Cassell v. Collins, 344 N.C. 160, 472 S.E.2d 770, 772 (1996). A necessary factor in proving negligence is the existence of a duty of care owed to the particular plaintiff by the defendant. Pinnix v. Toomey, 242 N.C. 358, 87 S.E.2d 893, 897 (1955) ("Actionable negligence presupposes the existence of a legal relationship between parties by which the injured party is owed a duty by the other, and such duty must be imposed by law."). We consider whether a bank owes a duty of care to a noncustomer who is defrauded by the bank's customer through use of its services. We cannot find an applicable precedent from a North Carolina court and look to case law from other jurisdictions. We conclude that the North Carolina Supreme Court, if it were to decide this issue, would hold that Wachovia did not owe Eisenberg a duty of care under the facts presented.

Whether Wachovia owes a duty of care to Eisenberg depends on the relationship between them. See W. Page Keeton et al., Prosser and Keeton on Torts § 53 at 356 (5th ed. 1984) ("It is better to reserve 'duty' for the problem of the relation between individuals which imposes upon one a legal obligation for the benefit of the other"); cf. Newton v. New Hanover Co. Bd. of Educ., 342 N.C. 554, 467 S.E.2d 58, 63 (1996) (holding nature and scope of duty owed by owner of land depends upon status of injured person as invitee, licensee or trespasser). Eisenberg had no direct relationship with Wachovia. He was not a Wachovia bank customer and, so far as the allegations indicate, has never conducted business with Wachovia. Eisenberg instead transacted with Reid, a Wachovia bank customer.

Courts in numerous jurisdictions have held that a bank does not owe a duty of care to a noncustomer with whom the bank has no direct relationship. See Weil v. First Nat'l Bank of Castle Rock, 983 P.2d 812, 815 (Colo.Ct.App.1999); Volpe v. Fleet Nat'l Bank, 710 A.2d 661, 664 (R.I.1998); Miller-Rogaska, Inc. v. Bank One, 931 S.W.2d 655, 664 (Tex.App.1996); Software Design & Application, Ltd. v. Hoefer & Arnett, Inc., 49 Cal.App.4th 472, 56 Cal.Rptr.2d 756, 760-63 (1996); Portage Aluminum Co. v. Kentwood Nat'l Bank, 106 Mich.App. 290, 307 N.W.2d 761, 764-65 (1981); Pa. Nat'l Turf Club, Inc. v. Bank of W. Jersey, 158 N.J.Super. 196, 385 A.2d 932, 936 (1978); Gesell v. First Nat'l City Bank, 24 A.D.2d 424, 260 N.Y.S.2d 581, 581-82 (1965).

McCallum v. Rizzo, 1995 WL 1146812 (Mass.Super.Ct. Oct. 13, 1995), presents highly analogous facts. Plaintiff McCallum loaned money to the Tsongas Committee, an organization advocating the election of presidential candidate Paul Tsongas. Id. at *1. Rizzo, the chief fund raiser for the Tsongas Committee, opened a bank account at Andover Bank bearing the committee's name and listed himself as sole signatory. Id. The bank did not verify that Rizzo was authorized to transact business on behalf of the Tsongas Committee. Id. Rizzo used the bank account to convert the proceeds of contributions and loans to the Tsongas Committee to his own use. McCallum's funds were converted by Rizzo. Id.

McCallum sued Andover Bank on a theory of negligence. He argued that the bank "owed a duty to contributors to the Tsongas committee to exercise due care in the opening and handling of the Tsongas Committee account." Id. The McCallum court disagreed and followed cases in other jurisdictions which held "a bank's failure to investigate a customer's suspicious activity does not give rise to liability to the third party who is injured by the customer's fraud." Id. at *2. The court explained:

> The mere fact that a bank account can be used in the course of perpetrating a fraud does not mean that banks have a duty to persons other than their own customers. To the contrary, the duty is owed exclusively to the customer, not to the persons with whom the customer has dealings.
>
> Id.

Beyond the McCallum rule it has been held that banks do not owe a duty of care to noncustomers even when the noncustomer is the person in whose name an account was fraudulently opened. In Software Design a financial consultant embezzled money from Software Design through a bank account he opened bearing the company name. 56 Cal.Rptr.2d at 759-60. The California Court of Appeal dismissed Software Design's negligence claim against the bank. Id. at 760-63. According to the court, "the primary flaw" in Software Design's negligence theory was the lack of a relationship between it and the bank. Id. at 760. Even though the bank account used to defraud Software Design bore its own name, the court held that a bank does not owe a duty of care to protect noncustomers against fraud. Id.; see also Volpe, 710 A.2d at 664 ("[A] bank is not liable in negligence to a noncustomer payee for having failed to ascertain whether a check paid by it bears the payee's genuine indorsement."). But see Patrick v. Union State Bank, 681 So.2d 1364, 1371 (Ala.1996) (holding bank owed duty of care to person in whose name account was opened to ensure that person opening account is not imposter).

Eisenberg was neither a Wachovia customer nor the person in whose name Reid's fraudulent bank account was opened. Bear Stearns would be the beneficiary of any duty of care which Wachovia might owe to a noncustomer. See id. Eisenberg instead falls into the undefined and unlimited category of strangers who might interact with Wachovia's bank customer. In McCallum the Massachusetts Superior Court noted that the maintenance of a bank account was intended to benefit the person who opened the account. McCallum, 1995

WL 1146812 at *3. The court reasoned that to extend a duty of care to strangers like Eisenberg would be contrary to the normal understanding of the purpose of a bank account and would expose banks to unlimited liability for unforeseeable frauds. Id.

Several other courts have relied on similar policy considerations in rejecting an argument that banks owe a duty to noncustomers. See Software Design, 56 Cal.Rptr.2d at 763 ("Better that the one contemplating the services of a financial advisor do the background check and then monitor the services. It is that person who has the most control and the most to win or lose, and with whom the investigative tasks should rest."); Weil, 983 P.2d at 814 ("It would be unreasonable to require banks to make an independent investigation of their customers' authority to use any particular unregistered trade name; and a duty to inquire only of the customer would not prevent the kind of harm plaintiff suffered."); Pa. Nat'l Turf Club, 385 A.2d at 936 ("Plaintiff was the party who assumed the risk associated with that hazardous activity [and] cannot recoup by attempting to shift responsibility to the bank which had no relationship with it.").

We are persuaded by the reasoning articulated in the numerous cases holding that a bank does not owe noncustomers a duty of care. The reasoning and result in McCallum are particularly persuasive as the McCallum facts are indistinguishable from the facts of this case. We have no doubt that the North Carolina Supreme Court would reach a similar conclusion as that in McCallum and hold that Wachovia does not owe Eisenberg a duty of care.

A North Carolina Court of Appeals decision supports our view. In Carlson v. Branch Banking & Trust Co., 123 N.C.App. 306, 473 S.E.2d 631 (1996), plaintiffs executed a $500 000 letter of credit to help fund a stockbroker's purchase of a mutual fund company. Id. at 632-34. Plaintiffs intended that the stockbroker would use the letter of credit to obtain a loan to be used solely for the contemplated purchase. Id. at 632-33. The stockbroker obtained a loan from the defendant bank but did not use the proceeds as intended. Id. at 634. When the stockbroker defaulted on the loan, the bank drew from plaintiffs' letter of credit. Id. Plaintiffs sued the bank, alleging a negligent failure to monitor the proper use of the loan proceeds. Id. The North Carolina Court of Appeals denied the negligence claim, holding that the bank did not owe plaintiffs a duty of care to monitor the disbursement of the loan proceeds. Id. at 636. The court reasoned that, absent a contractual obligation arising from the letter of credit itself, there was no relationship between the bank and the plaintiffs to give rise to a duty of care. Id. at 637. Carlson suggests that the North Carolina Court of Appeals would not find a duty of care in this case, where there was no direct relationship at all between Eisenberg and Wachovia, much less a contractual obligation.

We hold that Wachovia did not owe Eisenberg a duty of care under the facts of this case. Eisenberg consequently cannot maintain a claim of negligence against Wachovia….

第六节 商业银行的监管

银行业是现代市场经济的核心，银行业务秩序直接关系到国民经济稳定健康地发展。由于其在国民经济中的特殊地位及本身的高风险，在世界范围内，各国都十分重视对商业银行的监管。

一、中国对商业银行的监管

在中国，早期由中国人民银行对商业银行进行监管。2003 年 4 月，中国银监会正式成立，并全面接管了对商业银行的监管职责。同年 12 月，《中华人民共和国银行业监督管理法》（下称《银行业监督管理法》）获得通过，为中国银监会依法履行监管职责进一步提供了明确的法律依据。目前，中国已经形成了以中国银监会为主、相关行业协会为辅的银行业监管体制。

根据中国《银行业监督管理法》的规定，中国银监会负责对包括商业银行在内的全国银行业金融机构及其业务活动进行监督管理，包括对经其批准在境外设立的金融机构以及境内金融机构在境外的业务活动实施监督管理。中国银监会可以根据履行职责的需要设立派出机构，并对派出机构实行统一领导和管理。派出机构在中国银监会的授权范围内履行监督管理职责。在中国，银行业监督管理的目标是促进银行业的合法、稳健运行，维护公众对银行业的信心。

根据中国《银行业监督管理法》的规定，中国银监会对商业银行的监管职责，主要包括如下几个方面的内容：（1）制定并发布对银行业金融机构及其业务活动监督管理的规章、规则；（2）审查批准银行业金融机构的设立、变更、终止以及业务范围；（3）依照法律、行政法规制定银行业金融机构的审慎经营规则（包括风险管理、内部控制、资本充足率、资产质量、损失准备金、风险集中、关联交易、资产流动性等内容）；（4）对银行业金融机构的业务活动及其风险状况进行非现场监管，建立银行业金融机构监督管理信息系统，分析、评价银行业金融机构的风险状况；（5）对银行业金融机构的业务活动及其风险状况进行现场检查；（6）对银行业金融机构实行并表监督管理；（7）建立银行业金融机构监督管理评级体系和风险预警机制，根据银行业金融机构的评级情况和风险状况，确定对其现场检查的频率、范围和需要采取的其他措施；（8）负责统一编制全国银行业金融机构的统计数据、报表，并按照国家有关规定予以公布；（9）开展与银行业监督管理有关的国际交流、合作活动。

根据中国《银行业监督管理法》的规定，中国银监会有权采取如下措施，以履行其对商业银行的监管职能。

第一，要求报送相关资料。中国银监会根据履行职责的需要，有权要求银行业金融机构按照规定报送资产负债表、利润表和其他财务会计、统计报表、经营管理资料以及注册会计师出具的审计报告。

第二，现场检查。根据审慎监管的要求，中国银监会可以采取下列措施进行现场检查：进入银行业金融机构进行检查；询问银行业金融机构的工作人员，要求其对有关检查事项作出说明；查阅、复制银行业金融机构与检查事项有关的文件、资料，对可能被转移、隐匿或者毁损的文件、资料予以封存；检查银行业金融机构运用电子计算机管理业务数据的系统。

第三，监管谈话。中国银监会根据履行职责的需要，可以与银行业金融机构董事、高级管理人员进行监督管理谈话，要求银行业金融机构董事、高级管理人员就银行业金融机构的业务活动和风险管理的重大事项作出说明。

第四，强制信息披露。中国银监会应当责令银行业金融机构按照规定，如实向社会公众披露财务会计报告、风险管理状况、董事和高级管理人员变更以及其他重大事项等信息。

第五，权利限制措施。银行业金融机构违反审慎经营规则且逾期未改正的，或者其行为严重危及该银行业金融机构的稳健运行、损害存款人和其他客户合法权益的，经中国银监会或者其省一级派出机构负责人批准，可以区别情形，采取下列措施：责令暂停部分业务、停止批准开办新业务；限制分配红利和其他收入；限制资产转让；责令控股股东转让股权或者限制有关股东的权利；责令调整董事、高级管理人员或者限制其权利；以及停止批准增设分支机构。

第六，接管或重组。银行业金融机构已经或者可能发生信用危机，严重影响存款人和其他客户合法权益的，中国银监会可以依法对该银行业金融机构实行接管或者促成机构重组。

第七，撤销。银行业金融机构有违法经营、经营管理不善等情形，不予撤销将严重危害金融秩序、损害公众利益的，中国银监会有权予以撤销。

当然，在政府机构中，除中国银监会以外，还有包括中国人民银行以及中国审计署在内的机构对商业银行亦有一定的监管职权。

此外，行业协会的自律监管在商业银行的监管中也扮演着重要的角色。中国银行业协会于 2000 年 5 月成立，其是全国性银行业自律组织。凡经中国银监会批准设立的、具有独立法人资格的银行业金融机构（含在华外资银行业金融机构）以及经相关监管机构批准、具有独立法人资格并在民政部门登记注册的各省（自治区、直辖市、计划单列市）

银行业协会均可申请加入中国银行业协会，成为其会员单位。依据协会章程，中国银行业协会履行自律、维权、协调、服务职能，维护银行业合法权益，维护银行业市场秩序，提高银行业从业人员素质，提高为会员服务的水平，促进银行业的健康发展。

二、美国对商业银行的监管

美国对商业银行的监管是建立在一系列法律、法规的基础之上的。其中，最主要的法律、法规包括:《1863 年国民银行法》、《1913 年联邦储备法》、《联邦存款保险法》、《1933 年银行法》、《1956 年银行控股公司法》、《1980 年存款机构放松管制与货币控制法》、《1991 年联邦存款保险公司改进法》、《1991 年外资银行监督改善法》、《1996 年联邦存款保险基金法》、《1999 年金融服务现代化法》以及《多德—弗兰克华尔街改革和消费者保护法案》。

经过两百多年的发展，美国银行业形成了独特的双重多头监管体系，成为世界上最复杂的银行监管体系。双重是指联邦和州均设置有相关的监管机构对商业银行进行监管，多头是指商业银行同时要受到多个监管机构的监管。

在联邦层面，主要有货币监理署、联邦储备系统以及联邦存款保险公司等机构履行商业银行的监管职能。其中，货币监理署是根据《1863 年国民银行法》而设立的，其设在美国财政部下，负责对所有国民银行以及联邦许可的非美国银行的分支机构或部门授予特许状及进行监管和检查。联邦储备系统，是独立的美国中央银行，其包括 12 个地区性的联邦储备银行，每一家联邦储备银行在其管辖地域范围内履行中央银行的职能。联邦储备系统的主要职责是制定及执行货币政策，但是其亦有重要的银行监管及检查的职能：联邦储备系统是州会员行的主要联邦监管者、银行控股公司的监管者以及外国银行在美国经营活动的监管者和会员行在国外活动的监管者。联邦存款保险公司则依据《联邦存款保险法》的授权管理联邦存款保险体系，对存款保险基金进行跟踪，并享有对投保商业银行广泛的执行权，包括有权终止任何从事不安全或不稳妥活动的任何机构的存款保险。联邦存款保险公司对所有其承保的存款机构都享有第二位的监管和检查权，同时还是投保的州非会员行和州储蓄银行的首要联邦监管者。此外，联邦存款保险公司在倒闭的金融机构解散的过程中扮演着主要的管理者角色，并且实际上还是所有其保险的存款机构的接管人或保护人。

除此之外，在联邦层面还有两个特殊的机构：储蓄机构管理局以及国家信用合作社管理局，前者主要负责对联邦特许的储贷机构进行监管，但是已于 2010 年并入货币监理署，后者则负责颁发联邦信用合作社的特许状并对之进行监管。

此外，各州均设有相应的银行业监管机构，履行对商业银行的监管职能。在美国，依据各州法律登记注册的银行，需要从州银行监管机构获取特许状，并受到州银行监管机构的监督和检查。在一定的情况下，州特许银行还同时受到联邦监管机构的监管：加入联邦储备系统的州会员行，受到联储的监管；在联邦保险公司投保的州特许银行，还受到联邦保险公司的监管。

由于同时存在联邦监管机构以及州监管机构，并且联邦的监管机构还存在多个，所以这些机构之间的监管协调就成了问题。在美国，有大量的正式和非正式的机制促进各个联邦监管机构之间以及联邦和州监管机构之间的协调。其中，根据《1978 年金融机构监管和利率控制法》成立的联邦金融机构检查理事会是一个促进监管协调的重要机构。该理事会是由货币监理署、储蓄机构管理局、联邦储备系统、联邦存款保险公司以及国家信用合作社管理局这五个联邦监管机构组成的一个跨机构组织，其目的是为金融机构的联邦检查制定统一的原则，并为增加监管中的统一性提出建议。

在美国，监管机构对商业银行的监管内容，主要包括如下几个方面：（1）市场准入的监管。注册不同性质的商业银行，要由不同的监管机构进行审批及颁发特许状。联邦或州的监管机构通常会对商业银行的营业宗旨、组织章程、资本结构、董事、高管资历、管理业务和风险、获利能力和所有权要求等因素进行考虑和调查以作出决定。（2）资本充足率的监管。监管机构参照《巴塞尔协议》的规定来评价商业银行的资本充足性。第（3）对风险损失准备金的监管。监管机构会根据美国商业银行坏账的具体情况要求商业银行计提风险准备金。（4）对存款保险的监管。美国联邦储备系统的会员行均被要求参加联邦存款保险，同时大多数州也要求州立银行参加联邦存款保险。联邦存款保险公司一身二任，既是保险公司，又是金融监管机构，将业务职能与监管职能紧密结合，以检查投保银行安全状况的方式，监管美国商业银行。此外，监管机构还对银行的经营范围、资产集中、银行流动性、银行合并及银行破产和倒闭等进行监管。

在美国，监管机构可采取的监管手段有多种，常见的包括发布监管规则、进行现场检查以及非现场检查、对监管对象发布命令（如禁制令）以及进行金钱处罚等。例如，货币监理署对国民银行履行监管职责时，有权采取如下手段：（1）贯彻执行有关法律、法规，对银行的经营活动状况进行跟踪研究；（2）检查、监管所辖银行，审批所辖银行设立分行、进行并购重组的申请；（3）对所辖银行违法、违规或进行非正常金融活动进行处罚，包括撤换银行高级职员的职务、与董事会协商改变银行运作方式、下达暂停和停止业务命令以及实施资金处罚等；（4）制定管理银行投资、借贷和其他活动的规章制度。

三、案例资料

美国很早就确立起联邦和州双重监管的银行业监管体制。近些年来，美国的一些州政府不断介入传统上被认为属于联邦政府部门监管的领域。尤其在 2008 年金融危机之后，美国有诸多州政府机构趁势调查华尔街，其中又以纽约检察长办公室最为卖力。对此，联邦政府保持高度警惕，拼命加以阻止，不让州政府染指。这场金融监管地盘之争，最终引发了诉讼。2009 年 6 月 29 日，美国最高法院在 Cuomo v. Clearing House Ass'n, L.L.C 案中作出判决：各州有权按照其本州的法律监管国民银行，即便州政府的执法与联邦政府在此领域的执法有重叠之处。

Cuomo 案的起因在于 2005 年纽约州检察长立案调查几家银行（均为国民银行）的贷款业务。纽约州检察长依据州的公平借贷法向银行发函，要求它们提供属于非公开性质的关于贷款操作的信息，以便确定它们是否违反州法的规定。几家银行表示异议，并由结算协会与货币监理署出面，向法院起诉，请求禁止纽约州检察长的调查，理由是货币监理署根据《国民银行法》制定的规章禁止此类州法对国民银行实施。美国联邦地区法院和联邦上诉法院均判决纽约州检察长败诉。最终，案件被上诉至美国联邦最高法院。

该案涉及的核心问题在于，纽约州检察长向银行发函的行为，是否属于《国民银行法》中的查视权（visitorial powers）。按照美国 1864 年《国民银行法》等法律的规定，美国联邦政府有权随时查视国民银行记录，但州政府无权进行这种查视。最高法院多数派法官认为，按照立法者的意图，查视权并不涵盖发送信函的行为。因此，纽约州检察长并非在行使查视权，而是在行使其执法权力，并没有染指联邦政府的"查视"权力。但是，少数派法官则认为，立法者意图不够清楚，有多种解释余地。既然是有多种解释，那么就必须尊重行政机构的解释，也就是尊重货币监理署的解释，禁止将相关州法适用于国民银行。该案最终以五票对四票通过，判决纽约州检察长胜诉。

美国联邦最高法院的这一判决，具有十分重要的意义。其使得州政府在银行业监管方面扩大了地盘，国民银行在经营过程中也要受到州的部分监管。这使得国民银行受到更多的约束，但对于金融消费者保护而言无疑更有利。

Cuomo v. Clearing House Ass'n, L.L.C.

129 S.Ct. 2710, 174 L.Ed.2d 464, (U.S.,2009)

Justice SCALIA delivered the opinion of the Court.

In 2005, Eliot Spitzer, Attorney General for the State of New York, sent letters to several national banks making a request "in lieu of subpoena" that they provide certain non-public information about their lending practices. He sought this information to determine whether the banks had violated the State's fair-lending laws. Spitzer's successor in office, Andrew Cuomo, is the petitioner here. Respondents, the federal Office of the Comptroller of the Currency ("Comptroller" or "OCC") and the Clearing House Association, a banking trade group, brought suit to enjoin the information request, claiming that the Comptroller's regulation promulgated under the National Bank Act prohibits that form of state law enforcement against national banks.

The United States District Court for the Southern District of New York entered an injunction in favor of respondents, prohibiting the attorney general from enforcing state fair-lending laws through demands for records or judicial proceedings. The United States Court of Appeals for the Second Circuit affirmed. 510 F.3d 105 (2007). We granted certiorari. 555 U.S._, 129 S.Ct. 987, 173 L.Ed.2d 171 (2009). The question presented is whether *2715 the Comptroller's regulation purporting to pre-empt state law enforcement can be upheld as a reasonable interpretation of the National Bank Act.

I

Section 484(a) of Title 12, U.S.C., a provision of the National Bank Act, 13 Stat. 99, reads as follows:

> "No national bank shall be subject to any visitorial powers except as authorized by Federal law, vested in the courts of justice or such as shall be, or have been exercised or directed by Congress or by either House thereof or by any committee of Congress or of either House duly authorized."

The Comptroller, charged with administering the National Bank Act, adopted, through notice-and-comment rulemaking, the regulation at issue here designed to implement the statutory provision. Its principal provisions read as follows:

"§ 7.4000 Visitorial powers.

> "(a) *General rule.* (1) Only the OCC or an authorized representative of the OCC may exercise visitorial powers with respect to national banks, except as provided in paragraph (b) of this section. State officials may not exercise visitorial powers with respect to national banks, such as conducting examinations, inspecting or requiring the production of books or records of national banks, or prosecuting enforcement actions, except in limited circumstances authorized by federal law. However, production of a bank's records (other than non-public OCC information under 12 CFR part 4, subpart C) may be required under normal judicial procedures.

"(2) For purposes of this section, visitorial powers include:

"(i) Examination of a bank;

"(ii) Inspection of a bank's books and records;

"(iii) Regulation and supervision of activities authorized or permitted pursuant to federal banking law; and

"(iv) Enforcing compliance with any applicable federal or state laws concerning those activities." 12 CFR § 7.4000 (2009).

By its clear text, this regulation prohibits the States from "prosecuting enforcement actions" except in "limited circumstances authorized by federal law."

[1] Under the familiar Chevron framework, we defer to an agency's reasonable interpretation of a statute it is charged with administering. Chevron U.S.A. Inc. v. Natural Resources Defense Council, Inc., 467 U.S. 837, 104 S.Ct. 2778, 81 L.Ed.2d 694 (1984). There is necessarily some ambiguity as to the meaning of the statutory term "visitorial powers," especially since we are working in an era when the prerogative writs-through which visitorial powers were traditionally enforced-are not in vogue. The Comptroller can give authoritative meaning to the statute within the bounds of that uncertainty. But the presence of some uncertainty does not expand Chevron deference to cover virtually any interpretation of the National Bank Act. We can discern the outer limits of the term "visitorial powers" even through the clouded lens of history. They do not include, as the Comptroller's expansive regulation would provide, ordinary enforcement of the law. Evidence from the time of the statute's enactment, a long line of our own cases, and application of normal principles of construction to the National Bank Act make that clear.

A

Historically, the sovereign's right of visitation over corporations paralleled the right of the church to supervise its institutions and the right of the founder of a *2716 charitable institution "to see that [his] property [was] rightly employed," 1 W. Blackstone, Commentaries on the Laws of England 469 (1765). By extension of this principle, "[t]he king [was] by law the visitor of all civil corporations," ibid. A visitor could inspect and control the visited institution at will.

When the National Bank Act was enacted in 1864, "visitation" was accordingly understood as "[t]he act of examining into the affairs of a corporation" by "the government itself." 2 J. Bouvier, A Law Dictionary 790 (15th ed. 1883). Lower courts understood "visitation" to mean "the act of a superior or superintending officer, who visits a corporation to examine into its manner of conducting business, and enforce an observance of its laws and regulations." First Nat. Bank of Youngstown v. Hughes, 6 F. 737, 740 (C.C.N.D.Ohio 1881). A State was the "visitor" of all companies incorporated in the State, simply by virtue of the State's role as sovereign: The "legislature is the visitor of all corporations founded by it." Guthrie v. Harkness, 199 U.S. 148, 157, 26 S.Ct. 4, 50 L.Ed. 130 (1905) (internal quotation marks omitted).

This relationship between sovereign and corporation was understood to allow the States to use prerogative writs-such as mandamus and *quo warranto*-to exercise control "whenever a corporation [wa]s abusing the power given it, or, ... or acting adversely to the public, or creating a nuisance." H. Wilgus, Private Corporations, in 8 American Law and Procedure § 157, pp. 224-225 (1910). State visitorial commissions were authorized to "exercise a general supervision" over companies in the State. I. Wormser, Private Corporations § 80, pp. 100, 101, in 4 Modern American Law (1921).

B

Our cases have always understood "visitation" as this right to oversee corporate affairs, quite separate from the power to enforce the law. In the famous *Dartmouth College* case, Justice Story, describing visitation of a charitable corporation, wrote that Dartmouth was "subject to the controlling authority of its legal visitor, who... may amend and repeal its statutes, remove its officers, correct abuses, and generally superintend the management of [its] trusts," and who are "liable to no supervision or control." Trustees of Dartmouth College v. Woodward, 4 Wheat. 518, 676, 681, 4 L.Ed. 629 (1819) (concurring opinion). This power of "genera[l] superintend[ence]" stood in contrast to action by the court of chancery, which acted "not as itself possessing a visitorial power... but as possessing a general jurisdiction... to redress grievances, and frauds." *Id.*, at 676.

In Guthrie, supra, we held that a shareholder acting in his role as a private individual was not exercising a "visitorial power" under the National Bank Act when he petitioned a court to force the production of corporate records, *id.,* at 159, 26 S.Ct. 4. *2717 "[C]ontrol in the courts of justice," we said, is not visitorial, and we drew a contrast between the nonvisitorial act of "su[ing] in the courts of the State" and the visitorial "supervision of the Comptroller of the Currency," *id.,* at 159, 157, 26 S.Ct. 4.

In First Nat. Bank in St. Louis v. Missouri, 263 U.S. 640, 44 S.Ct. 213, 68 L.Ed. 486 (1924), we upheld the right of the Attorney General of Missouri to bring suit to enforce a state anti-bank-branching law against a national bank. We said that only the United States may perform visitorial administrative oversight, such as "inquir[ing] by *quo warranto* whether a national bank is acting in excess of its charter powers." *Id.*, at 660, 44 S.Ct. 213. But if a state statute of general applicability is not substantively pre-empted, then "the power of enforcement must rest with the [State] and not with" the National Government, ibid.

Our most recent decision, Watters v. Wachovia Bank, N.A., 550 U.S. 1, 127 S.Ct. 1559, 167 L.Ed.2d 389 (2007), does not, as the dissent contends, *post,* at 2731, "suppor[t] OCC's construction of the statute." To the contrary, it is fully in accord with the well established distinction between supervision and law enforcement. Watters held that a State may not exercise "general supervision and control" over a subsidiary of a national bank, 550 U.S., at 8, 127 S.Ct. 1559, because "multiple audits and surveillance under rival oversight regimes" would cause uncertainty, *id.,* at 21, 127 S.Ct. 1559. "[G]eneral supervision and control" and "oversight" are worlds apart from law enforcement. All parties to the case agreed that Michigan's general oversight regime could not be imposed on national banks; the sole question was whether operating subsidiaries of national banks enjoyed the same immunity from state visitation. The opinion addresses and answers no other question.

The foregoing cases all involve enforcement of state law. But if the Comptroller's exclusive exercise of visitorial powers precluded law enforcement by the States, it would also preclude law enforcement by federal agencies. Of course it does not. See, e.g., Bank of America Nat. Trust & Sav. Assn. v. Douglas, 105 F.2d 100, 105-106 (CADC 1939) (Securities Exchange Commission investigation of bank fraud is not an exercise of "visitorial powers"); Peoples Bank of Danville v. Williams, 449 F.Supp. 254, 260 (W.D.Va.1978) (same).

In sum, the unmistakable and utterly consistent teaching of our jurisprudence, both before and after enactment of the National Bank Act, is that a sovereign's "visitorial powers" and its power to enforce the law are two different things. There is not a credible argument to the contrary. And contrary to what the Comptroller's regulation says, the National Bank Act pre-empts only the former.

C

The consequences of the regulation also cast doubt upon its validity. No one denies *2718 that the National Bank Act leaves in place some state substantive laws affecting banks. See Brief for Federal Respondent 20; Brief for Respondent Clearing House Association, L.L.C. 29; *post,* at 2730-2731. But the Comptroller's rule says that the State may not *enforce* its valid, non-pre-empted laws against national banks. Ibid. The bark remains, but the bite does not.

The dissent admits, with considerable understatement, that such a result is "unusual," *ibid.* "Bizarre" would be more apt. As the Court said in St. Louis:

> "To demonstrate the binding quality of a statute but deny the power of enforcement involves a fallacy made apparent by the mere statement of the proposition, for such power is essentially inherent in the very conception of law." 263 U.S., at 660, 44 S.Ct. 213.

In sharp contrast to the "unusual" reading propounded by the Comptroller's regulation, reading "visitorial powers" as limiting only sovereign oversight and supervision would produce an entirely commonplace result-the precise result contemplated by our opinion in St. Louis, which said that if a state statute is valid as to national banks, "the corollary that it is obligatory *and enforceable* necessarily results." *Id.,* at 659-660, 44 S.Ct. 213 (emphasis added). Channeling state attorneys general into judicial law-enforcement proceedings (rather than allowing them to exercise "visitorial" oversight) would preserve a regime of exclusive administrative oversight by the Comptroller while honoring in fact rather than merely in theory Congress's decision not to pre-empt substantive state law. This system echoes many other mixed state/federal regimes in which the Federal Government exercises general oversight while leaving state substantive law in place. See, e.g., Wyeth v. Levine, 555 U.S._, 129 S.Ct. 1187, 173 L.Ed.2d 51 (2009).

This reading is also suggested by § 484(a)'s otherwise inexplicable reservation of state powers "vested in the courts of justice." As described earlier, visitation was normally conducted through use of the prerogative writs of mandamus and *quo warranto*. The exception could not possibly exempt that manner of exercising visitation, or else the exception would swallow the rule. Its only conceivable purpose is to preserve normal civil and criminal lawsuits. To be sure, the reservation of powers "vested in the courts of justice" is phrased as an exception from the prohibition of visitorial powers. But as we have just discussed, it cannot possibly be that, and it is explicable only as an attempt to make clear that the courts' ordinary powers of enforcing the law are not affected.

On a pragmatic level, the difference between visitation and law enforcement is clear. If a State chooses to pursue enforcement of its laws in court, then it is not exercising its power of visitation and will be treated like a litigant. An attorney general acting as a civil litigant must file a lawsuit, survive a motion to dismiss, endure *2719 the rules of procedure and discovery, and risk sanctions if his claim is frivolous or his discovery tactics abusive. Judges are trusted to prevent "fishing expeditions" or an undirected rummaging through bank books and records for evidence of some unknown wrongdoing. In New York, civil discovery is far more limited than the full range of "visitorial powers" that may be exercised by a sovereign. Courts may enter protective orders to prevent "unreasonable annoyance, expense, embarrassment, disadvantage, or other prejudice," N.Y. Civ. Prac. Law Ann. § 3103(a) (West 2005), and may supervise discovery *sua sponte,* § 3104(a). A visitor, by contrast, may inspect books and records at any time for any or no reason.

II

The Comptroller's regulation, therefore, does not comport with the statute. Neither does the Comptroller's *interpretation* of its regulation, which differs from the text and must be discussed separately.

Evidently realizing that exclusion of state enforcement of *all* state laws against national banks is too extreme to be contemplated, the Comptroller sought to limit the sweep of its regulation by the following passage set forth in the agency's statement of basis and purpose in the Federal Register:

> "What the case law *does* recognize is that 'states retain some power to regulate national banks in areas such as contracts, debt collection, acquisition and transfer of property, and taxation, zoning, criminal, and tort law.' [citing a Ninth Circuit case.] Application of these laws to national banks and their implementation by state authorities typically does not affect the content or extent of the Federally-authorized business of banking... but rather establishes the legal infrastructure that surrounds and supports the ability of national banks... to do business." 69 Fed.Reg. 1896 (2004) (footnote omitted).

This cannot be reconciled with the regulation's almost categorical prohibition in 12 CFR § 7.4000(a)(1) of "prosecuting enforcement actions." Nor can it be justified by the provision in subsection (a)(2)(iv) which defines visitorial powers to include "[e]nforcing compliance with any applicable... state laws concerning" "activities authorized or permitted pursuant to federal banking law," § 7.4000(a)(2)(iii). The latter phrase cannot be interpreted to include only distinctively banking activities (leaving the States free to enforce nonbanking state laws), because if it were so interpreted subsection (a)(2)(iii), which uses the same terminology, would limit the Comptroller's exclusive visitorial power of "regulation and supervision" to distinctively banking activities-which no one thinks is the case. Anyway, the National Bank Act *does* specifically authorize and permit activities that fall within what the statement of basis and purpose calls "the legal *2720 infrastructure that surrounds and supports the ability of national banks... to do business." See, e.g., 12 U.S.C. § 24 Third (power to make contracts); § 24 Seventh ("all such incidental powers as shall be necessary to carry on the business of banking"). And of course a distinction between "implementation" of "infrastructure" and judicial enforcement of other laws can be found nowhere within the text of the statute. This passage in the statement of basis and purpose, resting upon neither the text of the regulation nor the text of the statute, attempts to do what Congress declined to do: exempt national banks from all state banking laws, or at least state enforcement of those laws.

III

The dissent fails to persuade us. Its fundamental contention-that the exclusive grant of visitorial powers can be interpreted to preclude state enforcement of state laws-rests upon a logical fallacy. The dissent establishes, *post,* at 2726, (and we do not at all contest), that in the course of exercising visitation powers the sovereign can compel compliance with the law. But it concludes from that, *post,* at 2727, that *any* sovereign attempt to compel compliance with the law can be deemed an exercise of the visitation power. That conclusion obviously does not follow. For example, in the course of exercising its visitation powers, the sovereign can assuredly compel a bank to honor obligations that are in default. Does that mean that the sovereign's taking the same action in executing a civil judgment for payment of those obligations can be considered an exercise of the visitation power? Of course not. Many things can be compelled through the visitation power that can be compelled through the exercise of other sovereign power as well. The critical question is not what is being compelled, but what sovereign power has been invoked to compel it. And the power to enforce the law exists separate and apart from the power of visitation.

The dissent argues that the Comptroller's expansive reading of "visitorial powers" does not intrude upon the, "the historic police powers of the States," *post,* at 2732, (quoting Rice v. Santa Fe Elevator Corp., 331 U.S. 218, 230, 67 S.Ct. 1146, 91 L.Ed. 1447 (1947)), because, like federal maritime law, federal involvement in this field dates to "the earliest days of the Republic," post, at 2733 (quoting United States v. Locke, 529 U.S. 89, 108, 120 S.Ct. 1135, 146 L.Ed.2d 69 (2000)). For that reason, the dissent concludes, this case does not raise the sort of federalism concerns that prompt a presumption against pre-emption. We have not invoked the presumption against pre-emption, and think it unnecessary to do so in giving force to the plain terms of the National Bank Act. Neither, however, should the incursion that the Comptroller's regulation makes upon traditional state powers be minimized. Although the sovereign visitorial power of assuring national-bank compliance with *all* laws inhered in the Federal Government from the time of its creation of national banks, the Comptroller was not given authority to enforce nonpre-empted state laws until 1966. See Financial Institutions Supervisory Act of 1966, Tit. III, 80 Stat. 1046-1055. A power first exercised during the lifetime of every current Justice is hardly involvement "from the earliest days of the Republic."

States, on the other hand, have always enforced their general laws against national banks-and have enforced their banking-related laws against national banks for at least 85 years, as evidenced by St. Louis, in which we upheld enforcement of a state anti-bank-branching law, 263 U.S., at 656, 44 S.Ct. 213. See also *2721 Anderson Nat. Bank v. Luckett, 321 U.S. 233, 237, 248-249, 64 S.Ct. 599, 88 L.Ed. 692 (1944) (state commissioner of revenue may enforce abandoned-bank-deposit law against national bank through "judicial proceedings"); State by Lord v. First Nat. Bank of St. Paul, 313 N.W.2d 390, 393 (Minn.1981) (state treasurer may enforce general unclaimed-property law with "specific provisions directed toward" banks against national bank); Clovis Nat. Bank v. Callaway, 69 N.M. 119, 130-132, 364 P.2d 748, 756 (1961) (state treasurer may enforce unclaimed-property law against national bank deposits); State v. First Nat. Bank of Portland, 61 Or. 551, 554-557, 123 P. 712, 714 (1912) (state attorney general may enforce bank-specific escheat law against national bank).

The dissent seeks to minimize the regulation's incursion upon state powers by claiming that the regulation does not "declare the pre-emptive scope of the [National Bank Act]" but merely "interpret[s] the term 'visitorial powers.' " *Post,* at 2732. That is much too kind. It is not without reason that the regulation is contained within a subpart of the Comptroller's regulations on Bank Activities and Operations that is entitled "Preemption." The purpose and function of the statutory term "visitorial powers" is to define and thereby limit the category of action reserved to the Federal Government and forbidden to the States. Any interpretation of "visitorial powers" necessarily "declares the pre-emptive scope of the NBA," ibid. What is clear from logic is also clear in application: The regulation declares that "[s]tate officials may not... prosecut[e] enforcement actions." 12 CFR § 7.4000(a). If that is not pre-emption, nothing is.

IV

[2] [3] Applying the foregoing principles to this case is not difficult. "Visitorial powers"

in the National Bank Act refers to a sovereign's supervisory powers over corporations. They include any form of administrative oversight that allows a sovereign to inspect books and records on demand, even if the process is mediated by a court through prerogative writs or similar means. The Comptroller reasonably interpreted this statutory term to include "conducting examinations [and] inspecting or requiring the production of books or records of national banks," § 7.4000, when the State conducts those activities in its capacity as supervisor of corporations.

[4] When, however, a state attorney general brings suit to enforce state law against a national bank, he is not acting in the role of sovereign-as-supervisor, but rather in the role of sovereign-as-law-enforcer. Such a lawsuit is not an exercise of "visitorial powers" and thus the Comptroller erred by extending the definition of "visitorial powers" to include "prosecuting enforcement actions" in state courts, § 7.4000.

[5] The request for information in the present case was stated to be "in lieu of" other action; implicit was the threat that if the request was not voluntarily honored, that other action would be taken. All parties have assumed, and we agree, that if the threatened action would have been unlawful the request-cum-threat could be enjoined. Here the threatened action was not the bringing of a civil suit, or the obtaining of a judicial search warrant based on probable cause, but rather the Attorney General's issuance of subpoena on his own authority under New York *2722 Executive Law, which permits such subpoenas in connection with his investigation of "repeated fraudulent or illegal acts... in the carrying on, conducting or transaction of business." See N.Y. Exec. Law Ann. § 63(12) (West 2002). That is not the exercise of the power of law enforcement "vested in the courts of justice" which 12 U.S.C. § 484(a) exempts from the ban on exercise of supervisory power.

Accordingly, the injunction below is affirmed as applied to the threatened issuance of executive subpoenas by the Attorney General for the State of New York, but vacated insofar as it prohibits the Attorney General from bringing judicial enforcement actions.

The judgment of the Court of Appeals is affirmed in part and reversed in part.

It is so ordered.

Justice THOMAS, with whom THE CHIEF JUSTICE, Justice KENNEDY, and Justice ALITO join, concurring in part and dissenting in part.

第四章

信托法律制度

第一节 信托概述

信托制度起源于英国，后在世界范围内传播。美国继受了英国的信托制度并发挥到极致，成为世界上信托业最发达的国家。迄今，美国已经建立了复杂而完备的信托法律制度，除了大量法院判例所确立的规则，还包括众多的成文法律。

英美法中的信托制度，也逐渐被大陆法系国家所接受。中国早在20世纪80年代就制定了有关信托的法律文件。2001年4月，《中华人民共和国信托法》获得通过，至此信托制度在中国以法律的形式确定了下来。

一、中国信托概述

依据中国《信托法》的规定，信托是指委托人基于对受托人的信任，将其财产权委托给受托人，由受托人按委托人的意愿以自己的名义，为受益人的利益或者特定目的，进行管理或者处分的行为。

建立信托关系，必须具备以下要件：（1）信托当事人，包括委托人、受托人和受益人；（2）信托目的，即将财产委托给受托人进行管理或处分的合法目的；（3）信托财产，即委托人合法所有的交付给受托人进行管理或处分的确定的财产（包括财产权利，如债权）；（4）信托文件，即说明信托关系的文字依据，包括信托合同、遗嘱或者法律、行政法规规定的其他书面文件等。

在中国，根据性质的不同，信托被划分为三种类型：公益信托、民事信托和营业信托。

公益信托是指为公共利益目的而设立的信托。依据中国《信托法》的规定，这种公共利益包括：（1）救济贫困；（2）救助灾民；（3）扶助残疾人；（4）发展教育、科技、文化、艺术、体育事业；（5）发展医疗卫生事业；（6）发展环境保护事业，维护生态环境；（7）发展其他社会公益事业。

民事信托是指信托事项所涉及的法律依据在民事法律范围之内的信托。例如涉及遗产的继承和管理等事项的信托，均为民事信托。由于民事信托不以营利为目的，又称为“非营业信托”。

营业信托是指以营利为目的，委托营业性的信托机构实施商事行为的信托。作为现代金融业支柱之一的信托业，即为营业信托。中国《信托公司管理办法》第2条将信托业务定义为“信托公司以营业和收取报酬为目的，以受托人身份承诺信托和处理信托事务的经营行为”。在中国，信托业是特许行业，只有得到政府部门批准设立的信托公司，才能经营。迄今为止，中国已经形成了以《中华人民共和国信托法》为中心，以《信托公司管理办法》和《信托公司集合资金信托计划管理办法》为基础，以中国银监会发布的一系列法规、规章及行政规范性文件为支撑的信托业法律体系。

二、美国信托概述

美国虽然不是信托业最早起源的国家，但却是当今世界金融行业最发达、信托业最丰富的国家。按照2003年通过并发布的《信托法重述（三）》第2条对于信托的定义，在美国，除回归信托（resulting trust）和推定信托（constructive trust）外，信托是指一种与财产有关的信义义务关系，其产生于一种建立此种信义义务关系的明示意图，使得持有财产所有权的人承担为慈善或为一个或多个人（其中至少有一个人并非为唯一的受托人）的利益处置财产的义务。从上述定义中可以看出，一项信托通常涉及三个要素：受托人、受益人以及信托财产，其中信托财产是最核心的因素。

在美国，根据设立信托意图明确与否，可将信托分为明示信托（express trust）、回归信托和推定信托，后两者因“委托人”的意图不明确而由法院推定信托关系的存在。根据受益人情况的不同，可将信托分为慈善信托和私人信托两类。作为金融业的信托业，属于明示信托中的私人信托。

信托业在美国同样也是特许行业，信托机构只有得到相关政府部门授予的经营信托业务的权力（trust power），方可从事信托业务经营。美国的信托业务的范围非常广泛。例如，根据加利福尼亚州《金融法典》第106条的规定，信托业务（Trust business）是指经法院指定或基于法律授权作为财产的执行人（executor）、管理人（administrator）、监护人（guardian）或接管人（conservator of estates），受让人（assignee）、接收人（receiver）、保管人（depositary）或受托人（trustee）所从事的业务或为任何法律所许可的目的作为受托人所从事的业务。

在美国，根据服务对象的不同信托业务一般划分为个人信托和机构信托两大块。个人信托包括：受托管理财产、受托处理财产、指定充当监护人或管理人以及私人代理账户。机构信托包括：管理企业雇员基金账户、发行公司债务信托、商务管理信托（又称为公司理财业务）、表决权信托以及代理股票经纪业务等。另外，美国还开发了许多新型的信托投资工具，比如 MMMF（货币市场互助基金）、CMA（现金管理账户）、MTF（共同信托基金）、融资租赁业务以及把信托资金投资于 CD（大额存单）、CP（商业汇票）和 TB（国库券）等短期资金市场等。

美国并未制定全国统一的信托法，有关信托的法律规定大都列入联邦储备银行法与各州的银行条例之中。同时，法院判例形成的丰富的判例法对信托活动形成约束。此外，美国法律协会出版的《信托法重述》，成为美国信托活动的法律指南。

三、案例资料

在美国，信托业的发展有近二百年的历史。作为特许行业，信托业同时受到联邦法和州法的约束。美国信托法律确立的一项基本原则是，州法在适用上具有优先性，即联邦法只能在不与州法或地方法律相违背之时授权国民银行经营信托业务。

获得联邦授权经营信托业务的机构，在州内提供信托服务时，可能会遭到州法对其施加的限制。尽管州有权对信托业务予以管理和限制，但是州的行为又受到宪法的约束。下面的 American Trust Co.，Inc. v. South Carolina State Bd. of Bank Control 案对限制信托经营的州法的合宪性进行了讨论。

在该案中，原告作为联邦注册的信托机构在南卡罗来纳州提供信托服务，其对南卡罗来纳州法律中的如下限制提出质疑：（1）禁止受外州控制的州内公司作为执行人、管理人以及遗嘱受托人提供服务；（2）排除位于毗邻州（北卡罗来纳州和佐治亚州）或在毗邻州注册的公司作为遗嘱受托人提供服务；（3）在该州从事信托业务需要获得州银行监管委员会的批准。

法院从平等保护条款出发，认定上述（1）、（2）项法律违宪。法院承认，只要证明符合州的利益，州有权对州内的信托机构进行分类并给予不同的对待。但是，依据宪法中的平等保护条款，州所作的分类应当是合理且非武断性的，应当与其立法所要达到的目标具有实质相关性。法院认为，尽管州声称作出上述的分类限制是为了更好地管理州内的信托机构，确保州内的信托机构更好地服务该州的人民，但是相关的立法与州所主张的这一目标之间并不具有实质相关性。同时，法院承认，出于公共利益州可以限制信托业经营的竞争，但是法院并不赞同州所提出的受外州公司控制的州内公司在该州经营信托业务所导致的竞争对公共利益有害的观点。总之，法院的意思很明确，州不得制定歧视性法律，使经营信托业务的机构在竞争上处于不平等的地位。

法院还从宪法的正当程序条款以及贸易条款（Commerce Clause）展开分析，但认为相关立法并未违反这两个条款。尤其从贸易条款出发，法院认为，位于毗邻州或在毗邻州注册的公司向该州提供信托服务，构成跨州贸易。根据国会的立法，国民银行和州立银行在经营信托业务的权限范围上应当是一致的，这是为了维护二者之间的平等竞争地位。但是，南卡罗来纳州的立法并未区分国民银行和州立银行，对二者予以同等地限制，不存在使其中一方获得不公平的竞争地位的问题，因此并不违反宪法的贸易条款。

American Trust Co., Inc. v. South Carolina State Bd. of Bank Control

381 F.Supp. 313 (D.C.S.C. 1974)

BUTZNER, Circuit Judge:

…

NCNB Corporation is organized under the laws of North Carolina as a bank holding company within the meaning of the Bank Holding Company Act. 12 U.S.C. § 1841 et seq. (1970). It owns all of the stock, except the directors' qualifying shares of North Carolina National Bank, which is organized under the laws of the United States and maintains its principal offices in Charlotte, North Carolina. In addition to being one of the largest commercial banks in the southeastern part of the country, North Carolina National operates an extensive trust department. Its customers include a number of residents of South Carolina, who, in conformity with South Carolina law in effect at the time, named North Carolina National as their testamentary trustee. However, in 1970, South Carolina excluded otherwise qualified corporations that are domiciled or licensed in North Carolina or Georgia from serving as testamentary trustees of estates of South Carolina decedents.

NCNB Corporation then formed a South Carolina corporation, American Trust Company, to transact trust business in South Carolina. Before NCNB could launch its proposal to provide trust services in South Carolina through American Trust, it was required by federal law to obtain the approval of the Board of Governors of the Federal Reserve System. Despite opposition from South Carolina banking interests, the Board of Governors concluded that it would be in the public interest for NCNB to engage in the trust business in South Carolina through its subsidiary, American Trust. The Board, however, was unable to give its unqualified *319 approval because, while NCNB's application was pending American Trust was prohibited by newly enacted laws from serving as an executor, administrator, or testamentary trustee. Accordingly, the Board approved NCNB's request to the extent permitted by South Carolina law. This litigation was then instituted to test the constitutionality of South Carolina's restrictive statutes.

At the outset it may be well to clarify the scope of the attack on South Carolina's statutes. The plaintiffs do not question the power of South Carolina to prohibit foreign corporations from serving as executors or administrators of the estates of South Carolina decedents. Nor do they challenge any South Carolina statutes governing the conduct of fiduciaries and prescribing their duties. The plaintiff's attack is directed against those portions of South Carolina statutes that (I) bar foreign controlled domestic corporations from serving as executors, administrators (§ 19-592) and testamentary trustees (§§ 67-53(a)(3) and (4)); (II) exclude corporations domiciled or licensed in contiguous states, i.e., North Carolina and Georgia, from serving as testamentary trustees (§ 67-53(a)(4)); and (III) require approval of the State Board to engage in the trust business (§ 8-580).

I. Equal Protection Clause

American Trust principally relies on the equal protection clause in attacking §§ 19-592 and 67-53(a)(3) and (4) which prohibit it, as a domestic corporation, from serving as executor, administrator, or testamentary trustee because it is controlled by a North Carolina corporation. It charges that the classification of domestic corporations by the domicile of their corporate owners is irrelevant to any constitutionally permissible exercise of South Carolina's police powers. South Carolina asserts that the prohibition of foreign controlled domestic trust companies assures local control over fiduciaries and prevents destructive competition to native controlled corporations for the ultimate benefit of the public. The state emphasizes that South Carolina's estates and trusts should be administered by persons trained in South Carolina law, that trust companies should serve small as well as large accounts, and that it is to the advantage of South Carolina's economy to retain within the state both commercial and trust deposits. All of these objectives, the state contends, will be impaired by the operation of foreign controlled domestic trust companies.

[1] [2] [3] [4] [5] We start by accepting three of the state's propositions: the classification of domestic trust companies according to the domicile of their corporate owners is not inherently suspect, and the state, therefore, need not justify the classification by proving a compelling *320 state interest; the trust business, like banking, is subject to pervasive state control; and the statutes are presumptively constitutional. The principles governing the

application of the equal protection clause have been succinctly restated in Reed v. Reed, 404 U.S. 71, 75, 92 S.Ct. 251, 253, 30 L.Ed.2d 225 (1971):

In applying (the equal protection) clause, this Court has consistently recognized that the Fourteenth Amendment does not deny to States the power to treat different classes of persons in different ways.... The Equal Protection Clause of that amendment does, however, deny to States the power to legislate that different treatment be accorded to persons placed by a statute into different classes on the basis of criteria wholly unrelated to the objective of that statute. A classification "must be reasonable, not arbitrary, and must rest upon some ground of difference having a fair and substantial relation to the object of the legislation, so that all persons similarly circumstanced shall be treated alike...."

[6] No similar case dealing with the application of the equal protection clause to a trust company has been called to our attention, but we perceive no reason for exempting this type of business. Despite the broad authority states have over banking and related business, a state may not deny the equal protection of the laws to a corporation engaged in check cashing and sale of money orders. Morey v. Doud, 354 U.S. 457 (1957). Moreover, several courts have held that the classification of domestic corporations according to the residence or domicile of their controlling stockholders bears no relation to the legitimate objective of state control over companies engaged in various aspects of financing. Consequently, courts dealing with the problem have ruled that classification by domicile of the owners is a form of invidious discrimination that violates the equal protection clause. Mid-Penn National Mtge. Co. v. Hughes, 258 A.2d 291 (Del.Super.Ct.1969), aff'd per curiam, 268 A.2d 876 (Del.Sup.1970) (mortgage company); Oxford Consumer Discount Co. v. Stefanelli, 102 N.J.Super. 549, 246 A.2d 460 (1968), aff'd per curiam, 55 N.J. 489, 262 A.2d 874, appeal dismissed, 400 U.S. 808, 91 S.Ct. 45, 27 L.Ed.2d 38 (1970) (mortgage company); Miskell v. Termplan, Inc., 381 S.W.2d 129 (Tex.Civ.App.1964) (small loan company).

[7] Undoubtedly, South Carolina has a legitimate interest in assuring that corporate fiduciaries serve the public faithfully. Laws prescribing the fiduciaries' financial resources, governing their conduct, and defining their responsibilities are appropriate means of controlling trust companies. The difficulty with the state's argument is that the challenged statutes do not bear a fair and substantial relation to the objectives that the state seeks. A domestic trust company, whether it be native or foreign owned, can be required to retain licensed South Carolina attorneys to conduct those aspects of its business which the state includes in the practice of law. But the challenged statutes do not contain this requirement.

Similarly, nothing *321 in the challenged statutes would prevent a native owned domestic corporation from seeking investment or legal advice from persons who have offices in other states. A native owned domestic corporation is not barred from refusing small, uneconomic accounts, or from transferring funds out of the state if this is in the best interests of a trust's beneficiaries. The challenged statutes address none of these business practices. Contrary to the state's contention, the record fails to establish that a domestic trust company owned by a corporation domiciled or licensed in a state contiguous to South Carolina would be a less suitable testamentary trustee than a domestic company owned by a corporation domiciled in some other state. Nor does the proof demonstrate that a locally owned domestic trust company would better serve the public, or be more amenable to regulation, than a domestic company owned by a foreign corporation. Classification of domestic trust companies by the domicile or licensing of their corporate ownership bears no rational relation to the lawful discharge of their fiduciary duties or to the state's control over them.

[8] [9] [10] The state also argues that the statute serves the public interest by preventing competition that would injure South Carolina's existing corporate fiduciaries. While the equal protection clause denies a state the power to arbitrarily favor one domestic corporation over a competitor, the state can curb competition when the public interest will be served. Compare Mayflower Farms Products Co. v. Ten Eyck, 297 U.S. 266, 56 S.Ct. 457, 80 L.Ed. 675 (1936) with Borden's Farms Products Co. v. Ten Eyck, 297 U.S. 251, 56 S.Ct. 453, 80 L.Ed. 669 (1936). Accordingly, we accept the legal premise on which the state bottoms its argument: a state may limit competition in the trust business if the public interest will be served. Philadelphia Savings Fund Soc'y v. Myers, 406 Pa. 438, 179 A.2d 209 (1962). Cf. Noble State Bank v. Haskell, 219 U.S. 104, 31 S.Ct. 186, 55 L.Ed. 112 (1911). But we reject the factual basis of the state's claim that foreign corporate control of domestic trust companies inherently creates competition that is detrimental to the public interest. The claim is based on speculative opinions that are directly in conflict with the conclusions reached by the Board of Governors of the Federal Reserve System. Moreover, we find no rational relationship between the state's classification of domestic trust companies and the protection of the public from competition. If the public welfare will suffer from injurious competition, nothing in the challenged statutes prevents such competition from native owned domestic trust companies.

We conclude, therefore, that the following statutes invidiously discriminate against South Carolina trust companies and deny them the equal protection of the laws:

The second paragraph of § 19-592, which bars a South Carolina trust company from serving as executor or administrator because it is controlled by a corporation domiciled in another state;

Those portions of §§ 67-53(a)(3) and (4), which bar a South Carolina trust company from serving as testamentary trustee because it is controlled by a corporation domiciled or licensed in a contiguous state.

[11] We, therefore, will grant an appropriate injunction restraining the enforcement of these laws against American Trust. In conformity with South Carolina law, we rule that the statutes are separable and therefore the remaining portions are not invalid. Parker v. Bates, 216 S.Ct. 52, 56 S.E.2d 723, 730 (1949).

II

North Carolina National, claiming that it is otherwise qualified as a foreign corporation to serve as a testamentary trustee for South Carolina decedents, charges that the exclusion of corporations domiciled or licensed in states contiguous to South Carolina causes § 67-53(a)(4) to violate both the due *322 process and commerce clauses of the Constitution. These contentions require only brief comment.

Due Process Clause

[12] [13] [14] [15] It is undisputed that the Bank is a foreign corporation. Therefore, without violating the fourteenth amendment, South Carolina can exclude it from doing business in the state. Asbury Hospital v. Cass County, 326 U.S. 207, 211, 66 S.Ct. 61, 90 L.Ed. 6 (1945). Moreover, the Constitution commits to the states the power to control the administration of their citizens' estates. Labine v. Vincent, 401 U.S. 532, 538, 91 S.Ct. 1017, 28 L.Ed.2d 288 (1971); Riley v. New York Trust Co., 315 U.S. 343, 355, 62 S.Ct. 608, 86 L.Ed. 885 (1942); see 1 Bogert, Trusts and Trustees 642 (1965). Because the due process clause no longer offers a substantive bar to state regulation of a business subject to state control, North Dakota Pharmacy Board v. Snyder's Drug Stores, Inc., 414 U.S. 156, 94 S.Ct. 407, 38 L.Ed.2d 379 (1973), we conclude that § 67-53(a)(4) does not deprive North Carolina National of due process of law.

Commerce Clause

[16] North Carolina National places a value in excess of $32 000 000 on the estates of South Carolina residents who have requested it to act as testamentary trustee or as trustee of

pour-over trusts into which the customers may eventually devise their estates. The Bank explained that it formerly transacted this business "through use of the mails, telephone, and personal visits between its trust officers and South Carolina residents establishing the trusts, the beneficiaries of such trusts, or their attorneys." We hold, for the purpose of this case, that the Bank's interstate activities as testamentary trustee for South Carolina decedents constituted interstate commerce. Cf. United States v. Philadelphia National Bank, 374 U.S. 321, 336 n.12, 83 S.Ct. 1715, 10 L.Ed.2d 915 (1963). This aspect of the case, therefore, turns on the question whether the ban against the Bank is an impermissible burden on interstate commerce.

[17] [18] [19] National banks can exercise only the authority that has been expressly or impliedly granted to them by Congress. Investment Company Institute v. Camp, 401 U.S. 617, 628, 91 S.Ct. 1091, 28 L.Ed.2d 367 (1971). Federal law, 12 U.S.C. §§ 92a(a) and (b), authorizes a national bank to act as a fiduciary only "when not in contravention of State or local law." But a national bank does not act in contravention of state or local law if a competing state bank can serve as a fiduciary. In this event, the national bank's authority is coextensive with the state bank's, but it is not enlarged. New Hampshire Bankers' Ass'n v. Nelson, 336 F.Supp. 1330 (D.N.H.), aff'd 460 F.2d 307 (1st Cir. 1972). The term, "local law," as used in § 92a is defined as "the law of the state... governing the fiduciary relationship," *323 12 C.F.R. § 9.1(f) (1974), which in this instance is the law of South Carolina. See 1 Bogert, Trusts and Trustees 642 (1965). Section 67-53(a)(4) prohibits both North Carolina state banks and national banks located in North Carolina from serving as testamentary trustees of South Carolina decedents. In this respect it treats both types of banks equally.

[20] [21] [22] [23] Congress has paramount authority over national banks. McCulloch v. Maryland, 17 U.S. (4 Wheat.) 316, 4 L.Ed. 579 (1819). It can exercise its authority by incorporating restrictions found in state law. In 1927, when the McFadden Act, 12 U.S.C. § 36 (1970), authorized national banks to operate branches to the same extent that a state bank located in the same state could operate them, it intended to create "competitive equality" between state and national banks located in the same state. First Nat'l Bank v. Walker Bank and Trust Co., 385 U.S. 252, 261, 87 S.Ct. 492, 17 L.Ed.2d 343 (1966). It is apparent that in enacting § 92a, Congress intended to create the same kind of "competitive equality" with regard to trust services. Since South Carolina's ban on foreign testamentary trustees operates equally against state and national banks located in North Carolina, the exclusion of North Carolina National is not an impermissible burden on interstate commerce; Congress has allowed it by enacting § 92a. Furthermore, because the commerce clause is a grant, not a

restriction, on the power of Congress “to regulate Commerce... among the several States...” the exclusion is constitutionally valid. Cf. Prudential Insurance Co. v. Benjamin, 328 U.S. 408, 423, 66 S.Ct. 1142, 90 L.Ed. 1342 (1946)….

第二节　信托组织机构

一、中国的信托组织机构

充当受托人从事信托业务的经济组织，即为信托机构。中国实行严格的分业经营体制，信托业务只能由得到政府部门批准依法设立的信托公司经营，其他组织（包括银行、证券公司及保险公司）均无权经营。中国《信托公司管理办法》规定，除非法律、法规另有规定，未经中国银监会批准，任何单位和个人不得经营信托业务。

在中国，信托公司应当采取有限责任公司或者股份有限公司的形式，不能采取其他的组织形式。设立信托公司，应当经中国银监会批准，并领取金融许可证。除非法律、法规另有规定，未经批准，任何经营单位不得在其名称中使用“信托公司”字样。

设立信托公司，应当具备下列条件：（1）有符合规定的公司章程；（2）有具备规定的入股资格的股东；（3）具有最低限额的注册资本（目前最低限额为3亿元人民币）；（4）有具备任职资格的董事、高级管理人员和与其业务相适应的信托从业人员；（5）具有健全的组织机构、信托业务操作规程和风险控制制度；（6）有符合要求的营业场所、安全防范措施和与业务有关的其他设施；（7）监管部门规定的其他条件。

信托公司设立后，可申请经营广泛的业务，包括以下人民币或外币业务：（1）资金信托；（2）动产信托；（3）不动产信托；（4）有价证券信托；（5）其他财产或财产权信托；（6）作为投资基金或者基金管理公司的发起人从事投资基金业务；（7）经营企业资产的重组、购并及项目融资、公司理财、财务顾问等业务；（8）受托经营国务院有关部门批准的证券承销业务；（9）办理居间、咨询、资信调查等业务；（10）代保管及保管箱业务；（11）法律、法规规定或中国银监会批准的其他业务。

二、美国的信托组织机构

美国的信托机构可以分为信托业务兼营机构和专营机构两大类别。信托业务的兼营机构主要是商业银行和储贷机构（thrift）内设的信托部门。信托业务的专营机构也即信托公司，可以直接采取信托公司的形式，也可以采取专营信托业务的银行或储贷机构的形式。

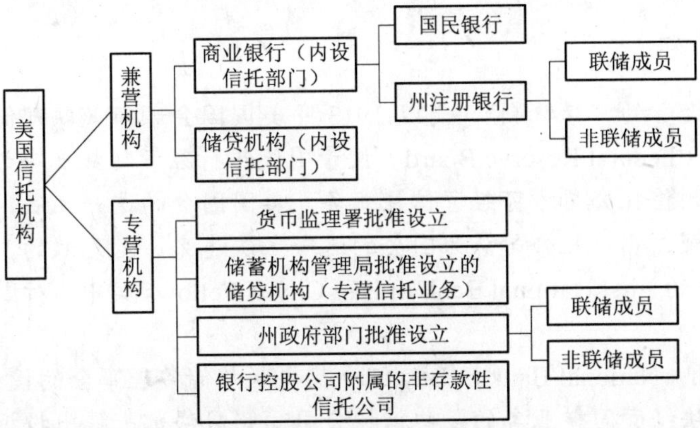

图 4-1 美国的信托机构

商业银行兼营信托业，是美国信托业的突出特点之一。事实上，美国在很大程度上对经营信托业务的信托公司和商业银行并未予以严格区分，甚至在概念上同等对待。例如，加利福尼亚州《金融法典》第 102 条将“银行”定义为“从事商业银行业务、工业银行业或信托业务的任何银行业机构”，第 107 条将“信托公司”定义为“被授权从事信托业务的公司、工业银行或商业银行”。目前，美国大部分商业银行都设立了自己的信托部门来经营信托业务，美国的信托业务基本上由大的商业银行设立的信托部所垄断。

在美国，欲从事信托业务的经营，必须获得相关机构授予的经营信托业务的权力（trust power）。有权作出授权的机构既包括联邦层级的货币监理署及储蓄机构管理局（2011 年 7 月储蓄机构管理局被并入货币监理署）等，也包括州层级的银行监管机构。申请经营信托业务的公司或银行，必须满足相关机构各自设置的相关条件，方可获得授权。

获得授权的信托机构，可以开展范围广泛的信托业务。依据委托人的不同，大体上可以将信托机构可经营的信托业务分为个人信托、法人信托及个人和法人混合信托三种类型。其中，个人信托是指委托人（自然人）基于财产规划的目的，将其财产权转移给受托人（信托机构），使受托人依据信托的本质为受益人的利益或特定目的，管理或处分信托财产的行为。它主要包括四种类型：（1）财产处理信托业务，包括契约信托和遗嘱信托等；（2）主要针对未成年人等的财产监护信托业务；（3）人寿保险信托业务；（4）以资助重度身心残疾者生活上的稳定为目的的特定赠与信托业务等。法人信托主要是代理企业发行股票和债券，进行财产管理，代办公司的设立、改组、合并及清理手续等的业务。个人和法人混合信托，有职工持股信托、年金信托、公益信托等。

三、案例资料

美国信托业经营的“双轨制”，是以 1913 年美国国会颁布《联邦储备银行法》授权联邦储备理事会（Federal Reserve Board）授予国民银行经营信托业务的权力而确立的。在此之前，只有州信托公司方可经营信托业务。美国国会的这一立法，遭到州信托公司的强烈反对和质疑。州信托公司认为国会的这一立法违宪，是无效的。美国联邦最高法院在 1917 年判决的 First National Bank of Bay City v. Fellows 案中，对国会立法的合宪性进行了裁决。

在该案中，First National Bank of Bay City 获得联邦储备理事会的授权经营信托业务。根据密歇根州州法经营同样业务的一些信托公司向州司法部长提出控诉，以国民银行获得经营信托的权力违背密歇根州州法并且联邦储备理事会的行为违反美国宪法为由，质疑国民银行经营信托业务的权力。密歇根州司法部长于是诉至州最高法院，欲以此试探国民银行经营信托业务的权力的合法性。密歇根州最高法院宣布国会的立法无效，联邦储备理事会无权授权国民银行经营信托业务。案件被上诉至美国联邦最高法院，联邦最高法院推翻了下级法院的判决。

联邦最高法院提出了四点理由，认定国会立法并未违宪：

第一，下级法院无视信托业作为银行经营的组成部分的关系，将信托业与银行的其他业务割裂开来并据此作出裁决，这是错误的。

第二，授予国民银行何种范围及性质的权力，属于国会行使自由裁量权的范围，不应再受到司法审查。

第三，下级法院据以作出裁决的假设是，经营信托的权力是由完全不与国民银行竞争的州个人或公司所享有，但实际情况是，享有经营信托业务权力的州的公司或多或少都是国民银行的竞争对手。

第四，下级法院认为，特定业务受到州法监管，因此国会无权授予国民银行经营该等业务的权力。这一观点是错误的。先例早已确定，尽管某项业务受到州的监管，但如果该业务的性质使其为国民银行开展业务活动所附带，那么国会有授予国民银行经营该等业务的权力。特定业务受到州的监管，这并不禁止国会授权国民银行经营该等业务。尽管州在宽泛意义上拥有监管该等业务的权力，但是州不得据此禁止国会特许该等业务的经营，否则无异于运用州的权力去禁止国会行使其依据宪法有权行使的权力。

通过此案的判决可以看出，美国信托业双轨制产生的一个重要原因在于，信托业被视作银行经营的一个部分，而非与银行的其他业务割裂开来对待。因此，存在于银行业经营及监管之中的平等竞争思想——维持联邦注册的国民银行与州注册的银行之间的“平等竞争地位”——自然被传导至信托行业：如果州法准许州注册的银行或其他机构经营信托业务，那么国会亦可授权国民银行在该州经营信托业务。由此，在美国，不仅出现了银行兼营信托业的局面，还形成了联邦注册和州注册的银行或公司经申请均可经营信托业务的竞争格局。

First National Bank of Bay City v. Fellows

244 U.S.416 （1917）

Mr. Chief Justice White delivered the opinion of the court:

…

Section 11(k) of the Act of Congress approved December 23, 1913, establishing the Federal Reserve Board (38 Stat. at L. 251, 262, chap. 6, Comp. Stat. 1916, §§ 9785, 9794), gives to that board authority "to grant by special permit to national banks applying therefor, when not in contravention of state or local law, the right to act as trustee, executor, administrator, or registrar of stocks and bonds under such rules and regulations as the said board may prescribe."

The First National Bank of Bay City, having obtained the certificate required, began the exercise of the powers stated. Thereupon certain trust companies which, under the laws of Michigan, had the authority to do the same character of business, petitioned the attorney general of the state to test the right of the national bank to use the functions, on the ground that its doing so was contrary to the laws of the state of Michigan, and that the action of the Federal Reserve Board, purporting to give authority, was in contravention of the Constitution of the United States. The attorney general then, on the relation of the trust companies, commenced in the supreme court of the state a proceeding in the nature of quo warranto to test the right of the corporation to exercise the functions. The bank, in defense, fully stated its Federal charter, the rights given by the act of Congress, and the action of the Federal Reserve Board taken thereunder. The attorney general demurred to this defense, first, because Congress had no power to confer the authority which was called in question; second, because if it had the power, it was without right to delegate to the Reserve Board the determination of when it should be used; and third, because the exercise of the powers was in contravention of the laws and authority of the state, and the Reserve Board, therefore, under the act, had no power to grant the certificate.

The case was heard by the full court. In an opinion of one judge, which, it would seem, was written before the opinion of the court was prepared, it was elaborately reasoned that the exercise by a national bank of the functions enumerated in the section of the act of Congress under consideration would be contrary to the laws of the state, and therefore the Reserve Board, under the terms of the act of Congress, had no power to authorize their exertion. The opinion of the court, however, fully examining the grounds thus stated and disagreeing with them, expressly decided that corporations were authorized by the state law to perform the functions in question, and that the mere fact that national banks were Federal corporations did not render them unfit to assume and perform such duties under the state law, because the mere difference existing between the general administrative rules governing national banks and state corporations afforded no ground for saying that it would be contrary to state law for national banks to exert the powers under consideration. The authority conferred by the act of Congress and the rights arising from the certificate from such point of view were therefore upheld. Looking at the subject, however, from a consideration of the legislative power of Congress in the light of the decisions in McCulloch v. Maryland and Osborn v. Bank of United States, and recognizing that it had been settled beyond dispute that Congress had power to organize banks and endow them with functions both of a public and private character, and in the assumed further light of the rule that every reasonable intendment must be indulged in in favor of the constitutionality of a legislative power exercised, it was yet decided that Congress had no authority to confer the powers embraced in the section of the act under consideration, and hence that the section was void. The court, following its reference to McCulloch v. Maryland and Osborn v. Bank of United States, and to passages in the opinions in those cases, upholding the rightful possession by the bank of both public functions and private banking attributes, stated the grounds which led it to conclude that the rulings in the decided cases were distinguishable and therefore not controlling....

But we are of opinion that the doctrine thus announced not only was wholly inadequate to distinguish the case before us from the rulings in McCulloch v. Maryland and Osborn v. Bank of United States, but, on the contrary, directly conflicted with what was decided in those cases; that is to say, disregarded their authority so as to cause it to be our duty to reverse for the following reasons:

1. Because the opinion of the court, instead of testing the existence of the implied power to grant the particular functions in question by considering the bank as created by Congress as an entity, with all the functions and attributes conferred upon it, rested the determination as to such power upon a separation of the particular functions from the other attributes and functions of the bank, and ascertained the existence of the implied authority to confer them by

considering them as segregated; that is, by disregarding their relation to the bank as component parts of its operations—a doctrine which, as we have seen, was in the most express terms held to be unsound in both of the cases.

2. Because while, in the premise to the reasoning, the right of Congress was fully recognized to exercise its legislative judgment as to the necessity for creating the bank, including the scope and character of the public and private powers which should be given to it, in application the discretion of Congress was disregarded or set aside by exercising judicial discretion for the purpose of determining whether it was relevant or appropriate to give the bank the particular functions in question.

3. Because even under this mistaken view the conclusion that there was no ground for implying the power in Congress was erroneous because it was based on a mistaken standard, since, for the purpose of testing how far the functions in question which were conferred by the act of Congress on the bank were relevant to its business, or had any relation to discrimination by state legislation against banks created by Congress, it considered not the actual situation, that is, the condition of the state legislation, but an imaginary or nonexisting condition; that is, the assumption that, so far as the state power was concerned, the particular functions were in the state enjoyed only by individuals or corporations not coming at all, actually or potentially, in competition with national banks. And the far-reaching effect of this error becomes manifest when it is borne in mind that, plainly, the particular functions enumerated in the statute were conferred upon national banks because of the fact that they were enjoyed as the result of state legislation, by state corporations, rivals in a greater or less degree of national banks.

4. In view of the express ruling that the enjoyment of the powers in question by the national bank would not be in contravention of the state law, it follows that the reference of the court below to the state authority over the particular subjects which the statute deals with must have proceeded upon the erroneous assumption that, because a particular function was subject to be regulated by the state law, therefore Congress was without power to give a national bank the right to carry on such functions. But if this be what the statement signifies, the conflict between it and the rule settled in McCulloch v. Maryland and Osborn v. Bank of United States is manifest. What those cases established was that although a business was of a private nature and subject to state regulation, if it was of such a character as to cause it to be incidental to the successful discharge by a bank chartered by Congress of its public functions, it was competent for Congress to give the bank the power to exercise such private business in co-operation with or as part of its public authority. Manifestly this excluded the power of the state in such case,

although it might possess in a general sense authority to regulate such business, to use that authority to prohibit such business from being united by Congress with the banking function, since to do so would be but the exertion of state authority to prohibit Congress from exerting a power which, under the Constitution, it had a right to exercise. From this it must also follow that even although a business be of such a character that it is not inherently considered susceptible of being included by Congress in the powers conferred on national banks, that rule would cease to apply if, by state law, state banking corporations, trust companies, or others which, by reason of their business, are rivals or quasi rivals of national banks, are permitted to carry on such business. This must be, since the state may not by legislation create a condition as to a particular business which would bring about actual or potential competition with the business of national banks, and at the same time deny the power of Congress to meet such created condition by legislation appropriate to avoid the injury which otherwise would be suffered by the national agency. Of course, as the general subject of regulating the character of business just referred to is peculiarly within state administrative control, state regulations for the conduct of such business, if not discriminatory or so unreasonable as to justify the conclusion that they necessarily would so operate, would be controlling upon banks chartered by Congress when they came, in virtue of authority conferred upon them by Congress, to exert such particular powers. And these considerations clearly were in the legislative mind when it enacted the statute in question. This result would seem to be plain when it is observed (a) that the statute authorizes the exertion of the particular functions by national banks when not in contravention of the state law; that is, where the right to perform them is expressly given by the state law; or, what is equivalent, is deducible from the state law because that law has given the functions to state banks or corporations whose business in a greater or less degree rivals that of national banks, thus engendering from the state law itself an implication of authority in Congress to do as to national banks that which the state law has done as to other corporations; and (b) that the statute subjects the right to exert the particular functions which it confers on national banks to the administrative authority of the Reserve Board, giving besides to that board power to adopt rules regulating the exercise of the functions conferred, thus affording the means of coordinating the functions when permitted to be discharged by national banks with the reasonable and nondiscriminating provisions of state law regulating their exercise as to state corporations—the whole to the end that harmony and the concordant exercise of the national and state power might result.

…

As it follows from what we have said that the court below erred in declaring the section of the act of Congress to be unconstitutional, the judgment must be reversed and the case remanded for further proceedings not inconsistent with this opinion.

And it is so ordered.

第三节 信托的运作

一、中国信托的运作

在中国，当委托人将信托财产交付给受托人并确立信托关系之时，信托公司作为受托人应当依照信托文件的约定，为受益人的最大利益处理信托事务。

信托公司管理、运用或者处分信托财产，必须恪尽职守，履行诚实、信用、谨慎、有效管理的义务，维护受益人的最大利益。这是信托公司开展业务活动必须遵守的基本原则。信托公司违反信托目的处分信托财产，或者因违背管理职责、处理信托事务不当致使信托财产受到损失的，应当承担赔偿责任。

为了更好地维护受益人利益，中国法律特别要求信托公司应当亲自处理信托事务。如果信托文件另有约定或有不得已事由时，信托公司可委托他人代为处理，但应尽足够的监督义务，并对他人处理信托事务的行为承担责任。

由于信托为基于信任而建立的委托关系，因此中国法律特别强调了信托公司的保密义务以及委托人、受益人的知情权。依照中国《信托法》以及《信托公司管理办法》的规定，信托公司对委托人、受益人以及所处理信托事务的情况和资料负有依法保密的义务；信托公司应当妥善保存处理信托事务的完整记录，定期向委托人、受益人报告信托财产及其管理、运用、处分及收支的情况；委托人、受益人有权向信托公司了解对其信托财产的管理、运用、处分及收支情况，并要求信托公司作出说明。

基于信托行业的特殊性，中国法律还要求信托公司应当将信托财产与其固有财产分别管理、分别记账，并将不同委托人的信托财产分别管理、分别记账；信托公司的信托业务部门应当独立于公司的其他部门，其人员不得与公司其他部门的人员相互兼职，业务信息不得与公司的其他部门共享。

信托终止的，信托公司应当依照信托文件的约定作出处理信托事务的清算报告。受益人或者信托财产的权利归属人对清算报告无异议的，信托公司就清算报告所列事项解除责任，但信托公司有不当行为的除外。

除了上述一般性要求以外，中国法律对信托公司开展某些特定的信托业务还有着其他特别的要求。尤其值得一提的是集合资金信托业务，即信托公司将两个以上（含两个）

委托人交付的资金进行集中管理、运用或处分的信托业务活动。信托公司开展这类资金信托业务，类似于向社会公众兜售其设计的证券产品，由于其风险性较高，因此受到严格监管。中国为此专门制定了《信托公司集合资金信托计划管理办法》，对这类信托产品的投资门槛、推介方式、信息披露、信托资金保管、信托计划的变更以及终止等都有着特殊的要求。

二、美国信托的运作

在美国，信托关系确立后，委托人除非在信托文件中保留了相应的权利，否则即退出信托关系，信托的内部关系仅表现为受托人与受益人之间的关系。

根据美国判例法所确定的原则，受托人取得信托财产名义上的所有权（legal title），有权以所有者的名义对信托财产进行管理、运用和处分；而受益人则享有信托财产“衡平法上的所有权”（equitable title），有权获取信托收益。

在信托存续期间，受托人对受益人负有两个主要义务：一是忠实义务（loyalty），二是谨慎义务（prudence）。前者要求受托人在管理、运用和处分信托财产之时，为受益人的最大利益服务，不得利用信托财产谋取私利；后者要求受托人管理、运用和处分信托财产应付诸合理的谨慎，避免信托财产因受托人的不当行为而遭受损失。

就信托业的经营而言，美国相关的法律特别注重对作为受托人的信托机构利用信托财产进行投资的规范。信托机构应当谨慎投资，这被监管部门当作重点来监管。

早期美国采取“法定清单”（legal list）制度，即信托机构只能在法律规定的清单所列举的投资品种目录中投资才符合谨慎投资的要求，除非在信托合同中另有授权。如在一些州规定的清单中，受托人只能投资一些债务工具和债券。

随着时代的发展，僵化的“法定清单”制度严重地限制了信托机构的投资选择，越来越不合时宜了。许多州转而采用更灵活的受托人投资标准——“谨慎人标准”（Prudent Man Standard）。《信托法重述（二）》对“谨慎人标准”作出如下的归纳：受托人对受益人负有谨慎义务，在管理信托的过程中，受托人应当像一个普通谨慎人处理自己的财产一样履行注意义务并行使技能；并且，如某个受托人自称拥有超过普通谨慎人的更高技能，则其有义务履行其声称的更高技能。“谨慎人标准”的确立，使得受托人有了更广泛的投资种类的选择。

进入20世纪下半叶，现代投资组合理论（Portfolio Theory）兴起。这一理论认为，一个谨慎的投资人应全面考虑投资面临的潜在风险，包括系统风险和具体风险，通过风险细分来平衡风险和收益的关系。多样化的投资组合反映了市场的总体情况，是谋求在不相关的多个市场内进行资产分配，通过分散投资来减少和回避市场的不确定性所带来的风险，稀释任何一个投资的不稳定性，把具体风险控制在相当低的水平，进而能获得更高的回报。[①]

投资组合理论对受托人谨慎义务标准也产生影响。美国许多州开始采纳“谨慎投资人规则”（Prudent Investor Rule）作为判断信托机构投资谨慎与否的标准。对这一规则，《信托法重述（三）》作出了如下的归纳：受托人对受益人有义务像谨慎投资人那样依照信托的目的、条款、分配要求及其他条件投资和管理信托基金。这一规则给予了受托人在投资方面更大的自由裁量权。

三、案例资料

实践中，信托机构在运用、管理或处分信托财产时是否履行了谨慎义务，比较难于判断。尤其在信托机构利用信托财产从事投资活动时，由于投资活动本身充满风险，要判断信托机构作出投资决策是否谨慎，并非易事。下面的 First Alabama Bank of Montgomery, N.A. v. Martin 案即涉及对信托机构的投资是否谨慎的判断。

在该案中，银行作为信托的受托人，将信托财产投资于两个共同信托基金、一个债券基金以及一个股权基金。银行的投资后来遭受重大损失，导致信托的受益人纷纷起诉银行，要求法院宣告银行的投资活动是不谨慎的，银行应承担赔偿责任。

对于银行所从事的投资活动是否谨慎，原被告都举出了诸多专家证人的证言。双方专家证人的证言针锋相对，从专业的角度予以论证，得出了完全不同的结论。

法院最终依据“谨慎人规则”（Prudent Man Rule）对银行的投资活动进行判断。“谨慎人规则”是由马萨诸塞州最高法院于 1830 年在 Harvard College v. Amory 案中创立的。依据该规则，对受托人投资方面的所有要求集中于一点，就是受托人应忠诚且依合理的判断行事。受托人应该考察一个谨慎、慎重、聪明的人是如何管理他自己的事务的，与是否投机无关，而要考虑资金的长远安排，在考虑可能的收入的同时也要考虑投资本金的安全性。运用这一规则，结合该案的证据，法院最终认定银行的投资是不谨慎的。

First Alabama Bank of Montgomery, N.A. v. Martin

425 So.2d 415, cert. denied, 461 U.S. 938 (1983)

TORBERT, Chief Justice.

This is a class action. The plaintiffs are beneficiaries of approximately 1 250 individual trusts, of which the bank is trustee. As trustee of these individual trusts, the bank invested certain assets comprising the principal of those trusts in participating units of two common

---

① 唐建辉. 美国信托法之受托人投资标准初探. 上海金融，2006（4）.

trust funds, a bond fund and an equity fund.

After First Alabama purchased and sold certain units and made certain investments that resulted in substantial losses to those funds, the plaintiffs sought a declaration as to the duty of the bank and its liability to account, a declaration that certain investments were imprudent, and affirmative relief requiring the bank to restore to the common trust funds the losses sustained because of the bank's allegedly improper investments.

...

I. Evidence as to Imprudence of Investments in the Equity Fund.

In regard to the equity fund, the court found that the purchase of seventeen of the twenty-four designated equity fund securities had been imprudent. As to these seventeen securities, the court found it unnecessary to decide whether their sale was imprudent but did conclude that the sale of five of the remaining seven securities had been imprudent.

Evidence was introduced showing that in 1973 the board of directors of First Alabama reduced to writing what it considered to be minimum standards of safety. Al Byrne, the vice president and senior trust officer of the bank admitted, however, that these standards were followed prior to 1973 as unwritten guidelines and were generally so followed at the time in which the sales and purchases in question were made. These standards were: (1) A rating of B+ or better by the Standard and Poor ratings (S & P) (B+ being an average rating and B being a speculative rating); (2) a minimum of 1 500 000 shares of stock in the hands of the public; and (3) annual sales of at least $100 million. Byrne testified that the bank generally invested in companies with at least ten years' experience in business and a record of increased earnings. He stated that the companies would generally be rated by one of the rating services. First Alabama claimed that the bank's minimum standards were primarily designed for individual trusts, rather than common trust funds, yet Byrne stated that when purchases were made for the two common funds, bank policy required that those minimum standards adopted by the bank be followed. Evidence was also presented showing that deviations were permitted from these standards adopted by the board of directors with the approval of the trust investment committee so as to accomplish its goals.

The plaintiffs offered evidence that these standards had not been followed. For example, Associated Coca-Cola, Cox Broadcasting, Rust Craft Greeting Cards and Sealed Power were rated B+ but failed to meet the Bank's requirement of one hundred million dollars in annual sales. In addition, the following stocks failed to meet the minimum requirement of a B+ rating: American Garden Products; Ames Department Stores; Beverage Canners; CNA Financial;

Elixir Industries; First Mortgage Investors; Hav-a-Tampa; Kinney Services; Loomis Corp.; Mortgage Associates; Transamerica Corp.; Universal Oil Products; and Wynn Oil Co.

…

II. Evidence as to Imprudence of Purchases in the Bond Fund.

Substantial questions arose in regard to the bond fund concerning the purchase of securities of six real estate investment trusts (REIT's). REIT's are entities primarily engaged in mortgage lending on security of real estate, or in a combination of lending with the ownership and commercial development of real estate. One witness called REIT's "the mutual funds of real estate." In September 1971, First Alabama *422 purchased the unsecured debentures of six REIT's for $2 608 443.00, which comprised 23.2 percent of the principal of the bond fund. First Alabama suffered a 47.03+% loss on these bonds when they were sold for $1 381 645.00, for a total loss of $1 226 798.00.

Questions were raised as to whether REIT's are safe trust investments. Kenneth Campbell, an expert witness for First Alabama, testified that the purchases of the REIT's were prudent investments. Yet he had called REIT's "shaky legal undertakings" in his book, New Opportunities in Real Estate Trusts 29 (1978)….

III. Special Defenses.

…

The principal issues to be determined on the merits of this case are whether the trial court erred (1) in finding that the bank acted imprudently in buying or selling the securities, and finding First Alabama to have breached its trust, (2) in assessing interest as a surcharge for imprudent investments, and (3) in ordering a distribution of money damages to the members of the class without identification of the recipients or calculation of their exact damages.

[14] The standard to be followed in determining whether a trustee has breached his duty to the trust was stated in Birmingham Trust National Bank v. Henley, 371 So.2d 883 (Ala.1979):

"The general definition of a trustee's investment duties was first stated by the Supreme Court of Massachusetts in Harvard College v. Amory, 9 Pick. 446, 461, 26 Mass. 446, 461 (1830):

> 'All that can be required of a trustee to invest, is, that he shall conduct himself faithfully and exercise a sound discretion. He is to observe how men of prudence, discretion and intelligence manage their own affairs, not in regard to speculation, but in regard to the

permanent disposition of their funds, considering the probable income, as well as the probable safety of the capital to be invested.'"

"The Restatement of the Law of Trusts 2d, § 227 (1959), states the rule in the following language:

'In making investments of trust funds the trustee is under a duty to the beneficiary
'(a) in the absence of provisions in the terms of the trust or of a statute otherwise providing, to make such investments and only such investments as a prudent man would make of his own property having in view the preservation of the estate and the amount and regularity of the income to be derived....'"

"BTNB is liable to the Trust in the Birmingham Realty matter only if it breached some duty to the Trust in refusing to make this investment at the time the decision was made. Was it an investment which a prudent man, managing his own affairs, would have made, based upon information then available? Liability cannot be based on the fact it subsequently developed that the investment would have been a good one. This is but the converse of the rule that a trustee is not liable if he makes an investment in a security which subsequently depreciates in value. III Scott on Trusts, § 204, supra, expresses the rule as follows:

'The failure to make a profit which does not result from a breach of trust does not subject the trustee to liability. Thus if by the terms of the trust he is permitted but is not directed to invest in certain securities, he is not liable for failure to make the investment, although the securities subsequently appreciate in value....' "

"The rule has also been summarized by Headley, Trust Investments, [97] Trusts & Estates 739 (1952), as follows:

'The first and all inclusive requirement of the law is that a trustee shall act with complete and undivided loyalty to his trust. Second is that a trustee shall act prudently in the selection and management of investments. The elements of prudence are:
'(1) Care-a trustee must gather and weigh the facts and base his decisions on them rather than on rumor or guesswork;

'(2) Skill-a trustee must exercise the skill of the average person as a minimum; and if he has more than average skill he must exercise such skill as he has;

*427 '(3) Caution-a trustee must not take chances which will imperil the accomplishment of the purposes of the trust.

'... There must be balance between security of principal and amount and regularity of income; and the governing motive of the trustee must be sound investment for a long period and not speculation for a profit....'"

"With specific reference to a trustee's investing in common stocks, this author says:

'... They represent no promise to return a dollar amount to the investor; their dividends are dependent on earnings and the action of a board of directors; they have always afforded an attractive vehicle for speculation. Nevertheless some of them have demonstrated, over a long period of years, the qualities required for sound permanent investments. Intrinsic values have been maintained and dividends have been adequate and regular. The principal has been reasonably safe for a number of reasons: competent management, sound financing, position in an essential industry, a successful record and an adequate market....' "

371 So.2d at 894-96.

Tested by this standard, we cannot say that the trial court committed reversible error in finding that the defendant did not fulfill its duty of caution, to preserve the trust corpus above all else, while striving for a regularity of income.

As to the imprudence of the equity fund, First Alabama contends that since Alabama is a "legal list" state, and since the beneficiaries had given their permission for the bank to invest in items not on the legal list, then the beneficiaries have no complaint for investments that have gone awry. This argument is without merit. As a trustee, First Alabama has a duty to preserve the trust property and make it productive. III Scott on Trusts § 227 (3rd ed. 1967).

First Alabama also contends that the only reason for holding it liable for the losses on the purchase and/or sale of the securities was that the ratings were below B+ on the S & P chart, and that the only reason for holding it liable for the losses on the REIT's was that there was no Moody's or similar rating. First Alabama asserts that to hold it liable here on such evidence would impose a duty upon trustees that would make them absolute insurers against a drop in market price. This, however, is not the case. First Alabama cannot be held liable for its failure to meet its own standards. This is only one factor in the decision. The evidence in this case supports the decision of the trial court that First Alabama failed to fulfill its primary responsibility which was to provide for the safety of the trust's principal. The secondary responsibility was to insure an adequate return.

The difference between speculation and investment is well described by Dr. Headley in Headley, Trust Investments, 97 Trusts & Estates 739 (1952), quoted above in the quotation from Birmingham Trust National Bank v. Henley, 371 So.2d at 895. As Dr. Headley states, one who buys common stocks with the idea of selling them on the market for higher prices is speculating. One who is making a prudent investment examines the stocks' intrinsic values and purchases them for a long-term investment. Walter McConnell, testifying for the defendant, stated that one approach adopted by trust managers is to pick established stocks and not worry about subsequent turns in the market price. It is obvious that neither Headley's standards, nor those mentioned by McConnell, were consistently used by First Alabama.

Dr. Robert Johnston, an expert witness for the plaintiffs, also testified as to how a trustee should conduct his investments. Dr. Johnston stated that, in his opinion, trustees should invest defensively and protect the principal. He testified that most of the seventeen stocks later found to be imprudent investments would fail to meet his tests. While Walter McConnell, an expert witness for the bank, stated that he believed the purchases to be prudent, he could not say that he, as an investment adviser for a number of trust companies, had ever *428 recommended the purchase of any of the twenty-four stocks at issue.

Finally, the testimony of Eldon Davis, who made the investments at issue, further strengthens the holding of the trial court. As stated above, Mr. Davis testified that he did not look at prospectuses, that he saw little difference between a stock rated B+, or median, and one rated B, or speculative, that he did not think the rating services understood their business, and that he tried to buy undervalued stocks instead of the higher priced, more established ones. All of this evidence, taken together, supports the holding of the trial court that First Alabama was imprudent with regard to purchases made for the equity fund.

[15] We also find no error in the trial court's holding that the sale of the five stocks was imprudent. Even Eldon Davis testified in his deposition that he was against the sale of these stocks and had recommended that they be held. Mr. McConnell, testifying for First Alabama, stated that during the recovery period after the recession the five stocks all had higher recovery rates than the S & P 500. It seems reasonable to state that had these stocks not been sold at the

bottom of the market, there would have been no loss. It is true that a trustee will not be held liable under ordinary circumstances for losses due to unforeseen depression or recession of the stock market. Yet, where the course of dealing of the trustee is such that it causes the loss, a trustee will be liable. First Nat. Bank of Birmingham v. Basham, 238 Ala. 500, 191 So. 873 (1939). Here, First Alabama sold these stocks at or near their lowest price levels, against the advice of its own trust officer, and at the time the country was just beginning to recover from the worst recession since the 1930's. We cannot hold as a matter of law that the trial court erred or was plainly and palpably wrong in its conclusion that a reasonable and prudent man would have held these stocks. We therefore affirm the trial court's decision that the sale of the five stocks was imprudent.

It does appear clear from the evidence before the trial court that the investment in six REIT's for the common bond fund was imprudent. The six REIT's were all three years old or less, they were not listed among the top REIT's in the country, and they were among the weakest of the nation's REIT's. They did not meet the standards of Al Byrne, Robert Johnston, and Kenneth Campbell, all experts in the case. Thus, we hold that the trial court committed no error in holding against First Alabama as to the purchase of the six REIT's.

...

After careful consideration of the many issues presented on appeal, this Court has determined that the trial court did not err in finding for the plaintiffs. We reaffirm the "prudent man rule," which states that a trustee must only exercise sound discretion, conduct himself faithfully, and manage funds entrusted to him as men of prudence, discretion, and intelligence would manage their own affairs, having due regard for the safety of the corpus and probable income. Harvard College v. Armory, 26 Mass. (9 Pick.) 446 (1830). See also, Birmingham Trust National Bank v. Henley, 371 So.2d 883 (Ala.1979). We conclude that the trial court applied the "prudent man rule." Based upon the foregoing principles and the ore tenus rule, the findings of the trial court are due to be affirmed.

AFFIRMED.

JONES, SHORES, EMBRY, BEATTY and ADAMS, JJ., concur.

FAULKNER, J., recused.

第四节 信托业的监管

一、中国对信托业的监管

信托业是与银行业、证券业、保险业并列的现代金融业四大支柱之一。在中国，针对银行业、证券业和保险业的监管，分别成立了中国银监会、中国证监会和中国保监会。对于信托业，中国并未单独成立一个专门的监管机构，而是将其划归中国银监会进行监管。中国《信托公司管理办法》规定，中国银监会对信托公司及其业务活动实施监督管理。

作为信托业的监管部门，中国银监会享有广泛的监管权力。一方面，欲从事信托业务经营，必须向中国银监会申请颁发金融许可证，并且信托公司的设立、重大变更以及终止解散等均需得到中国银监会的批准。另一方面，信托公司开展信托业务，受到中国银监会的严格监管。信托公司的经营活动，要符合中国银监会不时发布的相关监管规则的要求。中国银监会可以定期或者不定期对信托公司的经营活动进行检查，若发现信托公司违反审慎经营规则的，中国银监会有权责令限期改正，乃至采取暂停业务、限制股东权利等监管措施；情况严重的，中国银监会可责令停业整顿或者吊销其金融许可证甚至直接撤销该信托公司。

除中国银监会之外，信托行业自律组织——中国信托业协会在信托业监管方面也发挥着重要作用。根据《信托公司管理办法》的规定，信托公司可自愿选择加入中国信托业协会；一旦加入，则受到协会章程和规则的约束。

根据《中国信托业协会章程》（2010 年 11 月 18 日通过）的规定，中国信托业协会主要履行的职责在于，制定同业公约和自律制度并积极组织实施，协助制定营业性信托机构的业务经营规则，依法维护会员的合法权益，就有关政策法规和涉及营业性信托机构共同利益的问题向业务主管单位及其他监管部门及时反映并提出建议和要求，以及开展业务交流、收集行业信息、组织人员培训等。

中国信托业协会制定的诸多行业自律规则，如《信托公司证券投资信托业务自律公约》、《关于进一步规范和促进银信合作业务的自律公约》，对维护中国信托行业秩序、促进信托行业发展起着重要作用。作为行业自律组织，中国信托业协会发布的规则对会员单位形成一定的约束力，如会员单位有违反的，将会承担一定的不利后果。[①]

---

① 例如，中国信托业协会于 2009 年颁布的《信托公司证券投资信托业务自律公约》第 18 条规定：“……对于会员单位违反公约的行为，协会可采取内部通报、警示通知、限期整改、同业制裁等措施，协会采取的制裁措施将抄报银监会，作为监管评级的参考。对于涉嫌违规经营或触范法律法规的，协会可向监管部门或其他相关部门反映情况。”

二、美国对信托业的监管

在美国，由于实行信托业与银行业混业经营，信托业几乎是置于银行业内予以监管的。诸多负责银行监管的部门同时也对信托进行监管，信托业的监管具备诸多银行业监管的特色，尤其是双重多头监管的特点。

美国联邦和州两级监管机构，均有对信托的监管权限。并且，并非只有一家监管机构对信托实施监管，而是同时存在多个信托监管部门。在联邦层面，主要有货币监理署、储蓄机构管理局（现已并入货币监理署）、联邦储备系统及联邦存款保险公司（FDIC）等对信托机构进行监管；各州的监管机构是相关的金融监管部门。

对于国民银行、州立银行以及信托公司开展信托业务，各级监管机构的审批权力和遵循的程序也有所不同。国民银行要从事信托业务，需经过货币监理署批准。联储体系会员中的州立银行，需满足州法律有关从事信托业务的条件，并在得到州政府和联储董事会的许可后，才能获得信托权。非联储会员的州立银行或信托公司，只需得到州政府行政管理机构的许可，就可经营信托业务。如果信托机构在联邦存款保险公司进行了投保（大多数信托机构都在 FDIC 投了保），则还受到联邦存款保险公司的监管。

不同的信托机构需要遵守不同的监管机构发布的监管法规、规则及指南等。尽管如此，各监管部门之间的监管标准还是具有很大的相似性。如国民银行信托部门开展信托业务时，必须遵守货币监理署制定的信托法规，其中涉及信托业务的授权、审批，信托业务政策和程序，信托账户的审核，信托业务会计、审计、交易、资产保管及报酬、清算等内容，这些经营规则也往往被视作美国金融机构开展信托业务的行业标准。

监管部门对信托机构的监管，主要为实现两个目的：为信托客户提供保护以及确保信托机构的安全与稳健。为此，所有的信托机构都要接受监管部门定期和事先不通知的检查，检查的范围主要是看信托机构的业务经营和管理是否符合有关立法、条例等的规定。

除了特定的监管部门对信托机构实施监管以外，信托机构在从事特定的信托业务之时，还要受到其他相关法律以及监管部门的约束。例如，信托机构从事证券投资信托活动之时，要受到证券交易委员会的监管，必须遵守《1934 年证券交易法》、《1940 年投资顾问法》等相关证券类法规。

《1999 年金融服务现代化法》通过后，美国金融业开始进入全面混业经营的阶段。尽管如此，除了上层的银行控股公司由美联储监管外，下层的经营信托业务的附属机构依然受到信托业监管部门的分业监管。

三、案例资料

在美国，监管部门享有对信托机构广泛的监管权力。如果发现信托机构在经营过程中严重违反监管法规，监管部门甚至可以撤销已经授予的信托权力。下面的 Central National Bank of Mattoon v. U.S. Dept. of Treasury 案即涉及一家经营信托业务的国民银行因严重违规而被撤销信托权力的争议。

在该案中，国民银行的监管部门货币监理署（OCC）在发现原告的信托业务部门存在多项违法行为之后，决定撤销原告的信托权力。经过行政法官的审理，原告的违规经营得到认定，但是行政法官判定向原告颁布禁止令就足够了。OCC 认为禁止令的处罚过轻，依然撤销了原告的信托权力。原告认为，OCC 的处罚与其违规行为不相称，处罚过重，起诉要求法院撤销 OCC 的处罚决定。

对于原告的请求，法院表明了其基本的态度：只有在 OCC 违反了法律或监管规则，或者认定事实的实质性证据不足，或武断地（不合理地）作出处罚决定之时，法院才会撤销 OCC 的处罚决定。

法院认为，尽管撤销原告经营信托的权力确实会给其造成损害，但这是 OCC 裁量权行使的范围。即便承认 OCC 的处罚过于严厉（当然，法院并不这样认为），法院撤销 OCC 的处罚命令也没有正当理由。法院对监管部门的决定进行审查的一个基本姿态是，实行恭顺性（deferential）审查。恭顺到何种程度，视案件的具体性质而定。案件的性质越开放（由此越具有评判性），合理地作出决定就越需要专业知识，而这种专业知识可能为监管部门所有而肯定不为法院所有，那么司法介入的力度就应当越轻。在本案中，选择何种处罚措施是一种评判性的行为——一种应获得司法尊重的行政自由裁量权的行使，其依赖于银行业的特性，对此联邦司法机构并非作出评判的直接相关方。此外，尽管行政法官判定颁布禁止令便足够，但相关的裁量权属 OCC 所有，而非 OCC 聘请的行政法官，行政法官作出的结论对 OCC 而言仅仅只是一种建议。最终，法院驳回了原告的诉讼请求。

通过本案的判决可见，在美国，监管部门对信托机构的监管享有广泛的自由裁量权，其作出的监管决定通常都会受到法院的尊重，法院一般不会进行干预。

Central National Bank of Mattoon v. U.S. Dept. of Treasury

912 F.2d 897, 904-05 (7th Cir.1990)

POSNER, Circuit Judge.

Central National Bank is one of two national banks in Mattoon, a town of 20 000 in downstate Illinois. After an investigation of the bank's trust department, the Comptroller of the Currency, who regulates national banks, issued in 1987 a notice of intent to revoke the bank's permission to provide trust services to its customers. The notice was issued pursuant to 12 U.S.C. § 92a (k), which authorizes the Comptroller, upon notice and hearing, to revoke trust powers that the bank has "unlawfully or unsoundly exercised." After a hearing before an administrative law judge, the judge found that the bank had committed many violations of the Comptroller's regulations and engaged in many imprudent practices, but decided that it would be enough to order the bank to cease and desist. On review of the administrative law judge's order the Comptroller upheld the judge's findings, but considering the remedy imposed too weak revoked the bank's trust powers. The bank asks us to set aside the Comptroller's order. 12 U.S.C. § 1818(h)(2). We can do that only if the Comptroller has violated a statute or regulation, made findings of fact unsupported by substantial evidence, or exercised his judgment in an arbitrary, which is to say unreasonable, fashion. Id.; 5 U.S.C. §§ 706(2)(A), (E); Larimore v. Conover, 775 F.2d 890, 895-96 (7th Cir. 1985), reversed en banc on other grounds, 789 F.2d 1244 (7th Cir. 1986). These precepts apply to choice of remedy, id.; del Junco v. Conover, 682 F.2d 1338, 1340 (9th Cir. 1982); First National Bank v. Comptroller of Currency, 697 F.2d 674, 680 (5th Cir. 1983)—in spades, as we shall see.

…

We turn to the merits of the petition for review. The bank does not deny that it has engaged in improper practices in its trust department, but pleads a variety of mitigating circumstances. The improper practices not only are numerous but also reach back many years and were only partly corrected in previous remedial proceedings that resulted in the entry and subsequent dissolution of a cease and desist order in the early 1980s. The improprieties range in gravity from the technical (failure to comply with certain reporting requirements) through the mild (minor violations of the terms of trust instruments) to the grave (deliberately overvaluing securities in one of the bank's common trust funds, the consequence being to overcharge customers for units of the fund). The bank has very little to say in rebuttal to these charges, and nothing worth discussing. It trains all its guns on the alleged impropriety that precipitated the Comptroller's decision to order the bank to shut down its trust department—the purchase in 1985 of 20 000 shares of Eagle Bancorporation for a common trust fund administered by the bank's trust department.

The purchase price of $ 220 000 constituted more than 20 percent of the assets of the common trust fund. To finance the purchase, Malcolm O'Neill, the bank's trust officer, sold blue-chip stocks and bonds held in the common trust fund. Eagle was a modest (net worth of $ 14 million), unlisted company owning small, unlisted banks and seeking to acquire more of these; its stock was narrowly held and thinly traded. The president and (indirectly) principal stockholder of the Central National Bank of Mattoon, James Singer, owned stock in Eagle, as did another director of the bank and O'Neill himself. In addition, as O'Neill well knew, Eagle was trying to acquire another bank of which Singer was a major owner.

…

We have wandered a bit afield, for the Comptroller, perhaps prudently, does not emphasize the effect of the Eagle purchase in reducing the diversification of the common trust fund. So far as the trust services of the Central National Bank of Mattoon, Illinois, are concerned, the propriety of the bank's practices is determined by the Illinois law of trusts, 12 C.F.R. § 9.11(a); and while the duty of a fiduciary to diversify his investment portfolio is generally recognized, Restatement (Second) of Trusts, § 228 (1959); Hamilton v. Nielsen, 678 F.2d 709, 712 (7th Cir. 1982), leading us to hazard a guess in Hamilton that the duty was a part of the Illinois prudent man rule, we acknowledged that there were no Illinois cases on point. Id. The Illinois Appellate Court has misread Hamilton as holding that "Illinois law does not impose a duty on a trustee to diversify the trust assets." McCormick v. McCormick, 180 Ill. App. 3d 184, 198, 536 N.E.2d 419, 428, 129 Ill. Dec. 579 (1988). This leaves the status of the duty to diversify in Illinois law in a fog that neither the statute itself ("in... investing... property for any trust... the trustee shall exercise the 903 judgment and care under the circumstances then prevailing which men of prudence... exercise in the management of their own affairs," Ill. Rev. Stat. ch. 17, para. 1675(1)) nor the cryptic discussion of diversification in In re Estate of Pirie, 141 Ill. App. 3d 750, 755, 492 N.E.2d 884, 887, 97 Ill. Dec. 225 (1986), can penetrate. What is clear, though, is that the bank's failure to take reasonable steps to determine whether $ 11 was a fair estimate of the value of Eagle stock, and the fact that the bank was engaged in self-dealing in buying for the trust fund stock in a company in which the bank's insiders had a substantial stake, made the purchase imprudent, and therefore improper, under Illinois law and hence under federal law as well. Kinney v. Lindgren, 373 Ill. 415, 26 N.E.2d 471 (1940); Herget National Bank v. Lampitt, 133 Ill. App. 3d 418, 478 N.E.2d 904, 88 Ill. Dec. 413 (1985). Nor is this disputed by the bank; its argument is that the remedy is disproportionate to the wrong.

Yet the wrong was substantial. And while the remedy is severe, we disagree that the Comptroller has decreed the bank's demise. National banks are not trust companies, and only a minority of them (though a large one—40 percent) have trust departments. But while Central National Bank is wrong to argue that the revocation of its trust powers must endanger its survival, the Comptroller is equally wrong to argue that because the department is shown on the books of the bank as losing money the bank will be better off by the revocation. Unless the trust department is being run for the enrichment of the bank's officers—which the Comptroller does not argue—we can be confident that if the department is really conferring a net detriment on the bank it will be closed down voluntarily. Well, reasonably confident, for it is possible that the department is a loser but that revocation would be such a blow to public confidence in the bank (word of the Comptroller's order, and of the findings underlying it, would spread quickly in a town of 20 000 once the curtain of secrecy was lifted, as it now has been) that the losses in the department are worth bearing. More likely the trust department is a loss leader whose services generate other business for the bank that is profitable enough to more than cover the losses in the trust department. (We note in this connection that 80 percent of the bank's trust customers are also depositors, that they hold 30 percent of the total demand deposits in the bank, and that 10 to 20 percent of the bank's loans are to them.) In either event the trust department's losses would be illusory in an economic sense, being completely offset by the profits on other banking business that the operations of the trust department enable.

So probably the bank will be hurt by the revocation. Part of the hurt, however, will come not from the abolition of the trust department as such—for there should be other ways even in Mattoon to attract banking business besides offering cut-rate trust services (we are not even told whether the other national bank in the town has a trust department)—but from the negative inference concerning the quality of the bank's management that the public may draw from the Comptroller's order. But as should be evident from our earlier discussion of the bank's desire to conceal the nature and basis of the Comptroller's action from that same public, we consider this a private harm rather than a social one. The harm to the bank is offset—quite possibly more than offset—by benefits to others, namely consumers who will use the information to make an informed judgment on whether to take their banking business across the street to the other national bank in Mattoon, or to some other bank. The banking public of Mattoon is entitled to information concerning the prudence and probity of the bankers with whom it deals. Perhaps it will conclude that the mismanagement of the trust department bespeaks only an inability to attain the high fiduciary standards required of trust officers and not an inability to manage the other components of banking service. Then the damage to Central National Bank will be slight. The other possibility, of course, is that the bank's customers, or at least many of them, will decide to take their banking business elsewhere. Either way, the impact 904 of the Comptroller's order on the bank will be proportional to the gravity of the bank's misconduct as evaluated by the people of Mattoon in light of newspaper and other accounts of the Comptroller's, and this court's, action.

Even if the sanction is not so fell as the bank contends, it might still be disproportionate to the gravity of the wrongdoing. While admitting that O'Neill acted imprudently, the bank points out that there is no evidence that Singer or other members of the board of directors knew about the purchase of the Eagle shares until the repurchase agreement had expired. Suspicion, yes; evidence, no. And the Federal Reserve Board, which has final authority to determine whether O'Neill should be removed from his office or indeed excluded from banking, 12 U.S.C. § 1818(e)(4), has decided in an unpublished decision that he should not be removed or excluded, because he received no personal gain and demonstrated no personal dishonesty and because his action did not harm the bank, 12 U.S.C. § 1818(e)(1)(B)—directly. The harm came through the Comptroller's response to O'Neill's action, and this the Board, giving the statute a surprisingly narrow interpretation, thought too indirect. Meanwhile O'Neill has resigned from the bank, which argues that the problem has thus been solved (no other officers or employees having been implicated in O'Neill's actions) and that revocation of the bank's trust powers is overkill. It adds that no one has lost money because of the purchase of the Eagle shares, though it would be more accurate to say that no one knows whether in the end this imprudent purchase will yield a return equal to that of the securities that the bank sold to finance it. (A company's prospects are impounded in the market price of its shares, but we do not know whether shares in Eagle have a market price.) Crying unfair surprise, the bank points out that the Comptroller, perhaps in oblique response to the savings and loan scandal, has toughened his stance on the appropriate sanctions for imprudent practices. The bank also lays great weight on the refusal of the administrative law judge to order revocation, adding that it is unfair for the "prosecutor," as it describes the Comptroller, to impose on his own initiative the very punishment that the (administrative law) "judge" decided would be too severe.

The suggestion that revocation of the bank's trust powers was too drastic a sanction for an isolated lapse by one man whom the bank no longer employs ignores the fact that the purchase of the Eagle stock was the culmination of what the Comptroller, with much support in the evidence, describes as the bank's "escalating disregard" for the requirements of prudent management of trust accounts. The violations go back many years, with periodic improvements invariably being followed by serious backsliding. The bank has found it impossible to institutionalize prudence in its trust department, and one of its most egregious violations, the Eagle incident, was also the most recent. But even if we were inclined to agree that the Comptroller was being excessively severe (we are not so inclined), we would not be justified in setting aside his order. The general posture of a court reviewing agency decisions is deferential; how deferential depends among other things on the nature of the issue. The more open-ended it is, and hence judgmental, and the more a sound exercise of judgment requires specialized knowledge possibly possessed by the agency but certainly not by the court, the lighter the judicial hand. Here, as in general (for the Sentencing Guidelines do not apply here!), the choice of sanctions is judgmental—an exercise of administrative discretion entitled to judicial respect, American Power & Light Co. v. SEC, 329 U.S. 90, 112-18, (1946); Butz v. Glover Livestock Commission Co., 411 U.S. 182, 188, (1973); Carlson v. United States, 879 F.2d 261, 263 (7th Cir. 1989); Communication Workers of America v. NLRB, 784 F.2d 847, 852 (7th Cir. 1986); Panhandle Cooperative Ass'n v. EPA, 771 F.2d 1149, 1152 (8th Cir. 1985)—and depends on particulars of the banking industry to which the generalist federal judiciary is not privy. The relevant discretion, moreover, 905 is that of the Comptroller, not of the administrative law judges whom he employs to preside at hearings and make findings and conclusions that, so far as the appropriate remedy is concerned, are merely recommendations. Blackfoot Livestock Commission Co. v. Department of Agriculture, 810 F.2d 916, 922 (9th Cir. 1987); River Forest Pharmacy, Inc. v. Drug Enforcement Administration, 501 F.2d 1202, 1206 (7th Cir. 1974) (per curiam); Lorain Journal Co. v. FCC, 122 U.S. App. D.C. 127, 351 F.2d 824, 828 (D.C. Cir. 1965).

As for the supposed unfairness of casting the Comptroller in the role of a judge in his own cause, this disregards not only the precedent of the Federal Trade Commission, which both issues the complaint and on appeal from the administrative law judge decides whether the complaint has been sustained and a remedial order should issue, but subtle differences between the Comptroller's and Trade Commission's functions which should dissipate any lingering doubts concerning the propriety of combining prosecutorial and adjudicative functions in the Comptroller's person (if not the Commission's). The Commission—say, in policing under section 5 of the Federal Trade Commission Act the truth of advertising representations—does not assume responsibility for the welfare of the advertising industry. As a result it has a natural tendency to judge its success by the number of remedial orders that it issues, and in this tendency lies the potential bias in favor of upholding the complaint it has issued of which critics of the Commission have long, though so far unavailingly, complained. The Comptroller of the Currency, however, has comprehensive authority over national banks. First National Bank v. Smith, 610 F.2d 1258, 1263-65 (5th Cir. 1980). He charters them; he audits them; he enforces the laws relating to them; in short he "is charged by the national banking laws with the execution of all laws of the United States relating to the organization, operation, regulation and supervision of national banks." 12 C.F.R. § 1.1; see also 12 U.S.C. §§ 26, 93, 93a, 161. Those banks are his wards, and his only wards; if they fail in droves, he will be blamed. It is not in his self-interest, bureaucratic or otherwise, to endanger their solvency by amputating their powers to engage in profitable lines of business. It is in his interest, rather, in deciding whether to modify or uphold or throw out a remedial order against a bank recommended by one of his administrative law judges, to weigh the harm the order is likely to cause the bank against the order's deterrent effect, which will enhance the safety of the banking industry for the future. If the evidence presented to the administrative law judge points toward lenity in the exercise of the Comptroller's remedial powers, we can think of no reason why the Comptroller would be deflected by his initial prosecutorial role in the case from exercising lenity.

…

The petition to set aside the Comptroller's order revoking the bank's trust authority is DENIED.

第五章

证券法律制度

第一节　证券法概述

证券是多种经济权益凭证的统称，是证明持有人有权按券面所载内容取得相应权益的书面证明。证券有广义和狭义之分：广义证券是指以证明或设定权利为目的的一种法律凭证，狭义证券仅指有价证券。

证券法是调整有价证券的发行、交易、清算以及国家在证券监管过程中所发生的各种社会关系的法律规范。证券法律制度所调整的社会关系，既包括发行人、投资人以及证券中介服务机构相互之间所发生的民事关系，又包括国家证券监督管理机构对证券市场主体进行引导、组织、协调和监督过程中所发生的行政管理关系。

一、中国证券法概述

中国没有一部专门的法律对证券进行定义。但是，根据中国《证券法》第 2 条的规定，证券包括股票、公司债券、政府债券、证券投资基金份额以及中国国务院依法认定的其他证券。该条包含着“兜底条款”，但事实上，中国国务院迄今并未依法认定过“其他证券”。因此，在中国，股票、公司债券、政府债券、证券投资基金份额是最典型的证券。

中国的证券法律制度，是伴随着改革开放之后中国证券市场的不断建立和发展而确立和完善的。早在 20 世纪 80 年代，中国国内就已经有股票和国债的流通。20 世纪 90 年代初，上海证券交易所和深圳证券交易所相继成立，这是中国证券市场初步建立的一个重要标志。1992 年，中国证监会成立，这是中国证券市场发展的最重要事件之一，标志着中国证券市场开始逐步纳入全国统一监管框架。在中国证监会的推动下，一系列证券方面的法律、法规和规章制度被制定和发布，中国初步建立了证券市场的法规体系。

1993 年，中国制定了《股票发行与交易管理暂行条例》，对最重要的证券品种——股票的发行和交易作出了规定。1998 年 12 月，中国正式通过了《证券法》并于 1999 年 7 月实施，以法律形式确认了证券市场的地位。

2001 年 12 月，中国加入世界贸易组织，并就证券业的对外开放作出了相关承诺。由此，中国也加快了证券市场对外开放的步伐。对外开放推进了中国证券市场的市场化、国际化进程，促进了市场的成熟和发展壮大。为履行中国“入世”时有关证券市场对外开放的相关承诺，中国也相应修订了国内相关证券法律、法规，同时颁布了大量新的配套的证券法律、法规，从而建立起一套与国际接轨的证券法律体系。

2001 年之后，中国证券市场的发展突飞猛进。尤其是随着国有企业改革的深入，国有和非国有股份公司不断进入证券市场，成为证券市场新的组成部分，中国股票市场得到较快发展，上市公司数量快速增长。面对中国国内证券市场发展的新情况，2005 年 11 月，中国对《证券法》进行了大规模的修订并重新颁布。

修订后的中国《证券法》，是规范中国证券市场秩序和证券发行、交易行为的最重要、最基本的法律。其不仅对证券的发行、交易、上市公司的收购有着完善的规定，还对证券交易所、证券公司、证券登记结算机构、证券服务机构、证券业协会和证券监督管理机构的相关权利、义务和职责进行了全面的规定，并规定了相关的法律责任。以《证券法》为核心，中国又陆续颁布了诸多证券方面的法律、法规、规章以及规范性文件，建立起了健全的证券法律体制。

二、美国证券法概述

美国国会在《1933 年证券法》和《1934 年证券交易法》中对“证券”采取列举的方式进行了非常宽泛的定义。根据《1933 年证券法》第 2（a）（1）条，除非另有规定，“证券”指任何票据、股票、库存股票、证券期货、债券、公司（信用）债券、债务凭证、利润分享协议项下之权益或参与证书、担保信托证书、公司设立前之证书或认购权、可转让股份、投资契约、有表决权之信托证书、证券存托凭证、石油、天然气或其他矿产权之小额未分割权益，与证券、证券存托凭证、一组证券或证券指数有关的任何卖出权、买入权、买卖权、期权或优先权（包括其中或以其价值为基础的任何权益），或全国性证券交易所中与外币有关的任何卖出权、买入权、买卖权、期权或优先权，或被普遍视为“证券”的任何权益和工具，或与上述任何一项相关的权益或参与证书、暂时或临时证书、凭证、担保证书、认购、购买证或认购、购买权。[①]

由于美国制定法对“证券”的定义采用列举法，尽管该定义涵盖的范围广泛，但由于并未对“证券”的内涵进行抽象和概括，因而“为法院提供可预期的指导工作不断地带来麻烦”[②]，因此法院在司法实践中也采用多种标准不断地对“证券”进行重新界定或解释。

早在20世纪初，美国各州就开始制定各自的证券法律、法规，即所谓的“蓝天法”，对证券业务加以规制。各州的单独行动，面临着诸多问题：各州没有足够的人力、物力和财力来执行相关法律，同时也并不能有效打击证券跨州发行和销售的行为。1929年的股市暴跌以及随之而来的“大萧条”，最终促使美国国会通过了《1933年证券法》和《1934年证券交易法》，奠定了美国证券法的基石。

联邦政府的强力介入，促进了美国证券市场的高速发展，也推动着美国证券法律制度的不断完善。目前，美国已经形成由制定法和判例法组成的证券法律体系。其中，制定法既包括联邦的成文法，也包括各州根据其自身特定情况制定的适用于本州的证券法（目前所有的州都制定了不同形式的蓝天法适用于其境内和证券有关的活动），还包括诸如美国证券交易委员会这样的具有准立法权的机构根据证券交易法的授权制定调整美国证券市场及有关中介机构的各类规则。判例法，则为美国各级法院尤其是联邦最高法院通过生效的判决所确立的与证券相关的法律规则。

在美国，比较重要的证券法律均为联邦层面的成文法。例如，根据《1934年证券交易法》第3（a）（47）条，“证券法”指《1933年证券法》、《1934年证券交易法》、《2002年萨班斯—奥克斯利法》、《1935年公共事业控股公司法》（《美国法典》第15编第79a节及其后相关各节）、《1939年信托契约法》（《美国法典》第15编第77（aaa）节及其后相关各节）、《1940年投资公司法》、《1940年投资顾问法》以及《1970年证券投资者保护法》。

当今世界范围内，美国证券法处于领先地位，其立法原则和立法技术为世界上包括中国在内的诸多国家和地区所借鉴。

三、案例资料

一些典型的证券（如股票、债券）我们耳熟能详，而对于一些特殊的交易，该如何判断其是否属于证券法界定的“证券”？在下面的Teamsters v. Daniel案中，美国联邦最

---

① 与《1933年证券法》相比，《1934年证券交易法》对证券的定义有些许差别（例如，《1934年证券交易法》将短期商业票据排除在证券定义之外，而《1933年证券法》则将短期商业票据包括在内），但根据美国联邦最高法院在Tcherepnin v. Knight案中的判决，两法之间的定义应当按照“实质上完全相同”对待，即无论形式上如何，只要实质上与证券的本质相同，就需要按证券对待。See Tcherepnin v. Knight, 389U.S.332, 335 (1967).

② [美] 托马斯·李·哈森. 证券法. 张学安，等，译. 北京：中国政法大学出版社，2003：24.

高法院对养老金计划是否属于证券的问题进行了分析。

该案中，原告 Daniel 的雇主参与了一份养老金计划。根据该计划，雇主为自己所雇用的员工向养老基金出资而雇员无需出资，在员工退休时可以按月领取高额的养老金。但是，该计划的协议规定，只有连续工作满 20 年的雇员退休才有资格享受此收益。原告退休时，向该基金管理人申领退休金，但是遭到拒绝，理由是 Daniel 曾中断了几个月时间的工作。尽管 Daniel 进行了解释和申诉，但该基金还是裁定他没有资格领取养老金。最后，原告要求该基金的受托管理人放弃适用连续工作年限的规则，但是遭到拒绝。原告遂以该养老金计划存在虚假陈述和重大事实遗漏构成证券欺诈且违反了联邦证券法律为由，提起诉讼。

该案的一个主要争议焦点是：该养老金计划，是否构成美国证券法律中定义的“证券”。只有构成“证券”，才能进一步适用证券法去判定被告的行为是否构成证券欺诈。那么，何谓“证券”？美国《1933 年证券法》和《1934 年证券交易法》中对“证券”定义的规定相当宽泛，“证券”几乎无所不包。

在司法实践中，美国法院对于每一种证券都确定了一套与之相对应的概念和原则，从而用以区分“证券”和“非证券”。就该案中的养老金计划而言，因为《1933 年证券法》和《1934 年证券交易法》对证券的定义中，均未明确提到“养老金计划”，因而只能适用“Howey 标准”（Howey Test）来判定是否构成证券定义中的一种——“投资合同”（Investment Contract），进而判定其是否构成证券。事实上，投资合同是美国证券法上关于证券定义应用最广的一类，很多无名证券都被归入投资合同范畴。

“Howey 标准”是美国联邦最高法院在 1946 年 SEC v. W. J. Howey Co. 案中确立的判定“投资合同”的标准。联邦最高法院提出，判断某项特定的经济关系是否构成投资合同，其标准是：该交易或计划是否涉及向一个普通的企业投入资金，期望凭借他人的努力而获得收益。

本案中，初审法院支持 Daniel，认为该养老金计划符合“投资合同”的定义。联邦最高法院考察了“Howey 标准”的相关要件，认为员工参与的这项无需其出资的强制性的养老金计划（noncontributory, compulsory pension plan），并不构成证券类别中的“投资合同”。联邦最高法院的理由是：首先，从“投入资金”（investment of money）的要素来看，在这种养老金计划中，员工所谓的投入从经济实质上来看，是其出卖用以维持生计的劳动力，而非为未来所做的投资；从“期望凭借他人的努力而获得收益”的要素来看，在投资合同中，投资人投入资金，意图通过企业家的努力来实现收益，而在该养老金计划中，尽管养老基金在一定程度上依赖受托管理人的管理获得收益，但这只是养老基金获取收益微不足道的一方面，养老基金获取收益最主要的途径还是雇主的不断出资，这与企业家用别人的钱投资获取收益有本质的不同，况且员工能否获取收益，主要看其是否符合申领养老金的条件，而并不依赖该养老基金本身的投资收益状况。

Teamsters v. Daniel

439 U.S. 551 (1979)

MR. JUSTICE POWELL delivered the opinion of the Court.

This case presents the question whether a noncontributory, compulsory pension plan constitutes a "security" within the meaning of the Securities Act of 1933 and the Securities Exchange Act of 1934 (Securities Acts).

I

In 1954, multiemployer collective bargaining between Local 705 of the International Brotherhood of Teamsters, Chauffeurs, Warehousemen, and Helpers of America and Chicago trucking firms produced a pension plan for employees represented by the Local. The plan was compulsory and noncontributory. Employees had no choice as to participation in the plan, and did not have the option of demanding that the employer's contribution be paid directly to them as a substitute for pension eligibility. The employees paid nothing to the plan themselves.

The collective bargaining agreement initially set employer contributions to the Pension Trust Fund at $2 a week for each man-week of covered employment. The Board of Trustees of the Fund, a body composed of an equal number of employer and union representatives, was given sole authority to set the level of benefits, but had no control over the amount of required employer contributions. Initially, eligible employees received $75 a month in benefits upon retirement. Subsequent collective bargaining agreements called for greater employer contributions, which, in turn, led to higher benefit payments for retirees. At the time respondent brought suit, employers contributed $21.50 per employee man-week and pension payments ranged from $425 to $525 a month, depending on age at retirement. In order to receive a pension, an employee was required to have 20 years of continuous service, including time worked before the start of the plan.

The meaning of "continuous service" is at the center of this dispute. Respondent began working as a truckdriver in the Chicago area in 1950, and joined Local 705 the following year. When the plan first went into effect, respondent automatically received 5 years' credit toward the 20-year service requirement because of his earlier work experience.

He retired in 1973, and applied to the plan's administrator for a pension. The administrator determined that respondent was ineligible because of a break in service between December, 1960, and July, 1961. Respondent appealed the decision to the trustees, who affirmed. Respondent then asked the trustees to waive the continuous service rule as it applied to him. After the trustees refused to waive the rule, respondent brought suit in federal court against the International Union (Teamsters), Local 705 (Local), and Louis Peick, a trustee of the Fund.

Respondent's complaint alleged that the Teamsters, the Local, and Peick misrepresented and omitted to state material facts with respect to the value of a covered employee's interest in the pension plan. Count I of the complaint charged that these misstatements and omissions constituted a fraud in connection with the sale of a security in violation of § 10 (b) of the Securities Exchange Act of 1934, 48 Stat. 891, 15 U.S.C. § 78j(b), and the Securities and Exchange Commission's Rule 10b-5, 17 CFR § 240.10b-5 (1978). Count II charged that the same conduct amounted to a violation of § 17 (a) of the Securities Act of 1933, 48 Stat. 84, as amended, 15 U.S.C. § 77q. Other counts alleged violations of various labor law and common law duties. Respondent sought to proceed on behalf of all prospective beneficiaries of Teamsters pension plans and against all Teamsters pension funds.

The petitioners moved to dismiss the first two counts of the complaint on the ground that respondent had no cause of action under the Securities Acts. The District Court denied the motion. 410 F.Supp. 541 (ND Ill.1976). It held that respondent's interest in the Pension Fund constituted a security within the meaning of § 2 (1) of the Securities Act, 15 U.S.C. § 77b(1), and § 3 (a) (10) of the Securities Exchange Act, 15 U.S.C. § 78c(a) (10), because the plan created an "investment contract" as that term had been interpreted in SEC v. W. J. Howey Co., 328 U. S. 293 (1946). It also determined that there had been "sale" of this interest to respondent within the meaning of § 2 (3) of the Securities Act, as amended, 15 U.S.C. § 77b (3), and § 3 (a) (14) of the Securities Exchange Act, 15 U.S.C. § 77 (a) (14). It believed respondent voluntarily gave value for his interest in the plan, because he had voted on collective bargaining agreements that chose employer contributions to the Fund instead of other wages or benefits.

The order denying the motion to dismiss was certified for appeal pursuant to 28 U.S.C. § 1292 (b), and the Court of Appeals for the Seventh Circuit affirmed. 561 F.2d 1223 (1977). Relying on its perception of the economic realities of pension plans and various actions of

Congress and the SEC with respect to such plans, the court ruled that respondent's interest in the Pension Fund was a "security." According to the court, a "sale" took place either when respondent ratified a collective bargaining agreement embodying the Fund or when he accepted or retained covered employment instead of seeking other work. The court did not believe the subsequent enactment of the Employee Retirement Income Security Act of 1974 (ERISA), 88 Stat. 829, 29 U.S.C. § 1001 et seq., affected the application of the Securities Acts to pension plans, as the requirements and purposes of ERISA were perceived to be different from those of the Securities Acts. We granted certiorari, 434 U.S. 1061 (1978), and now reverse.

II

"The starting point in every case involving construction of a statute is the language itself." Blue Chip Stamps v. Manor Drug Stores, 421 U. S. 723, 421 U. S. 756 (1975) (POWELL, J., concurring); see Ernst Ernst v. Hochfelder, 425 U. S. 185, 425 U. S. 197, 425 U. S. 199, and n.19 (1976). In spite of the substantial use of employee pension plans at the time they were enacted, neither § 2 (1) of the Securities Act nor § 3 (a) (10) of the Securities Exchange Act, which define the term "security" in considerable detail and with numerous examples, refers to pension plans of any type. Acknowledging this omission in the statutes, respondent contends that an employee's interest in a pension plan is an "investment contract," an instrument which is included in the statutory definitions of a security.

To determine whether a particular financial relationship constitutes an investment contract, "[t] he test is whether the scheme involves an investment of money in a common enterprise with profits to come solely from the efforts of others." Howey, 328 U.S. at 328 U. S. 301. This test is to be applied in light of "the substance—the economic realities of the transaction—rather than the names that may have been employed by the parties." United Housing Foundation, Inc. v. Forman. 421 U. S. 837, 421 U. S. 851-852 (1975). Accord, Tcherepnin v. Knight, 389 U. S. 332, 389 U. S. 336 (1967); Howey, supra, at 328 U. S. 298. Cf. 359 U. S. Variable Annuity Life Ins. Co., 359 U. S. 65, 359 U. S. 80 (1959) (BRENNAN, J., concurring) ("[O]ne must apply a test in terms of the purposes of the Federal Acts..."). Looking separately at each element of the Howey test, it is apparent that an employee's participation in a noncontributory, compulsory pension plan such as the Teamsters' does not comport with the commonly held understanding of an investment contract.

A. Investment of Money

An employee who participates in a noncontributory, compulsory pension plan, by definition, makes no payment into the pension fund. He only accepts employment, one of the conditions of which is eligibility for a possible benefit on retirement. Respondent contends, however, that he has "invested" in the Pension Fund by permitting part of his compensation from his employer to take the form of a deferred pension benefit. By allowing his employer to pay money into the Fund, and by contributing his labor to his employer in return for these payments, respondent asserts he has made the kind of investment which the Securities Acts were intended to regulate.

In order to determine whether respondent invested in the Fund by accepting and remaining in covered employment, it is necessary to look at the entire transaction through which he obtained a chance to receive pension benefits. In every decision of this Court recognizing the presence of a "security" under the Securities Acts, the person found to have been an investor chose to give up a specific consideration in return for a separable financial interest with the characteristics of a security. See Tcherepnin, supra, (money paid for bank capital stock); SEC v. United Benefit Life Ins. Co., 387 U. S. 202 (1967) (portion of premium paid for variable component of mixed variable—and fixed-annuity contract); Variable Annuity life Ins. Co., supra, (premium paid for variable-annuity contract); Howey, supra, (money paid for purchase, maintenance, and harvesting of orange grove); SEC v. C. M. Joiner Leasing Corp., 320 U. S. 344 (1943) (money paid for land and oil exploration). Even in those cases where the interest acquired had intermingled security and nonsecurity aspects, the interest obtained had "to a very substantial degree elements of investment contracts...." Variable Annuity Life Ins. Co., supra at 359 U. S. 91 (BRENNAN, J., concurring). In every case, the purchaser gave up some tangible and definable consideration in return for an interest that had substantially the characteristics of a security.

In a pension plan such as this one, by contrast, the purported investment is a relatively insignificant part of an employee's total and indivisible compensation package. No portion of an employee's compensation other than the potential pension benefits has any of the characteristics of a security, yet these noninvestment interests cannot be segregated from the possible pension benefits. Only in the most abstract sense may it be said that an employee "exchanges" some portion of his labor in return for these possible benefits. He surrenders his labor as a whole, and, in return, receives a compensation package that is substantially devoid of aspects resembling a security. His decision to accept and retain covered employment may have only an attenuated relationship, if any, to perceived investment possibilities of a future pension. Looking at the economic realities, it seems clear that an employee is selling his labor primarily to obtain a livelihood, not making an investment.

Respondent also argues that employer contributions on his behalf constituted his investment into the Fund. But it is inaccurate to describe these payments as having been "on behalf" of any employee. The trust agreement used employee man-weeks as a convenient way to measure an employer's overall obligation to the Fund, not as a means of measuring the employer's obligation to any particular employee. Indeed, there was no fixed relationship between contributions to the Fund and an employee's potential benefits. A pension plan with "defined benefits," such as the Local's, does not tie a qualifying employee's benefits to the time he has worked. See n 3, supra. One who has engaged in covered employment for 20 years will receive the same benefits as a person who has worked for 40, even though the latter has worked twice as long and induced a substantially larger employer contribution. Again, it ignores the economic realities to equate employer contributions with an investment by the employee.

B. Expectation of Profits from a Common Enterprise

As we observed in Forman, the "touchstone" of the Howey test "is the presence of an investment in a common venture premised on a reasonable expectation of profits to be derived from the entrepreneurial or managerial efforts of others." at 421 U. S. 852. The Court of Appeals believed that Daniel's expectation of profit derived from the Fund's successful management and investment of its assets. To the extent pension benefits exceeded employer contributions and depended on earnings from the assets, it was thought they contained a profit element. The Fund's trustees provided the managerial efforts which produced this profit element.

As in other parts of its analysis, the court below found an expectation of profit in the pension plan only by focusing on one of its less important aspects to the exclusion of its more significant elements. It is true that the Fund, like other holders of large assets, depends to some extent on earnings from its assets. In the case of a pension fund, however, a far larger portion of its income comes from employer contributions, a source in no way dependent on the efforts of the Fund's managers. The Local 705 Fund, for example, earned a total of $31 million through investment of its assets between February, 1955, and January, 1977. During this same period, employer contributions totaled $153 million. Not only does the greater share of a pension plan's income ordinarily come from new contributions, but, unlike most entrepreneurs who manage other people's money, a plan usually can count on increased employer contributions, over which the plan itself has no control, to cover shortfalls in earnings.

The importance of asset earnings in relation to the other benefits received from employment is diminished further by the fact that, where a plan has substantial preconditions to vesting, the principal barrier to an individual employee's realization of pension benefits is not the financial health of the fund. Rather, it is his own ability to meet the fund's eligibility requirements. Thus, even if it were proper to describe the benefits as a "profit" returned on some hypothetical investment by the employee, this profit would depend primarily on the employee's efforts to meet the vesting requirements, rather than the fund's investment success. When viewed in light of the total compensation package an employee must receive in order to be eligible for pension benefits, it becomes clear that the possibility of participating in a plan's asset earnings "is far too speculative and insubstantial to bring the entire transaction within the Securities Acts," Forman, 421 U.S. at 421 U. S. 856.

III

The court below believed that its construction of the term "security" was compelled not only by the perceived resemblance of a pension plan to an investment contract, but also by various actions of Congress and the SEC with regard to the Securities Acts. In reaching this conclusion, the court gave great weight to the SEC's explanation of these events, an explanation which, for the most part, the SEC repeats here. Our own review of the record leads us to believe that this reliance on the SEC's interpretation of these legislative and administrative actions was not justified.

…

The court below believed, and it now is argued to us, that, almost from its inception, the SEC has regarded pension plans as falling within the scope of the Securities Acts. We are asked to defer to what is seen as a longstanding interpretation of these statutes by the agency responsible for their administration. But there are limits, grounded in the language, purpose, and history of the particular statute, on how far an agency properly may go in its interpretative role. Although these limits are not always easy to discern, it is clear here that the SEC's position is neither longstanding nor even arguably within the outer limits of its authority to interpret these Acts.

As we have demonstrated above, the type of pension plan at issue in this case bears no resemblance to the kind of financial interests the Securities Acts were designed to regulate.

Further, the SEC's present position is flatly contradicted by its past actions. Until the instant litigation arose, the public record reveals no evidence that the SEC had ever considered the Securities Acts to be applicable to noncontributory pension plans. In 1941, the SEC first articulated the position that voluntary, contributory plans had investment characteristics that rendered them "securities" under the Acts. At the same time, however, the SEC recognized that noncontributory plans were not covered by the Securities Acts because such plans did not involve a "sale" within the meaning of the statutes. Opinions of Assistant General Counsel, [1941-1944 Transfer Binder] CCH Fed.Sec.L.Serv. 75, 195 (1941); Hearings before the House Committee on Interstate and Foreign Commerce on Proposed Amendments to the Securities Act of 1933 and to the Securities Exchange Act of 1934, 77th Cong., 1st Sess., 895, 896-897 (1941) (testimony of Commissioner Purcell).

In an attempt to reconcile these interpretations of the Securities Acts with its present stand, the SEC now augments its past position with two additional propositions. First, it is argued, noncontributory plans are "securities" even where a "sale" is not involved. Second, the previous concession that noncontributory plans do not involve a "sale" was meant to apply only to the registration and reporting requirements of the Securities Acts; for purposes of the antifraud provisions, a "sale" is involved. As for the first proposition, we observe that none of the SEC opinions, reports, or testimony cited to us address the question. As for the second, the record is unambiguously to the contrary. Both in its 1941 statements and repeatedly since then, the SEC has declared that its "no sale" position applied to the Securities Acts as a whole. See opinions of Assistant General Counsel, [1941-1944 Transfer Binder] CCH Fed.Sec.L.Serv. 75, 195, p. 75, 387 (1941); Hearings before the House Committee on Interstate and Foreign Commerce, supra at 888, 896-897; Institutional Investor Study Report of the Securities and Exchange Commission, H.R.Doc. No. 92-14, pt. 3, p. 996 (1971) ("[T] he Securities Act does not apply..."); Hearings before the Subcommittee on Welfare and Pension Funds of the Senate Committee on Labor and Public Welfare on Welfare and Pension Plans Investigation, 84th Cong., 1st Sess., pt. 3, pp. 943 946 (1955). Congress acted on this understanding when it proceeded to develop the legislation that became ERISA. See, e.g., Interim Report of Activities of the Private Welfare and Pension Plan Study, 1971, S.Rep. No. 92-634, p. 96 (1972) ("Pension and profit-sharing plans are exempt from coverage under the Securities Act of 1933... unless the plan is a voluntary contributory pension plan and invests in the securities of the employer company an amount greater than that paid into the plan by the employer") (emphasis added). A far as we are aware, at no time before this case arose did the SEC intimate that the antifraud provisions of the Securities Acts nevertheless applied to noncontributory pension plans.

…

We hold that the Securities Acts do not apply to a noncontributory, compulsory pension plan. Because the first two counts of respondent's complaint do not provide grounds for relief in federal court, the District Court should have granted the motion to dismiss them. The judgment below is therefore.

Reversed.

第二节　证券组织机构

一、中国的证券组织机构

中国《证券法》第五章到第十章对证券组织机构进行了规定。依据中国《证券法》的规定，证券组织机构分为以下几种：证券交易所、证券登记结算结构、证券公司、证券服务机构、自律性组织和政府监管机构。

（一）证券交易所

依据中国《证券法》的规定，证券交易所是为证券集中交易提供场所和设施，组织和监督证券交易，实行自律管理的法人。中国《证券交易所管理办法》进一步规定，证券交易所是指以该办法规定条件设立的，不以营利为目的，为证券的集中和有组织的交易提供场所、设施，履行国家有关法律、法规、规章、政策规定的职责，实行自律性管理的法人。

在中国，证券交易所的设立和解散，由中国国务院决定，证券交易所设总经理一人，由中国证监会任免。中国目前已经设立了上海证券交易所和深圳证券交易所。

证券交易所为证券交易方提供平台服务，进入证券交易所参与集中交易的，必须是证券交易所的会员。证券交易所依照证券法律、行政法规制定上市规则、交易规则、会员管理规则和其他有关规则，并报中国证监会批准。在证券交易所内从事证券交易的人员，违反证券交易所有关交易规则的，证券交易所可以给予纪律处分；对情节严重的，撤销其资格，禁止其入场进行证券交易。

（二）证券登记结算机构

依据中国《证券法》的规定，证券登记结算机构是为证券交易提供集中登记、存管与结算服务，不以营利为目的的法人。设立证券登记结算机构必须经中国证监会批准。中国目前只设立了一家证券登记结算机构——中国证券登记结算有限责任公司。

在中国，证券登记结算机构履行下列职能：证券账户、结算账户的设立；证券的存管和过户；证券持有人名册登记；证券交易所上市证券交易的清算和交收；受发行人的委托派发证券权益；办理与上述业务有关的查询以及中国证监会批准的其他业务。

中国的证券登记结算采取全国集中统一的运营方式。证券登记结算机构章程、业务规则应当依法制定，并须经中国证监会批准。

（三）证券公司

证券公司是专门经营证券业务的机构，它具有证券交易所的会员资格，可以承销发行、自营买卖或自营兼代理买卖证券。

在中国，由于证券行业是特许行业，因此只有依法设立的证券公司才能经营证券业务。根据中国《证券法》的规定，设立证券公司，必须经中国证监会审查批准。未经中国证监会批准，任何单位和个人不得经营证券业务。

在中国，设立证券公司，应当具备一些条件，包括公司章程合法、主要股东具有持续盈利能力且信誉良好、有符合本法规定的注册资本、董事、监事、高级管理人员具备任职资格及从业人员具有证券从业资格、有完善的风险管理与内部控制制度和有合格的经营场所和业务设施等。得到中国证监会的批准，证券公司可以经营下列部分或者全部业务：证券经纪；证券投资咨询；与证券交易、证券投资活动有关的财务顾问；证券承销与保荐；证券自营；证券资产管理以及其他证券业务。

在中国，证券公司依法享有自主经营的权利，其合法经营不受干涉。但是，证券公司设立、收购或者撤销分支机构，变更业务范围或者注册资本，变更持有5%以上股权的股东、实际控制人，变更公司章程中的重要条款，合并、分立、变更公司形式、停业、解散、破产，必须经中国证监会批准。

（四）证券服务机构

证券服务机构是指依法设立的从事证券服务业务的法人机构。根据中国《证券法》的规定，经相关政府主管部门批准，投资咨询机构、财务顾问机构、资信评级机构、资产评估机构、会计师事务所可以从事证券服务业务。

其中，资信评级机构是非常重要的一类证券服务机构。在中国，资信评级机构从事证券市场资信评级业务，包括对下列评级对象开展资信评级服务：（1）中国证监会依法核准发行的债券、资产支持证券以及其他固定收益或者债务型结构性融资证券；（2）在证券交易所上市交易的债券、资产支持证券以及其他固定收益或者债务型结构性融资证券，国债除外；（3）第（1）项和第（2）项规定的证券的发行人、上市公司、非上市公众公司、证券公司、证券投资基金管理公司；（4）中国证监会规定的其他评级对象。资信评级机构从事证券市场资信评级业务，应当向中国证监会申请取得证券评级业务许可。未取得中国证监会的证券评级业务许可，任何单位和个人不得从事证券评级业务。

律师事务所为证券发行、上市和交易等证券业务活动提供法律服务（制作、出具法律意见书等文件），也是一类重要的证券服务机构。在中国，律师事务所从事证券服务业务，无需获得政府部门的特别批准。

（五）自律性组织和政府监管机构

在中国，证券业自律性组织主要是指证券业协会。1991 年 8 月，中国即已成立了中国证券业协会。根据中国《证券法》的规定，证券公司应当加入证券业协会。中国证券业协会对其会员实施自律性管理。此外，中国早在 1992 年便成立了专门的证券业监管机构——中国证监会。中国《证券法》中所称国务院证券监督管理机构即是指中国证监会。依据中国《证券法》的规定，中国证监会依法对证券市场实行监督管理，维护证券市场秩序，保障其合法运行。

二、美国的证券组织机构

美国是证券市场最为发达的国家，活跃在证券市场上的机构众多，不仅包括证券交易所、证券登记结算机构等平台中介，也包括证券公司、相关证券服务机构等市场参与主体，还包括行业自律性监管组织和政府监管机构。

（一）证券交易所

根据《1934 年证券交易法》的规定，“交易所”是指任何组织、协会或数人组成的小组，无论是否为股份有限，它为把证券买卖双方聚合在一起，或者为发挥其他与证券有关的、由众所周知的股票交易所正常发挥的那些作用而组成、维持或提供一个市场或设施，并且包括由这样的交易所维持的市场和市场设施。

《1934 年证券交易法》规定，美国境内的证券交易所包括两类：注册的全国性交易所和免于注册的交易所。符合一定的条件的交易所，经向美国证券交易委员会提出申请，可以获得注册。当交易所提出申请时，证券交易委员会认为，鉴于该交易所成交额有限，要求其注册是不可行、不必要或不合乎公众利益的，或为了保护投资方，而使该交易所免于注册，这种被免于注册交易所也是美国境内合法的交易所。

根据《1934 年证券交易法》的规定，除非在上述注册的全国性交易所和免于注册的交易所进行证券交易，否则任何经纪人、证券商或交易所为了利用合众国管辖的交易所的一切设施来促成证券的成交或通知成交的情况，以直接或间接手段使用邮件或任何一种州际商用媒介，均为违法行为。

（二）证券登记结算机构

美国的证券交易实行托管和结算制。根据《1934 年证券交易法》的规定，“结算机构”（clearing agency）是指作为中间人为与证券相关的交易付款或交付，或者两者兼做的任何人，或者是为涉及证券交易成交条件的资料比较而提供设施的任何人，或为证券成交偿付能力的划归提供设施的任何人；还指作为证券受托人的任何人。

美国证券托管与结算主要有两种模式，其中政府债券和抵押类债券托管于联邦储备银行电子划付系统（Fedwire）；股票、公司债券和市政债券集中托管于全美证券托管清算公司（DTCC）的全资子公司全美证券托管公司（DTC），DTC 为其中八个股票交易所和债券场外交易提供托管、清算、结算一体化服务。

美国主要的股票结算公司是国家证券结算公司（NSCC），集中了纽约交易所、美国交易所、NASDAQ 等市场的上市股份的清算业务。另外几家小的结算公司，都与 NSCC 实现联网，客户只需一个账户便可完成不同市场间交易的结算。[①]

（三）证券公司

在美国，证券公司等证券经营机构一般被称为证券商。美国《1933 年证券法》和《1934 年证券交易法》规定了两种类型的证券商：证券经纪人（broker）和交易商（dealer）。

证券经纪人是纯粹的中间人，充当买卖证券的代理人，为个人或机构投资者实施交易以获取经纪人手续费。《1933 年证券法》没有对“经纪人”作出定义。《1934 年证券交易法》规定，经纪人是指任何为他人从事证券交易业务的人。

与经纪人不同，证券交易商按照规定的价格买卖证券，以期从价差中获取收益。《1933 年证券法》规定，交易商指任何以代理人、经纪人或本人身份花费部分或全部时间，直接或间接从事他人发行证券的发行、买卖或交易的人。这个定义既包括了作为经纪人为他人交易证券的情形又包括了作为“本人”（principle）为自己交易证券的情形。《1934 年证券交易法》规定，交易商是指通过经纪人和其他方式为自己的账户从事买卖证券业务的任何人，但不包括任何个人直接还是通过信托为自己买卖证券却不把此活动作为其固定业务的人。比起《1933 年证券法》，这个定义只包括了为“本人自己账户”从事证券业务。

在美国，经纪人或交易商从事证券交易业务，必须满足一定的条件。

首先，经纪人或交易商必须获得 SEC 的登记注册。《1934 年证券交易法》规定，除非在 SEC 处登记，否则，任何经纪人或交易商（指非自然人或与非自然人经纪人交易商无关的自然人）利用州际商业信函或其他任何工具或手段从事证券交易的行为或者诱使别人买卖证券的行为都是违法行为。当然，如果该经纪人或交易商完全从事州内业务并且没有使用任何全国性证券交易设施，那么可以免除在 SEC 处注册登记的义务。此外，根据《1934 年证券交易法》的规定，SEC 可以从保护投资者及维护公众利益的角度出发，来附条件或不附条件地决定哪些经纪人或交易商可以免除上述注册登记义务。

---

① 丁化美，费兰静. 国际证券交易结算方式比较. 产权导刊，2011（4）.

其次，经纪人或交易商必须成为自律监管机构（SRO）成员或者（大多数情况下）成为证券投资者保护公司成员（Securities Investor Protection Corporation，SIPC）。此处的自律监管机构主要包括全国性的证券交易所和美国金融业监管局（FINRA）。经纪人或交易商必须成为 FINRA 会员，方可从事证券业务。此外，经纪人或交易商在任何一个证券交易所从事证券交易活动，就需要注册成为该交易所的会员。如果是从事柜台交易（over-the-counter transaction），则必须是 NASD 的成员。当然，如果经纪人或交易商同时在交易所和柜台市场交易，则必须同时成为交易所和 NASD 的成员。每个注册登记的经纪人或交易商必须成为证券投资者保护公司成员，除非其主要业务在美国之外发生或者完全是销售投资公司股份、可变养老年金或保险。

最后，经纪人或交易商还必须符合各州州法的注册登记要求。每个州都制定有适用于该州范围内证券交易的蓝天法，其中就有关于经纪人或交易商注册登记的具体规定。

三、案例资料

对于证券交易中的欺诈，通常而言民事责任主体主要包含四类人：发行人、上市公司，发行人、上市公司的董事、监事、高级管理人员和其他直接责任人员以及保荐人、承销的证券公司，会计师事务所等证券中介机构以及发行人、上市公司控股股东、实际控制人。在现实中，发行人、上市公司有时通过特定的商业交易安排来实现不实盈利或收入从而推高股价。那么，知情甚至是参与的交易对方应否也被要求承担证券欺诈责任？受损害的投资者是否可以直接对其提起诉讼？

这一话题在各国的证券法实践中都是比较有争议的。在美国，对参与公司欺诈阴谋的商业交易对方，投资者先后以其协助及教唆欺诈而应承担次要责任（secondary liability）和以其应承担欺诈的“首要责任”（primary liability）起诉到法院。美国法院对此意见不一，有支持投资者起诉的，也有反对者。最终，在 2008 年判决的 Stoneridge Inv. Partners, LLC v. Scientific-Atlanta 案中，美国联邦最高法院判定：投资者无权直接对此提起证券欺诈诉讼。

在该案中，被告是一家上市公司发行人的供货商，发行人与其商定：先由被告以其他借口提高供货价，随后将增加部分作为广告费返还给发行人，以记录为其收入和现金流并虚列成本，从而帮助达到市场分析师预期，误导审计师并发布虚假财报，抬高股价。该欺诈行为被曝光后，受损的上市公司投资者对被告提起证券欺诈的集团诉讼。该案的一审和二审法院均作出了驳回原告起诉的判决。原告继续上诉，最终美国联邦最高法院决定调卷终审。

该案的审理，在美国引起了广泛的关注。不同的个人、机构纷纷向联邦最高法院呈递意见，支持原告和支持被告的意见相互碰撞，争议空前，甚至连时任美国总统布什也发表意见，支持被告。2008年1月，联邦最高法院最终以5比3终审维持原判。联邦最高法院认为，类似被告的商业交易对方，不应承担证券欺诈的责任，并列出了三点理由：（1）原告必须满足10（b）规则有关私人民事诉权的全部要素方可对被告直接提起诉讼；（2）该案中，信赖要素并未得到满足，因为被告并未进行信息披露，也不能因为被告的行为导致了欺诈的产生从而判令其承担责任；（3）不能将普通法下的欺诈用在证券法下的证券欺诈诉讼中。联邦最高法院还进行了一系列的政策分析，声称如果允许原告起诉，那么将会带来一系列不良的后果。

该案是美国近年来最重要的证券法判例之一。判决作出后，争议仍旧不断。对参与发行人或上市公司欺诈阴谋的商业交易对方，投资者能否直接对其提起证券欺诈诉讼，在美国，无论是实务界还是理论界，仍旧众说纷纭。

Stoneridge Inv. Partners, LLC v. Scientific-Atlanta

552 U.S. 148, 128 S.Ct. 761 (U.S., 2008)

Justice KENNEDY delivered the opinion of the Court.

*152 We consider the reach of the private right of action the Court has found implied in § 10 (b) of the Securities Exchange Act of 1934, 48 Stat. 891, as amended, 15 U.S.C. § 78j(b), and SEC Rule 10b-5, 17 CFR § 240.10b-5 (2007). In this suit investors alleged losses after purchasing common stock. They sought to impose liability on entities who, acting both as customers and suppliers, agreed to arrangements that allowed the investors' company to mislead its auditor and issue *153 a misleading financial statement affecting the stock price. We conclude the implied right of action does not reach the customer/supplier companies because the investors did not rely upon their statements or representations. We affirm the judgment of the Court of Appeals.

I

This class-action suit by investors was filed against Charter Communications, Inc., in the United States District Court for the Eastern District of Missouri. Stoneridge Investment Partners, LLC, a limited liability company organized under the laws of Delaware, was the lead plaintiff and is petitioner here.

Charter issued the financial statements and the securities in question. It was a named defendant along with some of its executives and Arthur Andersen LLP, Charter's independent auditor during the period in question. We are concerned, though, with two other defendants, respondents here. Respondents are Scientific-Atlanta, Inc., and Motorola, Inc. They were suppliers, and later customers, of Charter.

For purposes of this proceeding, we take these facts, alleged by petitioner, to be true. Charter, a cable operator, engaged in a variety of fraudulent practices so its quarterly reports would meet Wall Street expectations for cable subscriber growth and operating cash flow. The fraud included misclassification of its customer base; delayed reporting of terminated customers; improper capitalization of costs that should have been shown as expenses; and manipulation of the company's billing cutoff dates to inflate reported revenues. In late 2000, Charter executives realized that, despite these efforts, the company would miss projected operating cash flow numbers by $15 to $20 million. To help meet the shortfall, Charter decided to alter its existing arrangements with respondents, Scientific-Atlanta and Motorola. Petitioner's*154 theory as to whether Arthur Andersen was altogether misled or, on the other hand, knew the structure of the contract arrangements and was complicit to some degree, is not clear at this stage of the case. The point, however, is neither controlling nor significant for our present disposition, and in our decision we assume it was misled.

Respondents supplied Charter with the digital cable converter (set top) boxes that Charter furnished to its customers. Charter arranged to overpay respondents $20 for each set top box it purchased until the end of the year, with the understanding that respondents would return the overpayment by purchasing advertising from Charter. The transactions, it is alleged, had no economic substance; but, because Charter would then record the advertising purchases as revenue and capitalize its purchase of the set top boxes, in violation of generally accepted accounting principles, the transactions would enable Charter to fool its auditor into approving a financial statement showing it met projected revenue and operating cash flow numbers. Respondents agreed to the arrangement.

**767 So that Arthur Andersen would not discover the link between Charter's increased payments for the boxes and the advertising purchases, the companies drafted documents to make it appear the transactions were unrelated and conducted in the ordinary course of business. Following a request from Charter, Scientific-Atlanta sent documents to Charter stating—falsely—that it had increased production costs. It raised the price for set top boxes for the rest of 2000 by $20 per box. As for Motorola, in a written contract Charter agreed to purchase from Motorola a specific number of set top boxes and pay liquidated damages of $20 for each unit it did not take. The contract was made with the expectation Charter would fail to purchase all the units and pay Motorola the liquidated damages.

To return the additional money from the set top box sales, Scientific-Atlanta and Motorola signed contracts with Charter*155 to purchase advertising time for a price higher than fair value. The new set top box agreements were backdated to make it appear that they were negotiated a month before the advertising agreements. The backdating was important to convey the impression that the negotiations were unconnected, a point Arthur Andersen considered necessary for separate treatment of the transactions. Charter recorded the advertising payments to inflate revenue and operating cash flow by approximately $17 million. The inflated number was shown on financial statements filed with the Securities and Exchange Commission (SEC) and reported to the public.

Respondents had no role in preparing or disseminating Charter's financial statements. And their own financial statements booked the transactions as a wash, under generally accepted accounting principles. It is alleged respondents knew or were in reckless disregard of Charter's intention to use the transactions to inflate its revenues and knew the resulting financial statements issued by Charter would be relied upon by research analysts and investors.

Petitioner filed a securities fraud class action on behalf of purchasers of Charter stock alleging that, by participating in the transactions, respondents violated § 10 (b) of the Securities Exchange Act of 1934 and SEC Rule 10b-5.

The District Court granted respondents' motion to dismiss for failure to state a claim on which relief can be granted. The United States Court of Appeals for the Eighth Circuit affirmed. In re Charter Communications, Inc., Securities Litigation, 443 F.3d 987 (2006). In its view the allegations did not show that respondents made misstatements relied upon by the public or that they violated a duty to disclose; and on this premise it found no violation of § 10 (b) by respondents. Id., at 992. At most, the court observed, respondents had aided and abetted Charter's misstatement of its financial results; but, it noted, there is no private right of action for aiding and abetting a § 10 (b) violation. See *156 Central Bank of Denver, N.A. v. First Interstate Bank of Denver, N. A., 511 U.S. 164, 191, 114 S.Ct. 1439, 128 L.Ed.2d 119 (1994). The court also affirmed the District Court's denial of petitioner's motion to amend the complaint, as the revised pleading would not change the court's conclusion on the merits. 443 F.3d, at 993.

Decisions of the Courts of Appeals are in conflict respecting when, if ever, an injured investor may rely upon § 10 (b) to recover from a party that neither makes a public misstatement nor violates a duty to disclose but does participate in a scheme to violate § 10 (b).

Compare Simpson v. AOL Time Warner Inc., 452 F.3d 1040 (C.A.9 2006), with **768 Regents of Univ. of Cal. v. Credit Suisse First Boston (USA), Inc., 482 F.3d 372 (C.A.5 2007). We granted certiorari. 549 U.S. 1304, 127 S.Ct. 1873, 167 L.Ed.2d 363 (2007).

II

[1] [2] Section 10 (b) of the Securities Exchange Act makes it

"unlawful for any person, directly or indirectly, by the use of any means or instrumentality of interstate commerce or of the mails, or of any facility of any national securities exchange... [t] o use or employ, in connection with the purchase or sale of any security... any manipulative or deceptive device or contrivance in contravention of such rules and regulations as the Commission may prescribe as necessary or appropriate in the public interest or for the protection of investors." 15 U.S.C. § 78j.

The SEC, pursuant to this section, promulgated Rule 10b-5, which makes it unlawful

"(a) To employ any device, scheme, or artifice to defraud,

"(b) To make any untrue statement of a material fact or to omit to state a material fact necessary in order to make the statements made, in the light of the circumstances under which they were made, not misleading, or

*157 "(c) To engage in any act, practice, or course of business which operates or would operate as a fraud or deceit upon any person,

"in connection with the purchase or sale of any security." 17 CFR § 240.10b-5.

Rule 10b-5 encompasses only conduct already prohibited by § 10 (b). United States v. O'Hagan, 521 U.S. 642, 651, 117 S.Ct. 2199, 138 L.Ed.2d 724 (1997). Though the text of the Securities Exchange Act does not provide for a private cause of action for § 10 (b) violations, the Court has found a right of action implied in the words of the statute and its implementing regulation. Superintendent of Ins. of N.Y. v. Bankers Life & Casualty Co., 404 U.S. 6, 13, n. 9, 92 S.Ct. 165, 30 L.Ed.2d 128 (1971). In a typical § 10 (b) private action a plaintiff must prove (1) a material misrepresentation or omission by the defendant; (2) scienter; (3) a connection between the misrepresentation or omission and the purchase or sale of a security; (4) reliance upon the misrepresentation or omission; (5) economic loss; and (6) loss causation. See Dura Pharmaceuticals, Inc. v. Broudo, 544 U.S. 336, 341-342, 125 S.Ct. 1627, 161 L.Ed.2d 577 (2005).

In Central Bank, the Court determined that § 10 (b) liability did not extend to aiders and abettors. The Court found the scope of § 10 (b) to be delimited by the text, which makes no mention of aiding and abetting liability. 511 U.S., at 177, 114 S.Ct. 1439. The Court doubted the implied § 10 (b) action should extend to aiders and abettors when none of the express causes of action in the securities Acts included that liability. Id., at 180, 114 S.Ct. 1439. It added the following:

> "Were we to allow the aiding and abetting action proposed in this case, the defendant could be liable without any showing that the plaintiff relied upon the aider and abettor's statements or actions. See also Chiarella [v. United States, 445 U.S. 222, 228, 100 S.Ct. 1108, 63 L.Ed.2d 348 (1980)]. Allowing plaintiffs to circumvent the reliance requirement would disregard the careful limits on 10b-5 recovery mandated by our earlier cases." Ibid.

*158 The decision in Central Bank led to calls for Congress to create an express cause of action for aiding and abetting within the Securities Exchange Act. Then-SEC Chairman Arthur Levitt, testifying before the Senate Securities Subcommittee, cited Central Bank and recommended that aiding**769 and abetting liability in private claims be established. S. Hearing No. 103-759, pp. 13-14 (1994). Congress did not follow this course. Instead, in § 104 of the Private Securities Litigation Reform Act of 1995 (PSLRA), 109 Stat. 757, it directed prosecution of aiders and abettors by the SEC. 15 U.S.C. § 78t(e).

[3] The § 10 (b) implied private right of action does not extend to aiders and abettors. The conduct of a secondary actor must satisfy each of the elements or preconditions for liability; and we consider whether the allegations here are sufficient to do so.

III

The Court of Appeals concluded petitioner had not alleged that respondents engaged in a deceptive act within the reach of the § 10 (b) private right of action, noting that only misstatements, omissions by one who has a duty to disclose, and manipulative trading practices (where "manipulative" is a term of art, see, e.g., Santa Fe Industries, Inc. v. Green, 430 U.S. 462, 476-477, 97 S.Ct. 1292, 51 L.Ed.2d 480 (1977)) are deceptive within the meaning of the rule. 443 F.3d, at 992. If this conclusion were read to suggest there must be a specific oral or written statement before there could be liability under § 10 (b) or Rule 10b-5, it would be erroneous. Conduct itself can be deceptive, as respondents concede. In this case, moreover, respondents' course of conduct included both oral and written statements, such as the backdated contracts agreed to by Charter and respondents.

A different interpretation of the holding from the Court of Appeals opinion is that the court was stating only that any deceptive statement or act respondents made was not actionable because it did not have the requisite proximate relation *159 to the investors' harm. That conclusion is consistent with our own determination that respondents' acts or statements were not relied upon by the investors and that, as a result, liability cannot be imposed upon respondents.

A

[4] [5] [6] Reliance by the plaintiff upon the defendant's deceptive acts is an essential element of the § 10 (b) private cause of action. It ensures that, for liability to arise, the "requisite causal connection between a defendant's misrepresentation and a plaintiff's injury" exists as a predicate for liability. Basic Inc. v. Levinson, 485 U.S. 224, 243, 108 S.Ct. 978, 99 L.Ed.2d 194 (1988); see also Affiliated Ute Citizens of Utah v. United States, 406 U.S. 128, 154, 92 S.Ct. 1456, 31 L.Ed.2d 741 (1972) (requiring "causation in fact"). We have found a rebuttable presumption of reliance in two different circumstances. First, if there is an omission of a material fact by one with a duty to disclose, the investor to whom the duty was owed need not provide specific proof of reliance. Id., at 153-154, 92 S.Ct. 1456. Second, under the fraud-on-the-market doctrine, reliance is presumed when the statements at issue become public. The public information is reflected in the market price of the security. Then it can be assumed that an investor who buys or sells stock at the market price relies upon the statement. Basic, supra, at 247, 108 S.Ct. 978.

[7] Neither presumption applies here. Respondents had no duty to disclose; and their deceptive acts were not communicated to the public. No member of the investing public had knowledge, either actual or presumed, of respondents' deceptive acts during the relevant times. Petitioner, as a result, cannot show reliance upon any of respondents' actions except in an indirect chain that we find too remote for liability.

****770 B**

Invoking what some courts call "scheme liability," see, e.g., In re Enron Corp. Securities, Derivative & "ERISA" Litigation, 439 F.Supp.2d 692, 723 (S.D.Tex.2006), petitioner*160 nonetheless seeks to impose liability on respondents even absent a public statement. In our view this approach does not answer the objection that petitioner did not in fact rely upon respondents' own deceptive conduct.

Liability is appropriate, petitioner contends, because respondents engaged in conduct with the purpose and effect of creating a false appearance of material fact to further a scheme to misrepresent Charter's revenue. The argument is that the financial statement Charter released to the public was a natural and expected consequence of respondents' deceptive acts; had respondents not assisted Charter, Charter's auditor would not have been fooled, and the financial statement would have been a more accurate reflection of Charter's financial condition. That causal link is sufficient, petitioner argues, to apply Basic's presumption of reliance to respondents' acts. See, e.g., Simpson, 452 F.3d, at 1051-1052; In re Parmalat Securities Litigation, 376 F.Supp.2d 472, 509 (S.D.N.Y.2005).

In effect petitioner contends that in an efficient market investors rely not only upon the public statements relating to a security but also upon the transactions those statements reflect. Were this concept of reliance to be adopted, the implied cause of action would reach the whole marketplace in which the issuing company does business; and there is no authority for this rule.

As stated above, reliance is tied to causation, leading to the inquiry whether respondents' acts were immediate or remote to the injury. In considering petitioner's arguments, we note § 10 (b) provides that the deceptive act must be "in connection with the purchase or sale of any security." 15 U.S.C. § 78j(b). Though this phrase in part defines the statute's coverage rather than causation (and so we do not evaluate the "in connection with" requirement of § 10 (b) in this case), the emphasis on a purchase or sale of securities does provide some insight into the deceptive acts that concerned the enacting Congress. See Black, Securities *161 Commentary: The Second Circuit's Approach to the "In Connection With" Requirement of Rule 10b-5, 53 Brooklyn L.Rev. 539, 541 (1987) ("[W] hile the 'in connection with' and causation requirements are analytically distinct, they are related to each other, and discussion of the first requirement may merge with discussion of the second"). In all events we conclude respondents' deceptive acts, which were not disclosed to the investing public, are too remote to satisfy the requirement of reliance. It was Charter, not respondents, that misled its auditor and filed fraudulent financial statements; nothing respondents did made it necessary or inevitable for Charter to record the transactions as it did.

The petitioner invokes the private cause of action under § 10 (b) and seeks to apply it beyond the securities markets—the realm of financing business—to purchase and supply contracts—the realm of ordinary business operations. The latter realm is governed, for the most part, by state law. It is true that if business operations are used, as alleged here, to affect securities markets, the SEC enforcement power may reach the culpable actors. It is true as well that a dynamic, free economy presupposes a high degree of integrity in all of its parts, an integrity that must be underwritten by rules enforceable in fair, independent, accessible courts. Were the implied cause of action to be extended to the practices described here, however, **771 there would be a risk that the federal power would be used to invite litigation beyond the immediate sphere of securities litigation and in areas already governed by functioning and effective state-law guarantees. Our precedents counsel against this extension. See Marine Bank v. Weaver, 455 U.S. 551, 556, 102 S.Ct. 1220, 71 L.Ed.2d 409 (1982) ("Congress, in enacting the securities laws, did not intend to provide a broad federal remedy for all fraud"); Santa Fe, 430 U.S., at 479-480, 97 S.Ct. 1292 ("There may well be a need for uniform federal fiduciary standards.... But those standards should not be supplied by judicial extension of § 10 (b) and Rule 10b-5 to 'cover the corporate universe' " (quoting Cary, *162 Federalism and Corporate Law: Reflections Upon Delaware, 83 Yale L.J. 663, 700 (1974))). Though § 10 (b) is "not 'limited to preserving the integrity of the securities markets,' " Bankers Life, 404 U.S., at 12, 92 S.Ct. 165, it does not reach all commercial transactions that are fraudulent and affect the price of a security in some attenuated way.

[8] [9] These considerations answer as well the argument that if this were a common-law action for fraud there could be a finding of reliance. Even if the assumption is correct, it is not controlling. Section 10 (b) does not incorporate common-law fraud into federal law. See, e.g., SEC v. Zandford, 535 U.S. 813, 820, 122 S.Ct. 1899, 153 L.Ed.2d 1 (2002) ("[Section 10 (b)] must not be construed so broadly as to convert every common-law fraud that happens to involve securities into a violation"); Central Bank, 511 U.S., at 184, 114 S.Ct. 1439 ("Even assuming... a deeply rooted background of aiding and abetting tort liability, it does not follow that Congress intended to apply that kind of liability to the private causes of action in the securities Acts"); see also Dura, 544 U.S., at 341, 125 S.Ct. 1627. Just as § 10 (b) "is surely badly strained when construed to provide a cause of action... to the world at large," Blue Chip Stamps v. Manor Drug Stores, 421 U.S. 723, 733, n. 5, 95 S.Ct. 1917, 44 L.Ed.2d 539 (1975), it should not be interpreted to provide a private cause of action against the entire marketplace in which the issuing company operates.

Petitioner's theory, moreover, would put an unsupportable interpretation on Congress' specific response to Central Bank in § 104 of the PSLRA. Congress amended the securities laws to provide for limited coverage of aiders and abettors. Aiding and abetting liability is authorized in actions brought by the SEC but not by private parties. See 15 U.S.C. § 78t(e).

Petitioner's view of primary liability makes any aider and abettor liable under § 10 (b) if he or she committed a deceptive act in the process of providing assistance. Reply Brief for Petitioner 6, n. 2; Tr. of Oral Arg. 24. Were we to adopt this construction of § 10 (b), it would revive in substance the implied cause of action against all aiders *163 and abettors except those who committed no deceptive act in the process of facilitating the fraud; and we would undermine Congress' determination that this class of defendants should be pursued by the SEC and not by private litigants. See Alexander v. Sandoval, 532 U.S. 275, 290, 121 S.Ct. 1511, 149 L.Ed.2d 517 (2001) ("The express provision of one method of enforcing a substantive rule suggests that Congress intended to preclude others"); FDA v. Brown & Williamson Tobacco Corp., 529 U.S. 120, 143, 120 S.Ct. 1291, 146 L.Ed.2d 121 (2000) ("At the time a statute is enacted, it may have a range of plausible meanings. Over time, however, subsequent acts can shape or focus those meanings"); see also Seatrain Shipbuilding Corp. v. Shell Oil Co., 444 U.S. 572, 596, 100 S.Ct. 800, 63 L.Ed.2d 36 (1980) ("[W] hile the views of subsequent Congresses**772 cannot override the unmistakable intent of the enacting one, such views are entitled to significant weight, and particularly so when the precise intent of the enacting Congress is obscure" (citations omitted)).

This is not a case in which Congress has enacted a regulatory statute and then has accepted, over a long period of time, broad judicial authority to define substantive standards of conduct and liability. Cf. Leegin Creative Leather Products, Inc. v. PSKS, Inc., 551 U.S. 877, 899, 127 S.Ct. 2705, 2720-21, 168 L.Ed.2d 623 (2007). And in accord with the nature of the cause of action at issue here, we give weight to Congress' amendment to the Act restoring aiding and abetting liability in certain cases but not others. The amendment, in our view, supports the conclusion that there is no liability.

The practical consequences of an expansion, which the Court has considered appropriate to examine in circumstances like these, see Virginia Bankshares, Inc. v. Sandberg, 501 U.S. 1083, 1104-1105, 111 S.Ct. 2749, 115 L.Ed.2d 929 (1991); Blue Chip, 421 U.S., at 737, 95 S.Ct. 1917, provide a further reason to reject petitioner's approach. In Blue Chip, the Court noted that extensive discovery and the potential for uncertainty and disruption in a lawsuit allow plaintiffs with weak claims to extort settlements from innocent companies. Id., at 740-741, 95 S.Ct. 1917. Adoption *164 of petitioner's approach would expose a new class of defendants to these risks. As noted in Central Bank, contracting parties might find it necessary to protect against these threats, raising the costs of doing business. See 511 U.S., at 189, 114 S.Ct. 1439. Overseas firms with no other exposure to our securities laws could be deterred from doing business here. See Brief for Organization for International Investment et al. as Amici Curiae 17-20. This, in turn, may raise the cost of being a publicly traded company under our law and shift securities offerings away from domestic capital markets. Brief for NASDAQ Stock Market, Inc., et al. as Amici Curiae 12-14.

C

[10] [11] [12] The history of the § 10 (b) private right and the careful approach the Court has taken before proceeding without congressional direction provide further reasons to find no liability here. The § 10 (b) private cause of action is a judicial construct that Congress did not enact in the text of the relevant statutes. See Lampf, Pleva, Lipkind, Prupis & Petigrow v. Gilbertson, 501 U.S. 350, 358-359, 111 S.Ct. 2773, 115 L.Ed.2d 321 (1991); Blue Chip, supra, at 729, 95 S.Ct. 1917. Though the rule once may have been otherwise, see J.I. Case Co. v. Borak, 377 U.S. 426, 432-433, 84 S.Ct. 1555, 12 L.Ed.2d 423 (1964), it is settled that there is an implied cause of action only if the underlying statute can be interpreted to disclose the intent to create one, see, e.g., Alexander, supra, at 286-287, 121 S.Ct. 1511; Virginia Bankshares, supra, at 1102, 111 S.Ct. 2749; Touche Ross & Co. v. Redington, 442 U.S. 560, 575, 99 S.Ct. 2479, 61 L.Ed.2d 82 (1979). This is for good reason. In the absence of congressional intent the Judiciary's recognition of an implied private right of action

> "necessarily extends its authority to embrace a dispute Congress has not assigned it to resolve. This runs contrary to the established principle that '[t] he jurisdiction of the federal courts is carefully guarded against expansion by judicial interpretation...,' American Fire & Casualty Co. v. Finn, 341 U.S. 6, 17[, 71 S.Ct. 534, 95 L.Ed. 702] (1951), and conflicts*165 with the authority of Congress under Art. III to set the limits of federal jurisdiction." **773 Cannon v. University of Chicago, 441 U.S. 677 746 99 S.Ct. 1946, 60 L.Ed.2d 560 (1979) (Powell, J., dissenting) (citations and footnote omitted).

The determination of who can seek a remedy has significant consequences for the reach of federal power. See Wilder v. Virginia Hospital Assn., 496 U.S. 498, 509, n. 9, 110 S.Ct. 2510, 110 L.Ed.2d 455 (1990) (requirement of congressional intent "reflects a concern, grounded in separation of powers, that Congress rather than the courts controls the availability of remedies for violations of statutes").

Concerns with the judicial creation of a private cause of action caution against its expansion. The decision to extend the cause of action is for Congress, not for us. Though it remains the law, the § 10 (b) private right should not be extended beyond its present boundaries. See Virginia Bankshares, supra, at 1102, 111 S.Ct. 2749 ("[T] he breadth of the [private right of action] once recognized should not, as a general matter, grow beyond the scope congressionally intended"); see also Central Bank, supra, at 173, 114 S.Ct. 1439 (determining that the scope of conduct prohibited is limited by the text of § 10 (b)).

This restraint is appropriate in light of the PSLRA, which imposed heightened pleading requirements and a loss causation requirement upon "any private action" arising from the Securities Exchange Act. See 15 U.S.C. § 78u-4 (b). It is clear these requirements touch upon the implied right of action, which is now a prominent feature of federal securities regulation. See Merrill Lynch, Pierce, Fenner & Smith Inc. v. Dabit, 547 U.S. 71, 81-82, 126 S.Ct. 1503, 164 L.Ed.2d 179 (2006); Dura, 544 U.S., at 345-346, 125 S.Ct. 1627; see also S.Rep. No. 104-98, p. 4-5 (1995), U.S.Code Cong. & Admin.News 1995, pp. 679, 684 (recognizing the § 10 (b) implied cause of action, and indicating the PSLRA was intended to have "Congress... reassert its authority in this area"); id., at 26 (indicating the pleading standards covered § 10 (b) actions). Congress thus ratified the implied right of action after the Court moved away from a broad willingness to imply private rights of action. See *166 Merrill Lynch, Pierce, Fenner & Smith, Inc. v. Curran, 456 U.S. 353, 381-382, and n. 66, 102 S.Ct. 1825, 72 L.Ed.2d 182 (1982); cf. Borak, supra, at 433, 84 S.Ct. 1555. It is appropriate for us to assume that when § 78u-4 was enacted, Congress accepted the § 10 (b) private cause of action as then defined but chose to extend it no further.

IV

[13] Secondary actors are subject to criminal penalties, see, e.g., 15 U.S.C. § 78ff, and civil enforcement by the SEC, see, e.g., § 78t(e). The enforcement power is not toothless. Since September 30, 2002, SEC enforcement actions have collected over $10 billion in disgorgement and penalties, much of it for distribution to injured investors. See SEC, 2007 Performance and Accountability Report, p. 26, http://www.sec.gov/about/secpar 2007. shtml (as visited Jan. 2, 2008, and available in Clerk of Court's case file). And in this case both parties agree that criminal penalties are a strong deterrent. See Brief for Respondents 48; Reply Brief for Petitioner 17. In addition some state securities laws permit state authorities to seek fines and restitution from aiders and abettors. See, e.g., Del.Code Ann., Tit. 6, § 7325 (2005). All secondary actors, furthermore, are not necessarily immune from private suit. The securities statutes provide an express private right of action against accountants and

underwriters in certain circumstances, see 15 U.S.C. § 77k, and the implied right of action in § 10 (b) continues to cover secondary actors who **774 commit primary violations. Central Bank, supra, at 191, 114 S.Ct. 1439.

[14] Here respondents were acting in concert with Charter in the ordinary course as suppliers and, as matters then evolved in the not so ordinary course, as customers. Unconventional as the arrangement was, it took place in the marketplace for goods and services, not in the investment sphere. Charter was free to do as it chose in preparing its books, conferring with its auditor, and preparing and then issuing its financial statements. In these circumstances the investors cannot be *167 said to have relied upon any of respondents' deceptive acts in the decision to purchase or sell securities; and as the requisite reliance cannot be shown, respondents have no liability to petitioner under the implied right of action. This conclusion is consistent with the narrow dimensions we must give to a right of action Congress did not authorize when it first enacted the statute and did not expand when it revisited the law.

The judgment of the Court of Appeals is affirmed, and the case is remanded for further proceedings consistent with this opinion.

It is so ordered.

Justice STEVENS, with whom Justice SOUTER and Justice GINSBURG join, dissenting….

第三节　证券发行与承销

证券发行是指证券发行人依照法定条件和程序发售证券的法律行为，是企业筹集资金的基本途径。关于证券发行制度，目前世界上主要有两种模式：一是核准制（substantive review），即证券发行不仅须满足信息公开等法定条件，而且还须在法定期限内通过证券监管机关的实质审查及核准；二是注册制（registration），即发行人在证券发行前向证券发行监管机关提交与发行有关的所有文件，在法定期限内如果证券监管机关未提出异议，其即可发行证券。

证券发行通过监管部门审查之后，具体的发售工作是由发行人聘请的承销商负责的。证券的承销，主要包括代销和包销两种方式。代销和包销的主要区别在于，对于未售出的证券，代销模式之下承销商可全部退还给发行人，而包销模式之下承销商则应当全部自行购入，不可退还给发行人。

一、中国的证券发行与承销

（一）证券发行

在中国，证券的发行包括公开发行和非公开发行。根据中国《证券法》的规定，有下列情形之一的，为公开发行：（1）向不特定对象发行证券的；（2）向特定对象发行证券累计超过 200 人的；（3）法律、行政法规规定的其他发行行为。除此之外的发行，则为非公开发行。无论是公开发行还是非公开发行，均需要有关主管部门的审核批准，而不存在任何审核豁免。

中国实行证券发行核准制度。对于公开发行证券，必须符合法律、行政法规规定的条件，并依法报经中国证监会或者国务院授权的部门核准；未经依法核准，任何单位和个人不得公开发行证券。对于非公开发行证券，只能向特定对象发行，且不得采用广告、公开劝诱和变相公开方式，同时还应当符合相关主管部门规定的条件，并报主管部门核准。中国证监会或者国务院授权的部门应当自受理证券发行申请文件之日起一定期限内，依照法定条件和法定程序作出予以核准或者不予核准的决定。

对于公开发行的证券，证券发行申请经核准，发行人应当依照法律、行政法规的规定，在证券公开发行前，公告公开发行募集文件，并将该文件置备于指定场所供公众查阅。发行证券的信息依法公开前，任何知情人不得公开或者泄露该信息。发行人不得在公告公开发行募集文件前发行证券。

中国证监会或者国务院授权的部门对已作出的核准证券发行的决定，发现不符合法定条件或者法定程序，尚未发行证券的，应当予以撤销，停止发行；已经发行尚未上市的，撤销发行核准决定，发行人应当按照发行价并加算银行同期存款利息返还证券持有人。

（二）证券承销

证券承销是指证券发行人委托具有证券承销资格的金融机构代为向社会公众发行证券的行为，它是证券经营机构最基础的业务活动之一。在中国，证券承销采取代销或者包销方式。证券代销是指证券公司代发行人发售证券，在承销期结束时，将未售出的证券全部退还给发行人的承销方式。证券包销是指证券公司将发行人的证券按照协议全部购入或者在承销期结束时将售后剩余证券全部自行购入的承销方式。

根据中国《证券法》的规定，发行人向不特定对象公开发行的证券，法律、行政法规规定应当由证券公司承销的，发行人应当同证券公司签订承销协议。公开发行证券的发行人有权依法自主选择承销的证券公司。证券公司不得以不正当竞争手段招揽证券承销业务。

证券公司实施证券承销前，应当向中国证监会报送发行与承销方案。证券公司承销证券，应当对公开发行募集文件的真实性、准确性、完整性进行核查；发现有虚假记载、误导性陈述或者重大遗漏的，不得进行销售活动；已经销售的，必须立即停止销售活动，并采取纠正措施。

证券发行由两家以上证券公司联合主承销的，所有担任主承销商的证券公司应当共同承担主承销责任，履行相关义务。承销团由三家以上承销商组成的，可以设副主承销商，协助主承销商组织承销活动。

二、美国的证券发行与承销

（一）证券发行

在美国，证券的发行采取注册制。发行人既要在证券交易委员会进行注册，又要在证券交易所注册。根据《1933 年证券法》的规定，任何人就未经注册的任何证券所为的任何销售均被禁止。发行注册申请获得批准的条件是，注册文件能够确保公众得到的有关发行人信息的充分性，并确保被注册证券的性质、发行人的资本结构以及证券持有人的权利被正确理解，以及对公众利益和保护投资者等方面给予应有的注意等。[①]

美国《1933 年证券法》规定了证券发行审核程序和行政程序。从审核程序看，证券发行注册分为三个阶段：

第一，注册申请提交之前阶段（Pre-Filing Period），即注册申报书送达 SEC 之前开始筹划发行证券，准备注册申请文件的阶段。在这一阶段，发行人、承销商和自营商不得有任何推销证券的行为，目的在于保证当信息未公开时，杜绝任何销售活动的存在。

第二，等待阶段（Waiting Period），即注册文件提交后，SEC 审核阶段。SEC 的审核时间为 20 天，自公司提交注册申报书之日算起。如果 SEC 认为注册文件有不充分、不准确之处，可以向申报人提出补充、修订的要求，申报人应进行补充、修订并延长注册生效期。如果 SEC 未提异议的，审核自提交申请 20 日后，或由 SEC 决定的更早的日子自动生效，发行人即可进入市场发行证券。在这一阶段，任何通过邮件或其他州际商务通讯手段发送招股说明书的行为都是违法的，但是以下行为则被允许：作出口头要约；作简单广告，其内容包括发行人、证券种类、价格及何处取得公开说明书等；制定初步公开说明书，该文件是申报注册文件的一部分，包括发行价格、承销报酬以外的公开说明书的全部内容。

第三，注册生效之后阶段（Post-Effective Period）。此阶段可从事证券发行并订立合同，但必须适时提交公开说明书。其他补充宣传文件也可于此阶段使用，但必须于事前或同时交付公开说明书，以防止投资者被夸大的宣传所迷惑。

在美国，并非所有证券的发行都要注册，有些证券实行发行豁免或交易豁免。根据

---

① 李朝晖. 证券市场法律监管比较研究. 北京：人民出版社，2000：94.

《1933 年证券法》的规定，以下证券豁免注册：

一是由特定机构或部门发行的证券，包括：（1）政府或银行发行或担保的证券；（2）短期商业票据；（3）非营利的宗教、教育或慈善团体发行的证券；（4）法定机构发行的证券；（5）受州际商务委员会监督的运送人发行的证券；（6）经法庭许可，由破产管理人发行的证券；（7）由政府机构监督下发行的担保单、捐款单及年金契约。由于发行人具有特殊性质，上述证券为永久性豁免。

二是特定情形或特定地域发行的证券，包括：（1）发行人及证券持有人间自愿的证券交换行为；（2）于公司重整时，由公司法或行政当局许可的证券发行；（3）在向某一州或准州居民发行或出售的证券。此类证券的发行，属豁免交易，即只有本次发行出售行为豁免，其第二次发行行为仍然要依法注册。

豁免交易还包括：（1）小额交易豁免（500 万美元以下的证券发行）；（2）私募发行豁免。私募发行豁免是美国《1933 年证券法》中的一项重要制度。在美国，构成私募发行，主要需要满足两个条件：一是发行对象的人数。依照 SEC 的观点，对 25 人以下进行招募构成私募，可豁免注册；二是发行对象的特定性，如果被招募人或被劝诱人与发行公司关系密切，甚至可以接近发行公司及其证券信息，可以保护自己，则构成私募。

在美国，证券发行过程中最重要的一环是信息披露。SEC 通过登记和披露制度，以确保发行公司准确地披露其财务状况、业务发展计划、实现计划目标的条件和可能性以及潜在的风险因素等。发行公司必须确保其披露信息的全面、真实和准确。如果披露的信息中存在重大遗漏或隐瞒或者存在重大的虚假信息，投资者有权提起诉讼，并可得到 SEC 的支持，直至追究有关当事人的民事或刑事责任。有关责任人主要包括：证券发行人；承销并分销证券的投资银行；参与申报书起草和审定并在其上签章属实的会计师、审计师和其他专家。对于证券发行欺诈，美国还允许投资者提起集团诉讼，这对于发行证券的公司形成巨大的威慑力。

（二）证券承销

美国的有价证券承销方式主要包括确定包销（firm-commitment underwriting）、余额包销（stand-by underwriting）、代销或称尽力销售（best-efforts underwriting）和竞价（competitive bidding）等方式，其中确定包销是主要的方式。

在确定包销方式下，证券承销机构先是其承销证券的唯一买方，后来又成为唯一的卖方。证券承销机构要将证券先行全部购入，其收益主要取决于承销折扣。因此，其倾向于订定一个对所发行证券更合适的价格从而保证自身的利益，从而也保证了发行人的利益。总体上，确定包销的方式更容易达到证券发行人和证券承销机构之间利益的一致性，因而确定包销在美国的证券承销中占据了主要地位。

余额包销同确定包销一样，也能给证券发行人提供某种保障，但是两者有着一定的区别。在余额包销中，证券承销机构主要承担一种经纪职能。在这里，证券发行人的风险转移得更为彻底。证券承销机构倾向于订定较高的承销价格，并议定一旦不能完全销售，其将以一个相同的价格购入剩余证券以作为其长期投资。

在代销方式中，一个承销商或者承销团同意尽最大努力将一定数量的证券向公众销售。承销商可能只是简单地承诺销售它们能做到的任何比例，它们的协议可能是完全不产生效果的。很明显，比起包销来，这种承销方式下承销商的风险较小，因此它几乎完全为小型承销商所使用。

竞价是确定包销的一种特殊方式。根据SEC发布的规定，凡是受《公用事业控股公司法》（Public Utility Holding Company Act）规范的公司所发行的证券的销售，必须采用竞价的方式。这主要是为了防止在涉及公共利益的公司股票销售时，承销机构以低于股票实际价值的承销价格取得股票，侵犯公众的利益。

三、案例资料

美国《1933年证券法》对于证券的公开发行采取注册制和信息强制披露，其目的是确保向投资者充分披露投资者认为形成投资决策所必需的信息，使其可以作出适当的投资决定，从而保护其正当利益。但是，根据《1933年证券法》的规定，对于不涉及公开发售的证券发行，发行人则被豁免了证券注册和信息强制披露的义务。在非公开发行之下，发行对象被认为有能力进行自我保护，而无须得到证券法中有关证券注册和信息强制披露制度的保护。非公开发行的证券投资者要承担更大的风险，这就对非公开发行的投资者提出了一定的资格限制。

在下面的Doran v. Petroleum Management Corp. 案中，美国联邦第五巡回上诉法院对非公开发行的对象的资格要求进行了深入分析。

在该案中，被告组建了一个有限合伙去开发油井。为了筹集资金，被告邀请原告以“特别参与人”（special participant）的身份参与该油井开发计划，原告同意并进行出资。后因该油井产量下降，导致原告作为出资而开具的本票到期未能承兑付款。本票的持票人起诉原告，并获得胜诉判决。原告则起诉被告，主张被告向其兜售证券时，虚假陈述及遗漏重大事实，违反了美国证券法的相关规定，要求撤销其出资的合约并责令被告承担违约责任。

该案的核心在于，被告邀请原告出资参与油井开发计划的行为是否构成证券的非公开发行。一审法院认定，因为原告自己是一名经验丰富的投资者，其无须得到证券法的保护，所以被告的行为属于非公开发行从而得到豁免，故驳回了原告的诉讼请求。原告遂提出上诉。

二审法院重点从发行对象的资格方面入手，分析了该案中的发行是否满足非公开发行豁免的要求。二审法院认为，就发行对象而言，只要其作为富有经验的投资者能在占有充分、真实的信息基础上正常行使其投资技能即满足立法要求。发行对象所能获得的信息，必须达到一个成熟的投资者足以运用其知识、技能作出投资判断的程度。对此，如何予以证明？二审法院提供了两条路径：发行人的披露（disclosure）或发行对象获取信息的途径（access）。即发行人要么证明其实际上已向所有的发行对象提供了注册声明书所能提供的全部信息，或者证明发行对象有获得包含此类相关信息的公司档案和记录的途径。从信息途径入手，发行人必须证明，发行对象相比于发行人处于优势地位，这种优势地位给发行对象提供了有效获取所需信息的途径。但是，这种优势地位并不要求发行对象必须是公司内部人（insider）。

该案确立了判定是否满足非公开发行豁免的标准，尤其是认定非公开发行的发行对象并非必须是公司内部人，这对充分发挥非公开发行的融资功能具有重要的促进作用。在该案之后，又有诸多判例对非公开发行的对象进行了讨论。最终，SEC 在总结法院判例的基础上，对非公开发行的对象类型进行了归纳，在“条例 D”（Regulation D）下“规则 501” (Rule 501) 的定义条款中，详细列举了“经认定的投资者”的种类。如果发行对象属于“经认定的投资者”，非公开发行的豁免就可以得到确认。

Doran v. Petroleum Management Corp.

545 F.2d 893 (5 Cir. 1977)

GOLDBERG, Circuit Judge:

In this case a sophisticated investor who purchased a limited partnership interest in an oil drilling venture seeks to rescind. The question raised is whether the sale was part of a private offering exempted by s 4 (2) of the Securities Act of 1933, 15 U.S.C. s 77d(2) (1970), from the registration requirements of that Act. See Securities Act of 1933, ss 5, 12 (1), 15 U.S.C. ss 77e, 77l (1). We hold that in the absence of findings of fact that each offeree had been furnished information about the issuer that a registration statement would have disclosed or that each offeree had effective access to such information, the district court erred in concluding that the offering was a private placement. Accordingly, we reverse and remand.

I. Facts

Prior to July 1970, Petroleum Management Corporation (PMC) organized a California limited partnership for the purpose of drilling and operating four wells in Wyoming. The limited partnership agreement provided for both “participants,” whose capital contributions were to be used first to pay all intangible expenses incurred by the partnership, and "special participants," whose capital contributions were to be applied first to pay tangible drilling expenses.

*898 PMC and Inter-Tech Resources, Inc., were initially the only "special participants" in the limited partnership. They were joined by four "participants." As found by the district court, PMC contacted only four other persons with respect to possible participation in the partnership. All but the plaintiff declined.

During the late summer of 1970, plaintiff William H. Doran, Jr., received a telephone call from a California securities broker previously known to him. The broker, Phillip Kendrick, advised Doran of the opportunity to become a "special participant" in the partnership. PMC then sent Doran the drilling logs and technical maps of the proposed drilling area. PMC informed Doran that two of the proposed four wells had already been completed. Doran agreed to become a "special participant" in the Wyoming drilling program. In consideration for his partnership share, Doran agreed to contribute $125 000 toward the partnership. Doran was to discharge this obligation by paying PMC $25 000 down and in addition assuming responsibility for the payment of a $113 643 note owed by PMC to Mid-Continent Supply Co. Doran's share in the production payments from the wells was to be used to make the installment payments on the Mid-Continent note.

Pursuant to this arrangement, on September 16, 1970, Doran executed a promissory note, already signed by the President and Vice President of PMC in their individual capacities, for $113 643 payable to Mid-Continent. On October 5, 1970, Doran mailed PMC a check for $25 000. He thereby became a "special participant" in the Wyoming drilling program.

On July 16, 1971, the balance on the note to Mid-Continent became due. The parties renegotiated the loan. A new note for $66 292.24 was executed by PMC, the two PMC officers, and Doran. Pursuant to a written agreement of February 9, 1971, however, Doran had agreed to hold PMC and its officers harmless for any liability arising from the Mid-Continent note. The July renegotiation did not alter Doran's obligation.

During 1970 and 1971, PMC periodically sent Doran production information on the completed wells of the limited partnership. Throughout this period, however, the wells were deliberately overproduced in violation of the production allowances established by the Wyoming Oil and Gas Conservation Commission. As a consequence, on November 16, 1971, the Commission ordered the partnership's wells sealed for a period of 338 days. On May 1, 1972, the Commission notified PMC that production from the wells could resume on August 9,

1972. After August 9, the wells yielded a production income level below that obtained prior to the Commission's order.

Following the cessation of production payments between November 1971 and August 1972 and the decreased yields thereafter, the Mid-Continent note upon which Doran was primarily liable went into default. Mid-Continent subsequently obtained a state court judgment against Doran, PMC, and the two signatory officers of PMC for $50 815.50 plus interest and attorney's fees.

On October 16, 1972, Doran filed this suit in federal district court seeking damages for breach of contract, rescission of the contract based on violations of the Securities Acts of 1933 and 1934, and a judgment declaring the defendants liable for payment of the state judgment obtained by Mid-Continent.

The court below found that the offer and sale of the "special participant" interest was a private offering because Doran was a sophisticated investor who did not need the *899 protection of the Securities Acts. The court also found that there was no evidence that PMC, its officers, or Kendrick made any misrepresentation or omissions of material facts to Doran. Finally, the court found that the overproduction of the wells was not a breach of the partnership agreement, but in any event there was no evidence that Doran suffered any losses as a result of the overproduction. The court concluded that all relief requested by Doran should be denied. Doran filed this appeal.

II. The Private Offering Exemption

[1] [2] No registration statement was filed with any federal or state regulatory body in connection with the defendants' offering of securities. Along with two other factors that we may take as established that the defendants sold or offered to sell these securities, and that the defendants used interstate transportation or communication in connection with the sale or offer of sale the plaintiff thus states a prima facie case for a violation of the federal securities laws. See Hill York Corp. v. American International Franchises, Inc., 448 F.2d 680, 686 (5th Cir. 1971).

[3] The defendants do not contest the existence of the elements of plaintiff's prima facie case but raise an affirmative defense that the relevant transactions came within the exemption from registration found in s 4 (2), 15 U.S.C. s 77d(2). Specifically, they contend that the offering of securities was not a public offering. The defendants, who of course bear the burden of proving this affirmative defense, must therefore show that the offering was private. See SEC v. Ralston Purina Co., 346 U.S. 119, 126, 73 S.Ct. 981, 985, 97 L.Ed. 1494 (1953); Hill York

Corp. v. American International Franchises, Inc., supra, 448 F.2d at 690; Lively v. Hirschfeld, 440 F.2d 631, 632 (10th Cir. 1971); United States v. Custer Channel Wing Corp., 376 F.2d 675, 678 (4th Cir.), cert. denied, 389 U.S. 850, 88 S.Ct. 38, 19 L.Ed.2d 119 (1967).

[4] This court has in the past identified four factors relevant to whether an offering qualifies for the exemption. The consideration of these factors, along with the policies embodied in the 1933 Act, structure the inquiry. *900 Hill York Corp. v. American International Franchises, Inc., supra, 448 F.2d at 687-88; Henderson v. Hayden, Stone Inc., 461 F.2d 1069, 1071 (5th Cir. 1972); SEC v. Continental Tobacco Co. of South Carolina, 463 F.2d 137, 158 (5th Cir. 1972); see also Woolf v. S. D. Cohn & Co., 515 F.2d 591, 609 (5th Cir. 1975), vacated on other grounds, 426 U.S. 944, 96 S.Ct. 3161, 49 L.Ed.2d 1181 (1976). The relevant factors include the number of offerees and their relationship to each other and the issuer, the number of units offered, the size of the offering, and the manner of the offering. Consideration of these factors need not exhaust the inquiry, nor is one factor's weighing heavily in favor of the private status of the offering sufficient to ensure the availability of the exemption. Rather, these factors serve as guideposts to the court in attempting to determine whether subjecting the offering to registration requirements would further the purposes of the 1933 Act.

[5] [6] The term, "private offering," is not defined in the Securities Act of 1933. The scope of the s 4 (2) private offering exemption must therefore be determined by reference to the legislative purposes of the Act. In SEC v. Ralston Purina Co., supra, the SEC had sought to enjoin a corporation's offer of unregistered stock to its employees, and the Court grappled with the corporation's defense that the offering came within the private placement exemption. The Court began by looking to the statutory purpose:

> Since exempt transactions are those as to which "there is no practical need for... (the bill's) application," the applicability of (s 4 (2)) should turn on whether the particular class of persons affected need the protection of the Act. An offering to those who are shown to be able to fend for themselves is a transaction "not involving any public offering."

346 U.S. at 124, 73 S.Ct. at 984. According to the Court, the purpose of the Act was "to protect investors by promoting full disclosure of information thought necessary to informed investment decisions." Id. at 124, 73 S.Ct. at 984. It therefore followed that "the exemption question turns on the knowledge of the offerees." Id. at 126-27, 73 S.Ct. at 985. That

formulation remains the touchstone of the inquiry into the scope of the private offering exemption. It is most nearly reflected in the first of the four factors: the number of offerees and their relationship to each other and to the issuer.

In the case at bar, the defendants may have demonstrated the presence of the latter three factors. A small number of units offered, relatively modest financial stakes, and an offering characterized by personal contact between the issuer and offerees free of public advertising or intermediaries such as investment bankers or securities exchanges these aspects of the instant transaction aid the defendants' search for a s 4 (2) exemption.

Nevertheless, with respect to the first, most critical, and conceptually most problematic factor, the record does not permit us to agree that the defendants have proved that they are entitled to the limited sanctuary afforded by s 4 (2). We must examine more closely the importance of demonstrating both the number of offerees and their relationship to the issuer in order to see why the defendants have not yet gained the s 4 (2) exemption.

A. The Number of Offerees

Establishing the number of persons involved in an offering is important both in order to ascertain the magnitude of the offering and in order to determine the characteristics and knowledge of the persons thus identified.

[7] [8] [9] [10] The number of offerees, not the number of purchasers, is the relevant figure in considering the number of persons involved in an offering. Hill York Corp. v. American International Franchises, Inc., supra, 448 F.2d at 691. A private placement *901 claimant's failure to adduce any evidence regarding the number of offerees will be fatal to the claim. SEC v. Continental Tobacco Co., supra, 463 F.2d at 161; Henderson v. Hayden, Stone Inc., supra, 461 F.2d at 1071-72; Repass v. Rees, 174 F.Supp. 898, 904 (D.Colo.1959). The number of offerees is not itself a decisive factor in determining the availability of the private offering exemption. Just as an offering to few may be public, so an offering to many may be private. SEC v. Ralston Purina Co., supra, 346 U.S. at 125, 73 S.Ct. at 984-85. Nevertheless, "the more offerees, the more likelihood that the offering is public." Hill York Corp. v. American International Franchises, Inc., supra, 448 F.2d at 688. In the case at bar, the record indicates that eight investors were offered limited partnership shares in the drilling program a total that would be entirely consistent with a finding that the offering was private.

The defendants attempt to limit the number of offerees even further, however. They argue that Doran was the sole offeree because all others contacted by PMC were offered "participant" rather than "special participant" interests. The district court, which did not issue a finding of fact or conclusion of law with respect to this argument, appears to have assumed that there were eight offerees.

[11] [12] [13] The argument is, in any event, unsupported by the record. The only evidence that the defendants adduced to show the number of offerees established merely that offers of "participant" interests were made to four investors who accepted, and that offers of "limited partnership" interests were made to three other prospective investors who declined. Because both "participant" and "special participant" interests were limited partnership interests, we are unable to discern from the record whether the three declining investors were offered "special participant" interests. Moreover, we have no evidence that the four "participants" were not also offered "special participant" interests. The defendants have the burden of proof regarding the number of offerees. We must therefore reject the argument that Doran was the sole offeree.

*902 [14] In considering the number of offerees solely as indicative of the magnitude or scope of an offering, the difference between one and eight offerees is relatively unimportant. Rejecting the argument that Doran was the sole offeree is significant, however, because it means that in considering the need of the offerees for the protection that registration would have afforded we must look beyond Doran's interests to those of all his fellow offerees. Even the offeree-plaintiff's 20-20 vision with respect to the facts underlying the security would not save the exemption if any one of his fellow offerees was in a blind.

B. The Offerees' Relationship to the Issuer

Since SEC v. Ralston, supra, courts have sought to determine the need of offerees for the protections afforded by registration by focusing on the relationship between offerees and issuer and more particularly on the information available to the offerees by virtue of that relationship. Id., 346 U.S. at 126-27, 73 S.Ct. at 985. Once the offerees have been identified, it is possible to investigate their relationship to the issuer.

[15] The district court concluded that the offer of a "special participant" interest to Doran was a private offering because Doran was a sophisticated investor who did not need the protections afforded by registration. It is important, in light of our rejection of the argument that Doran was the sole offeree, that the district court also found that all four " participants" and all three declining offerees were sophisticated investors with regard to oil ventures.

[16] The need of the offerees for the protection afforded by registration is, to be sure, a question of fact dependent upon the circumstances of each case. Hill York Corp. v. American

International Franchises, Inc., supra, 448 F.2d at 687. Nevertheless, the trial court's conclusion with respect to the availability of the private offering exemption may be set aside if induced by an erroneous view of the law. See SEC v. Continental Tobacco Co., supra, 463 F.2d at 156-57; Henderson v. Hayden, Stone Inc., supra, 461 F.2d at 1071.

1. The role of investment sophistication

[17] The lower court's finding that Doran was a sophisticated investor is amply supported by the record, as is the sophistication of the other offerees. Doran holds a petroleum engineering degree from Texas A&M University. His net worth is in excess of $1 000 000. His holdings of approximately twenty-six oil and gas properties are valued at $850 000.

[18] [19] Nevertheless, evidence of a high degree of business or legal sophistication on the part of all offerees does not suffice to bring the offering within the private placement exemption. We clearly established that proposition in Hill York Corp. v. American International Franchises, Inc., supra, 448 F.2d at 690. We reasoned that "if the plaintiffs did not possess the information requisite for a registration statement, they could not bring their sophisticated knowledge of business affairs to bear in deciding whether or not to invest...." Sophistication is not a substitute for access to the information that registration would disclose. United States v. Custer Channel Wing Corp., supra, 376 F.2d at 678. As we said in Hill York, although the evidence of the offerees' expertise "is certainly favorable to the defendants, the level of sophistication will not carry the point. In this context, the relationship between the promoters and the purchasers and the 'access to the kind of information which registration would disclose' become highly relevant factors." 448 F.2d at 690.

*903 [20] In short, there must be sufficient basis of accurate information upon which the sophisticated investor may exercise his skills. Just as a scientist cannot be without his specimens, so the shrewdest investor's acuity will be blunted without specifications about the issuer. For an investor to be invested with exemptive status he must have the required data for judgment.

2. The requirement of available information

The interplay between two factors, the relationship between offerees and issuer and the offerees' access to information that registration would disclose, has been a matter of some conceptual and terminological difficulty. For purposes of this discussion, we shall adopt the following conventions: We shall refer to offerees who have not been furnished registration information directly, but who are in a position relative to the issuer to obtain the information registration would provide, as having "access" to such information. By a position of access we mean a relationship based on factors such as employment, family, or economic bargaining power that enables the offeree effectively to obtain such information. See SEC Rule 146 (e), 17 C.F.R. s 280.146 (e) (1976). When offerees, regardless of whether they occupy a position of access, have been furnished with the information a registration statement would provide, we shall say merely that such information has been disclosed. When the offerees have access to or there has been disclosure of the information registration would provide, we shall say that such information was available.

[21] The requirement that all offerees have available the information registration would provide has been firmly established by this court as a necessary condition of gaining the private offering exemption. Our decisions have been predicated upon Ralston Purina, supra, where the Supreme Court held that in the absence of a showing that the "key employees" to whom a corporation offered its common stock had knowledge obviating the need for registration, the offering did not qualify for the private offering exemption. The Court said that an employee offering would come within the exemption if it were shown that the employees were "executive personnel who because of their position have access to the same kind of information that the act would make available in the form of a registration statement." Id., 346 U.S. at 125-26, 73 S.Ct. at 985.

[22] In Hill York Corp. v. American International Franchises, Inc., supra, 448 F.2d at 689, this court approved jury instructions that "correctly stated the ultimate test... that every offeree had to have information equivalent to that which a registration statement would disclose." In subsequent cases we have adhered to that test. See Woolf v. S. D. Cohn & Co., supra, 515 F.2d at 613; SEC v. Continental Tobacco Co., supra, 463 F.2d at 158-61; Henderson v. Hayden, Stone Inc., supra, 461 F.2d at 1071. Because the district court failed to apply this test to the case at bar, but *904 rather inferred from evidence of Doran's sophistication that his purchase of a partnership share was incident to a private offering, we must remand so that the lower court may determine the extent of the information available to each offeree.

More specifically, we shall require on remand that the defendants demonstrate that all offerees, whatever their expertise, had available the information a registration statement would have afforded a prospective investor in a public offering. Such a showing is not independently sufficient to establish that the offering qualified for the private placement exemption, but it is necessary to gain the exemption and is to be weighed along with the sophistication and number of the offerees, the number of units offered, and the size and manner of the offering.

See SEC v. Continental Tobacco Co., supra, 463 F.2d at 160; see also Woolf v. S. D. Cohn & Co., supra, 515 F.2d at 610-613. Because in this case these latter factors weigh heavily in favor of the private offering exemption, satisfaction of the necessary condition regarding the availability of relevant information to the offerees would compel the conclusion that this offering fell within the exemption.

[23] The cornerstone of the regulatory structure envisaged by the authors of the Securities Act is disclosure. The Act is practical and pragmatic, not dogmatic and doctrinaire. It is designed to give a panoply of protection to the investor, but also to allow play in the marts of trade for offers of securities that do not require the oversight of the Securities and Exchange Commission. In suggesting the scope of that exemption, we cannot divine all the variables of a formula that might enable a trial court precisely to determine whether a given offering falls within or without its perimeter. There are few certitudes, and in interpreting the statute we must permit ourselves room for the ifs, the perhapses, and the maybes in commercial relationships and variegated investor postures. The question of exemption remains one of fact reserved in the first instance for the trial court. Nevertheless, it cannot be doubted that within or without the perimeter of the private offering exemption, the policies of the Securities Act mandate that the courts focus on the information available to the offerees of a security.

C. On Remand: The Issuer-Offeree Relationship

[24] In determining on remand the extent of the information available to the offerees, the district court must keep in mind that the "availability" of information means either disclosure of or effective access to the relevant information. The relationship between issuer and offeree is most critical when the issuer relies on the latter route.

[25] To begin with, if the defendants could prove that all offerees were actually furnished the information a registration statement would have provided, whether the offerees occupied a position of access pre-existing such disclosure would not be dispositive of the status of the offering. If disclosure were proved and if, as here, the remaining factors such as the manner of the offering and the investment sophistication of the offerees weigh heavily in favor of the private status of the offering, the absence of a privileged relationship between offeree and issuer would not preclude a finding that the offering was private. Any other conclusion would tear out of context this court's earlier discussions of the s 4 (2) exemption and would conflict with the policies of the exemption.

Alternatively it might be shown that the offeree had access to the files and record of the company that contained the relevant information. Such access might be afforded merely by the position of the offeree or by the issuer's promise to open appropriate files and records to the offeree as well as to answer inquiries regarding material information. In either case, the relationship between offeree and issuer now becomes critical, for it must be shown that the offeree could realistically have been expected to take advantage of his access to ascertain *905 the relevant information. Similarly the investment sophistication of the offeree assumes added importance, for it is important that he could have been expected to ask the right questions and seek out the relevant information.

[26] In sum, both the relationship between issuer and offeree and the latter's investment sophistication are critical when the issuer or another relies on the offeree's "access" rather than the issuer's "disclosure" to come within the exemption. We shall first show that this formulation is consistent with the current state of private offering law in this and other circuits. Second, we shall examine the misconception that our cases require a privileged or "insider" relationship between issuer and offeree as a necessary condition of coming within the s 4 (2) exemption. Once the distinction between "access" and "disclosure" is fully recognized, our caselaw should not be construed to embody such a requirement.

1. Disclosure or access: a disjunctive requirement

That our cases sometimes fail clearly to differentiate between "access" and "disclosure" as alternative means of coming within the private offering exemption is, perhaps, not surprising. Although the Ralston Purina decision focused on whether the offerees had "access" to the required information, 346 U.S. at 127, 73 S.Ct. at 981, the holding that "the exemption question turns on the knowledge of the offerees," id. at 126, 73 S.Ct. at 981, could be construed to include possession as well as access. Such an interpretation would require disclosure as a necessary condition of obtaining a private offering notwithstanding the offerees' access to the information that registration would have provided.

Both the Second and the Fourth Circuits, however, have interpreted Ralston Purina as embodying a disjunctive requirement. Thus, for example, in Gilligan, Will & Co. v. SEC, 267 F.2d 461, 466 (2nd Cir. 1959), cert. denied, 361 U.S. 896, 80 S.Ct. 200, 4 L.Ed.2d 152 (1960), the court observed that Ralston Purina "held that the governing fact is whether the persons to whom the offering is made are in such a position with respect to the issuer that they either actually have such information as a registration would have disclosed, or have access to such information." See also SEC v. Tax Service, Inc., 357 F.2d 143, 144 (4th Cir. 1966).

The cases in this circuit are not inconsistent with this view. In Woolf v. S.D. Cohn & Co., supra, 515 F.2d at 612-13, we admittedly read Continental as "requiring that there be disclosure of the information registration would have revealed to each offeree...." Because the court in Continental found neither disclosure to all offerees of the information registration would provide nor their access to such information, however, the case does not hold that when sophisticated offerees have access to the requisite information by virtue of their privileged relationship to the issuer, actual disclosure is nonetheless necessary. Only if the defendants in Continental had demonstrated that all offerees were sophisticated and that all had access to the relevant information, but the court had nevertheless required actual disclosure, could Continental foreclose the view we express in the case at bar.

Similarly, in Woolf we found that because it was not clear "what information was disclosed to whom at what time," we were obliged to remand the case. Because the defendants in Woolf did not argue that *906 the offerees' access to information qualified the offering for private status even without actual disclosure, we did not and could not hold that disclosure was the only means of coming within the exemption.

Woolf refers to Rule 146 as a "useful frame of reference to an appellate court in assessing the validity of s 4 (2) exemptions claimed... prior to its effective date." 515 F.2d at 612. Since Woolf elsewhere notes specifically that Rule 146 would permit the issuer to show either access or disclosure, it is inconceivable that the court in Woolf would establish more stringent requirements for this circuit or would interpret Continental to establish such requirements. Rather, Woolf observes correctly that Rule 146 does not purport to be an exclusive definition of the circumstances under which the exemption is available, implying that there will be a class of placements that do not satisfy the more stringent criteria of the Rule 146 safe harbor but are nevertheless to be accorded private status. Id. at 612.

[27] Although Rule 146 cannot directly control the case at bar, we think its disjunctive requirement that the private offering claimant may show either "access" or "disclosure" expresses a sound view that this court has in fact implicitly accepted. For example, in Hill York Corp. v. American International Franchises, Inc., supra, 448 F.2d at 690-91, this court thought it necessary to show that the offerees neither possessed the information registration would afford nor had access to such information. See also 1 Loss, Securities Regulation 657 n.53 (2d ed. 1961), quoted in Hill York, supra, 448 F.2d at 698. And in Henderson v. Hayden, Stone Inc., supra, 461 F.2d at 1072, the court clearly separates the questions: "Did (the offerees) possess the same information as would be found in a registration statement? Did they have

access to such information?"

2. The role of insider status

[28] [29] [30] Once the alternative means of coming within the private placement exemption are clearly separated, we can appreciate the proper role to be accorded the requirement that the offerees occupy a privileged or "insider" status relative to the issuer. That is to say, when the issuer relies on "access" absent actual disclosure, he must show that the offerees occupied a privileged position relative to the issuer that afforded them an opportunity for effective access to the information registration would otherwise provide. When the *907 issuer relies on actual disclosure to come within the exemption, he need not demonstrate that the offerees held such a privileged position. Although mere disclosure is not a sufficient condition for establishing the availability of the private offering exemption, and a court will weigh other factors such as the manner of the offering and the investment sophistication of the offerees, the "insider" status of the offerees is not a necessary condition of obtaining the exemption.

Because the line between access and disclosure has sometimes been obscured, some have interpreted this court's decision in Continental as limiting the s 4 (2) exemption to insider transactions. As we pointed out in our recent decision in Woolf, however, such fears are unfounded. 515 F.2d at 610.

The language from Continental that gave rise to those fears consists in the court's findings that "Continental did not affirmatively prove that all offerees of its securities had received both written and oral information concerning Continental, that all offerees of its securities had access to any additional information which they might have required or requested, and that all offerees of its securities had personal contacts with the officers of Continental." 463 F.2d at 160. It is possible to read this as a list of the necessary conditions for coming within the s 4 (2) exemption, and therefore to infer that a private placement claimant must show the "insider" status of the offerees. Properly viewed in context, however, these statements were not clearly intended to establish necessary conditions, but only to point to the manifold weaknesses of the defendant's claim which, taken together, precluded private offering status.

In Continental, the court admittedly agreed with the SEC's position that even if the prospectus that Continental had sent to purchasers contained all the information registration would disclose, that fact alone would not justify the exemption. 463 F.2d at 160. That is doubtless true, since even if all the purchasers of Continental's securities had received full disclosure, the defendant would not have established that all offerees had received full disclosure. Because Continental had failed to sustain its burden of demonstrating the number of offerees, moreover, even the fact that all known offerees might have received disclosure would still have been insufficient to ensure the availability of the exemption. But the court's language in Continental should not be read as requiring in addition to full disclosure to all offerees a demonstration of the offerees' insider status.

Rather, the court's language regarding Continental's failure to show that all offerees had access to the requisite information and that all offerees had personal contacts with Continental's officers may be read as foreclosing the possible alternative route to the s 4 (2) exemption. Because the prospectus did not contain all the information registration would provide and because it was not established that all offerees received the prospectus, it was clear that Continental could not rely upon actual disclosure. The additional language in Continental, though admittedly subject to other interpretations, may be read as making clear that there was in that case no privileged *908 relationship between the offerees and the issuer that might have compensated for the defendant's palpable failure to disclose.

Although the disjunctive nature of the requirement is, to be sure, not made explicit in Continental, it is important that the pertinent conclusion of fact held clearly erroneous in that case was that "the offerees... were furnished and/or provided access to the same type of information that would have been provided in a registration statement...." 463 F.2d at 159. In order to hold this conclusion clearly erroneous, it was thus necessary to show that the defendant had failed to prove either disclosure or access.

[31] In any event, absent a clear and unambiguous indication to the contrary, we do not read Continental as requiring insider status. We think that any such requirement would inhibit the ability of business to raise capital without the expense and delay of registration under circumstances in which the offerees did not need the protection of registration. The enactment of Rule 146 represents the SEC's recognition of this legitimate business need. We think that it would be unwise to adopt in this circuit a requirement of insider status notwithstanding disclosure or that of actual disclosure notwithstanding effective access. Such requirements would constrict the scope of the private offering exemption more narrowly than does Rule 146 and would retard necessary capital investment without a corresponding benefit to those investors who need the protection of registration.

Rule 146 offers some rays of sunlight into the limbos and uncertain depths of s 4 (2). The cases cast at best a faint beacon toward the horizon of decision. While we appreciate full well that the test we have fashioned remains too fluid to enable the would-be private offering issuer to feel entirely secure, we are confident that, at long last, the safe harbor of Rule 146 will provide that security and that few private placement claimants will stray far from that harbor. Rule 146 is a serotine development. More than two decades passed after Ralston before the SEC sufficiently elaborated on the definitional concepts behind s 4 (2). With respect to those transactions that antedate the effective date of Rule 146, this case and those preceding it in this circuit establish as the critical factor in determining whether the exemption applies to a particular offering the availability of information to all offerees. The privileged status of the offerees must be demonstrated only when it is necessary to the claimant's efforts to establish that the requisite information was in fact available.

…

第四节 证券交易

证券交易是指证券持有人依照交易规则，将证券转让给其他投资者的行为。[1]证券交易是一种特殊的买卖行为，除须遵守一般的商事交易法律规定（如《合同法》）之外，还要遵守相关证券法律、法规的规定。

一、中国的证券交易

在中国，证券交易主要受到中国《证券法》的管辖。中国《证券法》对证券交易有着全面的规定。

首先，证券交易当事人依法买卖的证券，必须是依法发行并交付的证券。非依法发行的证券，不得买卖。同时，对于某些特殊身份的人士（如上市公司董事、监事、高级管理人员、持有上市公司股份5%以上的股东），法律对其所持证券的转让期限有限制性规定，在限定的期限内不得买卖。

其次，证券只能在依法设立的证券交易所上市交易或者在国务院批准的其他证券交易场所转让。中国尚未建立场外证券交易制度，因此证券无法进行场外交易。证券在证券交易所上市交易，应当采用公开的集中交易方式或者中国证监会批准的其他方式。申请证券上市交易，应当向证券交易所提出申请，由证券交易所依法审核同意，并由双方签订上市协议。特定情形下，证券交易所有权暂停相关证券上市交易。

再次，证券发行人必须满足相关的信息披露要求。发行人要保证其依法披露的信息

---

① 徐孟州. 金融法. 北京：高等教育出版社，2007：123.

真实、准确、完整，无虚假记载、误导性陈述或者重大遗漏。在相关证券上市交易后，发行人或上市公司还必须进行持续的信息披露。尤其是发生可能对上市公司股票交易价格产生较大影响的重大事件，投资者尚未得知时，上市公司应当立即将有关该重大事件的情况向中国证监会和证券交易所报送临时报告，并予公告。

最后，就证券交易中的几类典型的违法行为，中国《证券法》对其都有着规定：

一是内幕交易行为。证券交易内幕信息的知情人和非法获取内幕信息的人不得利用内幕信息从事证券交易活动。因从事内幕交易行为给投资者造成损失的，行为人应当依法承担赔偿责任。其中，证券交易活动中，涉及公司的经营、财务或者对该公司证券的市场价格有重大影响的尚未公开的信息，为内幕信息。证券交易内幕信息的知情人包括：证券交易内幕信息的知情人和非法获取内幕信息的人，在内幕信息公开前，不得买卖该公司的证券，或者泄露该信息，或者建议他人买卖该证券。

二是操纵证券市场行为。中国《证券法》将如下几类行为界定为操纵证券市场行为：（1）单独或者通过合谋，集中资金优势、持股优势或者利用信息优势联合或者连续买卖，操纵证券交易价格或者证券交易量；（2）与他人串通，以事先约定的时间、价格和方式相互进行证券交易，影响证券交易价格或者证券交易量；（3）在自己实际控制的账户之间进行证券交易，影响证券交易价格或者证券交易量；（4）以其他手段操纵证券市场。因操纵证券市场行为给投资者造成损失的，行为人应当依法承担赔偿责任。

三是证券欺诈行为。证券欺诈行为，既包括发行人和上市公司的欺诈行为，也包括证券公司及其从业人员的欺诈行为。

其中，发行人、上市公司公告的招股说明书、公司债券募集办法、财务会计报告、上市报告文件、年度报告、中期报告、临时报告以及其他信息披露资料，有虚假记载、误导性陈述或者重大遗漏，致使投资者在证券交易中遭受损失的，发行人、上市公司应当承担赔偿责任；发行人、上市公司的董事、监事、高级管理人员和其他直接责任人员以及保荐人、承销的证券公司，应当与发行人、上市公司承担连带赔偿责任，但是能够证明自己没有过错的除外；发行人、上市公司的控股股东、实际控制人有过错的，应当与发行人、上市公司承担连带赔偿责任。

证券公司及其从业人员从事下列损害客户利益的欺诈行为受到禁止：（1）违背客户的委托为其买卖证券；（2）不在规定时间内向客户提供交易的书面确认文件；（3）挪用客户所委托买卖的证券或者客户账户上的资金；（4）未经客户的委托，擅自为客户买卖证券，或者假借客户的名义买卖证券；（5）为牟取佣金收入，诱使客户进行不必要的证券买卖；（6）利用传播媒介或者通过其他方式提供、传播虚假或者误导投资者的信息；（7）其他违背客户真实意思表示，损害客户利益的行为。欺诈客户行为给客户造成损失的，行为人应当依法承担赔偿责任。

二、美国的证券交易

在美国，证券交易既可以在交易所进行，也可以通过场外交易市场（OTC 市场）进行。

美国国内已建立有多个全国性及地区性的证券交易所。在交易所进行证券交易的，除必须遵守证券法律的规定之外，还应当遵守交易所制定的相关规则，尤其是信息披露方面的规则。美国的 OTC 市场包括四个层次：NASDAQ 全国资本市场、NASDAQ 小型资本市场、OTCBB 和 Pink Sheets。在 OTC 市场进行证券交易的，受到的监管相对较小。OTC 市场交易品种以未能在证券交易所上市的证券为主，主要包括不符合交易所上市标准的证券、符合在证券交易所上市标准但不愿在交易所上市的证券、债券、美国存托凭证等。

在证券交易过程中，各国证券法律均将以下三类行为作为重点打击的对象：欺诈（deceptive devices）、内幕交易（insider trading）和市场操纵（manipulative devices）。对此，美国也不例外。

就证券市场操纵和欺诈交易而言，美国《1934 年证券交易法》第 9 节规定从事上市证券市场操纵行为是非法的，并详细列举了证券市场操纵的行为，还规定了因市场操纵行为而遭受损失的投资者的私法救济。[①] 第 10 节授权 SEC 颁布规则防止操纵性和欺诈性交易行为：SEC 为了公共利益或保护投资者而必须适当地制定规则和规章，以防止使用操纵的和欺骗的手段和方法购买或出售在国内证券交易所登记注册的证券和没有登记注册的证券。第 15 节禁止经纪人、交易商的欺诈性和操纵性行为，这是对第 9 节规定的补充。

就内幕交易而言，《1934 年证券交易法》并未有直接的规定。但是，SEC 根据《1934 年证券交易法》第 10 节（b）款的授权制定了规则 10b-5（Rule 10b-5）。该规则规定，任何人在买卖证券时不得就任何与交易有关的重大信息作虚假陈述或隐瞒该信息（misrepresentation or omission），或从事其他与交易有关的欺骗行为，否则即构成证券欺诈，将承担民事乃至刑事法律责任。实际上规则 10b-5 也没有出现内幕交易的字眼，它主要是将第 10 节（b）款中操纵的和欺骗的手段和方法加以细化。但是，由于内幕交易

---

① 关于投资者的私法救济的具体规定是：凡故意参加证券市场操纵的个人，应对按受该行为或交易影响的价格购买或出售任何证券的个人负有法律责任，受到损失的个人可向任何具有足够权限的法院起诉或提出权益要求，以补偿因此种行为或交易而遭受的损失。在此种诉讼中，法院可以以其自由裁量，要求双方诉讼当事人担保支付诉讼费用，并且估计合理的费用，包括合理的律师费。凡根据本款负有法律责任进行支付的个人，在订有合同的情况下，可以从参与原来诉讼、有责任进行相同支付的个人取得分担的费用。

属于隐瞒重大信息，因此规则 10b-5 自然适用于内幕交易。为了加强对内幕交易的处罚及加强对违反内幕交易法律和规则的起诉，美国国会先后又制定了《内幕人交易制裁法》（Insider Trading Sanction Act of 1984）和《内幕人交易与证券欺诈执行法》（Insider Trading and Securities Fraud Enforcement Act of 1988）。

三、案例资料

美国规范证券交易行为的法律主要是《1934 年证券交易法》。当时，全球经济尚未进入全球化时代，证券交易行为的地域范围相对有限。现如今，随着全球化时代的到来，各国证券市场紧密相连，证券交易也跨出国界。在这一背景下，必然会产生一国证券法律的域外效力问题。

在美国，近年来，针对非美国公司的证券欺诈诉讼不断增加。以往美国法院多采用具体案件具体处理的方式，通过审查受害投资者的所在地、被指控的不当行为的发生地以及该行为对美国市场的影响等因素，作出不同的判决。这种基于个案分析的处理方式，使得《1934 年证券交易法》域外管辖权的问题缺乏明确性及可预测性。对于是否只要认定证券不在美国全国性交易所交易以及买卖地不在美国，外国发行人便不受美国证券法中集团诉讼的规制这个问题，美国法院并没有清楚确定的答案。最终，美国联邦最高法院在 2010 年的 Morrison v. National Australia Bank Ltd. 案中，对此问题作出了最终的解答。

在该案中，包括 Morrison 在内的三名澳大利亚人在纽约对澳大利亚国民银行及其美国子公司 HomeSide 提起了集体诉讼，指责 HomeSide 在美国使用伪造账册，并将虚假财务数据发送给母公司澳大利亚国民银行，后者将该信息纳入在澳的申报文件中，误导了投资者，给原告造成了经济损失。原告称，被告违反了《1934 年证券交易法》第 10 节（b）款和第 20 节（b）款以及《美国证券交易委员会规则》第 10b-5 条的规定，即被告涉嫌使用和操纵虚假信息，要求法院判令被告赔偿损失。

由于三名原告是非美国居民，且他们购买的是在澳大利亚的证券交易所上市的公司的股票，股票的发行地和交易地都在澳大利亚，所以案件在美国起诉，涉及美国《1934 年证券交易法》域外管辖权的问题。在该案中，美国第二巡回上诉法院采用一种强调事实的“行为测试”来确定是否继续审理该案，在具体分析案情的基础之上最终驳回了原告的起诉。

美国联邦最高法院维持了第二巡回上诉法院驳回原告起诉的判决。但是，联邦最高法院并非是在个案分析的基础之上作出的上述判决，而是通过对《1934 年证券交易法》立法背景的分析，直接认定：在制定《1934 年证券交易法》时，并没有任何证据表明当时的国会有意图将此法适用于美国域外。联邦最高法院表示，美国《1934 年证券交易法》

关于虚假信息使用和操纵的规定仅适用于在美国证券交易所上市或交易的股票及公司，不具有域外适用的效力。由此，联邦最高法院确立了一项明确的法律规则，即证券不在美国全国性交易所交易以及买卖地不在美国的外国发行人不受美国证券集团诉讼的规制。

该案的判决具有重要的现实意义。对于在美国拥有业务活动且决定在美国境外进行证券上市的公司而言，该案判决提供了更多的保护，使其免于遭受在外国证券交易所购买证券的投资者在美国对其提起的诉讼。外国发行人将不会受到根据第 10 节（b）款提起的证券集体诉讼，除非其证券是在美国证券交易所上市或者是在美国境内交易。

Morrison v. National Australia Bank Ltd.

561 U.S. __ (2010)

Justice Scalia delivered the opinion of the Court.

We decide whether §10 (b) of the Securities Exchange Act of 1934 provides a cause of action to foreign plaintiffs suing foreign and American defendants for misconduct in connection with securities traded on foreign exchanges.

I

Respondent National Australia Bank Limited (National) was, during the relevant time, the largest bank in Australia. Its Ordinary Shares—what in America would be called "common stock"—are traded on the Australian Stock Exchange Limited and on other foreign securities exchanges, but not on any exchange in the United States. There are listed on the New York Stock Exchange, however, National's American Depositary Receipts (ADRs), which represent the right to receive a specified number of National's Ordinary Shares. 547 F. 3d 167, 168, and n. 1 (CA2 2008).

The complaint alleges the following facts, which we accept as true. In February 1998, National bought respondent HomeSide Lending, Inc., a mortgage servicing company headquartered in Florida. HomeSide's business was to receive fees for servicing mortgages (essentially the administrative tasks associated with collecting mortgage payments, see J. Rosenberg, Dictionary of Banking and Financial Services 600 (2d ed. 1985)). The rights to receive those fees, so-called mortgage-servicing rights, can provide a valuable income stream. See 2 The New Palgrave Dictionary of Money and Finance 817 (P. Newman, M. Milgate, & J. Eatwell eds. 1992). How valuable each of the rights is depends, in part, on the likelihood that the mortgage to which it applies will be fully repaid before it is due, terminating the need for servicing. HomeSide calculated the present value of its mortgage-servicing rights by using valuation models designed to take this likelihood into account. It recorded the value of its assets, and the numbers appeared in National's financial statements.

From 1998 until 2001, National's annual reports and other public documents touted the success of HomeSide's business, and respondents Frank Cicutto (National's managing director and chief executive officer), Kevin Race (HomeSide's chief operating officer), and Hugh Harris (HomeSide's chief executive officer) did the same in public statements. But on July 5, 2001, National announced that it was writing down the value of HomeSide's assets by $450 million; and then again on September 3, by another $1.75 billion. The prices of both Ordinary Shares and ADRs slumped. After downplaying the July write-down, National explained the September write-down as the result of a failure to anticipate the lowering of prevailing interest rates (lower interest rates lead to more refinancings, i.e., more early repayments of mortgages), other mistaken assumptions in the financial models, and the loss of goodwill. According to the complaint, however, HomeSide, Race, Harris, and another HomeSide senior executive who is also a respondent here had manipulated HomeSide's financial models to make the rates of early repayment unrealistically low in order to cause the mortgage-servicing rights to appear more valuable than they really were. The complaint also alleges that National and Cicutto were aware of this deception by July 2000, but did nothing about it.

As relevant here, petitioners Russell Leslie Owen and Brian and Geraldine Silverlock, all Australians, purchased National's Ordinary Shares in 2000 and 2001, before the write-downs. They sued National, HomeSide, Cicutto, and the three HomeSide executives in the United States District Court for the Southern District of New York for alleged violations of §§10 (b) and 20 (a) of the Securities and Exchange Act of 1934, 48 Stat. 891, 15 U. S. C. §§78j(b) and 78t(a), and SEC Rule 10b-5, 17 CFR §240.10b-5 (2009), promulgated pursuant to §10 (b). They sought to represent a class of foreign purchasers of National's Ordinary Shares during a specified period up to the September write-down. 547 F. 3d, at 169.

Respondents moved to dismiss for lack of subject-matter jurisdiction under Federal Rule of Civil Procedure 12 (b) (1) and for failure to state a claim under Rule 12 (b) (6). The District Court granted the motion on the former ground, finding no jurisdiction because the acts in this country were, "at most, a link in the chain of an alleged overall securities fraud scheme that culminated abroad." In re National Australia Bank Securities Litigation, No. 03 Civ. 6537 (BSJ), 2006 WL 3844465, *8 (SDNY, Oct. 25, 2006). The Court of Appeals for the Second

Circuit affirmed on similar grounds. The acts performed in the United States did not "compris [e] the heart of the alleged fraud." 547 F. 3d, at 175-176. We granted certiorari, 558 U. S. ___ (2009)...

III

A

It is a "longstanding principle of American law 'that legislation of Congress, unless a contrary intent appears, is meant to apply only within the territorial jurisdiction of the United States.'" EEOC v. Arabian American Oil Co., 499 U. S. 244, 248 (1991) (Aramco) (quoting Foley Bros., Inc. v. Filardo, 336 U. S. 281, 285 (1949)). This principle represents a canon of construction, or a presumption about a statute's meaning, rather than a limit upon Congress's power to legislate, see Blackmer v. United States, 284 U. S. 421, 437 (1932). It rests on the perception that Congress ordinarily legislates with respect to domestic, not foreign matters. Smith v. United States, 507 U. S. 197, n. 5 (1993). Thus, "unless there is the affirmative intention of the Congress clearly expressed" to give a statute extraterritorial effect, "we must presume it is primarily concerned with domestic conditions." Aramco, supra, at 248 (internal quotation marks omitted). The canon or presumption applies regardless of whether there is a risk of conflict between the American statute and a foreign law, see Sale v. Haitian Centers Council, Inc., 509 U. S. 155, 173-174 (1993). When a statute gives no clear indication of an extraterritorial application, it has none.

Despite this principle of interpretation, long and often recited in our opinions, the Second Circuit believed that, because the Exchange Act is silent as to the extraterritorial application of §10 (b), it was left to the court to "discern" whether Congress would have wanted the statute to apply. See 547 F. 3d, at 170 (internal quotation marks omitted). This disregard of the presumption against extraterritoriality did not originate with the Court of Appeals panel in this case. It has been repeated over many decades by various courts of appeals in determining the application of the Exchange Act, and §10 (b) in particular, to fraudulent schemes that involve conduct and effects abroad. That has produced a collection of tests for divining what Congress would have wanted, complex in formulation and unpredictable in application.

As of 1967, district courts at least in the Southern District of New York had consistently concluded that, by reason of the presumption against extraterritoriality, §10 (b) did not apply when the stock transactions underlying the violation occurred abroad. See Schoenbaum v. Firstbrook, 268 F. Supp. 385, 392 (1967) (citing Ferraoli v. Cantor, CCH Fed. Sec. L. Rep.

91615 (SDNY 1965) and Kook v. Crang, 182 F. Supp. 388, 390 (SDNY 1960)). Schoenbaum involved the sale in Canada of the treasury shares of a Canadian corporation whose publicly traded shares (but not, of course, its treasury shares) were listed on both the American Stock Exchange and the Toronto Stock Exchange. Invoking the presumption against extraterritoriality, the court held that §10 (b) was inapplicable (though it incorrectly viewed the defect as jurisdictional). 268 F. Supp., at 391-392, 393-394. The decision in Schoenbaum was reversed, however, by a Second Circuit opinion which held that "neither the usual presumption against extraterritorial application of legislation nor the specific language of [§]30 (b) show Congressional intent to preclude application of the Exchange Act to transactions regarding stocks traded in the United States which are effected outside the United States ...." Schoenbaum, 405 F. 2d, at 206. It sufficed to apply §10 (b) that, although the transactions in treasury shares took place in Canada, they affected the value of the common shares publicly traded in the United States. See id., at 208-209. Application of §10 (b), the Second Circuit found, was "necessary to protect American investors," id., at 206.

The Second Circuit took another step with Leasco Data Processing Equip. Corp. v. Maxwell, 468 F. 2d 1326 (1972), which involved an American company that had been fraudulently induced to buy securities in England. There, unlike in Schoenbaum, some of the deceptive conduct had occurred in the United States but the corporation whose securities were traded (abroad) was not listed on any domestic exchange. Leasco said that the presumption against extraterritoriality apples only to matters over which the United States would not have prescriptive jurisdiction, 468 F. 2d, at 1334. Congress had prescriptive jurisdiction to regulate the deceptive conduct in this country, the language of the Act could be read to cover that conduct, and the court concluded that "if Congress had thought about the point," it would have wanted §10 (b) to apply.Id., at 1334-1337.

With Schoenbaum and Leasco on the books, the Second Circuit had excised the presumption against extraterritoriality from the jurisprudence of §10 (b) and replaced it with the inquiry whether it would be reasonable (and hence what Congress would have wanted) to apply the statute to a given situation. As long as there was prescriptive jurisdiction to regulate, the Second Circuit explained, whether to apply §10 (b) even to "predominantly foreign" transactions became a matter of whether a court thought Congress "wished the precious resources of United States courts and law enforcement agencies to be devoted to them rather than leave the problem to foreign countries." Bersch v. Drexel Firestone, Inc., 519 F. 2d 974, 985 (1975); see also IIT v. Vencap, Ltd., 519 F. 2d 1001, 1017-1018 (CA2 1975).

The Second Circuit had thus established that application of §10 (b) could be premised upon either some effect on American securities markets or investors(Schoenbaum) or significant conduct in the United States (Leasco). It later formalized these two applications into (1) an "effects test," "whether the wrongful conduct had a substantial effect in the United States or upon United States citizens," and (2) a "conduct test," "whether the wrongful conduct occurred in the United States." SEC v. Berger, 322 F. 3d 187, 192-193 (CA2 2003). These became the north star of the Second Circuit's §10 (b) jurisprudence, pointing the way to what Congress would have wished. Indeed, the Second Circuit declined to keep its two tests distinct on the ground that "an admixture or combination of the two often gives a better picture of whether there is sufficient United States involvement to justify the exercise of jurisdiction by an American court." Itoba Ltd. v. Lep Group PLC, 54 F. 3d 118, 122 (1995). The Second Circuit never put forward a textual or even extratextual basis for these tests. As early as Bersch, it confessed that "if we were asked to point to language in the statutes, or even in the legislative history, that compelled these conclusions, we would be unable to respond," 519 F. 2d, at 993.

As they developed, these tests were not easy to administer. The conduct test was held to apply differently depending on whether the harmed investors were Americans or foreigners: When the alleged damages consisted of losses to American investors abroad, it was enough that acts "of material importance" performed in the United States "significantly contributed" to that result; whereas those acts must have "directly caused" the result when losses to foreigners abroad were at issue. See Bersch, 519 F. 2d, at 993. And "merely preparatory activities in the United States" did not suffice "to trigger application of the securities laws for injury to foreigners located abroad." Id., at 992. This required the court to distinguish between mere preparation and using the United States as a "base" for fraudulent activities in other countries.Vencap, supra, at 1017-1018. But merely satisfying the conduct test was sometimes insufficient without "some additional factor tipping the scales" in favor of the application of American law. Interbrew v. Edperbrascan Corp., 23 F. Supp. 2d 425, 432 (SDNY 1998) (quoting Europe & Overseas Commodity Traders, S. A. v. Banque Paribas London, 147 F. 3d 118, 129 (CA2 1998)). District courts have noted the difficulty of applying such vague formulations. See, e.g., In re Alstom SA, 406 F. Supp. 2d 346, 366-385 (SDNY 2005). There is no more damning indictment of the "conduct" and "effects" tests than the Second Circuit's own declaration that "the presence or absence of any single factor which was considered significant in other cases… is not necessarily dispositive in future cases." IIT v. Cornfeld, 619

F. 2d 909, 918 (1980) (internal quotation marks omitted).

Other Circuits embraced the Second Circuit's approach, though not its precise application. Like the Second Circuit, they described their decisions regarding the extraterritorial application of §10 (b) as essentially resolving matters of policy. See, e.g., SEC v. Kasser, 548 F. 2d 109, 116 (CA3 1977);Continental Grain, 592 F. 2d, at 421-422; Grunenthal GmbH v. Hotz, 712 F. 2d 421, 424-425 (CA9 1983); Kauthar SDN BHD v. Sternberg, 149 F. 3d 659, 667 (CA7 1998). While applying the same fundamental methodology of balancing interests and arriving at what seemed the best policy, they produced a proliferation of vaguely related variations on the "conduct" and "effects" tests. As described in a leading Seventh Circuit opinion: "Although the circuits… seem to agree that there are some transnational situations to which the antifraud provisions of the securities laws are applicable, agreement appears to end at that point." Id., at 665. See also id., at 665-667 (describing the approaches of the various Circuits and adopting yet another variation).

At least one Court of Appeals has criticized this line of cases and the interpretive assumption that underlies it. In Zoelsch v. Arthur Andersen & Co., 824 F. 2d 27, 32 (1987) (Bork, J.), the District of Columbia Circuit observed that rather than courts' "divining what 'Congress would have wished' if it had addressed the problem [, a] more natural inquiry might be what jurisdiction Congress in fact thought about and conferred." Although tempted to apply the presumption against extraterritoriality and be done with it, see id., at 31-32, that court deferred to the Second Circuit because of its "preeminence in the field of securities law," id., at 32. See also Robinson v. TCI/US West Communications Inc., 117 F. 3d 900, 906-907 (CA5 1997) (expressing agreement with Zoelsch's criticism of the emphasis on policy considerations in some of the cases).

Commentators have criticized the unpredictable and inconsistent application of §10 (b) to transnational cases. See, e.g., Choi & Silberman, Transnational Litigation and Global Securities Class-Action Lawsuits, 2009 Wis. L. Rev. 465, 467-468; Chang, Multinational Enforcement of U. S. Securities Laws: The Need for the Clear and Restrained Scope of Extraterritorial Subject-Matter Jurisdiction, 9 Fordham J. Corp. & Fin. L. 89, 106-108, 115-116 (2004); Langevoort, Schoenbaum Revisited: Limiting the Scope of Antifraud Protection in an Internationalized Securities Marketplace, 55 Law & Contemp. Probs. 241, 244-248 (1992). Some have challenged the premise underlying the Courts of Appeals' approach, namely that Congress did not consider the extraterritorial application of §10 (b) (thereby leaving it open to the courts, supposedly, to determine what Congress would have wanted). See, e.g., Sachs, The International Reach of Rule 10b-5: The Myth of Congressional Silence, 28 Colum. J. Transnat'l L. 677 (1990) (arguing that Congress considered, but rejected, applying the Exchange Act to transactions abroad). Others, more fundamentally, have noted that using congressional silence as a justification for judge-made rules violates the traditional principle that silence means no extraterritorial application. See, e.g., Note, Let There Be Fraud (Abroad): A Proposal for A New U. S. Jurisprudence with Regard to the Extraterritorial Application of the Anti-Fraud Provisions of the 1933 and 1934 Securities Acts, 28 Law & Pol'y Int'l Bus. 477, 492-493 (1997).

The criticisms seem to us justified. The results of judicial speculation made law divining what Congress would have wanted if it had thought of the situation before the court demonstrate the wisdom of the presumption against extraterritoriality. Rather than guess anew in each case, we apply the presumption in all cases, preserving a stable background against which Congress can legislate with predictable effects.

B

Rule 10b-5, the regulation under which petitioners have brought suit, was promulgated under §10 (b), and "does not extend beyond conduct encompassed by §10 (b)'s prohibition." United States v. O'Hagan, 521 U. S. 642, 651 (1997). Therefore, if §10 (b) is not extraterritorial, neither is Rule 10b-5.

On its face, §10 (b) contains nothing to suggest it applies abroad:

"It shall be unlawful for any person, directly or indirectly, by the use of any means or instrumentality of interstate commerce or of the mails, or of any facility of any national securities exchange... [t]o use or employ, in connection with the purchase or sale of any security registered on a national securities exchange or any security not so registered... any manipulative or deceptive device or contrivance in contravention of such rules and regulations as the [Securities and Exchange] Commission may prescribe…." 15 U. S. C. 78j(b).

Petitioners and the Solicitor General contend, however, that three things indicate that §10 (b) or the Exchange Act in general has at least some extraterritorial application.

First, they point to the definition of "interstate commerce," a term used in §10 (b), which includes "trade, commerce, transportation, or communication... between any foreign country and any State." 15 U. S. C. §78c (a) (17). But "we have repeatedly held that even statutes that contain broad language in their definitions of 'commerce' that expressly refer to '*foreign* commerce' do not apply abroad." Aramco, 499 U. S., at 251; see id., at 251-252 (discussing cases). The general reference to foreign commerce in the definition of "interstate commerce" does not defeat the presumption against extraterritoriality.

Petitioners and the Solicitor General next point out that Congress, in describing the purposes of the Exchange Act, observed that the "prices established and offered in such transactions are generally disseminated and quoted throughout the United States and foreign countries." 15 U. S. C. §78b(2). The antecedent of "such transactions," however, is found in the first sentence of the section, which declares that "transactions in securities as commonly conducted upon securities exchanges and over-the-counter markets are affected with a national public interest." §78b. Nothing suggests that this *national* public interest pertains to transactions conducted upon *foreign* exchanges and markets. The fleeting reference to the dissemination and quotation abroad of the prices of securities traded in domestic exchanges and markets cannot overcome the presumption against extraterritoriality.

Finally, there is §30 (b) of the Exchange Act, 15 U. S. C. §78dd (b), which does mention the Act's extraterritorial application: "The provisions of [the Exchange Act] or of any rule or regulation thereunder shall not apply to any person insofar as he transacts a business in securities without the jurisdiction of the United States," unless he does so in violation of regulations promulgated by the Securities and Exchange Commission "to prevent… evasion of [the Act]." (The parties have pointed us to no regulation promulgated pursuant to §30 (b).) The Solicitor General argues that "[this] exemption would have no function if the Act did not apply in the first instance to securities transactions that occur abroad." Brief for United States as Amicus Curiae 14.

We are not convinced. In the first place, it would be odd for Congress to indicate the extraterritorial application of the whole Exchange Act by means of a provision imposing a condition precedent to its application abroad. And if the whole Act applied abroad, why would the Commission's enabling regulations be limited to those preventing "evasion" of the Act, rather than all those preventing "violation"? The provision seems to us directed at actions abroad that might conceal a domestic violation, or might cause what would otherwise be a domestic violation to escape on a technicality. At most, the Solicitor General's proposed inference is possible; but possible interpretations of statutory language do not override the presumption against extraterritoriality. See Aramco, supra, at 253.

The Solicitor General also fails to account for §30 (a), which reads in relevant part as follows:

"It shall be unlawful for any broker or dealer… to make use of the mails or of any means or instrumentality of interstate commerce for the purpose of effecting on an exchange not within or subject to the jurisdiction of the United States, any transaction in any security the issuer of which is a resident of, or is organized under the laws of, or has its principal place of business in, a place within or subject to the jurisdiction of the United States, in contravention of such rules and regulations as the Commission may prescribe…." 15 U. S. C. §78dd(a).

Subsection 30 (a) contains what §10 (b) lacks: a clear statement of extraterritorial effect. Its explicit provision for a specific extraterritorial application would be quite superfluous if the rest of the Exchange Act already applied to transactions on foreign exchanges—and its limitation of that application to securities of domestic issuers would be inoperative. Even if that were not true, when a statute provides for some extraterritorial application, the presumption against extraterritoriality operates to limit that provision to its terms. See Microsoft Corp. v. AT&T Corp., 550 U. S. 437, 455-456 (2007). No one claims that §30 (a) applies here.

The concurrence claims we have impermissibly narrowed the inquiry in evaluating whether a statute applies abroad, citing for that point the dissent in Aramco, see post, at 6. But we do not say, as the concurrence seems to think, that the presumption against extraterritoriality is a "clear statement rule,"ibid., if by that is meant a requirement that a statute say "this law applies abroad." Assuredly context can be consulted as well. But whatever sources of statutory meaning one consults to give "the most faithful reading" of the text, post, at 7, there is no clear indication of extraterritoriality here. The concurrence does not even try to refute that conclusion, but merely puts forward the same (at best) uncertain indications relied upon by petitioners and the Solicitor General. As the opinion *for the Court* in Aramco (which we prefer to the dissent) shows, those uncertain indications do not suffice.

In short, there is no affirmative indication in the Exchange Act that §10 (b) applies extraterritorially, and we therefore conclude that it does not.

…

Section 10 (b) reaches the use of a manipulative or deceptive device or contrivance only in connection with the purchase or sale of a security listed on an American stock exchange, and the purchase or sale of any other security in the United States. This case involves no securities listed on a domestic exchange, and all aspects of the purchases complained of by those petitioners who still have live claims occurred outside the United States. Petitioners have therefore failed to state a claim on which relief can be granted. We affirm the dismissal of petitioners' complaint on this ground.

It is so ordered.

第五节 证券业的监管

证券监管，是指证券市场监管机构根据证券法律、法规的授权，对证券发行、交易以及证券经营机构等市场主体及其行为实施的监督与管理活动。证券市场投资者多、投机性强、敏感性高、突发性强、传导快、社会影响大，因此对证券市场实行有效监管，才能促进证券市场有序、合理、高效运行。

一、中国对证券业的监管

中国的证券业监管体制确立于20世纪90年代。经过多轮金融改革，中国逐渐建立了以中国证监会为核心、政府监管与自律性监管相结合、集中统一的证券业监管体制。

根据中国《证券法》的规定，国务院证券监督管理机构依法对全国证券市场实行集中统一监督管理。其中，“国务院证券监督管理机构”是指中国证监会。中国证监会依法对证券市场实行监督管理，维护证券市场秩序，保障其合法运行。中国证监会根据需要可以设立派出机构，派出机构按照授权履行监督管理职责。

中国证监会在对证券市场实施监督管理中，履行下列职责：（1）依法制定有关证券市场监督管理的规章、规则，并依法行使审批或者核准权；（2）依法对证券的发行、上市、交易、登记、存管、结算，进行监督管理；（3）依法对证券发行人、上市公司、证券公司、证券投资基金管理公司、证券服务机构、证券交易所、证券登记结算机构的证券业务活动，进行监督管理；（4）依法制定从事证券业务人员的资格标准和行为准则，并监督实施；（5）依法监督检查证券发行、上市和交易的信息公开情况；（6）依法对证券业协会的活动进行指导和监督；（7）依法对违反证券市场监督管理法律、行政法规的行为进行查处；（8）法律、行政法规规定的其他职责。中国证监会可以和其他国家或者地区的证券监督管理机构建立监督管理合作机制，实施跨境监督管理。

为依法履行职责，实现监管目的，中国证监会有权采取下列措施：（1）对证券发行人、上市公司、证券公司、证券投资基金管理公司、证券服务机构、证券交易所、证券登记结算机构进行现场检查；（2）进入涉嫌违法行为发生场所调查取证；（3）询问当事人和与被调查事件有关的单位和个人，要求其对与被调查事件有关的事项作出说明；（4）查阅、复制与被调查事件有关的财产权登记、通讯记录等资料；（5）查阅、复制当事人和与被调查事件有关的单位和个人的证券交易记录、登记过户记录、财务会计资料及其他相关文件和资料；对可能被转移、隐匿或者毁损的文件和资料，可以予以封存；（6）查询当事人和与被调查事件有关的单位和个人的资金账户、证券账户和银行账户；对有证据证明已经或者可能转移或者隐匿违法资金、证券等涉案财产或者隐匿、伪造、毁损重要证据的，经中国证监会主要负责人批准，可以冻结或者查封；（7）在调查操纵证券市场、内幕交易等重大证券违法行为时，可以限制被调查事件当事人的证券买卖。

在自律性监管方面，主要是由成立的行业协会对会员实施管理。根据中国《证券法》规定，证券业协会是证券业的自律性组织，是社会团体法人。证券公司应当加入证券业协会，成为其会员。中国已于 1991 年成立了中国证券业协会。

根据中国《证券法》的规定，证券业协会履行下列职责：（1）教育和组织会员遵守证券法律、行政法规；（2）依法维护会员的合法权益，向证券监督管理机构反映会员的建议和要求；（3）收集整理证券信息，为会员提供服务；（4）制定会员应遵守的规则，组织会员单位的从业人员的业务培训，开展会员间的业务交流；（5）对会员之间、会员与客户之间发生的证券业务纠纷进行调解；（6）组织会员就证券业的发展、运作及有关内容进行研究；（7）监督、检查会员行为，对违反法律、行政法规或者协会章程的，按照规定给予纪律处分；（8）证券业协会章程规定的其他职责。

二、美国对证券业的监管

20 世纪 30 年代以前，美国证券监管主要由各州自行负责，各州纷纷制定了所谓的“蓝天法”对本州的证券业务进行监管。各州分散的监管，存在诸多弊端。在 1929 年股灾后，美国相继颁布了《1933 年证券法》和《1934 年证券交易法》。这两部法律，是美国证券监管最重要的法律。随后，美国联邦层面又制定了多部证券监管法律、法规，与各州的蓝天法和法院判例，共同构成美国证券监管法律体系。这一套法律体系为政府监管提供了明确的法律依据和法定权力。

为保证证券监管立法的有效实施，除了各州分别设立的对本州证券业务进行监管的机构外，美国还设立了一个强有力的联邦证券监管机构——证券交易委员会（SEC）。其中，SEC 在证券业监管中发挥着最为重要的作用。

SEC 是依据《1933 年证券法》和《1934 年证券交易法》创建的，是一个独立的、超党派的、准司法的管理机关，行使着美国证券监管法律所赋予的职责，其地位类似于中国证监会。SEC 在组织设置上为一个独立的机构，不隶属于总统、国会、最高法院或者任何一个行政部门，只在法律规定的范围内独立行使其保证证券市场信息公开、保护投资者的合法权益的职权。

SEC 总部设在华盛顿市，此外还在全国各地的多个城市中设有地方或地区办公室，负责当地的证券执法。SEC 的职责和职权包括：（1）负责制定并调整有关证券活动的管理政策，制定并解释证券市场的各种规章制度，并组织贯彻执行；（2）管理全国范围内的一切证券发行和交易活动，根据授权对证券交易中的投诉和其他可能违法的迹象展开调查；（3）当案件涉及证券交易所或证券商协会会员、注册的经纪人或中间商时，SEC 有权进行行政诉讼并作出判决，对其进行行政处罚；（4）当有证据证明确实存在欺诈或者其他违法事件时，SEC 可以诉诸法院要求给予民事罚款或将证据移交司法部，请求对当事人予以刑事诉讼。①

2010 年 7 月，作为反思 2008 年金融危机的成果，美国国会通过了《多德—弗兰克华尔街改革和消费者保护法案》。尽管 SEC 之前在次贷衍生产品和麦道夫骗局中因监管缺位、反应迟缓而深受诟病，但其权限在最终的改革法案中却得以加强，监管的机构和产品范围均有所扩大。法案不仅将对冲基金、私募股权基金及其他投资顾问机构和信用评级机构纳入 SEC 的监管，而且还授权 SEC 对部分衍生产品和上市公司高管薪酬进行管理。

除政府部门的监管外，行业自律性组织（self-regulatory agency）在证券监管中也发挥着重要的作用。行业自律性组织通过对其会员进行监督、指导，实施自我教育、自我管理，从而保护市场的完整性，维持公平、高效和透明的市场秩序。

在美国，行业自律主体包括行业协会、证券交易所和其他团体。自律组织的自律活动需在证券法律框架内开展，并接受 SEC 的监管。SEC 既可以对自律组织颁布的规则条例进行修订、补充和废止，也可以要求自律组织制定新的规章。

交易所是最早出现的自律组织，主要通过制定上市规则、交易规则、信息披露等方面的标准，对其会员和上市公司进行管理，并实时监控交易活动，防止异常交易行为的发生。行业协会则是另一类重要的自律组织。一般而言，市场主体在注册成为该协会会员之前，不能进入这一行业。行业协会主要通过制定行业准则和行业标准，推广行业经验来实施自我管理、自我规范，并对其会员进行监督。此外，还有其他一些团体参与证券市场，发挥自律监管的作用。

在美国，最大的非政府证券业自律监管机构莫过于美国金融业监管局（the Financial Industry Regulatory Authority，FINRA）。2007 年 7 月 30 日，美国证券商协会（NASD）与纽约证券交易所中有关会员监管、执行和仲裁的部门合并成立了 FINRA。FINRA 的使命是投资者保护和市场诚信，履行五大职能：制定和组织实施自律规则；负责会员的合规检查；承担投资者教育，并管理投资者教育基金；编制行业报告；负责投资者和会员争议仲裁。

在美国，所有与公众开展业务的证券公司不仅必须是 FINRA 的成员，还应当遵守其

① 周知群. 试论美国的证券监管体制及其对中国的启示. 天府新论，2001（6）.

制定的规则。如果认定其成员和/或相关的成员的代表人不遵守联邦证券法律、法规及其制定的规则，FINRA将对违反者采取适当的处罚措施。因此，FINRA在维护证券市场健康发展方面起着非常重要的作用。

三、案例资料

FINRA是美国最重要的证券业自律监管机构，其拥有对从事证券业的相关中介机构和人士广泛的监管权限。但是，美国第二巡回上诉法院在Fiero v. Financial Industry Regulatory Authority, Inc. 案中的判决，却令FINRA有些尴尬：FINRA能够作出罚款的处罚，但是如果被处罚人不交罚款，FINRA却不能起诉到法院要求判令其交纳罚款。

在该案中，Fiero Brothers（其是FINRA的成员）及其所有人John Fiero在1998年因为从事“裸卖空”（“naked short-selling”）行为而受到FINRA的前身NASD的调查。2000年12月6日，NASD认定，Fiero违反了美国《1934年证券交易法》等的相关规定，因此撤销了Fiero及Fiero Brothers的成员资格，同时还对Fiero及Fiero Brothers处以100万美元的罚款。但是，Fiero拒绝支付罚款。因此，FINRA向法院提起诉讼，要求法院判令Fiero支付罚款。

该案的审理可谓是一波三折。从2003年12月22日起诉到纽约州最高法院，历经纽约州上诉分庭、纽约州上诉法院（该院驳回了FINRA的起诉，认为此案应由联邦法院审理，州法院无管辖权），随即又转移至纽约南部地区法院并最终上诉至美国第二巡回上诉法院。2011年10月5日，第二巡回上诉法院判决FINRA败诉。

在美国第二巡回上诉法院对该案的审理中，FINRA提出，无论是依据《1934年证券交易法》还是依据其1990年发布的一项规则，其均有权通过诉讼的方式来征收其已经科处的罚金。第二巡回上诉法院对此予以了反驳。

首先，第二巡回上诉法院审查了《1934年证券交易法》第15A（b）条的规定。依据该条规定，类似FINRA的行业自律组织有法定的权力和义务“对其成员的任何违法违规行为，包括违反证券交易法的任何规定、违反依据证券交易法而颁布的规则或规章或违反其自己制定的规则，给予适当的处罚，这种处罚包括撤销成员资格、中止成员资格，限制活动、功能及经营，罚款，审查，被中止或禁止与任何成员往来，或任何其他适当的处罚措施”。但是，法院从立法语言和立法意图角度分析，发现该条法律规定并未明确授权FINRA提起司法诉讼以执行罚金处罚的权力。

其次，法院对FINRA于1990年发布的一项规则修正案（该修正案授权FINRA征收罚款的权力）进行了审查。法院认为，依据《1934年证券交易法》的相关规定，行业自律性组织更改其内部规则必须遵守一定的程序，即在对规则进行修改之前，如果该规则的修改实质性地影响到公众利益或投资者的保护，那么应当先发布正式的通知，向公众征求意见。而 1990 年的那一项规则修正案的发布并未遵守这一程序，因此不能援引该规则的授权。

第二巡回上诉法院通过严格解释《1934 年证券交易法》的相关规定以及攻击 FINRA1990 年发布的规则的程序性缺陷，否定了 FINRA 通过诉讼执行罚款的权力，这显得有些牵强。此案的判决，在一定程度上会对券商不支付 FINRA 的罚款形成一定的鼓励。当然，这并不意味着 FINRA 对违规的券商没有威慑力。尽管不能通过诉讼的方式征收罚金，但是对不支付罚金的券商，FINRA 有权撤销其成员资格。如果不是 FINRA 的成员，就无法涉足证券行业。因此，大多数遭受处罚的券商还是会主动支付罚金。当然，违规的券商也可能进行成本—收益分析。基于各种因素的考量，如果认定继续从事证券业的收益要小于支付罚金的成本，那么被处罚的券商可能会选择被吊销成员资格而不愿支付罚金。此时，尽管不能从事证券交易活动，但违法的券商却仍能保留其违法所得，这似乎还是有失公正。

Fiero v. Financial Industry Regulatory Authority, Inc.

No. 09-1556-CV, 2011 WL 4582436 (2d Cir. Oct. 5, 2011)

WINTER, Circuit Judge:

John J. Fiero ("Fiero") and Fiero Brothers, Inc. ("Fiero Brothers") (together, "Fieros") appeal from Judge Marreros dismissal of their complaint, which sought a declaratory judgment that, inter alia, the Financial Industry Regulatory Authority, Inc. ("FINRA") lacks the authority to bring court actions to collect disciplinary fines it has imposed. We hold that FINRA lacks such authority. We therefore reverse the dismissal of the complaint and vacate the money judgment on FINRA's counterclaim.

BACKGROUND

a) FINRA's Role

FINRA is a "self-regulatory organization" ("SRO") as a national securities association registered with the SEC pursuant to the Maloney Act of 1938, 15 U.S.C. § 78o-3, et seq. See Desiderio v. Nat'l Ass'n of Sec. Dealers, Inc., 191 F.3d 198, 201 (2d Cir. 1999). FINRA is the successor to the National Association of Securities Dealers ("NASD"). It "is responsible for conducting investigations and commencing disciplinary proceedings against [FINRA] member firms and their associated member representatives relating to compliance with the federal securities laws and regulations." D.L. Cromwell Invs., Inc. v. NASD Regulation, Inc., 279

F.3d 155, 157 (2d Cir. 2002) (quoting Datek Sec. Corp. v. Nat'l Ass'n of Sec. Dealers, Inc., 875 F.Supp. 230, 232 (S.D.N.Y.1995) (internal quotation marks omitted)). As a practical matter, all securities firms dealing with the public must be members of FINRA. See Sacks v. SEC, 648 F.3d 945, 948 (9th Cir. 2011) (citing 72 Fed.Reg. 42, 169, 42, 170 (Aug. 1, 2007); 15 U.S.C. §§ 78c (a) 26, 78s (b)) (noting that FINRA is "responsible for regulatory oversight of all securities firms that do business with the public"); see also note 1, supra. FINRA's disciplinary proceedings are governed by the FINRA Code of Procedure ("FINRA COP"). The FINRA COP has been approved by the SEC, as required by Section 19 of the Securities Exchange Act of 1934. 15 U.S.C. § 78s(b) (describing the required procedure for approval of proposed SRO rule changes).

FINRA has the power to initiate a disciplinary proceeding against any FINRA member or associated person for violating any FINRA rule, SEC regulation, or statutory provision. Id. § 78s(h) (3). To issue a complaint, FINRA's Department of Enforcement or Department of Market Regulation must obtain authorization from the FINRA Regulation Board or FINRA Board. FINRA COP § 9211. After a complaint is filed, a hearing panel conducts a hearing and issues a decision. Id. § 9231. Final decisions of the hearing panel may be appealed to the FINRA National Adjudicatory Council ("NAC"), which can affirm, modify, or reverse the hearing panel's decision. Id. §§ 9311, 9349 (a), 9268-9269. NAC decisions may then be appealed to the SEC, pursuant to 15 U.S.C. § 78s(d), and from the SEC to the United States Court of Appeals, pursuant to 15 U.S.C. § 78y. 15 U.S.C. §§ 78s(d), 78y(a); see also Mister Discount Stockbrokers v. SEC, 768 F.2d 875, 876 (7th Cir. 1985).

b) The Disciplinary Action Against the Fieros

Fiero Brothers, a New York corporation, was a FINRA member firm and broker-dealer registered with the SEC. John J. Fiero was the sole registered representative of Fiero Brothers. As such, the Fieros were subject to the regulations and discipline of NASD.

On February 6, 1998, NASD's Department of Enforcement initiated disciplinary proceedings against the Fieros, the merits of which are not pertinent to this appeal. On December 6, 2000, an NASD hearing panel held that the Fieros had violated Section 10 (b) of the Exchange Act, Rule 10b-5, and FINRA Conduct Rules 2110, 2120, and 3370. The hearing panel expelled Fiero Brothers, barred Fiero from associating with any FINRA-member firm in any capacity, and fined the Fieros $1 000 000 plus costs, jointly and severally.

On appeal, the NAC affirmed the hearing panel's decision in its entirety. John Fiero, Nat'l Adjudicatory Council No. CAF980002, 2002 WL 31476976, at *34 (Oct. 28, 2002). The

Fieros did not appeal the NAC's decision to the SEC.

…

DISCUSSION

We review a district court's grant of a motion to dismiss de novo. Chase Grp. Alliance v. City of N.Y. Dep't of Fin., 620 F.3d 146, 150 (2d Cir. 2010). Our review of a district court's legal conclusions, including the interpretation of a federal statute, is also de novo. United States v. Fuller, 627 F.3d 499, 503 (2d Cir. 2010).

The Fieros argue that while the Exchange Act and FINRA's rules and bylaws authorize FINRA to impose sanctions on its members, it has no authority to bring judicial actions to collect monetary sanctions. FINRA argues that it has this authority under the Exchange Act and from a FINRA rule submitted to, and not disapproved by, the SEC in 1990 ("1990 Rule Change"). See Notice of Filing and Immediate Effectiveness of Proposed Rule Change by NASD Relating to the Collection of Fines and Costs in Disciplinary Proceedings, Exchange Act SEC Release No. 28227, 46 S.E.C. Docket 1049 (July 18, 1990) (hereinafter "SEC Notice of 1990 Rule Change"). We discuss each argument seriatim.

a) FINRA's Authority Under the Exchange Act

The first question is whether the Exchange Act provides FINRA with the necessary authority. We hold that it does not.

Under Section 15A(b) of the Exchange Act, SRO's have a statutory authority and obligation to "appropriately discipline" their members for violation of any provision of the Exchange Act, the rules or regulations promulgated thereunder, or their own rules, "by expulsion, suspension, limitation of activities, functions, and operations, fine, censure, being suspended or barred from being associated with a member, or any other fitting sanction." 15 U.S.C. § 78o-3 (b) (7). However, there is no express statutory authority for SRO's to bring judicial actions to enforce the collection of fines.

In the present context the omission is not insignificant. The core issue, of course, is congressional intent, Touche Ross & Co. v. Redington, 442 U.S. 560, 568 (1979), and, in the discussion that follows, we explain why we believe that Congress did not intend to empower FINRA to bring judicial actions to enforce its fines.

The statutory scheme carefully particularizes an array of available remedies, including permissible actions in the federal courts. These include, of course, a variety of actions by private parties for damages. 15 U.S.C. §§ 77k-77l, 78i(f), 78t(b); see Redington, 442 U.S. at 571-72 (discussing generally private rights of action in the Securities Exchange Act).

Also, Section 21 (d) of the Exchange Act provides express statutory authority for the SEC to seek judicial enforcement of penalties. See 15 U.S.C. § 78u(d). More specifically, the SEC "may in its discretion bring an action" to enjoin any person who "is engaged or is about to engage in acts or practices constituting a violation" of, inter alia, any provision of the Exchange Act, the rules or regulations thereunder, or the rules of a national securities exchange or registered securities association of which such person is a member from such practices. Id. § 78u(d) (1). Moreover, the SEC has explicit authority to seek monetary penalties for violations of the Exchange Act, the rules and regulations promulgated thereunder, or for the violation of a cease and desist order. Id. § 78u(d) (3) (A). Under Section 21 (e) of the Exchange Act, the SEC may also seek "writs of mandamus, injunctions, and orders" from the federal courts commanding any person to comply with, inter alia, "the provisions of [the Exchange Act], the rules, regulations, and orders thereunder, the rules of a national securities exchange or registered securities association of which such person is a member or person associated with a member." Id. § 78u(e). Under Section 21 (f), however, the SEC is prohibited from bringing "any action pursuant to subsection (d) or (e) of this section against any person for violation of, or to command compliance with, the rules of a self-regulatory organization unless it appears to the Commission that (1) such self-regulatory organization. is unable or unwilling to take appropriate action against such person in the public interest and for the protection of investors, or (2) such action is otherwise necessary or appropriate in the public interest or for the protection of investors." Id. § 78u (f).

Therefore, when Congress passed the Exchange Act, and to this date, Sarbanes-Oxley Act of 2002, § 3 (b), (amending 15 U.S.C. § 78u); Dodd-Frank Wall Street Reform Act, Pub.L. No. 111-203, § 929P, 124 Stat. 1376, 1862-63 (2010) (amending 15 U.S.C. § 78u), it was well aware of how to grant an agency access to the courts to seek judicial enforcement of specific sanctions, including monetary penalties. 15 U.S.C. § 78u(d) (3) (A); see, e.g., SEC v. Rosenthal, Nos. 10-1204-cv(L); 10-1253 (con.), 2011 WL 2271743 (2d Cir. June 9, 2011); SEC v. Tx. Gulf Sulphur Co., 446 F.2d 1301, 1307 (2d Cir. 1971).

In contrast, there are no explicit provisions in the statute authorizing SRO's to seek judicial enforcement of the variety of sanctions they can impose. This is significant evidence that Congress did not intend to authorize FINRA to seek judicial enforcement to collect its disciplinary fines. Redington, 442 U.S. at 571-72 (not implying a private right of action where elsewhere in the Exchange Act Congress demonstrated the ability and explicit intent to create private rights of action).

We need not rely upon negative implications alone, however, because there are statutory provisions that weigh heavily against FINRA's claim of enforcement powers through court actions alleging breach of contract. First, FINRA's sanctions are appealable by an aggrieved party to the SEC and thereafter to the United States Courts of Appeals. Had Congress intended judicial enforcement, it would surely have provided for some specific relief other than leaving SRO's to commonlaw proceedings in state courts or in federal district courts under diversity jurisdiction. Second, where FINRA enforces statutory or administrative rules, or enforces its own rules promulgated pursuant to statutory or administrative authority, it is exercising the powers granted to it under the Exchange Act. Indeed, FINRA's powers in that regard are subject to divestment by the SEC under Section 19 (g) (2) of that Act. However, Congress gave the federal courts exclusive jurisdiction to enforce the Exchange Act, 15 U.S.C. § 78aa, and FINRA's breach of contract theory undermines that provision. FINRA contract enforcement actions may bristle with Exchange Act legal issues because the most serious fines levied by FINRA will be for member violations of the Act. For example, the Fieros were charged with a violation of Section 10 (b) of that Act. State court enforcement of FINRA fines might well, therefore, entail interpretation of the Exchange Act notwithstanding the exclusive jurisdiction of the federal courts.

One might argue that an inference of congressional intent to authorize such legal actions by FINRA can be drawn from the seemingly inexplicable nature of a gap in the FINRA enforcement scheme: fines may be levied but not collected. However, the gap does not support an inference of inadvertent omission because significant under enforcement of the securities laws and FINRA rules is hardly the inevitable result of FINRA's inability to bring fine-enforcement actions. FINRA fines are already enforced by a draconian sanction not involving court action. One cannot deal in securities with the public without being a member of FINRA. When a member fails to pay a fine levied by FINRA, FINRA can revoke the member's registration, resulting in exclusion from the industry. Moreover, where a fine is based on a violation of the Exchange Act, the violator will also face a panoply of private and SEC remedies. See, e.g., 15 U.S.C. §§ 77k-77l, 78i, 78j (b).

Finally, our conclusion is amply supported by NASD's longstanding practices. It has always relied exclusively upon its powers to revoke the registration of or deny reentry into the industry to punish members who do not comply with sanctions. U.S. Gen. Accounting Office, SEC and CFTC: Most Fines Collected, But Improvements Needed in the Use of Treasury's Collection Service 11 (2001). So far as we can tell, it was not until 1990 that the NASD sought to enforce fines or any other sanction through judicial actions in its own right. NASD (or any other SRO) may never even have claimed to have the power to do so until 1990. In that year, as discussed infra, NASD proposed a rule and successfully asked the SEC not to disapprove it. The rule notified the public of a new NASD policy of bringing court actions in its name to collect fines. NASD, Notice to Members 90-21, available at http://www.finra.org/Industry/Regulation/Notices/Pre-1996/. This rule, and its effect, are discussed in the next subsection. And, even after the change in policy in 1990—the effect of which turns in part on the question of statutory authority—the action against the Fieros is said to be the first case brought under that policy. Appellant's Br. at 10.

Such a longstanding practice supports an inference that NASD believed that it lacked judicial enforcement power. As the Supreme Court has stated,

> Authority actually granted by Congress of course cannot evaporate through lack of administrative exercise. But just as established practice may shed light on the extent of power conveyed by general statutory language, so the want of assertion of power by those who presumably would be alert to exercise it, is equally significant in determining whether such power was actually conferred.

Fed. Trade Comm'n v. Bunte Bros., 312 U.S. 349, 352 (1941); see also Bankamerica Corp. v. United States, 462 U.S. 122, 131 (1983) (finding that "the Government's failure for over 60 years to exercise the power it now claims strongly suggests that it did not read the statute as granting such power").

Moreover, NASD's longstanding reliance upon these other substantial enforcement methods was known to Congress, and Congress left that reliance unaltered. This lack of action further indicates that FINRA is not authorized to enforce the collection of its fines through the courts. See Merrill Lynch, Pierce, Fenner & Smith, Inc. v. Curran, 456 U.S. 353, 381-82 (1982) (noting that "an implied cause of action under the [Commodities Exchange Act] was a part of the 'contemporary legal context' in which Congress legislated," and that "[i] n that context, the fact that a comprehensive reexamination and significant amendment of the [Commodities Exchange Act] left intact the statutory provisions under which the federal courts had implied a cause of action is itself evidence that Congress affirmatively intended to preserve that remedy" (internal citations omitted)). The situation here is different from Merrill Lynch in that a failure to bring actions, rather than the bringing of actions, was involved, but the principle of congressional acquiescence is the same.

In sum, the issue is one of legislative intent, and we conclude that the heavy weight of evidence suggests that Congress did not intend to empower FINRA to bring court proceedings to enforce its fines.

b) FINRA's Authority Under the 1990 Rule

On April 10, 1990, and as amended on June 20, 1990, FINRA filed a rule with the SEC pursuant to Section 19 (b) (1) of the Exchange Act. Self-Regulatory Organizations; Notice of Filing and Immediate Effectiveness of Proposed Rule Change by National Association of Securities Dealers, Inc. Relating to the Collection of Fines and Costs in Disciplinary Proceedings, Exchange Act Release No. 28227, 46 SEC Docket 1049 (July 18, 1990), 1990 WL 320480. The proposal provided notification that the NASD "intends to pursue other available means for the collection of fines and costs imposed in disciplinary decisions" on or after July 1, 1990. Id. at *1. The NASD advised that should "its own internal efforts for the collection of fines. fail," it may refer a matter "to external collection agencies and in appropriate situations, seek to reduce such fines to a judgment." Id. at *1 n.2. Along with its SEC filing, the NASD issued a notice to its members in April 1990, informing them of its new policy and outlining how the policy would be implemented. See NASD, Notice to Members 90-21, available at http:// www.finra.org/Industry/Regulation/Notices/Pre-1996/. The notice became effective on July 1, 1990. Id. (noting that the "NASD will not pursue the collection of fines and costs assessed in cases concluded prior to July 1, 1990").

In October 1999, NASD sent a second notice to its members notifying them that it would "pursue the collection of any fine in sales practice cases, even if an individual is barred, if there has been widespread, significant, and identifiable customer harm; or the respondent has retained substantial ill-gotten gains." NASD, Notice to Members 99-86, available at http:// www.finra.org/Industry/Regulation/Notices/1999/p004067.

FINRA claims that the 1990 Rule Change constitutes authority for judicial enforcement of its fines. This claim is something of an exaggeration. The 1990 Rule Change does not even purport to be newly granted authorization from the SEC to FINRA to bring such judicial actions. Rather, it appears to assume a pre-existing power and to serve only as a notice of a new policy under that power.

Having found no such pre-existing power, we may nevertheless assume for purposes of analysis that the 1990 Rule Change, if properly obtained, constitutes such authorization. However, for FINRA to have obtained authority under the 1990 Rule Change to enforce the collection of its disciplinary fines through judicial proceedings, the rule must have been properly promulgated under the procedures established by the Exchange Act. It was not.

Section 19 (b) of the Exchange Act establishes the mechanism by which SRO's can change their governing rules. See 15 U.S.C. § 78s(b). To initiate the process, an SRO must file any proposed rule change with the SEC, "accompanied by a concise general statement of the basis and purpose of such proposed rule change." Id. § 78s(b) (1). The SEC is then required to publish notice of the proposed rule change and give interested individuals an opportunity to comment prior to either approving or disapproving the rule. Id.

Under this system, established by Congress in 1975, all new substantive rules and modification of existing rules for SRO's must go through a notice and comment period and obtain SEC approval before becoming effective. Securities Acts Amendments of 1975, Pub.L. No. 94-29, 89 Stat. 97 (codified as amended at 15 U.S.C. §§ 78a to 80b-4 (1975)); Credit Suisse First Boston Corp. v. Grunwald, 400 F.3d 1119, 1130 (9th Cir. 2005). A substantive rule—or legislative one, as it is sometimes called in this Circuit—creates "new law, right, or duties, in what amounts to a legislative act." N.Y. State Elec. & Gas Corp. v. Saranac Power Partners, L.P., 267 F.3d 128, 131 (2d Cir. 2001) (citations and internal quotation mark omitted) (defining substantive rule in the context of the Administrative Procedure Act).

Congress also included an exception to the comment and notice requirement of § 19 (b) (1) for "'House-Keeping' rules and other rules which do not substantially affect the public interest or the protection of investors." 121 Cong. Rec. 700-183 (1975) (comments of Sen. Harrison Williams); see also Saranac Power Partners, 267 F.3d at 131 (defining interpretive rules as those which "do not create rights, but merely clarify an existing statute or regulation" (citations and internal quotation marks omitted)); Grunwald, 400 F.3d at 1130 n.11. Such proposed rule changes take immediate effect upon filing with the SEC. 15 U.S.C. § 78s(b) (3) (A). In particular, the rule change becomes effective on filing with the SEC if the SRO designates the proposed rule as:

> (i) constituting a stated policy, practice, or interpretation with respect to the meaning, administration, or enforcement of an existing rule of the self-regulatory organization, (ii) establishing or changing a due, fee, or other charge imposed by the self-regulatory organization on any person, whether or not the person is a member of the self-regulatory organization, or (iii) concerned solely with the administration of the self-regulatory

organization or other matters which the Commission [may specify].

Id.

In proposing the 1990 Rule Change, the NASD designated it as such a "House-Keeping" rule, "one constituting a stated policy with respect to the enforcement of an existing rule of the NASD under § 19 (b) (3) (A) (i) of the [Exchange] Act." See Self-Regulatory Organizations; Notice of Filing and Immediate Effectiveness of Proposed Rule Change by National Association of Securities Dealers, Inc. Relating to the Collection of Fines and Costs in Disciplinary Proceedings, Exchange Act Release No. 28227, 46 SEC Docket 1049 at *1, 1990 WL 320480. Thus, the rule was to become effective upon the SEC's receipt of the filing. 15 U.S.C. § 78s (b) (3) (A).

We, however, are not bound by the NASD's characterization as to whether the 1990 Rule Change affected the substantive rights of members. Brodsky v. U.S. Nuclear Regulatory Comm'n, 578 F.3d 175, 182 (2d Cir.2009) ("The particular label placed upon [an order] by [an agency] is not necessarily conclusive, for it is the substance of what the [agency] has purported to do and has done which is decisive." (quoting Columbia Broad. Sys., Inc. v. United States, 316 U.S. 407, 416 (1942))).

Prior to the 1990 Rule Change, as discussed, there was no existing SEC rule or statute that authorized the NASD to initiate judicial proceedings to enforce the collection of its disciplinary fines. Furthermore, the NASD had a longstanding practice of not seeking to enforce collection through judicial actions. Indeed, even subsequent to the 1990 Rule Change, NASD did not rely on it to ask courts to enter judgments based on its disciplinary fines. For example, in 1998, it sought the SEC's assistance in obtaining court orders to direct violators owing NASD fines to pay these amounts. See U.S. Gen. Accounting Office, SEC and CFTC: Most Fines Collected, But Improvements Needed in the Use of Treasury's Collection Service 11 (2001). In response, the SEC agreed to seek court orders under Exchange Act § 21 (e) (1) to enforce the NASD's disciplinary fines, but only for cases that it affirmed on appeal and that met other specific requirements. Id.

This background and the various statutory provisions discussed above demonstrate that the 1990 Rule Change was not simply a stated policy change under 15 U.S.C. § 78s(b) (3) (A) that could bypass the required notice and comment period of Section 19 (b). Rather, it was a new substantive rule that affected the rights of barred and suspended members to stay out of the industry and not pay the fines imposed on them in prior disciplinary proceedings. As a result, the NASD was required to file the new substantive rule with the SEC under 15 U.S.C. § 78s(b) (1) for publication of a notice and comment period. Because the NASD improperly designated the 1990 Rule Change, it was never properly promulgated and cannot authorize FINRA to judicially enforce the collection of its disciplinary fines.

CONCLUSION

For the foregoing reasons, we reverse the judgment dismissing the appellants' declaratory judgment complaint and vacate the judgment entered in favor of the appellee.

第六章

证券投资基金法律制度

第一节　证券投资基金概述

证券投资基金是适应市场发展和社会对专业化理财服务日益增长的需求而产生的，是在证券市场的长期实践中逐步演化形成的，反映了社会经济发展的必然趋势。

证券投资基金是一种集合投资制度，即通过发行基金份额集中投资者的资金，由基金托管人托管，由基金管理人管理和运用资金，从事股票、债券等金融工具投资，并将投资收益按基金投资者的投资比例进行分配的一种间接投资方式。它发行的凭证即基金券（或受益凭证、基金单位、基金股份及基金份额）与股票、债券一起构成有价证券的三大品种。投资者通过购买基金券完成投资行为，并凭之分享证券投资基金的投资收益，承担证券投资基金的投资风险。

作为一种现代化的投资工具，证券投资基金具有集合投资、分散风险及专业理财等特征。证券投资基金具有强大的募集基金能力，一方面为中小投资者拓宽了投资渠道，另一方面，作为资本市场上最重要的机构投资者参与证券投资活动，有利于证券市场的稳定与发展。

一、中国的证券投资基金

中国立法上并未对证券投资基金进行定义。但是，中国《证券投资基金法》第 2 条对证券投资基金进行了抽象的描述，即在中国境内，通过公开发售基金份额募集资金，由基金管理人管理，基金托管人托管，为基金份额持有人的利益，以资产组合方式进行证券投资的活动。

中国证券投资基金业起步于 20 世纪 90 年代初期。在早期，证券投资基金的设立、管理、托管等环节均缺乏明确有效的监管机构和监管规则，大部分基金的设立由中国人民银行地方分行或者由地方政府根据一些地方性法规审批，没有统一的法律、法规予以规范。

1997 年 10 月，《证券投资基金管理暂行办法》出台，该暂行办法对证券投资基金的设立、募集与交易，基金托管人、基金管理人和基金持有人的权利和义务，投资运作与管理等都作出了明确的规范。这是中国第一个全面规范证券投资基金的法规，标志着中国证券投资基金业进入了规范发展的阶段。

随后，中国人民银行、中国证监会、财政部、国家税务总局等陆续发布了多项法律文件等，内容涉及基金的组织制度、市场制度、监管制度各个方面。法律、法规不断完善，监管力量加强，为基金业的运作创造出良好的外部环境。中国证券投资基金业逐渐进入快速发展时期，各种专业的基金管理公司纷纷组建起来，不同形式的证券投资基金也不断设立，且规模日益壮大。

2003 年 10 月，中国通过了《证券投资基金法》，并于 2004 年 6 月 1 日正式实施。《证券投资基金法》的颁布和实施，确立了基金业的法律地位，为基金业的发展创造出广阔的空间，有利于加强对投资者权益的保护，增强基金投资者的信心。这一法律的颁布，还标志着中国已经初步建立起完善的证券投资基金法律体系，并最终以法律的形式确定了以中国证监会为核心的监管体系。

《证券投资基金法》颁布后，中国证券投资基金进入了蓬勃发展时期。在中国设立的证券投资基金越来越多，各种封闭式基金和开放式基金吸引了众多投资者的目光，募集资金的规模越来越庞大。同时，证券投资基金已经成为中国资本市场上最重要的机构投资者。

二、美国的证券投资基金

美国的投资基金业非常发达，基金的种类也很多，大致可以分为：私募基金（包括对冲基金）、封闭基金、共同基金、交易基金和属于某一机构或面向特定人群的基金。其中，跟中国的证券投资基金最为近似的是其中的共同基金（Mutual Funds）。

美国并没有专门的法律对共同基金进行定义。根据美国证券交易委员会网站的介绍，共同基金是指汇集从诸多投资者那里募集的资金并将资金投资于股票、债券、货币市场工具以及其他证券甚至现金之上的一种投资公司。[①]按照美国 1940 年《投资公司法》的定义，投资公司是指：事实上或者宣称自己主要从事证券的投资、再投资或交易；从事或准备从事证券的投资、再投资、拥有、持有或交易，并拥有或准备获得超过发行者总资产价值 40%投资证券的任何一个实体。

自从 1924 年发行第一支共同基金到现在，美国共同基金业已经有八十多年的发展历程。美国共同基金业的低进入门槛和不断创新，使得不断有新的发起人进入到行业中来，

① 参见美国证券交易委员会网站：［2011-12-30］. http://www.sec.gov/answers/mutfund.htm.

这些新鲜血液的加入使得整个行业一直处于相当激烈的竞争状态下，且并不因为行业已经成熟而降低竞争。多年来，美国一直是世界上最大的共同基金市场，共同基金管理的资金已达到数万亿美元。

美国共同基金按不同的标准可分为不同的种类：按持有证券类型可以分为股票型基金、债券型基金、混合型基金和货币市场基金；按投资地域可以分为国内基金、国外基金和国际基金，其中，国际基金既可以投资于国外市场，也可以投资于国内市场，国外基金只投资于国外市场；按投资决策可以分为主动交易基金（由基金经理根据基金的既定投资方向选择所持有的证券）和被动交易基金（基金经理不得自行选择持有证券，只是确保投资组合与基金跟踪的指数的构成尽量一致）。此外，按照不同的组织形态和法律基础，共同基金可以分为公司型和信托型。公司型共同基金是依据美国公司法组成，以营利为目的投资于有价证券的投资公司，共同基金本身即为投资公司；信托型共同基金是依据一定的信托合同而组织起来的代理投资行为。

美国共同基金业的发展壮大，得益于其完善的基金法律制度和较为强大的监管体制。

在美国，以联邦法律为基础，加上各州制定的蓝天法以及法院生效判决所形成的判例法，共同构成了一套严密的共同基金业法律体系。其中，最为核心的是《1933 年证券法》、《1934 年证券交易法》、《1940 年投资公司法》以及《1940 年投资顾问法》这四部法律，它们是管理美国基金业的主要法律。其中，《1940 年投资公司法》对基金信息披露及运作，投资公司独立董事的组成和选举要求，托管人安排及会计师选择，有关基金运作纪录的存档要求等，均有详细规定。《1940 年投资顾问法》则对共同基金中最重要的主体——投资顾问有着详细的规定。《1933 年证券法》和《1934 年证券交易法》则对基金的销售与交易活动作出明确规定。而各州政府发布的蓝天法，为管理在各州的基金销售活动提供了法律依据。

此外，美国建立了以证券交易委员会监管为核心的共同基金监管体制。在完善的法律体系之下，美国证券交易委员会对共同基金业进行着严密而高效的监管，促进了美国基金业健康、迅速的发展。

三、案例资料

证券投资基金是一种集中资金、专家管理、分散投资、降低风险的投资工具。在证券投资基金中，基金在获取投资收入后，必须先扣除相关的费用，然后才能将利润分配给投资者。扣除的费用中，很重要的一部分为基金管理费。投资者和基金管理人在基金管理费数额的确定上往往会产生争议。争议发生后，投资者可以“用脚投票”，把高费率的基金转换到低费率的基金，或者是直接赎回基金。但是，也有投资者选择以诉讼的方式寻求法律上的保护。

在下面的 Jones v. Harris Associates L.P. 案中，围绕基金的管理费问题，基金的个人投资者将基金的投资顾问告上法庭。诉讼的争议焦点为，投资顾问 Harris Associates L.P. 是否违背其信义义务收取了过高的管理费。投资者认为，投资顾问收取个人投资者的管理费是其收取机构投资者的两倍，这种行为违背了信义义务，违反了《投资公司法》中第 36 (b)条的规定（该条就收取管理费问题对投资顾问施加了一种信义义务）。

初审法院适用 Gartenberg v. Merrill Lynch Asset Management, Inc. 案中确立的标准（Gartenberg 标准），认定被告并未违反其信义义务，驳回了原告的诉讼。依据 Gartenberg 标准，如果投资顾问的收费计划处于基于所有的背景情况经过双方协商谈判所能达到的收费范围之内，那么该项收费计划并不导致投资顾问违反其信义义务。只有投资顾问收取的费用过高且高额的费用与其所提供的服务并无合理的关系以及高额的费用并非双方协商的结果，才能认定投资顾问违反了《投资公司法》中第 36（b）条的规定。第七巡回上诉法院拒绝适用 Gartenberg 标准，而是从信息披露的角度认定被告并未违反其信义义务。第七巡回上诉法院认为，就管理费的收取而言，投资顾问所要做的是充分的信息披露，只要投资顾问在协商管理费时是诚实的且进行了充分的信息披露，那么司法机关就不应再介入管理费的纷争。

案件最后被上诉至联邦最高法院。最高法院认为，尽管第 36（b）条并未有明确的规定，但是根据该条的立法语言以及投资者就投资顾问违反信义义务起诉在《投资公司法》整体结构中的地位，Gartenberg 标准是判断管理费高低的正确标准。根据最高法院的判决，国会并未计划让法院在共同基金领域拥有设定费率的权力，国会认识到，法庭不具备进行如此精确计算的能力。法院在审查共同基金顾问收取服务费的问题上仅可发挥有限的裁决作用，只有在共同基金所收取的服务费过高且“与其提供的服务之间存在着不合理的关系”时，法院才能介入。

最高法院的这一判决，对美国的共同基金业有着重要的影响。一方面，判决给了投资者挑战投资顾问收取过高服务费寻求司法保护的武器；另一方面，判决将服务费的设定权留给了基金管理人，这又有助于缓解共同基金业所面临的减少投资顾问每年所收取之高额服务费的压力。

Jones v. Harris Associates L.P.

559 U.S. —, 130 S.Ct. 1418, 176 L.Ed.2d 265 (U.S., 2010)

Justice ALITO delivered the opinion of the Court.

We consider in this case what a mutual fund shareholder must prove in order to show that a mutual fund investment adviser breached the "fiduciary duty with respect to the receipt of compensation for services" that is imposed by § 36 (b) of the Investment Company Act of 1940, 15 U.S.C. § 80a-35 (b) (hereinafter § 36 (b)).

I

A

The Investment Company Act of 1940 (Act), 54 Stat. 789, 15 U.S.C. § 80a-1 et seq., regulates investment companies, including mutual funds. "A mutual fund is a pool of assets, consisting primarily of [a] portfolio [of] securities, and belonging to the individual investors holding shares in the fund." Burks v. Lasker, 441 U.S. 471, 480, 99 S.Ct. 1831, 60 L.Ed.2d 404 (1979). The following arrangements are typical. A separate entity called an investment adviser creates the mutual fund, which may have no employees of its own. See Kamen v. Kemper Financial Services, Inc., 500 U.S. 90, 93, 111 S.Ct. 1711, 114 L.Ed.2d 152 (1991); Daily Income Fund, Inc. v. Fox, 464 U.S. 523, 536, 104 S.Ct. 831, 78 L.Ed.2d 645 (1984); Burks, 441 U.S., at 480-481, 99 S.Ct. 1831. The adviser selects the fund's directors, manages the fund's investments, and provides other services. See id., at 481. Because of the relationship between a mutual fund and its investment adviser, the fund often "cannot, as a practical matter sever its relationship with the adviser. Therefore, the forces of arm's-length bargaining do not work in the mutual fund industry in the same manner as they do in other sectors of the American economy." Ibid. (quoting S.Rep. No. 91-184, p. 5 (1969) (hereinafter S. Rep.)).

"Congress adopted the [Investment Company Act of 1940] because of its concern with the potential for abuse inherent in the structure of investment companies." Daily Income Fund, 464 U.S., at 536, 104 S.Ct. 831 (internal quotation marks omitted). Recognizing that the relationship between a fund and its investment adviser was "fraught with potential conflicts of interest," the Act created protections for mutual fund shareholders. Id., at 536-538, 104 S.Ct. 831 (internal quotation marks omitted); Burks, supra, at 482-483, 99 S.Ct. 1831. Among other things, the Act required that no more than 60 percent of a fund's directors could be affiliated with the adviser and that fees for investment advisers be approved by the directors and the shareholders of the fund. See §§ 10, 15 (c), 54 Stat. 806, 813.

The growth of mutual funds in the 1950's and 1960's prompted studies of the 1940 Act's effectiveness in protecting investors. See Daily Income Fund, 464 U.S., at 537-538, 104 S.Ct. 831. Studies commissioned or authored by the Securities and Exchange Commission (SEC or Commission) identified problems relating to the independence of investment company boards and the compensation received by investment advisers. See ibid. In response*1423 to such concerns, Congress amended the Act in 1970 and bolstered shareholder protection in two primary ways.

First, the amendments strengthened the "cornerstone" of the Act's efforts to check conflicts of interest, the independence of mutual fund boards of directors, which negotiate and scrutinize adviser compensation. Burks, supra, at 482, 99 S.Ct. 1831. The amendments required that no more than 60 percent of a fund's directors be "persons who are interested persons," e.g., that they have no interest in or affiliation with the investment adviser. 15 U.S.C. § 80a-10 (a); § 80a-2 (a) (19); see also Daily Income Fund, supra, at 538, 104 S.Ct. 831. These board members are given "a host of special responsibilities." Burks, 441 U.S., at 482-483, 99 S.Ct. 1831. In particular, they must "review and approve the contracts of the investment adviser" annually, id., at 483, 99 S.Ct. 1831, and a majority of these directors must approve an adviser's compensation, 15 U.S.C. § 80a-15 (c). Second, § 36 (b), 84 Stat. 1429, of the Act imposed upon investment advisers a "fiduciary duty" with respect to compensation received from a mutual fund, 15 U.S.C. § 80a-35 (b), and granted individual investors a private right of action for breach of that duty, ibid.

The "fiduciary duty" standard contained in § 36 (b) represented a delicate compromise. Prior to the adoption of the 1970 amendments, shareholders challenging investment adviser fees under state law were required to meet "common-law standards of corporate waste, under which an unreasonable or unfair fee might be approved unless the court deemed it 'unconscionable' or 'shocking,' " and "security holders challenging adviser fees under the [Investment Company Act] itself had been required to prove gross abuse of trust." Daily Income Fund, 464 U.S., at 540, n. 12, 104 S.Ct. 831. Aiming to give shareholders a stronger remedy, the SEC proposed a provision that would have empowered the Commission to bring actions to challenge a fee that was not "reasonable" and to intervene in any similar action brought by or on behalf of an investment company. Id., at 538, 104 S.Ct. 831. This approach was included in a bill that passed the House. H.R. 9510, 90th Cong., 1st Sess., § 8 (d) (1967); see also S. 1659, 90th Cong., 1st Sess., § 8 (d) (1967). Industry representatives, however, objected to this proposal, fearing that it "might in essence provide the Commission with ratemaking authority." Daily Income Fund, 464 U.S., at 538, 104 S.Ct. 831.

The provision that was ultimately enacted adopted "a different method of testing management compensation," id., at 539, 104 S.Ct. 831 (quoting S.Rep., at 5 (internal quotation marks omitted)), that was more favorable to shareholders than the previously available remedies but that did not permit a compensation agreement to be reviewed in court for "reasonableness." This is the fiduciary duty standard in § 36 (b).

***1424 B**

Petitioners are shareholders in three different mutual funds managed by respondent Harris Associates L.P., an investment adviser. Petitioners filed this action in the Northern District of Illinois pursuant to § 36 (b) seeking damages, an injunction, and rescission of advisory agreements between Harris Associates and the mutual funds. The complaint alleged that Harris Associates had violated § 36 (b) by charging fees that were "disproportionate to the services rendered" and "not within the range of what would have been negotiated at arm's length in light of all the surrounding circumstances." App. 52.

The District Court granted summary judgment for Harris Associates. Applying the standard adopted in Gartenberg v. Merrill Lynch Asset Management, Inc., 694 F.2d 923 (C.A.2 1982), the court concluded that petitioners had failed to raise a triable issue of fact as to "whether the fees charged... were so disproportionately large that they could not have been the result of arm's-length bargaining." App. to Pet. for Cert. 29a. The District Court assumed that it was relevant to compare the challenged fees with those that Harris Associates charged its other clients. Id., at 30a. But in light of those comparisons as well as comparisons with fees charged by other investment advisers to similar mutual funds, the Court held that it could not reasonably be found that the challenged fees were outside the range that could have been the product of arm's-length bargaining. Id., at 29a-32a.

A panel of the Seventh Circuit affirmed based on different reasoning, explicitly "disapprov[ing] the Gartenberg approach." 527 F.3d 627, 632 (2008). Looking to trust law, the panel noted that, while a trustee "owes an obligation of candor in negotiation," a trustee, at the time of the creation of a trust, "may negotiate in his own interest and accept what the settlor or governance institution agrees to pay." Ibid. (citing Restatement (Second) of Trusts § 242, and Comment f). The panel thus reasoned that "[a] fiduciary duty differs from rate regulation. A fiduciary must make full disclosure and play no tricks but is not subject to a cap on compensation." 527 F.3d, at 632. In the panel's view, the amount of an adviser's compensation would be relevant only if the compensation were "so unusual" as to give rise to an inference "that deceit must have occurred, or that the persons responsible for decision have abdicated." Ibid.

The panel argued that this understanding of § 36 (b) is consistent with the forces operating in the contemporary mutual fund market. Noting that "[t]oday thousands of mutual funds compete," the panel concluded that "sophisticated investors" shop for the funds that produce the best overall results, "mov[e] their money elsewhere" when fees are "excessive in relation to the results," and thus "create a competitive pressure" that generally keeps fees low. Id., at 633-634. The panel faulted Gartenberg on the ground that it "relies too little on markets." 527 F.3d, at 632. And the panel firmly rejected a comparison between the fees that Harris Associates charged to the funds and the fees that Harris Associates charged other types of clients, observing that "[d]ifferent clients call for different commitments of time" and that costs, such as research, that may benefit several categories of clients "make it hard to draw inferences from fee levels." Id., at 634.

The Seventh Circuit denied rehearing en banc by an equally divided vote. 537 F.3d 728 (2008). The dissent from the denial of rehearing argued that the panel's rejection of Gartenberg was based "mainly on an economic analysis that is ripe for reexamination." *1425 537 F.3d, at 730 (opinion of Posner, J.). Among other things, the dissent expressed concern that Harris Associates charged "its captive funds more than twice what it charges independent funds," and the dissent questioned whether high adviser fees actually drive investors away. Id., at 731.

We granted certiorari to resolve a split among the Courts of Appeals over the proper standard under § 36 (b). 556 U.S. —, 129 S.Ct. 1579, 173 L.Ed.2d 675 (2009).

II

A

Since Congress amended the Investment Company Act in 1970, the mutual fund industry has experienced exponential growth. Assets under management increased from $38.2 billion in 1966 to over $9.6 trillion in 2008. The number of mutual fund investors grew from 3.5 million in 1965 to 92 million in 2008, and there are now more than 9 000 open—and closed-end funds.

During this time, the standard for an investment adviser's fiduciary duty has remained an open question in our Court, but, until the Seventh Circuit's decision below, something of a consensus had developed regarding the standard set forth over 25 years ago in Gartenberg, supra. The Gartenberg standard has been adopted by other federal courts, and "[t]he SEC's regulations have recognized, and formalized, Gartenberg-like factors." Brief for United States as Amicus Curiae 23. See 17 CFR § 240.14a-101, Sched. 14A, Item 22, para. (c) (11) (i) (2009); 69 Fed.Reg. 39801, n.31, 39807-39809 (2004). In the present case, both petitioners and respondent generally endorse the Gartenberg approach, although they disagree in some respects about its meaning.

In Gartenberg, the Second Circuit noted that Congress had not defined what it meant by a "fiduciary duty" with respect to compensation but concluded that "the test is essentially whether the fee schedule represents a charge within the range of what would have been negotiated at arm's-length in the light of all of the surrounding circumstances." 694 F.2d, at 928. The Second Circuit elaborated that, "[t]o be guilty of a violation of § 36 (b) ... the adviser-manager must charge a fee that is so disproportionately large that it bears no reasonable relationship to the services rendered and could not have been the product of arm's-length bargaining." Ibid. "To make this determination," the Court stated, "all pertinent facts must be weighed," id., at 929, and the Court specifically mentioned*1426 "the adviser-manager's cost in providing the service... the extent to which the adviser-manager realizes economies of scale as the fund grows larger, and the volume of orders which must be processed by the manager." Id., at 930. Observing that competition among advisers for the business of managing a fund may be "virtually non-existent," the Court rejected the suggestion that "the principal factor to be considered in evaluating a fee's fairness is the price charged by other similar advisers to funds managed by them," although the Court did not suggest that this factor could not be "taken into account." Id., at 929. The Court likewise rejected the "argument that the lower fees charged by investment advisers to large pension funds should be used as a criterion for determining fair advisory fees for money market funds," since a "pension fund does not face the myriad of daily purchases and redemptions throughout the nation which must be handled by [a money market fund]." Id., at 930, n. 3.

B

[1] The meaning of § 36 (b)'s reference to "a fiduciary duty with respect to the receipt of compensation for services" is hardly pellucid, but based on the terms of that provision and the role that a shareholder action for breach of that duty plays in the overall structure of the Act, we conclude that Gartenberg was correct in its basic formulation of what § 36 (b) requires: to face liability under § 36 (b), an investment adviser must charge a fee that is so disproportionately large that it bears no reasonable relationship to the services rendered and could not have been the product of arm's length bargaining.

1

We begin with the language of § 36 (b). As noted, the Seventh Circuit panel thought that the phrase "fiduciary duty" incorporates a standard taken from the law of trusts. Petitioners agree but maintain that the panel identified the wrong trust-law standard. Instead of the standard that applies when a trustee and a settlor negotiate the trustee's fee at the time of the creation of a trust, petitioners invoke the standard that applies when a trustee seeks compensation after the trust is created. Brief for Petitioners 20-23, 35-37. A compensation agreement reached at that time, they point out, "'will not bind the beneficiary' if either 'the trustee failed to make a full disclosure of all *1427 circumstances affecting the agreement'" which he knew or should have known or if the agreement is unfair to the beneficiary. Id., at 23 (quoting Restatement (Second) of Trusts § 242, Comment i). Respondent, on the other hand, contends that the term "fiduciary" is not exclusive to the law of trusts, that the phrase means different things in different contexts, and that there is no reason to believe that § 36 (b) incorporates the specific meaning of the term in the law of trusts. Brief for Respondent 34-36.

[2] We find it unnecessary to take sides in this dispute. In Pepper v. Litton, 308 U.S. 295, 60 S.Ct. 238 (1939), we discussed the meaning of the concept of fiduciary duty in a context that is analogous to that presented here, and we also looked to trust law. At issue in Pepper was whether a bankruptcy court could disallow a dominant or controlling shareholder's claim for compensation against a bankrupt corporation. Dominant or controlling shareholders, we held, are "fiduciar[ies]" whose "powers are powers [held] in trust." Id., at 306, 60 S.Ct. 238. We then explained:

"Their dealings with the corporation are subjected to rigorous scrutiny and where any of their contracts or engagements with the corporation is challenged the burden is on the director or stockholder not only to prove the good faith of the transaction but also to show its inherent fairness from the viewpoint of the corporation and those interested therein.... *The essence of the test is whether or not under all the circumstances the transaction carries the earmarks of an arm's length bargain*. If it does not, equity will set it aside." Id., at 306-307[, 60 S.Ct. 238] (emphasis added; footnote omitted); see also Geddes v. Anaconda Copper Mining Co., 254 U.S. 590, 599, 41 S.Ct. 209, 65 L.Ed. 425 (1921) (standard of fiduciary duty for interested directors).

We believe that this formulation expresses the meaning of the phrase "fiduciary duty" in § 36 (b), 84 Stat. 1429. The Investment Company Act modifies this duty in a significant way: it shifts the burden of proof from the fiduciary to the party claiming breach, 15 U.S.C. § 80a-35 (b) (1), to show that the fee is outside the range that arm's-length bargaining would produce.

The Gartenberg approach fully incorporates this understanding of the fiduciary duty as set out in Pepper and reflects § 36 (b) (1)'s imposition of the burden on the plaintiff. As noted,

Gartenberg insists that all relevant circumstances be taken into account, see 694 F.2d, at 929, as does § 36 (b) (2), 84 Stat. 1429 ("[A] pproval by the board of directors... shall be given such consideration by the court as is deemed appropriate under *all the circumstances*" (emphasis added)). And Gartenberg uses the range of fees that might result from arm's-length bargaining as the benchmark for reviewing challenged fees.

2

Gartenberg's approach also reflects § 36 (b)'s place in the statutory scheme and, in particular, its relationship to the other protections that the Act affords investors.

Under the Act, scrutiny of investment adviser compensation by a fully informed mutual fund board is the "cornerstone of the... effort to control conflicts of interest within mutual funds." Burks, 441 U.S., at 482, 99 S.Ct. 1831. The Act interposes disinterested directors as "independent watchdogs" of the relationship between a mutual fund and its adviser. Id., at 484, 99 S.Ct. 1831 (internal quotation marks omitted). To provide these directors with the information needed to judge whether an adviser's compensation *1428 is excessive, the Act requires advisers to furnish all information "reasonably... necessary to evaluate the terms" of the adviser's contract, 15 U.S.C. § 80a-15 (c), and gives the SEC the authority to enforce that requirement. See § 80a-41. Board scrutiny of adviser compensation and shareholder suits under § 36 (b), 84 Stat. 1429, are mutually reinforcing but independent mechanisms for controlling conflicts. See Daily Income Fund, 464 U.S., at 541, 104 S.Ct. 831 (Congress intended for § 36 (b) suits and directorial approval of adviser contracts to act as "independent checks on excessive fees"); Kamen, 500 U.S., at 108, 111 S.Ct. 1711 ("Congress added § 36 (b) to the [Act] in 1970 because it concluded that the shareholders should not have to rely solely on the fund's directors to assure reasonable adviser fees, notwithstanding the increased disinterestedness of the board" (internal quotation marks omitted)).

In recognition of the role of the disinterested directors, the Act instructs courts to give board approval of an adviser's compensation "such consideration... as is deemed appropriate under all the circumstances." § 80a-35 (b) (2). Cf. Burks, 441 U.S., at 485, 99 S.Ct. 1831 ("[I]t would have been paradoxical for Congress to have been willing to rely largely upon [boards of directors as] 'watchdogs' to protect shareholder interests and yet, where the 'watchdogs' have done precisely that, require that they be totally muzzled").

From this formulation, two inferences may be drawn. First, a measure of deference to a board's judgment may be appropriate in some instances. Second, the appropriate measure of deference varies depending on the circumstances.

[3] Gartenberg heeds these precepts. Gartenberg advises that "the expertise of the independent trustees of a fund, whether they are fully informed about all facts bearing on the [investment adviser's] service and fee, and the extent of care and conscientiousness with which they perform their duties are important factors to be considered in deciding whether they and the [investment adviser] are guilty of a breach of fiduciary duty in violation of § 36 (b)." 694 F.2d, at 930.

III

While both parties in this case endorse the basic Gartenberg approach, they disagree on several important questions that warrant discussion.

[4] [5] The first concerns comparisons between the fees that an adviser charges a captive mutual fund and the fees that it charges its independent clients. As noted, the Gartenberg court rejected a comparison between the fees that the adviser in that case charged a money market fund and the fees that it charged a pension fund. 694 F.2d, at 930, n. 3 (noting the "[t]he nature and extent of the services required by each type of fund differ sharply"). Petitioners contend that such a comparison is appropriate, Brief for Petitioners 30-31, but respondent disagrees. Brief for Respondent 38-44. Since the Act requires consideration of all relevant factors, 15 U.S.C. § 80a-35 (b) (2); see also § 80a-15 (c), we do not think that there can be any categorical rule regarding the comparisons of the fees charged different types of clients. See Daily Income Fund, supra, at 537, 104 S.Ct. 831 (discussing concern with investment advisers' practice of charging higher fees to mutual funds than to their other clients). Instead, courts may give such comparisons the weight that they merit in light of the similarities and differences between the services that the clients in question require, but courts must be wary of inapt comparisons. As the panel below noted, there may be significant differences between the *1429 services provided by an investment adviser to a mutual fund and those it provides to a pension fund which are attributable to the greater frequency of shareholder redemptions in a mutual fund, the higher turnover of mutual fund assets, the more burdensome regulatory and legal obligations, and higher marketing costs. 527 F.3d, at 634 ("Different clients call for different commitments of time"). If the services rendered are sufficiently different that a comparison is not probative, then courts must reject such a comparison. Even if the services provided and fees charged to an independent fund are relevant, courts should be mindful that the Act does not necessarily ensure fee parity between mutual funds and institutional clients contrary to petitioners' contentions. See id., at 631. ("Plaintiffs maintain that a fiduciary may charge its

controlled clients no more than its independent clients").

[6] By the same token, courts should not rely too heavily on comparisons with fees charged to mutual funds by other advisers. These comparisons are problematic because these fees, like those challenged, may not be the product of negotiations conducted at arm's length. See 537 F.3d, at 731-732 (opinion dissenting from denial of rehearing en banc); Gartenberg, supra, at 929 ("Competition between money market funds for shareholder business does not support an inference that competition must therefore also exist between [investment advisers] for fund business. The former may be vigorous even though the latter is virtually non-existent").

[7] Finally, a court's evaluation of an investment adviser's fiduciary duty must take into account both procedure and substance. See 15 U.S.C. § 80a-35 (b) (2) (requiring deference to board's consideration "as is deemed appropriate under all the circumstances"); cf. Daily Income Fund, 464 U.S., at 541, 104 S.Ct. 831 ("Congress intended security holder and SEC actions under § 36 (b), on the one hand, and directorial approval of adviser contracts, on the other, to act as independent checks on excessive fees"). Where a board's process for negotiating and reviewing investment-adviser compensation is robust, a reviewing court should afford commensurate deference to the outcome of the bargaining process. See Burks, 441 U.S., at 484, 99 S.Ct. 1831 (unaffiliated directors serve as "independent watchdogs"). Thus, if the disinterested directors considered the relevant factors, their decision to approve a particular fee agreement is entitled to considerable weight, even if a court might weigh the factors differently. Cf. id., at 485, 99 S.Ct. 1831. This is not to deny that a fee may be excessive even if it was negotiated by a board in possession of all relevant information, but such a determination must be based on evidence that the fee "is so disproportionately large that it bears no reasonable relationship to the services rendered and could not have been *1430 the product of arm's-length bargaining." Gartenberg, supra, at 928.

[8] In contrast, where the board's process was deficient or the adviser withheld important information, thc court must take a more rigorous look at the outcome. When an investment adviser fails to disclose material information to the board, greater scrutiny is justified because the withheld information might have hampered the board's ability to function as "an independent check upon the management." Burks, supra, at 484, 99 S.Ct. 1831 (internal quotation marks omitted). "Section 36 (b) is sharply focused on the question of whether the fees themselves were excessive." Migdal v. Rowe Price-Fleming Int'l, Inc., 248 F.3d 321, 328 (C.A.4 2001); see also 15 U.S.C. § 80a-35 (b) (imposing a "fiduciary duty with respect to the

receipt of compensation for services, or of payments of a material nature" (emphasis added)). But an adviser's compliance or noncompliance with its disclosure obligations is a factor that must be considered in calibrating the degree of deference that is due a board's decision to approve an adviser's fees.

[9] [10] It is also important to note that the standard for fiduciary breach under § 36 (b) does not call for judicial second-guessing of informed board decisions. See Daily Income Fund, supra, at 538, 104 S.Ct. 831; see also Burks, 441 U.S., at 483, 99 S.Ct. 1831 ("Congress consciously chose to address the conflict-of-interest problem through the Act's independent-directors section, rather than through more drastic remedies"). "[P]otential conflicts [of interests] may justify some restraints upon the unfettered discretion of even disinterested mutual fund directors, particularly in their transactions with the investment adviser," but they do not suggest that a court may supplant the judgment of disinterested directors apprised of all relevant information, without additional evidence that the fee exceeds the arm's-length range. Id., at 481, 99 S.Ct. 1831. In reviewing compensation under § 36 (b), the Act does not require courts to engage in a precise calculation of fees representative of arm's-length bargaining. See 527 F.3d, at 633 ("Judicial price-setting does not accompany fiduciary duties"). As recounted above, Congress rejected a "reasonableness" requirement that was criticized as charging the courts with rate-setting responsibilities. See Daily Income Fund, supra, at 538-540, 104 S.Ct. 831. Congress' approach recognizes that courts are not well suited to make such precise calculations. Cf. General Motors Corp. v. Tracy, 519 U.S. 278, 308, 117 S.Ct. 811, 136 L.Ed.2d 761 (1997) ("[T]he Court is institutionally unsuited to gather the facts upon which economic predictions can be made, and professionally untrained to make them"); Verizon Communications Inc. v. FCC, 535 U.S. 467, 539, 122 S.Ct. 1646, 152 L.Ed.2d 701 (2002); see also Concord v. Boston Edison Co., 915 F.2d 17, 25 (CA1 1990) (opinion for the court by Breyer, C.J.) ("[H]ow is a judge or jury to determine a 'fair price'?"). Gartenberg's "so disproportionately large" standard, 694 F.2d, at 928, reflects this congressional choice to "rely largely upon [independent director] 'watchdogs' to protect shareholders interests." Burks, supra, at 485, 99 S.Ct. 1831.

By focusing almost entirely on the element of disclosure, the Seventh Circuit panel erred. See 527 F.3d, at 632 (An investment adviser "must make full disclosure and play no tricks but is not subject to a cap on compensation"). The Gartenberg standard, which the panel rejected, may lack sharp analytical clarity, but we believe that it accurately reflects the compromise that is embodied in § 36 (b), and it has provided a workable standard for nearly three decades. The debate between*1431 the Seventh Circuit panel and the dissent from the denial of rehearing regarding today's mutual fund market is a matter for Congress, not the courts.

IV

For the foregoing reasons, the judgment of the Court of Appeals is vacated, and the case remanded for further proceedings consistent with this opinion.

It is so ordered.

Justice THOMAS, concurring.

第二节　证券投资基金主体

一、中国证券投资基金主体

在中国境内，通过公开发售基金份额募集的证券投资基金，由基金管理人管理，基金托管人托管，基金份额持有人享有相关收益，基金份额由相关基金销售机构负责销售。目前，中国相关的法律、法规已经涵盖了上述四类证券投资基金主体：基金管理人、基金托管人、基金份额持有人以及基金销售机构。

（一）基金管理人

基金管理人是指为基金份额持有人的利益按照基金合同的规定运用基金资产投资并管理基金资产的人。在中国，担任基金管理人，应当经中国证监会核准。根据中国《证券投资基金法》的规定，基金管理人只能由依法设立的基金管理公司担任。设立基金管理公司，应当具备一定的条件，并经中国证监会批准。

依照中国《证券投资基金法》的规定，基金管理人应当履行下列职责：（1）依法募集基金，办理或者委托经中国证监会认定的其他机构代为办理基金份额的发售、申购、赎回和登记事宜；（2）办理基金备案手续；（3）对所管理的不同基金财产分别管理、分别记账，进行证券投资；（4）按照基金合同的约定确定基金收益分配方案，及时向基金份额持有人分配收益；（5）进行基金会计核算并编制基金财务会计报告；（6）编制中期和年度基金报告；（7）计算并公告基金资产净值，确定基金份额申购、赎回价格；（8）办理与基金财产管理业务活动有关的信息披露事项；（9）召集基金份额持有人大会；（10）保存基金财产管理业务活动的记录、账册、报表和其他相关资料；（11）以基金管理人名义，代表基金份额持有人利益行使诉讼权利或者实施其他法律行为；（12）中国证监会规定的其他职责。

基金管理人在对基金进行管理的过程中，负有忠实和勤勉的义务。为履行该义务，基金管理人被禁止从事以下行为：（1）将其固有财产或者他人财产混同于基金财产从事证券投资；（2）不公平地对待其管理的不同基金财产；（3）利用基金财产为基金份额持有人以外的第三人牟取利益；（4）向基金份额持有人违规承诺收益或者承担损失；（5）依照法律、行政法规有关规定，由中国证监会规定禁止的其他行为。

基金管理人因各种原因职责终止的，基金份额持有人大会应当在一定期限内选任新基金管理人；新基金管理人产生前，由中国证监会指定临时基金管理人。职责终止的基金管理人，应当妥善保管基金管理业务资料，及时办理基金管理业务的移交手续，新基金管理人或者临时基金管理人应当及时接收。基金管理人职责终止的，还应当按照规定聘请会计师事务所对基金财产进行审计，并将审计结果予以公告，同时报中国证监会备案。

（二）基金托管人

基金托管人是投资人权益的代表，是基金资产的名义持有人或管理机构。在中国，基金托管人由依法设立并取得基金托管资格的商业银行担任。申请取得基金托管资格，应当符合一定条件，并经中国证监会和中国银监会核准。为了保持基金托管人的独立性及保证基金资产的安全，中国《证券投资基金法》规定基金托管人与基金管理人不得为同一人，不得相互出资或者持有股份。

依照中国《证券投资基金法》的规定，基金托管人应当履行下列职责：（1）安全保管基金财产；（2）按照规定开设基金财产的资金账户和证券账户；（3）对所托管的不同基金财产分别设置账户，确保基金财产的完整与独立；（4）保存基金托管业务活动的记录、账册、报表和其他相关资料；（5）按照基金合同的约定，根据基金管理人的投资指令，及时办理清算、交割事宜；（6）办理与基金托管业务活动有关的信息披露事项；（7）对基金财务会计报告、中期和年度基金报告出具意见；（8）复核、审查基金管理人计算的基金资产净值和基金份额申购、赎回价格；（9）按照规定召集基金份额持有人大会；（10）按照规定监督基金管理人的投资运作；（11）中国证监会规定的其他职责。

基金托管人只是基金资产的名义持有人，其对基金资产的最终所有人——基金份额持有人也负有忠实和勤勉义务。因此，前述基金管理人被禁止从事的行为也适用于基金托管人。此外，为保证基金资产的安全，基金托管人还有义务监督基金管理人的行为。基金托管人发现基金管理人的投资指令（包括依据交易程序已经生效的投资指令）违反法律、行政法规和其他有关规定，或者违反基金合同约定的，应当拒绝执行，立即通知基金管理人，并及时向中国证监会报告。

基金托管人因各种原因职责终止的，基金份额持有人大会应当在一定期限内选任新基金托管人；新基金托管人产生前，由中国证监会指定临时基金托管人。职责终止的基金托管人，应当妥善保管基金财产和基金托管业务资料，及时办理基金财产和基金托管业务的移交手续，新基金托管人或者临时基金托管人应当及时接收。基金托管人职责终止的，还应当按照规定聘请会计师事务所对基金财产进行审计，并将审计结果予以公告，同时报中国证监会备案。

（三）基金份额持有人

基金份额持有人是证券投资基金的投资人，通过购买基金份额，成为基金份额持有人。基金的一切投资活动都是为了增加投资者的收益，一切风险管理都是围绕保护投资者利益来考虑的。因此，基金份额持有人是基金一切活动的中心。

依照中国《证券投资基金法》的规定，基金份额持有人按其所持基金份额享受收益和承担风险。基金份额持有人是基金资产的最终所有人。基金合同终止时，经清算后的剩余基金财产，应当按照基金份额持有人所持份额比例进行分配。

为了保障基金份额持有人的合法利益，中国《证券投资基金法》赋予了基金份额持有人如下权利：（1）分享基金财产收益；（2）参与分配清算后的剩余基金财产；（3）依法转让或者申请赎回其持有的基金份额；（4）按照规定要求召开基金份额持有人大会；（5）对基金份额持有人大会审议事项行使表决权；（6）查阅或者复制公开披露的基金信息资料；（7）对基金管理人、基金托管人、基金份额发售机构损害其合法权益的行为依法提起诉讼；（8）基金合同约定的其他权利。

（四）基金销售机构

基金销售机构是指向社会公众销售基金份额的机构。在中国，只有基金管理人以及经中国证监会认定的其他机构才能担任基金销售机构。其中，基金管理人可以办理其募集的基金产品的销售业务。此外，符合一定条件的商业银行（含在华外资法人银行）、证券公司、证券投资咨询机构、独立基金销售机构以及中国证监会规定的其他机构可以向中国证监会申请基金销售业务资格。

根据中国证监会发布的《证券投资基金销售管理办法》（2010年修订）的规定，证券投资基金销售，包括基金销售机构宣传推介基金，发售基金份额，办理基金份额申购、赎回等活动。在基金销售过程中，还有其他相关机构与基金销售业务的环节。此类机构包括为基金销售机构提供支付结算服务、基金销售结算资金监督、注册登记服务等与基金销售业务相关服务的机构。

二、美国证券投资基金主体

在美国，根据共同基金组织形态的不同，所涉及的当事人不尽相同。信托型共同基金主要涉及基金管理公司（委托人）、基金保管机构（受托人）和投资人（受益人）三方当事人。而公司型共同基金，共同基金本身即为投资公司，除此之外，还涉及另外四方的当事人：基金持有人、承销商、基金托管人和基金管理人。

在美国，根据《1940 年投资公司法》的规定，投资公司必须向美国证券交易委员会登记注册，其主要目的在于由证券交易委员会审查证券投资公司的资格经营范围和方针，以防止投资公司同投资者发生利益冲突。当然，《1940 年投资公司法》还规定了若干豁免登记注册的情形。投资公司在注册登记时，必须向投资者提供一份共同基金投资说明书，在说明书中应向投资者进行详细的信息披露。此外，投资公司还必须定期向投资者寄发共同基金经营状况报告。同时，投资公司亦须依照《1933 年证券法》和《1934 年证券交易法》的规定，对其营业状况和财务状况加以公开。

基金持有人是共同基金的出资人，拥有资金资产的所有权以及资金投资的收益权。共同基金持有人的权利并未在美国《1940 年投资公司法》中进行专门的界定，而是伴随着基金重大事项的决定权的相关规定而散见于各条款中。如《1940 年投资公司法》第 13 条（关于投资政策的改变）、第 15 条（关于投资顾问契约与承销契约）、第 16 条（关于董事会的变化及关于严格信托）等条款中都对基金持有人的权利进行了规定。

承销商主要负责基金股份的销售，对基金的成功至关重要。为把基金推向市场，吸引投资者来投资基金，承销商要准备销售材料、宣传手册和咨询材料，同时需要设计激励机制，鼓励各式各样的销售代理来促进销售。它们可以直接售卖基金份额，也可以通过经纪商、银行、保险公司或者共同基金超市等来销售。

基金托管人是投资人权益的代表，是基金资产的名义持有人或管理机构。为了保护基金资产的安全，基金托管人应当为基金开设独立的账户，按照基金管理人的指令负责资金划拨、款项收付、分红派息、证券清算等事宜。根据美国《1940 年投资公司法》的规定，每一家注册的管理公司均应将其证券和类似投资置于和维持在托管机构下，可充当托管人（美国各州的实践不大一样）的有商业银行、经纪商、证券交易所、证券公司、期货公司、储蓄公司及投资公司本身。基金托管人必须由符合条件的商业银行或投资信托公司担任，它们必须得到联邦或州监管部门的特许并受到监管部门的检查。

基金管理人是指凭借专门的知识与经验，根据法律、法规及基金章程或契约的规定，运用所管理基金的资产进行投资决策，使所管理的基金资产不断增值、基金持有人获取收益的机构。美国共同基金的管理人必须注册为投资顾问，投资顾问受托管理该基金和设计证券投资组合。投资顾问既可以是机构也可以是个人。美国《1940 年投资顾问法》中对投资顾问的定义为：为获得报酬从事就证券价值或投资、买卖证券的可行性直接或通过出版物和书面材料向他人提供咨询业务的人，或为获得报酬作为常规业务组成部分发布或公布与证券有关的分析或报告的人。

三、案例资料

在美国，基金管理人管理基金，必须尽到信义义务（fiduciary duty）。为监督信义义务的履行，美国实行基金管理人的独立董事制度，在基金管理公司的董事会中引进一定比例的外部董事（又称为非关联董事），制衡大股东的力量、监视基金管理人的行为，以保护基金份额持有人的利益。此外，作为履行信义义务很重要的一个方面，基金管理人必须尽到充分的信息披露义务，尤其是涉及自身利益冲突的信息。如果没有进行相关的信息披露，基金管理人可能需要为此承担相应的赔偿责任。

在下面的 Rose MOSES v. C. Rodgers BURGIN et al. 案中，原告 MOSES 是一家开放型基金的股东，其将该基金诉至法庭。一同作为被告的还有该基金的投资顾问 Fidelity 公司以及该投资顾问的全资子公司 Crosby，该基金份额的承销商，该基金的两名关联董事以及该基金的其他非关联董事。

该案的起因是，基金向承销商返还了部分佣金。在美国，为招揽业务，承销商通常愿意放弃一部分佣金或就其收取的佣金给予折扣。在该案中，承销商将从 Crosby 公司购买的基金份额向公众销售。为了激励承销商更多地销售基金份额，基金根据承销商的销售情况向承销商按比例返还了其放弃的佣金。原告对此提出了两点异议：

首先，基金向承销商返还佣金，导致基金损失了本可获得的收益。原告声称，通过设立关联的承销商以参与承销或者将放弃的佣金支付给关联方，都可以使得基金不用损失该笔收益。其次，该返还行为使得 Fidelity 公司和 Crosby 公司受益，因为销售更多的基金份额将增加 Crosby 获得的佣金以及 Fidelity 公司的顾问费。因此，原告认为，Fidelity 公司及其董事使用基金的财产谋取私利。原告还声称，基金的董事会从未考虑过获取该损失的收益的可能性，因为 Fidelity 公司不当地占有相关信息而并未向基金的非关联董事披露。

法院判决认定，Fidelity 公司并非只是存在疏忽。它明知道获取承销商放弃的佣金在行业里是一件严肃且尚未解决的问题，它也知道，这是一件涉及他们自身利益以及基金股东利益之间潜在冲突的问题。但是，Fidelity 公司并未将自己所知的信息披露给非关联董事。因此，Fidelity 公司及两名关联董事应当对由此造成的损失承担赔偿责任。另一方面，非关联的董事无需为此承担责任。尽管关联董事有义务就基金的管理运作进行独立调查监督，但是在该案中，对于取回佣金一事，他们一无所知（他们有权依赖基金管理人通知他们取回佣金的问题），并且他们对此也不存在任何个人利益冲突。

Rose MOSES v. C. Rodgers BURGIN et al.

445 F.2d 369 (1st Cir. 1971)

ALDRICH, Chief Judge.

Plaintiff Moses, a shareholder of Fidelity Fund, Inc. (Fund), a Massachusetts-incorporated investment company, in December 1967 filed a complaint, and in November 1968 an amended complaint, in this derivative action. Fund is an open-end mutual fund, registered under the Investment Company Act of 1940, 15 U.S.C. §§ 80a-1 et seq. Defendants, in addition to Fund, are Fidelity Management and Research Company (Management), Fund's investment adviser; the Crosby Corporation (Crosby), a wholly owned subsidiary of Management and sometimes included within that term, an underwriter whose sole business is selling shares of Fund to independent broker-dealers; E. C. Johnson 2d, president and director of Fund, and president, director and principal voting stockholder of Management; E. C. Johnson 3d, director of Fund since April 1968, and director and substantial voting stockholder of Management; and C. R. Burgin, G. R. Harding, G. H. Hood, Jr., R. Jones, G. K. McKenzie and H. Schermerhorn, who are or were directors of Fund who claim not to be "affiliated" within the meaning of section 10 (a) of the Act, 15 U.S.C. § 80a-10 (a), hereinafter the unaffiliated directors. Although the last two were named as defendants, the action has been dismissed against them for lack of service of process. Other dramatis personae, not defendants, include D. G. Sullivan, a vice-president of Management and Fund and since April 1968 a director of Fund; C. Loring, Jr., an officer of Fund and counsel for, and a non-voting stockholder of, Management; and S. H. Babcock, retained in December 1966 as counsel to advise the unaffiliated directors.

Plaintiff complained of various breaches of fiduciary duty allegedly imposed by the Investment Company Act and the common law. Following an extensive trial on liability only, the district court resolved all ultimate issues against her. 316 F.Supp. 31. Plaintiff appeals. The record is voluminous, the briefs lengthy and detailed, and the sums of money involved substantial. Many of the claims advanced in the district court are no longer pressed. Before us plaintiff makes one principal complaint, that Fund could, and should, have recovered a portion of the brokerage commissions it was obliged to pay on its so-called portfolio business, viz., on the purchases and sales of the securities in which it invested its assets. Plaintiff's proposals as to how this should have been accomplished require a considerable review of Fund's method of operation.

Fund's shareholders are numbered in five, and its assets in the upper nine, figures. The amount of its assets, apart from changes in the market value of its investments, depends upon the number of shares that it can sell as against the number it must redeem. Both activities are continual. The purchasers of individual participating interests, or shares, pay their net worth in terms of the current value of Fund's assets, plus a 1½% sales charge to Crosby and a brokerage commission of 6%. In reponse to advice by Management, Fund is constantly changing its portfolio. This is done through independent broker-dealers, and mostly involves trading by them on the New York and regional stock exchanges. The conclusion of a trade is commonly referred to as execution. A claim made in the district court was that defendants, in choosing their brokers, or other trading methods not presently pertinent, did not always obtain best execution. The court resolved this issue against plaintiff, from which no appeal is taken.

The exchanges, at all relevant times, set required commission rates, with no quantity discounts. Because of the size of many mutual fund transactions brokers competing for business were willing to give up a portion of the commissions they received from the fund. "Anti-rebate" rules adopted by every exchange prevented any rebate or discount, direct or indirect, that would bring the net commission paid below the minimum level set by the exchange. As will be described, the total effect of these rules was in doubt, but they at least prevented direct cash refunds to the customer. On Fund's instructions, at Management's behest, the so-called customer-directed give-ups were paid over to brokers who sold shares of Fund acquired from Crosby to the public, in proportion to their success, in order to stimulate sales. Customer-directed give-ups are to be distinguished from broker-directed give-ups, a long-recognized practice whereby two or more brokers who have shared in the work divide the commission between themselves. Give-ups which are customer-directed (which is what we shall mean by the term "give-up" hereafter) are inherently and necessarily, as the district court found, in the nature of a refund, or rebate to the customer.

Plaintiff's complaint is double-barreled. First, she complains of Fund's give-up practices because they resulted in the loss of the value of brokerage commissions which could have been recaptured. She claims recapture was possible either by creation of a broker affiliate that could participate in Fund portfolio transactions, or by channeling present give-ups to an affiliate, with the result that in either case the sums involved would be credited to Fund. Second, she complains that the give-up practices, pursued to the exclusion of either course she suggests, benefitted Management and Crosby, since stimulating sales of Fund's shares increased Crosby's commissions, and increased Management's advisory fee, which was measured by the size of Fund's portfolio. Accordingly, plaintiff claims that Management and the two Johnsons, who together owned 90% of its voting stock, were using Fund's assets to their own private advantage. More pointedly, she claims in particular that Fund's board never considered these possibilities because relevant information regarding them was improperly withheld from the unaffiliated directors by the Management defendants. Recovery is sought, inter alia, under section 36 of the Investment Company Act, 15 U.S.C. § 80a-35. To prevail on this appeal plaintiff must persuade us that the district court's rulings were wrong and that its factual findings in defendants' favor were clearly erroneous. Plaintiff openly accepts this burden.

…

The Duty To Recapture

The brief filed on behalf of Management, Crosby and the two Johnsons states, "The court found that it was the directors' common business judgment that encouraging sales would promote a net cash inflow and growth of the Fund beneficial to the shareholders."

Calling this a "policy decision to promote sales" the brief added that the court found that the directors believed that Fund's awards of give-ups to brokers who sold its shares to the public enhanced its sales. Management's implication, which in oral argument it emphasized to the point of affirmation, was that, if recapture was in fact practical, the directors still had a right to choose between recapture of the give-ups for Fund's direct benefit, and awarding them to brokers for its indirect benefit. We hold, however, that if recovery was freely available to Fund, the directors had no such choice.

Fund's charter required that upon sale of its shares it receive their full asset value. The obvious purpose was to prevent the value of the existing shareholders' interest in the assets from being diminished by the addition of further participants. If Fund receives the asset value of new shares, but at the same time rewards the selling broker with give-ups that it has a right to recapture for itself, then the net income Fund receives from the process of selling a share is less than asset value. The existing shareholders have contributed—by paying more than otherwise necessary on Fund's portfolio transactions—to the cost of the sale, which was supposed to have been borne by the new member alone. We cannot, therefore, consider absolving the defendants, if we find that they have violated any duty owed the Fund, by finding that directing give-ups to brokers benefitted Fund by stimulating sales of its shares. Such application violated its charter if it would have been practicable to obtain the give-ups for the direct benefit of its treasury.

Management counsel ultimately conceded this during oral argument. We have dwelt upon it to show that the concession was correct. This is not, of course, to say that the court was not justified in finding that it was beneficial to existing shareholders to promote sales of Fund's shares, as well as being beneficial to Management and to Crosby. It is merely that, by the terms of the charter, Fund cannot use free money, or credit, to pay brokers for sales. Sales are

Crosby's business. Whether, during the period covered by the complaint, it was practical for Fund to recover commissions for its direct use is another matter.

Broker Affiliation

There are a number of methods of mutual fund operation. In general, as has been pointed out, management is placed in the hands of an independent entity. Beyond that, some funds sell their participating shares through a captive sales force and others, including Fund, through independent brokers. Some conduct their portfolio business through the same entity that furnishes them with investment advice, while many, like Fund, use independent brokers. There are basic, fundamental differences in the operational problems, and risks to the fund, resulting from the use of affiliated, versus independent, brokers for portfolio transactions. Some of these are dealt with in detail in the district court's comprehensive opinion. We see no purpose in further elaboration. Suffice it to say that a change from independent brokerage to an affiliated broker is not a matter to be lightly undertaken.

It is in this vein that we must see plaintiff's contention that Fund should have decided to have an affiliated broker since recapture could have been effected by having Crosby, or some new subsidiary of Management, become a broker member of an exchange. Plaintiff puts this point with something less than full clarity. Insofar as a fund has a broker affiliate which acts as its executing broker, no question of give-ups arises at all; the issue is the possibility of recapture of the affiliate's profits. It is true that if the broker-affiliate was not used as the fund's exclusive trader, there would in addition be the possibility of using the affiliate to recover give-ups resulting from trading through other houses, and recapturing these as well. It is only too clear, as the court found, that the unaffiliated directors had noted the general risks attendant upon a brokerage operation, especially the risk of loss of best execution, and they had long decided against it. The court found, on adequate evidence, that there were sound business reasons for this decision. We agree; the directors had no duty to pursue plaintiff's suggested course of action, and without their doing so, recapture was not freely available. Plaintiff knew of Fund's practice when she bought her shares; she could have chosen a fund that did have an affiliated broker.

While the court found that the unaffiliated directors learned, in 1965, of the Pacific exchange's admission of broker-affiliates and had in fact rejected such an operation, there is evidence that some of them did not consider, when deciding, the full possibility of thereby recapturing the broker's profits and give-ups accruing from trading with other houses. The court did not specifically address itself to that question. We cannot find in the evidence, however, any reason to suppose that this difference would have swung the balance in the other direction. Plaintiff has not met her burden of showing the court plainly wrong.

Alternatively, plaintiff suggests that Crosby might have become a more limited type of broker, on the New York Stock Exchange, known as an introducing broker. This itself would not have required substantial operational changes, in fact, plaintiff's suggestion is really that Crosby could become, under this label, a conduit for give-ups though not in any way engaged in normal brokerage activities. But the court found that NYSE required that all brokers, to be members, must be engaged primarily in brokerage, and that in the application of this principle the exchange regarded the broker and its affiliates as one. It found that Management and Crosby, accordingly, would not have been able to qualify for membership. (F. 56). Plaintiff has not successfully attacked this finding.

NASD Recapture

We turn, accordingly, to plaintiff's second major claim, that without the necessity of a broker affiliate, or changing Crosby's methods of operations, give-ups could have been channeled to Crosby—already eligible to receive them—to be applied against Management's advisory fee, a process that has been described as indirect recapture.

Six of the seven regional exchanges permitted members of the National Association of Securities Dealers (NASD) who were not exchange members, either by joining the exchange as special members, or even without the formality of any membership, to receive customer-directed give-ups. Crosby was a member of NASD. Plaintiff asserts that Crosby, without making any changes in its structure or any basic commitments, was or could have become qualified to receive give-ups on these exchanges, and that Fund could have directed such receipts, having agreed with Management to set them off against its advisory fee. Management responds that if Fund had so directed, Crosby's crediting Fund would have violated the anti-rebate rules of the exchanges, and hence would not have been permitted. To this plaintiff replies that by 1965 the Pacific Exchange was allowing funds to recapture brokerage commissions from their broker-affiliates via setoffs against advisory fees owed to management, and that there was no reason to expect that it would draw a distinction, under its anti-rebate rule, against similar recapture of commissions funnelled from independent brokers to NASD members connected with Fund; that Management failed to investigate, or even to inform the unaffiliated directors of the possibility of this indirect recapture; that in 1967 the Philadelphia-Baltimore-Washington Exchange (PBW) did permit a fund to recapture its give-ups through NASD membership of its adviser-underwriters; and that in 1968, when

Management finally pursued this subject, a second exchange, Pacific, agreed to essentially this procedure. The balance of this opinion deals with this subject.

Management's Duty of Disclosure

Plaintiff's argument criticizing the Management defendants for not effecting NASD recapture is based on her finding implicit in the Investment Company Act the familiar general principles governing fiduciaries in the area of self-dealing. We do not denigrate these principles, though we need hold relevant only their expression through the federally imposed standard under section 36, which may vary from the state common law. We believe, however, that the Act imposes a more fundamental and pervasive requirement where, because of the structure of investment trusts, self-dealing is not the exception but, so far as management is concerned, the order of the day. One of the primary reasons for Congress' enactment of the Investment Company Act was its finding that,

> "the national public interest and the interest of investors are adversely affected * * * (2) when investment companies are organized, operated, managed * * * in the interest of directors, officers, investment advisers * * * underwriters * * * rather than in the interest of all classes of such companies' security holders. * * *" 15 U.S.C. § 80a-1 (b).

Unlike an ordinary trust, or a business, management's normal activities are frequently touched with self-interest, as the example of give-ups, universally used, and benefitting management at least as much as fund shareholders, clearly shows. Management defendants admit that they gained from the give-up practice, while asserting that Fund also benefitted from the resulting growth. To the extent that they, or the court in finding for them without finding full disclosure, imply that their self-interest could not influence the decisions to be made on behalf of Fund, Congress had an answer. It responded to this problem by enacting a mandatory provision for unaffiliated, that is, independent, watchdog directors. 15 U.S.C. § 80a-10 (a).

Whatever may be the duty of disclosure owed to ordinary corporate directors, we think the conclusion unavoidable that Management defendants were under a duty of full disclosure of information to these unaffiliated directors in every area where there was even a possible conflict of interest between their interests and the interests of the fund. This duty could not be put more clearly than was stated by the SEC in 1965.

"The Investment Company Act's requirement as to unaffiliated directors, if its purposes are not to be subverted, carries with it the obligation on the part of the affiliated directors, and the investment adviser itself, to insure that unaffiliated directors are furnished with sufficient information so as to enable them to participate effectively in the management of the investment company." Imperial Financial Services, Inc., CCH Fed.Sec.L.Rep. 77, 287 at 82, 464 (SEC 1965).

Except where it may be fairly assumed that every unaffiliated director will have such knowledge, effective communication is called for. And, in testing that assumption, it must be borne in mind that they are not full time employees of the fund and it may be—as with Fund's unaffiliated directors—that neither their activities nor their experience are primarily connected with the special and often technical problems of fund operation. If management does not keep these directors informed they will not be in a position to exercise the independent judgment that Congress clearly intended. The only question can be whether the matter is one that could be thought to be of possible significance.

Management's Failure To Disclose

The district court found untrue plaintiff's claim that Management "consistently kept from the directors any of the information which might have aroused them from their inaction." This finding is supportable only in the sense that the concealment was not "consistent." In any other sense it is plainly erroneous as to NASD recapture in the light of the knowledge Management concededly possessed which could well have aroused the unaffiliated directors. As will be developed, the inescapable fact is that Management defendants did, for an extended period of time, keep to themselves possibly, we would say probably, stimulating information.

In June 1965, two representatives of the SEC, Silver and Eisenberg, conducted an inquiry of Fund representatives, trading on the Detroit Stock Exchange and Off-Board Trading by Exchange Members. Sullivan, together with Hamilton, another officer of Management, and Belash, a law partner of Loring, attended. In the course of the proceedings Silver suggested that Crosby, though not an exchange member, could receive give-ups through its NASD membership which could then be set off against the advisory fee. Hamilton responded that directing any give-ups to Crosby would conflict with Illinois blue-sky laws, thus affecting Fund's sales there. Silver replied that the Illinois rule was obviously designed to prevent underwriters from benefitting at the expense of the fund, and asked whether Illinois would object if the give-ups were applied to credit Fund. Sullivan in disregard of the charter obligation not to use money or credits that were available to Fund to support sales of its shares, stated that the change would irritate dealers who had been receiving give-ups and have a consequent bad effect upon sales. Silver inquired whether the need to compete with the funds that had joined the Pacific exchange, and were reducing brokerage commissions that way, might change their view of the economics of the situation, which we interpret as a suggestion that Fund's asset loss of recapturable give-ups might have a more adverse effect on sales than would the loss of rewards for dealers. The SEC had already indicated in its 1963 Special Study, n. 5, ante, that the principal beneficiaries of fund-paid portfolio commissions are not the funds, but the advisers and underwriters. What was new was the suggestion of how, in fact, the interests of Fund could be better served. The suggestion by Silver should clearly have imparted to Management the idea that its benefit could now conflict with Fund's interest—and should, in turn, have made these defendants sensitive to the need for passing the suggestion along to the unaffiliated directors. However, as the court found, this was not done. Nor was anything else done.

In September 1966, three SEC representatives, Rotberg, Eisenberg and Archie conducted further SEC inquiries, this time entitled Commission Rate Structure. The same Management representatives attended. There was a general discussion of NASD recapture of give-ups. Rotberg suggested, inter alia, that Fund should recapture through Crosby. Sullivan and Belash again mentioned the depressing effect upon sales. It was added that such conduct would conflict with Crosby's contract, and it was again stated that it raised problems under Illinois blue-sky laws. Rotberg pointedly asked what Fund had done since the staff's same suggestions had been made at the previous proceeding. The Fund representatives replied, "Nothing," explicitly adhering to the position that Fund needed the friendship of the small brokers more than it needed the money. No one suggested the possible illegality of recapture under the anti-rebate rules upon which all defendants now rely.

Again, although by this time the conflict was clearly laid out, the court found that nothing was reported by the Management defendants to the unaffiliated directors. In their brief the Management defendants say, seemingly to imply that no communication was necessary, that they "investigated the substance of these questions," and concluded that nothing could be done. "Investigation" seems a palpable exaggeration of what was done. All the record shows is that they discussed it among themselves.

In sum, we can only conclude that the Management defendants saw a question, that they knew it to be in an area where there was a conflict between their personal interests and the direct interests of the Fund treasury, and that they did not inform the unaffiliated directors or submit it to their consideration.

Nor was this all. On December 2, 1966 the House Committee on Interstate and Foreign Commerce released an SEC report entitled Public Policy Implications of Investment Company Growth (PPI); H.R.Rep. No. 2337, 89th Cong., 2d Sess. (1966). At page 173, in a subsection entitled, "Reducing advisory fees," it was stated,

> "It would not be inconsistent with those rules for dealer-distributed funds to direct give-ups to their advisor-underwriters, all of whom are NASD members, for the purpose of applying these give-ups to reduce the advisory fees payable by the funds."

Loring, Johnson 2d, and Sullivan discussed this among themselves, but did nothing further. While the Management defendants now claim that they communicated this information to the unaffiliated directors, they face insuperable obstacles to establishing that assertion. In the first place, the court made the following general finding.

> "Before this action was brought [the unaffiliated directors] did not have knowledge of any other methods of so-called recapture [than through a broker-affiliate]."

We cannot believe that the court meant by this finding that it believed that the unaffiliated directors were given the information, but forgot about it. Nor are Management defendants helped by the evidence they cite to support their claim. They list four matters.

a) That McKenzie, on his own, obtained and read a copy of the PPI report. Even if this can be taken to mean that McKenzie noted and understood the meaning of the two relevant pages in this 346 page report, McKenzie was only one of five unaffiliated directors.

b) That, as the district court found, a copy of the report was given by Loring to Babcock. There is no evidence, however, that the matter of NASD recapture was called to his attention. Babcock did not take the stand. No unaffiliated director testified to any communication with him at that time on the subject of recapture, and there was no evidence to indicate that his retainer included consideration of the possibility of, or the duty to, recapture until his opinion was asked in August 1968.

c) That, as the court found, a summary of the report, prepared by the SEC, was given to all of the unaffiliated directors. The summary, however, did not refer to the portion of the report dealing with NASD recapture.

d) That McKenzie testified that following the issuance of the report, he discussed recovery of give-ups at the December 14, 1966 meeting. The minutes of the meeting state, "Excerpts from the [PPI report] was read, including the factors to be considered in determining the reasonableness of management fees." Determining management fees is the subject of Chapter III, "The Management Function and Its Cost," which occupies some 70 pages of the report. "Reducing advisory fees" by credits through NASD recapture is a short subsection in another chapter. It was never mentioned. Examination of McKenzie's testimony, including all references made in Management's brief, clearly reveals that he was talking about fixing the advisory fee and giving some consideration in connection therewith to recapture through West Coast broker affiliation, the method we have already dealt with. The district court, likewise, did not accept it as showing that NASD recapture was discussed or it would not have made the general finding, previously adverted to, that the unaffiliated directors had no ante litem knowledge of this method of recapture.

On the basis of the above, Management's brief makes the bald statement, "[B]oth the [PPI] report itself and, in particular, the relevant passage, captioned 'Reducing advisory fees' * * * were put before the board." How they could say this, passes our understanding.

Post Litem

With the commencement of this suit in December 1967, a year after the PPI report, the matter of recapture of give-ups was sharply brought to the unaffiliated directors' attention. The suit was followed shortly by Securities Exchange Act of 1934 Release No. 8239, dated January 26, 1968, proposing a new rule, 10b-10. In its introductory portion the release stated that the purpose of the proposed rule was to "prohibit investment company managers from directing brokers executing transactions for an investment company to divide their compensation in any way with other brokers unless the benefits of such division accrue to the investment company and its shareholders." It stated that the rule "had its antecedents" in the PPI report, citing specifically the sentence at page 173 which we have quoted ante, and added, "The reasoning on which the proposed rule is based is that if, as pointed out above, a mutual fund manager has various means at his disposal to recapture for the benefit of the fund a portion of the commissions paid by the fund, he is under a fiduciary duty to do so."

The presently relevant portion of the rule is the first subsection.

"Rule 10b-10

"(1) It shall be unlawful for any registered investment company or affiliated person of such registered investment company to directly or indirectly, to [sic] order or request any broker or dealer:

"(a) to pay or arrange for the payment, directly or indirectly, of all or any portion of a commission on any securities transaction to any broker, dealer or any other person *unless* pursuant to a written contract the full amount of such remittance is required to be paid over to such registered investment company, or fees owed by or charged to such registered investment company are required to be reduced in an amount equal to the remittance; * * *"

The directors, shown the release by Sullivan on February 5, 1968, appointed Sullivan and Loring, both of whom, it will be recalled, represented Management, to advise them what they should do. They, in turn, designated Belash and Reilly of Loring's law firm to investigate the practices and possibilities of recapture on various regional exchanges. Reilly's resulting report was submitted to Sullivan and Loring in late March, and the unaffiliated directors were shortly told of it, and advised that detailed letters of inquiry would be addressed to the exchanges. At this time Reilly's report showed that Pro Fund, Inc., had already been recapturing give-ups on the PBW Exchange, with the exchange's permission, since December 1967, and that, based on information from the Pacific Exchange's president, Reilly thought that Crosby could receive give-ups there "to reduce fund expenses." Neither of these facts were communicated to the unaffiliated directors. It was thought that "they might not see the forest for the trees." No reason was given why it was not immediately decided to "bank" (escrow in the hands of the giving-up brokers) give-ups on those apparently favorable exchanges pending a final resolution of the issue—a procedure not detrimental to the existing give-up procedures if Fund ultimately decided not to recapture.

Two months later Loring's office, characterized by the court as "moving slowly," sent out the promised letters to the exchanges. At the May 29 meeting Loring informed the directors that the manager of the security transactions had been directed to use PBW, when consistent with best execution, and that give-ups on that exchange were being banked pending final determination of whether they were recapturable. By August 1 the same arrangements were instituted with regard to the Pacific Exchange, after it had formally replied that NASD recapture was permissible. The Midwest Exchange ultimately wrote that recapture there was not possible. No written replies appear to have been received from the Detroit and Boston Exchanges; oral replies from the president of Boston, and a vice-president of Detroit, had been in the negative. On November 27 the directors voted to recapture the banked PBW and Pacific give-ups. On December 5, give-ups were abolished on all exchanges.

These post litem events, if they do not justify plaintiff's charge of misrepresentation to the unaffiliated directors, at least compel the conclusion that the Management defendants' regard for the need of keeping them abreast in the matter of recapture was minimal, and their persistence in continuing to avoid doing so, to prevent injury to Crosby's relationship with its broker-dealers, consciously maximal. We are obliged to reject their brief's protest that they were always open in their disclosure in matters of self-interest just as we do Johnson's testimonial description of the January 1968 SEC release as being "in the nature of a bombshell that hit us." After the 1965 SEC proceedings, the 1966 proceedings, and the 1966 PPI report, the bomb's fuse had been audible to Management for a long time.

Illegality of Recapture

Turning to defendants' asserted excuses for any failure to disclose, we commence with their single most important point, as it would be a short answer to plaintiff's NASD recapture claim if defendants could support the district court's findings and rulings as to its illegality. The district court held,

> "Insofar as it is a question of fact, this court finds that any scheme involving [Fund's] use of its underwriter Crosby as a recipient of a give-up on the understanding that Crosby's parent would give [Fund] a credit against charges for investment advisory services is manifestly a rebate within the meaning of the anti-rebate constitutions and rules of the NYSE and other exchanges." (F. 84)
>
> "Inasmuch as an anti-rebate rule is the type of stock exchange rule which has the force of law and is binding alike upon members and customers of the exchange [Silver v. New York Stock Exchange, 373 U.S. 341, 360-361, 83 S.Ct. 1246, 10 L.Ed.2d 389; Colonial Realty Corporation v. Bache & Co., 358 F.2d 178, 181-182 (2nd Cir.)] all recapture devices which are contrary to the anti-rebate provisions of exchange constitutions are illegal." 316 F.Supp. at 57. (Brackets court's)

It is not clear what the court meant by its statement that the anti-rebate rule "has the force of law." Certainly no criminal sanction attaches to conduct at variance with such a rule, unless the rule happens to parallel a prohibition of the statute or a SEC rule, which this one does not. If the court's phrase, and use of the word "illegal," implies possible criminality we could not agree, and doubt that it was intended to do so. Of course, in a lower key, the violation of exchange rules by Fund might give rise to civil causes of action based on contract. Roberts v. Criss, 2 Cir., 1920, 266 F. 296, holds that the constitution and rules of an exchange are a contract between the members. Colonial Realty Corp. v. Bache & Co., 2 Cir., 1966, 358 F.2d 178, refers to the authority of exchanges to make and enforce their own rules, subject to only broad limitations, as "supervised self-regulation." Whatever the terminology, the nature of the obligations imposed by such rules is to be determined primarily on the basis of the construction which the exchanges that adopted the rules give to them. A court is not free to regard the problem as a statutory interpretation issue of first impression.

The district court, analyzing the issue as an original question, dismissed as irrelevant the wide-spread, accepted use of give-ups, despite its conclusion that they are also rebates, by saying that "a customer-directed give-up which was not used to establish a credit for a customer is no precedent for a customer-directed give-up which does establish such a credit." Recapture, it said, has "the evil consequence of giving back to the customer a dollar credit traceable directly or indirectly to the commission he paid." The fact that there may be some logic in this analysis does not mean that it is correct. The very fact that one type of rebate was uniformly tolerated by the exchanges despite their anti-rebate rules in itself shows that logic alone cannot supply the answer. The controlling answer must be found in how the exchanges, who were the rule-makers, themselves translated their rules. We have seen that the Pacific and PBW Exchanges, when confronted with proposals for recapture, chose to permit it. We do not accept the district court's disregard of that fact, based on its pronouncement that these exchanges were simply mistaken in doing so. This is not to say that the federal courts cannot review an exchange's interpretation of its rules and overrule those that are arbitrary or subjective. Bright v. Philadelphia-Baltimore-Washington Stock Exchange, E.D.Pa., 5/11/71, 327 F.Supp. 495. The district court perceived a distinction between recapturing give-ups for the benefit of the customer and its underwriter in terms of selling its shares, and recapturing to pay the fee of the adviser who had generated the transaction from which the give-up arose. Accepting that, we could not think it arbitrary, in view of the common factors shared by these two kinds of rebates, for an exchange to say that the distinction did not compel a difference in result. We reject the district court's ruling that the decision was illegal.

Management's Defenses

a) *Self-Dealing*

Management says that it is a "fallacious premise that this is a 'self-dealing' case. It is not." However, after discussing plaintiff's cases on self-dealing, these defendants eventually conclude with the statement that this is not a self-dealing case because they had in fact made disclosure to the unaffiliated directors. This position eliminates the necessity of our demonstrating, beyond what we already have done, that this is a self-dealing case if the Management defendants breached their duty of disclosure. On this assumption we may omit discussion of the legal authorities. At the same time we note that Management defendants' position appears to be an open acceptance of what we hold to be the fact, that this is a clear conflict of interest case that routinely calls for disclosure quite apart from any special burden that may be implicit in the Investment Company Act.

b) *The Duty To Experiment*

We pass with equal brevity the court's ruling which it stated disposed of any obligation to recapture even if it was not clearly unlawful. The court said,

> "A fiduciary is under no duty to engage in legally doubtful experiments virtually unsupported by custom or convention or court decision." 316 F. Supp. at 57.
>
> In so stating the court answered a wise observation it had made during the course of the trial.
>
> "It may be that we are moving into an era in which the duty of a trustee is not to rely upon custom, habit and practice of his neighbor, but when he has a sufficiently large interest to make it economically perhaps desirable for him to go and make sure that he has moved in a way which is to the greatest benefit of his beneficiary."

We are not so sure that the court's answer was correct. But in any event, it was the directors of Fund, not Management, who were the ones to make the decision. That they need not have decided to experiment is irrelevant. The court's ruling does not excuse Management from its failure to disclose and so permit the unaffiliated directors to decide.

c) *Management's Awareness*

The Management defendants are accordingly in chancery unless non-disclosure on their part was reasonable, or at least not grossly unreasonable. Primarily they point to the district court's finding that it is "hard to fault" them for not informing the unaffiliated directors of SEC proceedings conducted by "subordinate SEC employees." The court added that these employees "obviously did not see the technical difficulties with suggestions they informally threw out." As to the level of their experience, Silver, Eisenberg and Rotberg, who conducted the proceedings, were associate directors and assistant general counsel of the SEC. They were subordinate only in the narrow sense that they did not speak as the Commission. Nor is there any evidence that Management representatives were struck, either in June 1965, or in September 1966, by the staff's ignorance of technical difficulties. (*Cf.* n. 14, ante.) Be that as it may, the September 1966 proceedings were shortly followed by the Commission's own, formal, PPI report. Management defendants, whatever their own views on the feasibility of recapture, were then on full notice that the possibility of recapture was a substantial issue that directly involved their self-interest. Any contention that the Commission's views were off-hand or so inconsequential that Management defendants were entitled to keep their own counsel and not even mention the issue to the unaffiliated directors is, to put it bluntly, little short of extraordinary. We may add that Management's willingness to disregard the Commission itself casts some doubt on the bona fides of a claim that the earlier expressed views of the staff were ignored because of its inferior position.

Liability

Enough has been said to show that Management defendants were not guilty of mere negligence. They knew, seemingly in June 1965, and at least after the publication of PPI, that the possibility of recapture was a serious and unresolved issue in the industry. They also knew that it was an issue that involved a potential conflict between their interests and the interests of Fund's shareholders. Their failure to disclose the information available to them to the unaffiliated directors was the result of neither inadvertence nor misapprehension of the facts. Among the abuses enumerated in section 1 (b) of the Act, quoted ante, is the operation of investment companies in the interest of advisers, underwriters, and other affiliated persons rather than that of the shareholders. By intentionally pursuing a course of non-disclosure these defendants made the effective functioning of the mechanism protecting Fund from their overreaching impossible. We do not believe that Congress intended that the SEC and the federal courts should be powerless to deal with this kind of conduct, or should excuse it on facts such as those disclosed in the case at bar. See Aldred Inv. Trust v. SEC, 1 Cir., 1945, 151 F.2d 254, 260, cert. denied 326 U.S. 795, 66 S.Ct. 486, 90 L.Ed. 483. Such a construction of the Act would be inconsistent with Congress' direction in section 1 (b) that the provisions of the Act be interpreted in accordance with its purpose to "mitigate and, so far as is feasible, to eliminate the conditions enumerated in this section." To hold otherwise would render the benefits Congress sought to obtain through the provisions for unaffiliated directors merely precatory, rather than positive. We therefore conclude that the Management defendants were guilty of gross misconduct within the meaning of the Act in failing to disclose the possibility of NASD recapture to the unaffiliated directors. The two individual management defendants, and the Management corporations, must be held liable for damages under section 36.

On the other hand, the unaffiliated directors, with the possible exception of McKenzie, who is not a defendant here, have not been shown to have had any knowledge of the possibility of NASD recapture. Nor did they have any personal conflicting interest which should have sharpened their attention. Plaintiff has not shown that they violated any duty to discover and explore the issue on their own; recapture was a new problem, and they were entitled to rely on the Management defendants, who devoted full time to the investment industry, to advise them of its emergence. While the unaffiliated directors are not free of all obligations to consider matters on their own, we see no basis for holding them in this case.

…

第三节 证券投资基金的运行规则

证券投资基金自设立至终止，均需遵循法律确定的规则。在设立过程中，基金的募集、基金份额的销售及申购等；在运作过程中，相关信息的披露、基金份额的交易及赎回等；在基金终止时，基金财产的清算和分配等，相关法律都对其确定了相应的规则。

一、中国证券投资基金的运行规则

中国《证券投资基金法》对通过公开发售基金份额募集的证券投资基金的设立、运作及终止进行了全面的规定。

（一）基金的设立

在中国，设立基金并发售基金份额，应当向中国证监会提交相关文件，并经中国证监会核准。所提交的文件中，最重要的是基金合同草案和招募说明书草案。前者主要规定了基金份额持有人、基金管理人和基金托管人等各方的权利、义务，后者主要是进行相关的信息披露。中国证监会在受理基金募集申请之日起一定期限内依照相关法律、法规及审慎监管原则进行审查，作出核准或者不予核准的决定，并通知申请人。

基金募集申请经核准后，方可发售基金份额，由社会公众申购。基金份额的发售，由基金管理人负责办理；基金管理人还可以委托经中国证监会认定的其他机构代为办理。基金管理人应当自收到核准文件之日起一定期限内进行基金募集，不得超过核准的基金募集期限。

基金募集期限届满，封闭式基金募集的基金份额总额达到核准规模的80%以上，开放式基金募集的基金份额总额超过核准的最低募集份额总额，并且基金份额持有人人数符合中国证监会规定的，基金管理人应当自募集期限届满之日起一定期限内办理基金备案手续，并予以公告。由此，基金才能合法设立。

基金募集期限届满，如果募集的基金份额总额不能满足法律规定的条件的，基金管理人应当：（1）以其固有财产承担因募集行为而产生的债务和费用；（2）在基金募集期限届满后一定期限内返还投资人已缴纳的款项，并加计银行同期存款利息。

（二）基金的运作

根据中国《证券投资基金法》的规定，基金运作方式主要为封闭式和开放式。为对证券投资基金日后的创新发展预留空间，中国《证券投资基金法》还规定基金运作方式可以采取其他方式，采用其他运作方式的基金的基金份额发售、交易、申购、赎回的办法，由国务院另行规定。但是，中国国务院尚未制定其他方式运作的基金的相关法律、法规。

采用封闭式运作方式的基金（封闭式基金），是指经核准的基金份额总额在基金合同期限内固定不变，基金份额可以在依法设立的证券交易场所交易，但基金份额持有人不得申请赎回的基金。封闭式基金的基金份额，经基金管理人申请，中国证监会核准，可以在证券交易所上市交易。中国证监会还可以授权证券交易所依照法定条件和程序核准基金份额上市交易。基金份额上市交易规则由证券交易所制定，报中国证监会核准。

采用开放式运作方式的基金（开放式基金），是指基金份额总额不固定，基金份额可以在基金合同约定的时间和场所申购或者赎回的基金。开放式基金的基金份额的申购、赎回和登记，由基金管理人负责办理；基金管理人也可以委托经中国证监会认定的其他机构代为办理。开放式基金应当保持足够的现金或者政府债券，以备支付基金份额持有人的赎回款项。基金财产中应当保持的现金或者政府债券的具体比例，由中国证监会规定。基金份额的申购、赎回价格，依据申购、赎回日基金份额净值加、减有关费用计算。

在基金的运作过程中，基金管理人、基金托管人依照法律和基金合同的约定，履行受托职责。基金份额持有人按其所持基金份额享受收益和承担风险。基金财产应独立于基金管理人、基金托管人的固有财产，基金管理人、基金托管人不得将基金财产归入其固有财产。基金管理人、基金托管人因基金财产的管理、运用或者其他情形而取得的财产和收益，归入基金财产。基金财产的债权，不得与基金管理人、基金托管人固有财产的债务相抵销；不同基金财产的债权债务，不得相互抵销。

基金管理人、基金托管人管理、运用基金财产，应当恪尽职守，履行诚实信用、谨慎勤勉的义务。基金管理人运用基金财产进行证券投资，应当采用资产组合的方式。资产组合的具体方式和投资比例，依照法律和中国证监会的规定在基金合同中约定。根据中国《证券投资基金法》的规定，基金财产只能用于投资上市交易的股票、债券以及中国证监会规定的其他证券品种，不得用于其他投资活动。

基金管理人、基金托管人和其他基金信息披露义务人应当依法披露基金信息，并保证所披露信息的真实性、准确性和完整性。基金信息披露义务人应当确保应予披露的基金信息在中国证监会规定时间内披露，并保证投资人能够按照基金合同约定的时间和方式查阅或者复制公开披露的信息资料。公开披露基金信息，不得有下列行为：（1）虚假记载、误导性陈述或者重大遗漏；（2）对证券投资业绩进行预测；（3）违规承诺收益或者承担损失；（4）诋毁其他基金管理人、基金托管人或者基金份额发售机构；（5）依照法律、行政法规有关规定，由中国证监会规定禁止的其他行为。

（三）基金的终止

出现基金合同期限届满而未延期的、基金份额持有人大会决定终止以及基金管理人、基金托管人职责终止，在6个月内没有新基金管理人、新基金托管人承接等情况的，基金合同终止。基金合同终止时，基金管理人应当组织清算组对基金财产进行清算。清算组由基金管理人、基金托管人以及相关的中介服务机构组成。清算组作出的清算报告经会计师事务所审计，律师事务所出具法律意见书后，报中国证监会备案并公告。清算后的剩余基金财产，应当按照基金份额持有人所持份额比例进行分配。

二、美国证券投资基金的运行规则

美国《1933年证券法》和《1934年证券交易法》均将共同基金纳入证券的范畴，因此共同基金在运作的过程中，除了要适用《1940年投资公司法》和《1940年投资顾问法》外，还应适用相关证券法律、法规。

根据《1940年投资公司法》的规定，设立共同基金之前，必须向证券交易委员会提交一份全面介绍该基金情况的文件，申请注册。这项注册文件将成为共同基金的招募书，在其中要说明基金的发起人、董事会、投资目标、允许投资的类型、基金费率以及风险等。

在公开发行股份之前，共同基金还必须满足证券法的信息披露要求。《1933年证券法》对共同基金的注册、内容和广告宣传均加以明确规定，从而实现两个目的：一是要求发行人向投资者充分披露其财务状况和其他有关资料；二是禁止虚假陈述以及欺诈销售证券。基金股份如果要在交易所上市交易，必须满足《1934年证券交易法》的定期信息披露要求。

依法设立之后，共同基金各项具体事务的运作主要是通过委托其他公司来完成。其中，基金的日常行政管理和投资的具体运作通常委托给投资管理人，而商业银行等基金托管人通常受委托来负责共同基金资产的保管以及进行财务监督，基金证券的销售工作则委托给证券承销商，过户代理人则受托负责基金证券的日常买卖（申购与赎回）等。

所有这些业务的委托，都由投资公司董事会负责与受托方签订契约。投资公司的董事会在履行其职责时，除要遵守《1940 年投资公司法》的特别要求外，还要履行普通法所规定的信义义务，如有违反，受损失的投资者可以此为诉因对其提起诉讼。

（一）基金资产运用

根据《1940 年投资公司法》的规定，投资公司不允许用差价买卖证券，不许卖空，不允许参与联合交易账户。在进行承销活动时，包销总量不允许超过其总资产的一定比例。除非由有表决权的基金持有人（投资者）的大多数通过，投资公司不允许借贷、发行优先权证券、包销证券、买卖不动产或提供贷款、改变其分散或集中投资的投资策略、改变机构设置或改变其经营性质使其不再成为投资公司。投资公司经理人在作出投资决策时，不对某些失败的投资而导致的损失承担责任，或者因某个保守的投资者认为其不谨慎而承担责任。

（二）基金资产的托管

根据《1940 年投资公司法》的规定，基金应将基金资产交由高质量的美国银行来保管，或者全国性证券交易所的会员证券商来保管。投资公司也可以自己保管基金资产，但必须遵守美国证券与交易委员会严格的规则要求。此外，证券中央托管系统也可保管投资公司的证券。美国证券监管部门对于全国性证券交易所会员的保管，投资公司的自我保管，或使用证券托管系统来保管基金资产都制定了严格的管理规则。

（三）基金管理费

基金管理人因管理基金资产而有权向基金会收取费用。为了激励基金管理人更有效地运用基金资产，有的基金会还规定基金在支付基金管理费后可向基金管理人支付基金业绩报酬。无论联邦法律还是证券交易委员会的监管条例，都没有明确地限定投资顾问收取的管理费的比例。《1940 年投资顾问法》对管理费的管理主要依赖于相关的信息披露。

（四）基金的信息披露

信息披露是共同基金运作过程中最重要的一个环节。除需遵守《1940 年投资公司法》中设定的强制信息披露的规定之外，共同基金还应遵守《1933 年证券法》和《1934 年证券交易法》中的信息披露规定。这些法规都要求，投资公司在投资者购买基金股份之前向其提供一份详细的招募说明书，此外，还有年度报告、征集代理投票权说明书以及其他持续信息披露。基金持续运作环节的信息披露文件主要包括公开说明书、定期报告、临时报告、澄清公告与说明以及其他公告等。

（五）文件保存

美国《1940 年投资顾问法》对已注册的基金管理人施加了宽泛的记账制度要求。基金管理人被要求保留两种账册和记录：（1）典型的商业会计记录；（2）某些被美国证券交易委员会认为基金管理人根据其业务中特定的受托性质应当保留的记录。

三、案例资料

在美国，为了保护投资者，作为基金主体的投资公司应遵守《1933年证券法》的规定，进行充分的信息披露。在发售基金份额前，投资公司应当向投资者提供一份详细的招股说明书、年度报告、征集代理投票权说明书等，还应当进行其他持续性信息披露。SEC制定了大量的监管规则，以保证这些官方规定的信息披露文件包含有关证券基金过去和将来预期的充分而可靠的信息。如果发行人或相关联的人在信息披露中出现了重大虚假陈述，将会面临着各种诉讼。

下面的 Hines v. ESC Strategic Funds, Inc. 案对投资公司的信息和风险披露问题进行了讨论。该案中，原告作为投资者购买了ESC公司发行的“Value Fund”基金。但由于受到亚洲金融风暴的影响，该基金无法实现预期的目标，后ESC停止了这一基金，并对其财产进行了清算。原告认为被告没有在1997年的招股说明书和年度报告中告知投资者如果该基金不能在短期内吸引足够多的投资者就可能停止运行的风险，而是强调了该基金长期投资的战略，指控被告违反了信义义务，存在错误和虚假陈述，对投资者产生误导，属于欺诈行为。原告因此提起了诉讼。

法院从保护投资者角度的利益出发，认为应该将招股说明书看成一个整体，基于整体背景情况来考察披露的信息是否会误导一个理性的投资者。原告称1997年招股说明书强调 Value Fund 的长期投资是误导性的，被告则认为不构成误导，因为紧随其后还有一个警示声明。法院认为，1997年招股说明书的警示语言只是一般性的陈述，说明基金可能不会达到其投资的目的，而没有表明在没有达到特定目的的时候会停止基金的风险；被告没有向投资者披露他们可能在短期的市场衰退中停止基金，相反却重复地强调长期的投资战略，这一误导性的陈述影响了投资者的投资行为和购买价格，因此认为ESC违反了其信息和风险披露的义务。

Hines v. ESC Strategic Funds, Inc

No. 3:99-0530, 1999 WL 1705503 (M.D.Tenn. Sept. 17, 1999)

TRAUGER, J.

...

Defendant ESC Strategic Funds, Inc. (“ESC”) is an open-end management registered investment company. Defendant SunTrust Equitable Securities Corporation (“Equitable

Securities") served as the investment advisor for the ESC Strategic Value Fund ("Value Fund"). Plaintiff Allison Hines invested $50 000 in Class A shares of the Value Fund in September 1997.

Defendants offered shares of the Value Fund to the public by way of a prospectus filed with the Securities and Exchange Commission ("SEC") on February 18, 1997. The defendants sold two classes of shares of the Value Fund. Class A shares carried a maximum front-end sales charge of 4.50% and annual operating expenses of approximately 1.80%, and Class D shares carried a maximum front-end sales charge of 1.50% and annual operating expenses of 2.30%. The Value Fund began operating on May 7, 1997.

...

On November 25, 1998, the defendants filed a Semi-Annual Report for all ESC funds, including the Value Fund, with the SEC. (Docket No. 6, Ex. B) The Semi-Annual Report provided the following information with respect to the Value Fund:

ESC Strategic Value Fund Like a Category 4 hurricane, the storm from Asia slammed into the world's financial markets-and wreaked havoc during the six months ended September 30, 1998. Damage was apparent across the spectrum and in all sectors-growth stocks, value stocks, large caps, small caps and international stocks-all suffered to some degree....

Our contrarian/value investment philosophy was sorely tested over the course of the period. But, we believe the key to successful investing is having the discipline to stick to the strategy in all market environments. Historically, the markets have handsomely rewarded such investors for their pain and suffering. Nonetheless, the period was a very disappointing and frustrating one....

Standing Strong，In recent weeks, many of the situations that so frightened investors earlier in the year have calmed. Asia's rate of decline has slowed, or possibly even flattened out. The Russian economy, while still very shaky, is no longer in complete free-fall. And, in an effort to spark activity overseas, the U.S. Federal Reserve has cut interest rates twice. As a result, the stock market has firmed and even gained back some of the ground lost.

Given this, while we aren't completely out of the woods yet, we believe the worst may be over. But uncertainty lingers-so new highs are rather unlikely in the near-term. Long-term, however, we believe prospects remain extremely bright for the market in general, and our holdings in particular. Which is why we have no plans to change our strategy-we believe it is a proven one. And we know "you've gotta dance with who brung ya' to succeed over the long-term." (Docket No. 3, at P 20; Docket No. 6, Ex. B, at 4)

On February 9, 1999, ESC sent a letter to all investors stating that, on the recommendation of Equitable Securities, the Board of Directors of ESC had decided to liquidate the assets and discontinue operation of the Value Fund effective March 26, 1999. (Docket No. 6, Ex. C) In the letter, ESC informed investors that "[d]uring the almost two years of its existence, the Value Fund has not attracted sufficient interest among prospective investors and is considered unlikely to do so in the future. Furthermore, because of the Fund's asset size, the Board of Directors is concerned that it cannot operate, on an ongoing basis, at a competitive or reasonable expense ratio." (Docket No. 6, Ex. C, at 1) In the letter, Plaintiff was also informed of her right to transfer her investment to another ESC Strategic Fund without incurring any front-end sales charge. Id.

Plaintiff did not exercise her transfer option. After the defendants liquidated the Value Fund, Plaintiff was sent a check in the amount of $35 000, the dollar value of a share in the Value Fund (at the time of liquidation) times the number of shares she owned.

On May 19, 1999, Plaintiff filed suit in the Circuit Court for Davidson County. On June 17, 1999, the defendants filed a Notice of Removal to the United States District Court for the Middle District of Tennessee. (Docket No. 1) On June 23, 1999, Plaintiff filed her First Amended Complaint. (Docket No. 3) …

2. Count Five: Violation of 12 (2) of the Securities Act of 1933

...

In Olkey v. Hyperion 1999 Term Trust, Inc., 98 F.3d 2 (2d Cir. 1996), the Second Circuit held that the cautionary statements in the prospectus precluded the plaintiffs' claim under Section 12 (2) of the Securities Act of 1933. In affirming the district court's dismissal of the suit under Fed. R. Civ. P. 12 (b) (6), the Second Circuit found that, despite the plaintiffs' claims that the prospectus misrepresented both the investment strategy and the risks involved in the investment, there were sufficient cautionary statements in the prospectus such that the "prospectuses warn[ed] investors of exactly the risk the plaintiffs claim was not disclosed." Olkey, 98 F.3d at 5. While the plaintiffs sought to have all cautionary language in the prospectuses disregarded as "boilerplate," the Second Circuit found that the cautionary language was "too prominent and specific to be disregarded." Id.

Here, the defendants claim that, as in Olkey, the termination of the Value Fund "fell well within the terms of these warnings." (Docket No. 6, at 18) The defendants claim that because the warnings in the 1997 Prospectus were "conspicuous, clear, and readily understandable, there can be no credible argument that Plaintiff was unaware of a material rick before she invested." (Docket No. 6, at 18)

However, the cautionary language in the 1997 Prospectus is not, as it was in Olkey, specific to the actual risks Plaintiff alleges were material. Indeed, the cautionary language from the 1997 Prospectus cited in (1) above only indicates that the Manager of the Value Fund expected to keep certain securities for a period of two to five years but may need to liquidate certain securities-not the fund as a whole-in a shorter period of time. Even if this language were to apply to the Value Fund as a whole (and it does not), the language would not put investors on notice of when and under what circumstances the Value Fund would be terminated. As for the cautionary language cited in (2)-(4) above, these warnings are only general statements that the Value Fund may not achieve its investment objective. The warnings do not indicate that there was a risk that the defendants would close the Value Fund in the event that it did not reach some unspecified goal for the number of investors or the amount of investment in the Value Fund. (Docket No. 12, at 13)

Accordingly, the defendants' motion to dismiss Plaintiff's Section 12 (2) claim is denied.

3. Count Six: Violation of Section 10 (b) of the Securities and Exchange Act

...

In order to state a claim under Section 10 (b) of the Securities and Exchange Act of 1934 and Rule 10 (b)-5, a plaintiff must allege "in connection with the purchase or sale of securities, the misstatement or omission of a material fact, made with scienter, upon which the plaintiff justifiably relied and which proximately caused the plaintiff's injury." In re Comshare, 1999 WL 460917, at *4 (July 8, 1999) (citing Aschinger v. Columbus Showcase Co., 934 F.2d 1402, 1409 (6th Cir. 1991)). To establish liability under Section 10 (b), a plaintiff "must, as a threshold matter, allege in his complaint that the defendant acted with sufficient scienter." Id.

Allegations of securities fraud, as with all allegations of fraud, must satisfy the requirements of Fed. R. Civ. P. 9 (b). Rule 9 (b) requires that when a plaintiff alleges fraud, "the circumstances constituting fraud or mistake shall be stated with particularity." FED. R. CIV. P. 9 (b). Despite the heightened pleading standard in Rule 9 (b), Congress passed the Private Securities Litigation Reform Act ("PSLRA") in 1995 after determining that Rule 9 (b) had not stemmed the abuse of the securities laws by private litigants. H.R. Conf. Rep. No. 104-369 (1995).

Pursuant to the amendments in the PSLRA, a plaintiff alleging a misstatement or omission must specify "each statement alleged to have been misleading, the reason or reasons why the statement is misleading, and, if an allegation regarding the statement or omission is made on information and belief, the complaint shall state with particularity all facts on which that belief is formed." 15 U.S.C. s 78u-4 (b) (1). Furthermore, "the complaint shall, with respect to each act or omission alleged to have violated this chapter, state with particularity facts giving rise to a strong inference that the defendant acted with the required state of mind." 15 U.S.C. s 78u-4 (b) (2) (1998).

The Sixth Circuit recently held that a plaintiff must plead scienter in a Section 10 (b) or Rule 10 (b)-5 case "by alleging facts giving rise to a strong inference of recklessness, but not by alleging facts merely establishing that a defendant had the motive and opportunity to commit securities fraud." In re Comshare, 1999 WL 460917, at *5. In defining recklessness, the Sixth Circuit looked to earlier opinions, stating that "recklessness [is] highly unreasonable conduct which is an extreme departure from the standards of ordinary care. While the danger need not be known, it must at least be so obvious that any reasonable man would have known of it." Id. at (citing Mansbach v. Prescott, 598 F.2d 1017, 1025 (6th Cir. 1979)). The Sixth Circuit further explained that recklessness is to be understood as a "mental state apart from negligence and akin to conscious disregard." Id. In applying this pleading standard to the facts of the case, the Sixth Circuit found that the plaintiff's allegations did not satisfy the standard because they merely alleged that the defendants had the motive and opportunity to commit securities fraud. Id. at * 9.

Here, the defendants contend that Plaintiff's allegations are also insufficient under the pleading standard set forth in In re Comshare. (Docket No. 6, at 11-14)

First, the defendants contend that Plaintiff has not alleged any "reason for the Court to believe that it is 'standard' in the mutual fund industry for prospectuses or other communications with shareholders to state that an investment company may liquidate a mutual fund if its fails to attract investors-or, as in this case, if it faces a precipitous decline in investors threatening the value of the remaining shareholders' assets." (Docket No. 6, at 12)

Although Plaintiff does not specifically allege that the defendants' omissions of material fact were clear departures from the standard of ordinary care in the mutual fund industry, her failure to make such an allegation is not fatal to her claim. Indeed, Plaintiff has alleged that the defendants failed to provide material information concerning the potential duration of the Value Fund and the risk of early termination, especially in light of the defendants' emphasis on the long-term nature of the investment and the high front-end sales charges. (First Amended Complaint at PP 25-28) Furthermore, there is circumstantial evidence in the February 1999 letter that the defendants were aware at the time the 1997 Prospectus was issued that there was a minimum investment amount needed to ensure the viability of the Value Fund. See Docket No. 6, Ex. C ("During the almost two years of its existence, the Value Fund has not attracted sufficient interest among prospective investors and is considered unlikely to do so in the future.")

The defendants also contend that Plaintiff has failed to allege that ESC had the required state of mind when ESC made the misleading statements or omitted to make material statements in the 1997 Prospectus. (Docket No. 6, at 13) Although the defendants point to the cautionary statements in the 1997 Prospectus as being sufficient to warn investors that they might liquidate the Value Fund if necessary, these cautionary statements do not inform Plaintiff of the risk that the Value Fund would not be able to successfully weather a short-term decline in the market if the Value Fund was unable to attract a minimum total investment.

In all, Plaintiff has alleged that the defendants failed to warn investors that they might terminate the Value Fund during a short-term decline in the market even though they repeatedly emphasized the long-term nature of the defendants' investment strategy. Plaintiff also alleges that, as a result of the misleading statements and omissions, Plaintiff invested in the Value Fund "at a price that was affected" by the misstatements and omissions because she invested in Class A shares which had a higher front-end sales charge but lower annual expenses.

Thus, in repeatedly emphasizing their long-term investment strategy, the defendants failed to warn investors of the risks that the defendants themselves would not be able to follow such a strategy in the event of a short-term decline in the market. Thus, Plaintiff has adequately alleged that the defendants acted with the requisite scienter and the allegations in her First Amended Complaint are sufficient to withstand a motion to dismiss. See Caremark, Inc. v. Coram Healthcare Corp., 113 F.3d 645, 650 n. 7 (7th Cir. 1997) (reversing district court's dismissal of complaint, finding that plaintiff had adequately alleged scienter where plaintiff had alleged that the defendant had represented that its business strategy was to focus on "core business" and to divest "non-strategic businesses" even though the defendant had been negotiating to acquire another business); see also Page v. Derrickson, 1997 WL 148558, at *4-6 (M.D.Fla. Mar. 25, 1997) (finding that plaintiffs had sufficiently alleged 10 (b) claim); Carley Capital Group v. Deloitte & Touche, L.L.P., 27 F. Supp. 2d 1324, 1339-40 (N.D. Ga.1998) (same).

...

第四节 证券投资基金的监管

一、中国对证券投资基金的监管

随着证券投资基金在中国发展的突飞猛进，2003 年 10 月，中国制定了《证券投资基金法》，以法律的形式对证券投资基金进行了全面规定。随着《证券投资基金法》的出台，中国相关政府部门以该法为依据，陆续颁布了一系列的法规、规章及规范性文件，形成了相对完善的证券投资基金监管法律制度。值得说明的是，中国目前证券投资基金相关法律、法规，规范的是公开发售基金份额募集的证券投资基金，对于私募证券投资基金尚未有规定。中国正在对《证券投资基金法》进行修订，以将私募证券投资基金纳入监管。

根据《证券投资基金法》的规定，一方面，中国证监会依法对证券投资基金活动实施监督管理；另一方面，基金管理人、基金托管人和基金份额发售机构，可以成立同业协会，加强行业自律。中国目前已经建立了以政府部门集中统一监管为主、行业自律组织自律监管为辅的证券投资基金监管体制。

（一）中国证监会的监管

为了规范证券投资基金活动，保护投资人及相关当事人的合法权益，促进证券投资基金和证券市场的健康发展，中国证监会根据《证券投资基金法》的授权对证券投资基金进行集中统一监管。中国证监会的监管职责，涵盖以下方面的内容：（1）依法制定有关证券投资基金活动监督管理的规章、规则，并依法行使审批或者核准权；（2）办理基金备案；（3）对基金管理人、基金托管人及其他机构从事证券投资基金活动进行监督管理，对违法行为进行查处，并予以公告；（4）制定基金从业人员的资格标准和行为准则，并监督实施；（5）监督检查基金信息的披露情况；（6）指导和监督基金同业协会的活动；（7）法律、行政法规规定的其他职责。

为了实现监管目标，达到监管效果，中国证监会在依法履行职责时，有权采取以下措施：（1）进入违法行为发生场所调查取证；（2）询问当事人和与被调查事件有关的单位和个人，要求其对与被调查事件有关的事项作出说明；（3）查阅、复制当事人和与被调查事件有关的单位和个人的证券交易记录、登记过户记录、财务会计资料及其他相关文件和资料，对可能被转移或者隐匿的文件和资料予以封存；（4）查询当事人和与被调查事件有关的单位和个人的资金账户、证券账户或者基金账户，对有证据证明有转移或者隐匿违法资金、证券迹象的，可以申请司法机关予以冻结；（5）法律、行政法规规定的其他措施。

为了保证中国证监会监管的合法性、有效性和独立性等，中国《证券投资基金法》规定，中国证监会工作人员依法履行职责，进行调查或者检查时，不得少于二人，并应当出示合法证件；对调查或者检查中知悉的商业秘密负有保密的义务。在中国证监会履行监管职责时，被调查、检查的单位和个人应当配合，如实提供有关文件和资料，不得拒绝、阻碍和隐瞒。在监管过程中，若发现违法行为涉嫌犯罪的，中国证监会应当将案件移送司法机关处理。同时，中国证监会工作人员不得在被监管的机构中兼任职务。

（二）行业自律监管

除了中国《证券投资基金法》规定基金管理人、基金托管人和基金份额发售机构可以成立同业协会进行自律监管以外，中国《证券投资基金管理公司管理办法》更是明确规定：基金行业的协会依据法律、行政法规、中国证监会的规定和自律规则，对基金管理公司及其业务活动进行自律管理。

中国证券投资基金业尚没有自己独立的自律组织，而是统一纳入中国证券业协会的自律管理体系中。2001 年 8 月，中国证券业协会基金公会成立。2002 年 12 月，中国证券业协会证券投资基金业委员会成立，承接了原基金公会的职能和任务，在证券业协会的领导下开展基金行业的自律管理工作。目前，证券投资基金业委员会的主要职责是调查、收集、反映业内意见和建议，研究、论证业内相关政策与方案，草拟或审议证券投资基金业务有关规则、职业标准、工作指引和自律公约，协助开展业内教育培训、国际交流与合作等，所能发挥的作用相对有限。

二、美国对证券投资基金的监管

美国共同基金采取注册制，即只要满足条件，任何机构和个人都可以通过注册的方式进入基金行业，因此加强监管就显得非常重要。事实上，美国共同基金的快速发展，与美国政府几十年来长期坚持保护投资者利益、建立起较完善的法律制度和监管体制是分不开的。

美国已经建立起以《1933 年证券法》、《1934 年证券交易法》、《1940 年投资公司法》和《1940 年投资顾问法》等联邦法律为基础包含各州的蓝天法以及法院判例法在内的规范共同基金业的完备法律体系。在这一法律体系之下，共同基金的设立、运作及有关参与主体的活动均有相关法律、法规予以规范，监管机构在实施监管过程中也有充分的法律依据。

除了完备的法律制度之外，美国还建立了以证券交易委员会为中心，依靠多种监管机制保护基金参与者的健全的基金业监管体系。

美国证券交易委员会是依据美国《1934 年证券交易法》于 1934 年成立的独立的联

邦政府机构，专门负责对美国证券市场进行监管，包括对共同基金的监管。证券交易委员会根据《1940年投资公司法》和《1940年投资顾问法》的规定，制定有关基金法规、规章，监管基金管理人、托管银行、过户代理商、分销商以及其他为基金提供服务的机构和人士是否合规经营，基金资产是否得到安全保管，基金信息披露是否及时、完整、充分。

美国基金业自律性组织主要有投资公司协会（ICI）、投资管理和研究协会（AIMR）以及美国证券交易商协会（NASD）。[①] 这些组织在维护基金行业的职业道德、督促会员机构及基金从业人员规范经营方面发挥着重要作用。美国基金业自律管理一般遵守以下原则：实施平等、公正的业务准则，维护投资者利益；禁止欺诈（包括公布虚假广告、发行虚假基金、设置虚假空盘等行为）和操纵市场行为；禁止收取不合理佣金和其他费用，坚持公开原则。

自律组织的主要功能为：颁布管理守则，包括统一业务守则、行为守则、程序守则和仲裁守则；对会员单位实施监管，监管的内容主要为对经理机构的资格管理和从业人员的资格管理；对基金资产投资范围的监管和基金资产投资结构的监管；对基金公司经营行为的管理和基金收益分配的管理。

此外，还有一个特殊的自律组织——美国证券投资者保护基金（SIPC）也发挥着重要的作用。该组织是一个非营利性质的、管理投资公司风险经营的保险组织，以保护广大投资者利益为管理目标。根据《证券投资者保护法》的规定，所有在证券交易委员会注册的投资公司都必须成为SIPC的会员，并上缴会费。SIPC将上缴的会费集中起来，形成一笔庞大的投资保险基金，主要用于投资公司遇到财务困难或破产时对客户的债务清偿。

除了上述外部机构监管以外，美国完善的外部审计和内部控制制度，对基金监管作用也很大。外部审计一般由著名的会计师事务所承担，这些事务所定期审查基金的账簿、交易记录以及投资公司的内部工作程序。美国基金业的内部控制体系也十分完善，如建立了投资公司董事会、基金独立董事制度。这些制度在防范基金经理从事关联交易及内幕交易、保护投资者利益等方面发挥了重要作用。

美国的这种既强调政府监管、又注重自律监管，既强调外部监管、又注重内部监管的体制，极大地推动了共同基金业的健康发展。

2008年，美国爆发金融危机。危机过后，美国对金融监管体制进行了大规模改革。此次改革将此前缺乏监管的场外衍生品市场、对冲基金、私募基金等均纳入了监管范畴，还专门针对对冲基金和私募基金建立了若干监管规则，制定了被称为《2010年私募基金

---

① 2007年7月，美国证券商协会与纽约证券交易所中有关会员监管、执行和仲裁的部门合并成立了美国金融业监管局。

投资顾问注册法案》的法律。其中，涉及投资顾问新的监管规则，对共同基金的发展亦产生重要的影响。

三、案例资料

2003年，美国共同基金接连暴露多宗丑闻，包括进行短线交易、市后交易、交易费用欺诈、交易信息不透明以及向提供信息发布服务的公司收取回扣等。这些丑闻极大地影响了基金投资人的信心，致使共同基金市场动荡不安。

丑闻被揭发后，作为监管者的SEC于2004年提出了加强对共同基金监管的条例，目的是通过保证共同基金的董事与基金管理公司的商业利益隔离，以应对基金业日益增多的损害基金持有人利益的事件，更有效地保护基金持有人的利益。条例要求，在基金公司董事会的独立董事席位由50%升至75%，并且董事长也要由独立董事担任。这条规定背后的理论依据是：更多的独立性能减少利益冲突，而且独立董事能保护基金持有人免受高费用和非理性行为的侵害。

作为监管对象，基金公司对这一条例强烈反对，他们称没有更多的证据表明这样对共同基金监管会更具有效率，而且这种新的人事安排成本是非常高昂的。最终，由美国商会（U.S. Chamber of Commerce）出面对SEC提起诉讼，要求法院审查SEC立法的合宪性。

案件被提交到美国哥伦比亚特区巡回上诉法院后，上诉法院认为，时任SEC主席唐纳森和SEC的两位民主党委员只花了8天时间研究就匆忙推出了这一规定，违反了《行政程序法》，违反了征集公众意见的要求。此外，SEC没有充分考虑到共同基金在适用这一规则时可能增加的潜在成本，也没有充分考虑除了设立独立董事长之外的其他方案。上诉法院声称，SEC的这一条例将对共同基金业产生实质性的破坏效应，因为它可能使美国基金业的管理实践出现前后不一的中断后果，并在广大的公众投资者心中产生极大的混乱。上诉法院决定，在判决书下达后90天内，SEC的这一条例暂时失效。在这段时间里，SEC应当再次向公众征询对这一条例所涉及的各项成本的意见。

可见，在美国，尽管SEC对共同基金拥有巨大的监管权限，但是这种监管权力的行使并非毫无边界，而是受到相应的限制。如果被监管的共同基金认为证券交易委员会的监管措施存在违法嫌疑，可以通过包括诉讼在内的各种途径提出质疑。

U.S. Chamber of Commerce v. SEC

443 F.3d 890 (D.C. Cir. 2006)

ROGERS, Circuit Judge.

This appeal concerns the continuing challenge by the Chamber of Commerce of the United States to the rule promulgated on July 27, 2004 ("the Rule") by the Securities and Exchange Commission amending the Exemptive Rules under the Investment Company Act of 1940 ("ICA"), 15 U.S.C. § 80a-1 et seq. (2000). The Rule requires that mutual funds relying on the Exemptive Rules adopt certain governance practices, including those set forth in two conditions: a fund must have (1) a board with no less than 75% independent directors and (2) an independent chair. See Investment Company Governance, Release No. 26, 520, 69 Fed.Reg. 46, 378, 46, 381 (Aug. 2, 2004) ("Adopting Release"). In Chamber of Commerce v. SEC, 412 F.3d 133 (D.C. Cir. 2005) ("Chamber I"), the court held that the Chamber had standing to challenge the Rule, the Commission had authority to promulgate the Rule, and the Commission had not violated the Administrative Procedure Act ("APA"), 5 U.S.C. 551 et seq., except when it failed, as required by the ICA, to determine the costs of the two conditions and when it failed to address a proposed alternative to the independent chair condition. The court remanded the case to the Commission.

The Chamber now challenges the Commission's decision not to modify the two conditions in response to Chamber I. See Investment Company Governance, Release No. 26, 985, 70 Fed.Reg. 39, 390, 39, 398 (July 7, 2005) ("Response Release"). We again hold that the Chamber has standing, and we hold that the Commission had authority to consider whether to modify the Rule prior to issuance of the mandate in Chamber I. We further hold that, although the Commission was not constrained by Chamber I in how to estimate the costs of the conditions, the Commission failed to comply with section 553 (c) of the APA, 5 U.S.C. 553(c), by relying on materials not in the rulemaking record without affording an opportunity for public comment, to the prejudice of the Chamber. On August 10, 2005, the court stayed the two conditions.

I

Section 2 (c) of the ICA requires that when the Commission "engage[s] in rulemaking and is required to consider or determine whether an action is consistent with the public interest,

[it] shall... consider... whether the action will promote efficiency, competition, and capital formation." 15 U.S.C. § 80a-2 (c). In Chamber I, the court held:

> With respect to the 75% independent director condition, the Commission, although describing three methods by which a fund might comply with the condition, claimed it was without a "reliable basis for determining how funds would choose to satisfy the [condition] and therefore it [was] difficult to determine the costs associated with electing independent directors." 69 Fed. Reg. at 46, 387. That particular difficulty may mean the Commission can determine only the range within which a fund's cost of compliance will fall, depending upon how it responds to the conditions but, as the Chamber contends, it does not excuse the Commission from its statutory obligation to determine as best it can the economic implications of the rule it has proposed.

412 F.3d at 143 (citing Pub. Citizen v. Fed. Motor Carrier Safety Admin., 374 F.3d 1209, 1221 (D.C. Cir. 2004)). With respect to the independent chair condition, the court noted that the Commission had stated that an independent chair may decide to hire more staff, but that it had no "reliable basis for estimating... th[ose] costs." Id. at 144 (citing Adopting Release, 69 Fed. Reg. at 46, 387 n. 81) The court held that "[a]lthough the Commission may not have been able to estimate the aggregate cost to the mutual fund industry of additional staff... it readily could have estimated the cost to an individual fund, which estimate would be pertinent to its assessment of the effect the condition would have upon efficiency and competition, if not upon capital formation." Id. The court also held that the Commission could not ignore a "facially reasonable" alternative suggested by the two dissenting Members of the Commission. See id. at 145 (citing standard set forth in Laclede Gas Co. v. FERC, 873 F.2d 1494, 1498 (D.C. Cir. 1989)).

The Commission responded within a matter of days to the release of Chamber I. The Commission explained that prompt action was required to avoid postponing the January 15, 2006 date for compliance with the Rule in order to ensure protection of fund investors "in the wake of the discovery of serious wrongdoing at many of the nation's largest fund complexes and by officials at the highest levels of those complexes." Response Release, 70 Fed. Reg. at 39, 391. This occurred, the Commission explained, because "[f]und managers acted in their own interests rather than in the interests of fund investors (which they are required to do), resulting in substantial investor losses that were well documented at the time [the Commission] adopted the [Rule]," and left investor confidence severely shaken, id.; see Adopting Release, 69 Fed. Reg. at 43, 378. In the Commission's view, prompt action could best be accomplished by having the same five Commissioners who had been considering mutual fund governance issues for more than a year and a half "bring the[ir] collective judgment and learning" to the issues identified by the court. See Response Release, 70 Fed. Reg. at 39, 391. Because the Chairman was scheduled to resign on June 30, 2005, the Commission decided to respond to Chamber I at its previously scheduled public meeting on June 29, 2005. See id. at 39, 391; see also id. at 39, 403 (Glassman, Comm'r, dissenting); id. at 39, 408 (Atkins, Comm'r, dissenting).

The Commission decided it was unnecessary to reopen the rulemaking record for further comment. Observing that it had previously given notice and called for comment on the costs of complying with the two conditions, the Commission concluded that "the information in the existing record, together with publicly available information on which we may rely, is a sufficient base on which to rest the Commission's consideration of the deficiencies identified by the Court." Id. at 39, 390-91 (emphasis added). Based on materials not in the rulemaking record, including what the Commission described as a "widely used industry survey" of mutual fund directors' compensation, the Commission determined a range of costs for each of the options that a fund might use to meet the 75% independent director condition. See id. at 39, 392 n. 28, 39, 391-94. The Commission viewed the costs to an individual fund of the independent chair condition to derive principally from the increased compensation for the independent chair and the costs of additional staff, the latter cost estimated based on extra-record salary surveys by the Securities Industry Association, a source on which the Commission stated it "commonly rel[ies] in its rulemakings." Id. at 39, 394. The Commission stated that it did not expect small funds would hire additional staff. See Id. The Commission concluded, based on these cost estimates, that the costs of complying with the two conditions "are extremely small relative to the fund assets for which fund boards are responsible, and are also small relative to the expected benefits of the two conditions." Id. at 39, 395. "Whether the two conditions are viewed separately or together," the Commission stated, "even at the high end of the ranges, the costs of compliance are minimal." Id. This was true as well for small funds. See id. at 39, 396 n. 77. Accordingly, regarding section 2 (c) of the ICA, the Commission concluded:"[W]e do not expect the amendments to the Exemptive Rules to have a significant adverse effect on efficiency, competition or capital formation because the costs associated with the amendments are minimal and many funds have already adopted the required practices." Id. at 39, 396. The Commission noted that as of the time it proposed the

Rule, it estimated that "nearly sixty percent of all funds currently me[t] [the 75% independent director] requirement." Adopting Release, 69 Fed. Reg. at 46, 387 n. 78; see Response Release, 70 Fed. Reg. at 39, 391 & n. 18.

The Commission also set forth its reasons for rejecting the alternative proposal to the independent chair condition: "[I]n light of the nature of investment companies and the purposes of the statutory prohibitions to which the Exemptive Rules apply," the Commission concluded that the condition requiring an independent chair was superior to an expansion of disclosure requirements. See Response Release, 70 Fed. Reg. at 39, 396-97. The Commission explained that mutual funds are "unique" because they are managed "by people whose primary loyalty and pecuniary interests lie outside the enterprise," which presents "inherent conflicts of interest and potential for abuses." Id. at 39, 396. The Commission reasoned that disclosure alone would not prevent self-dealing by managers. See id. at 39, 397. Further, the Commission observed, the independent chair was part of a package of regulatory reforms designed to change the "boardroom culture," id., that would result in benefits that could not be accomplished by disclosure alone, which to become meaningful faced several obstacles given the information that would need to be imparted to an investor, see id....

II

Section 553 of the APA requires that an agency give notice of a proposed rule setting forth "either the terms or substance of the proposed rule or a description of the subjects and issues involved," 5 U.S.C. 553(b), and "give interested persons an opportunity to participate in the rule making through submission of written data, views, or arguments with or without opportunity for oral presentation," id. § 553 (c). Among the information that must be revealed for public evaluation are the "technical studies and data" upon which the agency relies. See Solite Corp. v. EPA, 952 F.2d 473, 484 (D.C. Cir. 1991).

Congress may vest broad rulemaking authority in an agency, and even charge the agency with "swiftly and effectively implementing [a]national policy," Natural Res. Def. Council, Inc. v. SEC, 606 F.2d 1031, 1050 (D.C. Cir. 1979) ("NRDC"), but on remand the agency remains bound by the APA's notice and comment requirements, see Simmons v. ICC, 757 F.2d 296, 300 (D.C. Cir. 1985); cf. West Virginia v. EPA, 362 F.3d 861, 869 (D.C. Cir. 2004). Although judicial review of informal rulemaking is generally limited in scope, see NRDC, 606 F.2d at 1050, and is deferential when rulemaking implicates the agency's expertise, see Fresno Mobile Radio, Inc. v. FCC, 165 F.3d 965, 971 (D.C. Cir. 1999), more exacting review may be required when the presumption of regularity is rebutted, as may occur when the agency arrives at an identical result on remand under circumstances that throw into question the regularity of its proceedings, see NRDC, 606 F.2d at 1049 n. 23; Food Mktg. Inst. v. ICC, 587 F.2d 1285, 1289-90 (D.C. Cir. 1978); see also Citizens to Preserve Overton Park v. Volpe, 401 U.S. 402, 420, 91 S.Ct. 814, 28 L.Ed.2d 136 (1971). Reviewing the procedures through which agencies develop legislative rules falls within the court's "special area[s] of competence" and generally "contributes to the rationality and fairness of agency decisionmaking without detracting unduly from its effectiveness." NRDC, 606 F.2d at 1049; see Envtl. Def. Fund, Inc. v. Ruckelshaus, 439 F.2d 584, 598 (D.C. Cir. 1971).

Where the court does not require additional fact gathering on remand, as in Chamber I, 412 F.3d at 145, the agency is typically authorized to determine, in its discretion, whether such fact gathering is needed, see Sierra Club v. EPA, 325 F.3d 374, 382 (D.C. Cir. 2003) (citing Nat'l Grain & Feed Ass'n v. OSHA, 903 F.2d 308, 310-11 (5th Cir. 1990)), and how it should be accomplished, see NRDC, 606 F.2d at 1055. If the agency determines that additional fact gathering is necessary, then notice and comment are typically required. See Action on Smoking and Health v. Civil Aeronautics Bd., 713 F.2d 795, 799-800 (D.C. Cir. 1983); cf. Air Transp. Ass'n of Am. v. FAA, 169 F.3d 1, 7 (D.C. Cir. 1999); Ass'n of Data Processing Serv. Orgs., Inc. v. Bd. of Governors of the Fed. Reserve Sys., 745 F.2d 677, 684-85 (D.C. Cir. 1984).

However, further notice and comment are not required when additional fact gathering merely supplements information in the rulemaking record by checking or confirming prior assessments without changing methodology, see Solite, 952 F.2d at 485, by confirming or corroborating data in the rulemaking record, see Community Nutrition Inst. v. Block, 749 F.2d 50, 57-58 (D.C. Cir. 1984); cf. Building Indus. Ass'n of Superior Cal. v. Norton, 247 F.3d 1241, 1246 (D.C. Cir. 2001), or by internally generating information using a methodology disclosed in the rulemaking record, Air Transp. Ass'n of Am. v. Civil Aeronautics Bd., 732 F.2d 219, 224 (D.C. Cir. 1984); cf. Portland Cement Ass'n v. Ruckelshaus, 486 F.2d 375, 393 (D.C. Cir. 1973). For example, in Solite, the agency's explanation of a rule rested on a survey, which was not part of the rulemaking record, that the agency substituted for an older report in the rulemaking record. Solite, 952 F.2d at 481. The court stated that "consistent with the APA, an agency may use 'supplementary' data, unavailable during the notice and comment period, that 'expands on and confirms' information contained in the proposed rulemaking and addresses 'alleged deficiencies' in the pre-existing data, so long as no prejudice is shown." Id. at 484 (quoting Community Nutrition, 749 F.2d at 57-58) (alterations omitted). Such "supplementary" information, the court explained in Community Nutrition, is distinct from "provid[ing] entirely new information critical to the [agency]'s determination." Community Nutrition, 749 F.2d at 57-58 (citations omitted). When the agency relies on supplementary evidence without a showing of prejudice by an interested party, see Solite, 952 F.2d at 484; Community Nutrition, 749 F.2d at 58, the procedural requirements of the APA are satisfied without further opportunity for comment, provided that the agency's response constitutes a "logical outgrowth" of the rule initially proposed, see Envtl. Integrity Project v. EPA, 425 F.3d 992, 996 (D.C. Cir. 2005); Ne. Md. Waste Disposal Auth. v. EPA, 358 F.3d 936, 952 (D.C. Cir. 2004).

In essence, the question is whether "at least the most critical factual material that is used to support the agency's position on review... [has] been made public in the proceeding and exposed to refutation." Ass'n of Data Processing, 745 F.2d at 684; see Air Transp. Ass'n, 169 F.3d at 7. By requiring the "most critical factual material" used by the agency be subjected to informed comment, the APA provides a procedural device to ensure that agency regulations are tested through exposure to public comment, to afford affected parties an opportunity to present comment and evidence to support their positions, and thereby to enhance the quality of judicial review. See Int'l Union, United Mine Workers of Am. v. Mine Safety & Health Admin., 407 F.3d 1250, 1259 (D.C. Cir. 2005). These considerations are no less relevant when an agency on remand considers whether to modify a rule pending on appeal. See Simmons, 757 F.2d at 300.

The Commission maintains that section 553 did not require further notice and comment in response to Chamber I for two reasons: First, the Rule's two conditions were set out in materially the same terms in the notice of proposed rulemaking, see Investment Company Governance, Release No. 26, 323, 69 Fed. Reg. 3472, 3473 (Jan. 23, 2004) ("NOPR"), thus providing all interested parties the opportunity to comment on the proposed amendments and specifically on their costs, see id. at 3481. Second, although the Commission relied on materials not made subject to public comment under section 553 (c), the materials were "publicly available" and merely supplemented data in the rulemaking record that had been subject to public comment. See Response Release, 70 Fed. Reg. at 39, 391. We agree with the Commission's first point, because the NOPR provided adequate notice, but not the second, because the extra-record materials did not merely supplement the rulemaking record without prejudice to the Chamber, and the public availability of those materials, in this instance, does not merit an exception to the comment requirement of section 553 (c). We therefore do not reach the Chamber's contention that the Commission's decision to forgo further notice and comment and rely on extra-record materials was arbitrary and capricious under the APA. Cf. Air Transp. Ass'n, 169 F.3d at 8.

In Chamber I, the court held that the Commission, in order to satisfy "its statutory obligation" under ICA § 2 (c), 15 U.S.C. § 80a-2 (c), would need "to do what it can to apprise itself? and hence the public and the Congress? of the economic consequences of a proposed regulation before it decides whether to adopt the measure." Chamber I, 412 F.3d at 144. Given this general instruction, the Commission was not required under section 553 (b) to give further notice of the two conditions. The NOPR identified the amendments to the Exemptive Rules, proposed the 75% independent director and independent chair conditions, id., and solicited comments and empirical data on costs. See NOPR, 69 Fed. Reg. at 3473. In relevant part, the NOPR stated:

We do not anticipate that these proposals will have a significant effect on efficiency, competition and capital formation with regard to funds because the costs associated with the proposals are minimal and many funds have already adopted some of the proposed practices.... We request comments on whether the proposed rule amendments, if adopted, would promote efficiency, competition, and capital formation. Will the proposed amendments or their resulting costs materially affect the efficiency, competition, and capital formation of funds? Comments will be considered by the Commission in satisfying its responsibilities under section 2 (c) of the Investment Company Act. Commenters are requested to provide empirical data and other factual support for their views to the extent possible.

Id. The NOPR thus fully informed interested parties of the two conditions and expressly requested comments on costs so that the Commission would be in a position to comply with ICA section 2 (c). See Envtl. Integrity Project, 425 F.3d at 996.

The Commission's extensive reliance upon extra-record materials in arriving at its cost estimates, and thus in determining not to modify the two conditions, however, required further opportunity for comment under section 553 (c). The Commission justified its decision not to reopen the comment period on the ground that "the information in the existing record, together with publicly available information upon which we may rely, is a sufficient base on which to rest the Commission's consideration of the deficiencies identified by the Court." Response Release, 70 Fed. Reg. at 39, 391 (emphasis added); see also id. at 39, 392 n. 24. To the extent the Commission suggests that the "publicly available" extra-record materials merely supplemented the rulemaking record, which alone would have been sufficient to allow the

Commission to estimate the costs of the two conditions, it ignores what is obvious from the Response Release.

To develop cost estimates for the Rule's two conditions, the Commission relied on privately produced "Management Practice Inc. Bulletin[s]," id. at 39, 392 nn. 24, 28, 30; id. at 39, 393 nn. 33, 43; id. at 39, 394 n. 48; id. at 39, 395 n. 73, and a nonpublic survey of compensation and governance practices in the mutual fund industry that is summarized in one of these bulletins, id. at 39, 392 n. 28. Neither the bulletins nor the survey were part of the rulemaking record. Nor did the Commission identify the bulletins as materials on which it typically relies in rulemakings. Compare id. at 39, 394. Yet these extra-record materials supply the basic assumptions used by the Commission to establish the range of costs that mutual funds are likely to bear in complying with the two conditions. See id. at 39, 392. The bulletins constitute the only source of information on the number of directors serving on the boards of most mutual funds, id. n. 24, the median annual salaries for directors, id. n. 28 (summarizing the "widely used" survey), and the rough breakdown between boards overseeing a large number of individual funds and boards overseeing a small number of funds, id. n. 30. With these three assumptions? average number of board members, average salary, and average number of funds overseen by an individual director? the Commission was able to "estimate the annual compensation cost per fund" of the 75% independent director requirement from $4 779 for large fund complexes to $37 500 for boards overseeing only one fund. Id. at 39, 392-93.

When the Commission does refer to information in the rulemaking record with regard to the per fund cost calculation for the 75% independent director condition, see id. at 39, 393 n. 31, the Commission uses this data to bolster estimates based upon the extra-record materials, and not the other way around. Specifically, the Commission, in referring to two letters in the rulemaking record, "note[s] that commentators' estimated costs of paying new independent directors ranged from $4 000 to $20 000, which are roughly comparable with and do not exceed our estimated ranges." Id. (citing letters of New Alternatives Fund, Inc. (Feb. 9, 2004) and Independent Directors of Flaherty & Crumrine Preferred Income Opportunity Fund Inc. (Feb. 23, 2004)). But comparing the range derived from the record data with the range derived from the extra-record data implies that the two ranges are comparable. The ranges are not comparable because the two letters, which are cited as the source of the $4 000 and $20 000 figures, refer only to boards overseeing "small" and "small to mid-sized funds."

Hence, the $4 000 to $20 000 range derived from the rulemaking record is comparable only to the $37 500 figure that the Commission estimated as the per fund cost for boards overseeing a single fund. This comparison of the $37 500 estimate and the $4 000 to $20 000 range suggests that the Commission, acting conservatively, may have overestimated the per fund cost for boards overseeing only a few funds. See Response Release, 70 Fed. Reg. at 39, 392. However, the Commission points to no data in the rulemaking record to support its per fund cost estimate for compensation of independent directors overseeing a large number of funds. At best, the rulemaking record supports only one end of the Commission's estimated range; the cost estimate for boards overseeing a large number of funds appears entirely derived from the extra-record materials. See id. 39, 392 n. 28. The rulemaking record, then, serves to supplement the extra-record data by providing a cross-check for only the Commission's estimate for small fund families.

Other aspects of the Commission's decision illustrate that it treated extra-record data as primary, rather than supplementary, evidence. Extra-record sources are essential to the Commission's cost estimate for the independent chair condition, which is based on estimates of the cost of compensation for independent directors. See id. at 39, 395. With respect to the ancillary, non-compensation costs of the conditions, while the nature of the Commission's estimates is somewhat different? because they are largely based upon such things as the prevailing rates for legal, financial, and other services, matters with which Commission Members are likely to be familiar and which are less susceptible to reasonable disagreement? extra-record data is similarly essential to these estimations to the extent they are affected by the Commission's predictions about how funds would come into compliance and how independent directors will behave. See, e.g., id. at 39, 394. Thus, even with respect to ancillary costs, section 553 (c) required that interested parties have the opportunity to comment prior to the agency's final decision.

On appeal, the Commission maintains, relying on Solite, 952 F.2d at 484, and Building Industry, 247 F.3d at 1246, that the extra-record materials simply filled gaps in the rulemaking record and "only confirmed the findings delineated in the [NOPR]." Respondent's Br. at 46. By this, the Commission suggests that the extra-record materials were "supplementary"? not in the sense of being unnecessary support for the Commission's cost estimates? but in the sense of filling the gap left in the rulemaking record after the Commission had solicited public comment on the costs of the proposed amendments. The NOPR requested such cost data and stated that the Commission expected "the costs associated with the proposals to be minimal." 69 Fed. Reg. at 3473. However, neither Solite, 952 F.2d at 484, nor Building Industry, 247

F.3d at 1246, suggest that an agency generally may rely, without affording comment, on data critical to support a rule solely because the existing record contains a deficiency that extra-record data might cure.

Rather, for extra-record data to be "supplementary," it must clarify, expand, or amend other data that has been offered for comment. See Air Transp. Ass'n, 169 F.3d at 8. In Solite, the agency relied upon an updated and expanded extra-record study that was based upon a "methodology... that did not change significantly from the proposed notices," giving the petitioners "ample opportunity to criticize the [agency's] approach." See 952 F.2d at 485. In Building Industry, the agency relied upon a comprehensive empirical study that "confirmed the findings delineated in the proposal," was supported by data in the record, and "provided additional support for that hypothesis." See 247 F.3d at 1246 (emphasis added). Similarly, the Commission's reliance on the statement in Association of Data Processing "that the 'administrative record' might well include crucial material that was neither shown to nor known by the private parties in the proceeding," 745 F.2d at 684, is misplaced, for the court was addressing judicial review of all informal agency actions, including adjudications under the arbitrary and capricious standard, 5 U.S.C. 706, not addressing an agency's independent requirement to provide notice and comment under section 553 (c). See Ass'n of Data Processing, 745 F.2d at 683-84.

The Commission also maintains that it was free to use extra-record data in its response because the Chamber has not, as we have required, shown that it was prejudiced by its lack of opportunity to comment. See Solite, 952 F.2d at 484 (citing Community Nutrition, 749 F.2d at 57-58, and Air Transp. Ass'n, 732 F.2d at 224); see also Air Canada v. Dep't of Transp., 148 F.3d 1142, 1156-57 (D.C. Cir. 1998) (citing 5 U.S.C. 706). To show prejudice, those protesting the use of supplementary information might "point to inaccuracies in the [supplemental] data," Solite, 952 F.2d at 484, show that the agency "hid or disguised the information it used, or otherwise conducted the rulemaking in bad faith," id., or "indicate with 'reasonable specificity' what portions of the [data] it objects to and how it might have responded if given the opportunity," Air Transp. Ass'n, 169 F.3d at 8. The court has not required a particularly robust showing of prejudice in notice-and-comment cases, holding that "an utter failure to comply with notice and comment cannot be considered harmless if there is any uncertainty at all as to the effect of that failure." Sugar Cane Growers Co-op. of Fla. v. Veneman, 289 F.3d 89, 96 (D.C. Cir. 2002) (explaining the standard of McLouth Steel Prods. Corp. v. Thomas, 838 F.2d 1317, 1324 (D.C. Cir. 1988)); see also Sprint Corp. v. FCC, 315 F.3d 369, 376-77

(D.C. Cir. 2003). Although the instant case does not involve the outright dodge of APA procedures that led the court to permit a limited showing of prejudice, see McLouth Steel Prods. Corp., 838 F.2d at 1323-24, the Chamber has offered objections and studies creating enough "[un]certainty whether petitioner's comments would have had some effect if they had been considered," id. at 1324, to show prejudice.

To be clear, the requirement, deriving from sections 553 (c) and 706 that an agency may rely on supplemental materials to fill gaps in the rulemaking record only when there is no prejudice to the interested parties does not mean parties can withhold relevant data and blindside the agency on appeal. When, after an agency explains the basis for its preliminary conclusions by reference to the information on which it has relied and requests data regarding its conclusions, and the agency concludes no such data (or no data the agency concludes is reliable) has been produced during the comment period, the agency may develop data along the lines it has proposed to fulfill its statutory obligations without further public comment. See Solite, 952 F.2d at 484-85. In light of the notice provided, there is no fair-comment prejudice to interested parties under section 553 (c) even if the extra-record materials serve as the crucial confirmation of the agency's preliminary conclusions, see Building Indus., 247 F.3d at 1246, or even as the compelling reason for the agency's modification of its preliminary conclusion, see Solite 952 F.2d at 484-85. A contrary rule would provide a perverse incentive for parties opposing a rule to withhold data in order to seek vacation of the rule on appeal.

This is not the situation here. The Commission's bare request for information on costs and its expectation that these costs would be "minimal" did not place interested parties on notice that, in the absence of receiving reliable cost data during the comment period, the Commission would base its cost estimates on an extra-record summary of extra-record survey data that, although characterized as "a widely used survey," was not the sort, apparently, relied upon by the Commission during the normal course of its official business. For purposes of section 553 (c), it is one thing to suggest that members of the mutual fund industry are familiar with an extra-record survey and quite another thing to give notice that the Commission would rely on a summary of that survey as set forth in the bulletins. The Chamber's failure to critique the extra-record bulletins and summarized survey until this appeal indicates that it had no reason to anticipate the Commission's ultimate reliance on those materials.

Moreover, the rulemaking record closed almost a year before the Commission returned to the cost issue in July 2005, and during that period more funds had adopted the Rule's conditions. See Response Release, 70 Fed. Reg. at 39, 391, 39, 398; see id. at 39, 407 & n. 23

(Atkins, Comm'r, dissenting). When the Commission decided not to reopen the rulemaking record, individual mutual funds had offered to provide information on their actual implementation costs and the Investment Company Institute had offered to gather such data from its membership. See id. The Chamber alerted the Commission that the actual implementation data would identify how funds had adopted the 75% independent director condition and could indicate whether independent director's fees had increased and whether additional staff had been hired in light of the added costs for the fund.

The Commission would rebut the Chamber's assertions of prejudice by pointing out that the Chamber has not suggested the implementation cost data would show that the Commission's cost estimates are materially inaccurate. This is not the relevant test of prejudice under our precedent, which does not require a showing that the Commission would have reached a different result. See, e.g., Sprint, 315 F.3d at 376-77. While the Chamber's section 553 (c) challenge focuses on the procedural faults of the Commission's action, with respect to which the Chamber maintains it had no burden to show such prejudice because it had no knowledge of the specific extra-record information until the Commission relied upon such information in its final decision, see Air Transp. Ass'n, 169 F.3d at 8, the Chamber proffered specific and credible objections to the soundness of the Commission's estimates and hence to its decision not to modify the two conditions. See id.; Sprint, 315 F.3d at 377. Specifically, the Chamber maintains that the Commission's cost estimates were predicated upon an assumption that the extra-record survey summarized in an extra-record bulletin provides information on the salaries solely of independent directors, see Response Release, 70 Fed. Reg. at 39, 392 n. 28, which if incorrect "would have depressed the overall salary data and potentially seriously undermined this important cost of the rule," Petitioner's Br. at 46. Cf. Cent. & S. Motor Freight Tariff Ass'n v. ICC, 777 F.2d 722, 737 (D.C. Cir. 1985). Although the Chamber also identifies data regarding small funds that it would have presented had it been afforded an opportunity to comment, only data that was unavailable during the comment period is relevant here as the NOPR specifically requested cost data; the actual implementation data, however, would either lend support or not to the Chamber's position that the Commission understated the potential ill effects of the two conditions on smaller mutual funds. Cf. Air Transp. Ass'n, 169 F.3d at 8. Under our precedents, the Chamber need not prove that its comments would have persuaded the Commission to reach a different outcome. The Chamber's demonstration that it had something useful to say about this critical data is sufficient to establish prejudice.

In sum, the combination of circumstances? inadequate notice that the Commission would base its cost estimates for the two conditions on "publicly available" extra-record materials on which it did not typically rely in rulemakings; the Commission's acknowledgment that the rulemaking record contained gaps and did not include reliable cost data; the availability of additional implementation data for the period between the close of the rulemaking record and the Commission's response to Chamber I as more funds adopted the conditions; the Chamber's colorable claim that the Commission's failure to consider such implementation data harms its investment choices? suffices to show that the Chamber has been prejudiced by the Commission's reliance on materials not in, nor merely "supplementary" to, the rulemaking record. See Solite, 952 F.2d at 484; Community Nutrition, 749 F.2d at 57-58.

The Commission seeks to mitigate its procedural burdens in two ways. First, the Commission suggests that public comment was not necessary because the extra-record materials on which it relied were "publicly available." See Response Release, 70 Fed. Reg. at 39, 391. In some instances, "publicly available" information, such as "published literature in the fields relevant to the [agency's] proposal," may be so obviously relevant that requiring it be specifically noticed and included in the rulemaking record would advance none of the goals of the APA, see RICHARD J. PIERCE, ADMINISTRATIVE LAW TREATISE § 7.3, at 436-38 (2004), such as improving the quality of the information used by the agency, ensuring fairness to affected parties, or enhancing the quality of judicial review, cf. Sprint, 315 F.3d at 373. The public availability of such information might fall into an implied exception to the general requirement that extra-record data critical to support a legislative rule be subject to public comment, see Community Nutrition, 749 F.2d at 57-58, or, alternatively, go towards negating the petitioner's claims of prejudice when such extra-record information is used to cure deficiencies in the rulemaking record. Neither circumstance is present here.

On appeal, the Commission characterizes the extra-record survey as a "widely used industry survey," Response Release, 70 Fed. Reg. at 39, 392 n. 28; Respondent's Br. at 52, noting that an earlier version had been cited by the dissenting commissioners, id., and pointing to the Management Practice Inc. website as one public source for the bulletins summarizing the results of this survey. However, the mere availability of the extra-record bulletins on the internet is insufficient to demonstrate that these bulletins are generally considered reliable sources of information that should be treated as the inevitable background source of information on the mutual fund industry, as might be true, in other contexts, of a relevant study in a broadly cited scientific journal. See PIERCE, ADMINISTRATIVE LAW TREATISE § 7.3, at 436-38. Although the Commission points out that opponents of the two conditions, including the Investment Company Institute, have cited a broad array of publications as the principal sources on fund director compensation during the last decade, this does not explain why these particular privately produced bulletins are trustworthy or confirm that the survey is so reliable or ubiquitous that the procedural requirements for comment should be relaxed when these materials serve as the critical data on which the Commission relies to assess the costs of implementing the two conditions. See Building Indus., 247 F.3d at 1245-46; Ass'n of Data Processing, 745 F.2d at 684-85; see also Int'l Union, UAW v. OSHA, 938 F.2d 1310, 1324 (D.C. Cir. 1991) (citing Sierra Club v. Costle, 657 F.2d 298, 398 (D.C. Cir. 1981)). Unlike the salary surveys conducted by the Securities Industry Association, which the Commission identified as "a source on which we commonly rely in our rulemakings," Response Release, 70 Fed. Reg. at 39, 394, and the Mutual Fund Fact Book, which is a generally cited source of statistical information relied upon by the Commission in other rulemakings, see, e.g., Regulation NMS, Exchange Act Release No. 34-51808, 70 Fed. Reg. 37, 496, 37, 532 n. 300 (2005), the bulletins received no such commendation by the Commission in the Response Release.

Nor are the Chamber's claims of prejudice materially diminished because the bulletins are "publicly available." The NOPR did not indicate that the Commission intended to rely on these bulletins if reliable cost data was not produced during the comment period, much less indicate that the Commission considered the bulletins to be a source of reliable data for estimating the costs of the two conditions. The fact that the dissenting Commissioners cited a news article that summarized an extra-record survey conducted by the publisher of the bulletins, see Adopting Release, 69 Fed. Reg. at 46, 391 n. 24 (Glassman & Atkins, Comm'rs, dissenting), likewise does not indicate that interested parties would have treated a summary of the "widely used survey" as background information or focused their comments on the survey. At best, notice was given that surveys of the type typically relied upon by the Commission in rulemakings should be addressed. In fact, one of the bulletins was not in existence until after the rulemaking record had closed and thus was not "publicly available" for comment. See id. at 39, 393 n. 43.

Nor does public access to the bulletins alter the fact that the Commission had acknowledged the inadequacies of the rulemaking record with respect to estimating costs. The Commission's recourse to extra-record materials indicates that even for the more refined task of estimating direct costs described in Chamber I, 412 F.3d at 144, the Commission continued to view the rulemaking record as lacking reliable cost information. Nor, finally, does the availability of the "widely used survey" alleviate the prejudice to the Chamber when the Commission, in light of its prior acknowledgment of the inadequacies of the rulemaking record and the period during which more funds had adopted the conditions, declines to reopen the record to allow the Chamber to submit actual implementation cost data. Although the Commission's judgment in relying on these extra-record sources may be well-founded, the bulletins themselves acknowledge "wide divergence" among the funds represented in the summarized extra-record survey "in the methodologies used to calculate director compensation." Management Practice Inc. Bulletin: More Meetings Means More Pay for Fund Directors at 1 (April 2004) (cited at 70 Fed. Reg. at 39, 392 n. 28). In the absence of an explanation by the Commission, this caveat suggests that other, possibly more reliable estimates may exist that could have influenced the Commission's assumptions about director compensation, which supports the Chamber's claim of prejudice.

Second, the Commission justifies its choice to act without re-opening the record by invoking the need to act swiftly:

> We find that any further delay or ambiguity surrounding implementation of the rules would disadvantage not only investors but also fund boards and management companies, most of which have already begun the process of coming into compliance with the rules. By acting swiftly and deliberately to respond to the Court's remand order, the Commission will reduce uncertainty, facilitate better decision-making by funds, and ultimately serve the interests of fund shareholders.

Id. at 39, 398. The Commission's preference to proceed with the same five Commission Members who were familiar with the rulemaking in considering the cost estimates described in Chamber I, see id. at 39, 391, is not the type of exigent circumstance that comes within the narrow "good cause" exception of section 553 (b) (B). See Tennessee Gas Pipeline Co. v. FERC, 969 F.2d 1141, 1144 (D.C. Cir. 1992); Util. Solid Waste Activities Group v. EPA, 236 F.3d 749, 754 (D.C. Cir. 2001). The exception excuses notice and comment in emergency situations, Am. Fed'n of Gov't Employees v. Block, 655 F.2d 1153, 1156 (D.C. Cir. 1981), where delay could result in serious harm, see Jifry v. FAA, 370 F.3d 1174, 1179 (D.C. Cir. 2004) (citing Hawaii Helicopter Operators Ass'n v. FAA, 51 F.3d 212, 214 (9th Cir. 1995)), or when the very announcement of a proposed rule itself could be expected to precipitate activity by affected parties that would harm the public welfare, see Mobil Oil Corp. v. Dep't of Energy,

728 F.2d 1477, 1492 (Temp. Emer. Ct. App. 1983). These exigent circumstances are of a far different nature than the not uncommon circumstance facing commissions when their membership changes during the course of a rulemaking, which may involve appeals and remands and thus extend for a period of years. Although the Commission's membership would change after June 30, 2005, and the even division among the remaining Commissioners could delay further action on the Rule, which the Commission considered necessary to redress "a serious breakdown in management controls," Adopting Release, 69 Fed. Reg. at 43, 379, the risk of such delay is hardly atypical and does not satisfy the narrow exception.

Therefore, because the Commission relied on extra-record material critical to its costs estimates without affording an opportunity for comment to the prejudice of the Chamber, we hold that the Commission violated the comment requirement of section 553 (c).

…

Accordingly, we grant the Chamber's petition, without reaching its other challenges to the Remand Release, vacate the two conditions, but withhold the issuance of the mandate for ninety days as set forth in this opinion.

第七章

保险法律制度

第一节 保 险 简 介

现代意义的保险制度起源于欧洲中世纪的海上贸易，伴随着商品经济发展和资本主义制度的建立，现代保险逐步扩展到火灾险（陆上险）、人寿保险以及工业保险。目前，在商业领域，财产险和人寿险占据主要地位，同时保险业已经成为金融行业的重要一极。

一、中国保险简介

广义的保险，包括商业保险和社会保险。作为金融行业中的保险业，是指狭义的保险，即商业保险而不包括社会保险。根据中国《保险法》（2009 年修订）的规定，保险是指投保人根据合同约定，向保险人支付保险费，保险人对于合同约定的可能发生的事故因其发生所造成的财产损失承担赔偿保险金责任，或者当被保险人死亡、伤残、疾病或者达到合同约定的年龄、期限等条件时承担给付保险金责任的商业保险行为。

保险业是金融业的一个重要部门。在保险业经营之中，投保人向保险人支付的费用被称为“保险费”。大量客户所缴纳的保险费一部分被用来建立保险基金以应付预期发生的赔款，另一部分被保险人用做营业费用支出。如果自始至终保险人所支出的赔款和费用小于保险费收入，那么差额就成为保险公司的利润。当然，保险公司更重要的利润来源在于投资回报，即在保险公司收入保险费到保险公司支付赔款之间的时间，保险公司将保险费形成的保险基金进行投资赚取盈利。

在中国，保险业同银行业、证券业、信托业实行分业经营、分业管理，保险公司与银行、证券、信托业务机构分别设立。目前，中国保险市场已形成了全国性和区域性保险公司以及外资保险公司并存的多层次、多元化的竞争体系，逐步开放和扩展的保险业务也促使保险代理、保险经纪以及保险公估等中介机构日趋完善。

随着保险业在中国的蓬勃发展，中国已经建立起以《保险法》为核心的保险业法律体系。自1995年6月30日中国《保险法》正式颁布起，中国保险业就在法制化与规范化的道路上不断前行。中国《保险法》作为中国保险业基本法，确立了中国保险法律制度的基本原则，并对保险合同、保险业监督管理制度以及保险当事人权利保障作了明确的规定，是保障保险业健康发展的一部重要法律。同时，《保险公司管理规定》、《外资保险公司管理条例》及《外资保险公司管理条例实施细则》、《保险公估机构监管规定》、《保险专业代理机构监管规定》以及《保险经纪机构监管规定》等一系列配套的保险法规也相继颁布，形成了有中国特色的保险法律体系。

此外，中国于20世纪90年代成立中国保监会，目前已经形成了以中国保监会监管为核心的完善的保险业监管体系。中国对保险业的监管，注重以机构监管和功能监管相结合、微观审慎和宏观审慎监管相结合以及现场检查和非现场监管相结合。此外，中国保险业的监管实行专业监管和外部监督相结合，形成政府监管、行业自律、企业内控和社会监督“四位一体”的监管格局。

二、美国保险简介

美国保险业迄今已有一百多年的发展历史。由于美国人具有强烈的风险意识和保险意识，用于各类保险的支出在经济收入中占有很大比例，这促使了美国保险业的高速发展。当前，美国是世界上保险市场规模最大的国家，其保险业高度发达。

在美国，保险是一种金融产品，消费者通过购买这种金融产品，将不可预见事件导致的经济损失的不确定性转化为可以预期的特定数额的经营成本（即保费）。美国没有专门统一的立法对保险进行定义，保险的内涵通常是通过法院判例予以确立的。早在1938年的State ex rel. Duffy v. Western Auto Supply Co. 案中，俄亥俄州法院就对“保险”的定义作了这样的阐述：“从广义上讲，保险是一种合同，是一方以收取保险费的方式承担另一方的特定风险，并承诺当特定事故发生时，对另一方或其受益人给予一定或特定金额补偿的合同。对财产和责任保险而言，它是这样一种合同：一方通过收取对价，承诺当一方因特定原因蒙受损失时对其给予补偿或赔偿，或对其由此造成的损失提供保证、赔偿或保护。”

美国的经济深受放任自由主义的影响，市场不受政府监管本应是一种常态，然而所有州均禁止任何尚未得到正式批准的人在其领域内开展保险业务，即便获得批准也仍须持续满足法律特别规定的条件。但是，不同于银行、期货商、证券商以及其他金融机构，在美国保险业主要受各州的监管而非主要受到联邦层面的监管或联邦和州的双重监管。

美国没有全国统一的保险法，关于保险的立法散见于各州的保险法律之中。各州政府依据本州的保险法律，对本州范围内的保险经营活动进行管理。各州的保险法律虽不完全相同，但一般都包括保险公司的成立、保险业的财务监督、投保人的利益保护等方面的内容。各州还设有专门管理保险业的行政部门。

三、案例资料

在美国的司法实践中，法院经常碰到这样的问题：哪些经济交易应当被视为保险从而受到保险法的规制，而哪些经济交易仅仅只是普通的商业活动。下面的 State ex rel. Duffy v. Western Auto Supply Co. 案即涉及一家汽车配件公司在其零售业务中附加有关“保证”的合同是否是保险的争议。

在该案中，汽车配件公司在与客户订立的轮胎销售合同中提供了如下“保证”：对于除失火和失窃以外的几乎一切原因所造成的轮胎不适宜使用的情形，汽车配件公司将向顾客提供免费修理服务或是在顾客支付等价于已使用期限的使用费条件下免费更换。俄亥俄州检察长认为，这种“保证”是未经准许擅自开展保险业务的行为，故以汽车配件公司违反州法律中保险特许经营的规定而起诉。

州检察长承认，仅仅是对于产品的材料和工艺提供的“保证”并不构成保险，但是被告在合同中将“保证”的范围扩大到几乎所有外来原因，实际上是将独立于乃至与产品的材料和工艺无关的风险从买方转移到自己身上，这种“保证”本质上就是保险。被告则争辩称，对于“保证”原因的列举仅仅是为了解决纠纷的便利；况且自己仅对自己售出的产品提供“保证”，“保证”的内容也并不包括任何经济返还。

法院基本认同了原告的观点。法院首先对保险进行了界定：广义而言，保险是一种合同，基于该合同，一方为取得被称为保费的价款而承担了另一方的特别风险，并承诺在发生特定事件的情况下向另一方或其指定的人支付一定数额的金钱。随后，法院对保险和一般“保证”加以区别：一般“保证”的对象仅仅是产品本身，也就是仅在产品本身存在质量问题的时候给予赔偿；而保险所保障的对象是与产品自身缺陷无关的外来风险。虽然被告提供的“保证”仅仅是自身产品销售中的附加事项，但这并不影响它保险的本质。俄亥俄州的法律规定，除非有明确的法律授权，禁止直接或间接从事保险业务，也不得签订事实上的保险合同。本案中被告对于所售产品近乎无条件的保证，即使不构成保险业务，也是一种“事实上”的保险合同，应当受到州法律中有关特许经营规定的规制。

State ex rel. Duffy v. Western Auto Supply Co.

134 Ohio St. 163 (Ohio 1938)

MATTHIAS, Judge.

The sole question presented by the record is whether these oral or written agreements or statements or either of them as employed by the respondent in connection with its sale of automobile tires constitutes insurance. **258 It is contended by the relator that in the respect complained of the respondent is engaged in the business of insurance in violation of Section 665, General Code. Its provisions are as follows:

"No company, corporation, or association, whether organized in this state or elsewhere, shall engage either directly or indirectly in this state in the business of insurance, or enter into any contracts substantially amounting to insurance, or in any manner aid therein, or engage in the business of guaranteeing against liability, loss or damage, unless it is expressly authorized by the laws of this state, and the laws regulating it and applicable thereto, have been complied with.

"No person, firm, association, partnership, company and/or corporation shall publish or distribute, receive and print for publication or distribution any advertising matter wherein insurance business is solicited unless such advertiser has complied with the laws of this state regulating the business of insurance, and a certificate of such compliance is issued by the superintendent of insurance.

"Whoever violates the provisions of this section with reference to advertising, shall be deemed guilty *167 of a misdemeanor and upon conviction thereof, shall be fined not less than one hundred dollars nor more than five hundred dollars for each offense."

The relator concedes that any agreement in the sale of any product which is a warranty against defects in material or workmanship is not insurance, but contends that any agreement which goes further than to guarantee the material and workmanship is violative of the insurance laws of the state, and particularly of the section above quoted. Relator contends that the guarantee agreement is more than a warranty of material and workmanship because of the stipulation that tires are subject to injury and their failure may result from cuts, bruises, blow-outs and other road hazards. Relator further contends that the special guarantee of material and workmanship, unlimited as to time, shows that the general guarantee is for another and different purpose and relates to injuries sustained from exterior causes, and also that the clause, "should the tire fail within the replacement period," with no limitation as to cause, shifts from the buyer to the seller the risk of accidental damage or loss which is independent of and entirely unrelated to quality of material or workmanship.

The contention of the respondent is that the agreement of warranty in either of the forms it uses in the sale of its tires is intended only as a guarantee of material and workmanship and provides a method of carrying out and performing its contract of guarantee which, from its experience, has proved most satisfactory to its customers and the trade generally. It argues that in the absence of some such pre-determined method of adjustment, upon the failure of a tire to render the service expected of it if free from defects of workmanship and material, disputes between the manufacturer or dealer and the customer as to the cause of such failure are constant and annoying, and that it was by reason of the difficulties of reaching *168 satisfactory adjustments and for the purpose of eliminating these disputes and disagreements between dealer and customer and to preserve and promote good will of the users of a product which is subject to failure from various causes often difficult of ascertainment that the type of unconditional or road hazard guarantee was adopted as the fairest, most practical and satisfactory method available.

It argues also that these agreements of guaranty have to do only with the product sold by the respondent and are a part of the sale transaction between itself and its customer, and that the undertaking is limited to a guarantee that the tire will render service for a stipulated period and that in neither of the forms employed is there any promise of financial return to the purchaser in any event, but only to repair the damaged tire without charge or to replace it upon the payment of the specified proportion of the current price covering the remainder of the stipulated period of service guaranteed.

Are such agreements of guarantee permissible as incidental to the sale of automobile tires; or do they constitute "the business of insurance" or "the business of guaranteeing against liability, loss or damage" or are these agreements of guarantee "contracts substantially amounting to insurance" within the purview of Section 665, General Code, and therefore inhibited?

[1][2][3] What is insurance? "Broadly defined, insurance is a contract by which one party, for a compensation called the premium, assumes particular risks of the other party and promises to pay to him or his nominee a certain or ascertainable sum of money on a specified contingency. As regards property and liability insurance, it is a contract by which one party

promises on a consideration **259 to compensate or reimburse the other if he shall suffer loss from a specified cause, or to guarantee or indemnify or secure him against loss from that cause." 32 Corpus Juris, 975. It is a contract*169 "to indemnify the insured against loss or damage to a certain property named in the policy, by reason of certain perils to which it may be exposed." State ex rel. Sheets, Atty. Gen., v. Pittsburgh, C., C. & St. L. Ry. Co., 68 Ohio St. 9, 30, 67 N.E. 93, 96, 64 L.R.A. 405, 96 Am. St. Rep. 635; State ex rel. Physicians' Defense Co. v. Laylin, Secy. of State, 73 Ohio St. 90, 97, 76 N.E. 567.

[4][5] It seems well settled that to constitute insurance the promise need not be one for the payment of money, but may be its equivalent or some act of value to the insured upon the injury or destruction of the specified property. It is well settled, also that the business of insurance is impressed with a public use and consequently its regulation, supervision and control are authorized and required to protect the general public and safeguard the interests of all concerned. We are in accord with the suggestion that business and enterprise should not be unduly restricted or interfered with but should be permitted as great freedom in the conduct and management of their affairs as is consistent with the public interest and welfare. However, our conclusion of the issue presented in this case must be determined from the provisions of our own statutes and our especial inquiry is whether the guarantees in question constitute insurance or are contracts substantially amounting to insurance.

[6] Numerous decisions have been cited which deal with conditions and transactions so at variance with those involved in this case that they are of little assistance in reaching a conclusion of the legal question before us. It is essential that the distinction between warranty and insurance be clearly stated. Section 8392, General Code, defines an express warranty as follows:"Any affirmation of fact or any promise by the seller relating to the goods is an express warranty if the natural tendency of such affirmation or promise is to induce the buyer to purchase the goods, and if the *170 buyer purchases the goods relying thereon." A warranty promises indemnity against defects in the article sold, while insurance indemnifies against loss or damage resulting from perils outside of and unrelated to defects in the article itself.

[7] The respondent, in one of its forms of contract, specifically guarantees "against defects in material and workmanship without limit as to time, mileage or service;" but it goes further and undertakes to indemnify the owner of such tires against all road hazards (except fire and theft) which may render his tire unfit for service. The terms employed in the guarantee are sufficiently broad to include not only damage from blowouts, cuts and bruises, whether resulting from under-inflation, faulty brakes or misalignment, but any and every hazard,

including collisions, whether resulting from negligence of the owner or another. It clearly embraces insurance upon the property of the owner, such as is authorized by the provisions of Section 9556, General Code, to be written by companies required to comply with the insurance laws of the state.

The ultimate force and effect of the contract of indemnity embraced in this guarantee may be appreciated if extended to cover not only the automobile tire but the automobile itself. Surely no one would centend that an undertaking by an automobile manufacturer to replace an automobile damaged or destroyed (excepting only by fire and theft) within a specified period after its purchase is not a contract to reimburse one if he suffers loss from a specified cause or to indemnify him against such loss.

The fact that such contract of indemnity is made only with the purchaser of the indemnitor's product does not relieve the transaction of its insurance character. When the sale is complete, title passes and the property which is the subject of insurance of indemnity belongs to the purchaser. If the contracts of indemnity*171 involved here are not violative of the insurance laws, then every company may, in consideration of the purchase price paid therefor, furnish its product and also undertake to insure it against all hazards for a specified period. Even if such contract is an incident in the sale of merchandise and its use therein does not constitute the business of insurance, it in effect is a contract "substantially amounting to insurance" within the restrictive provisions of Section 665, General Code.

We are unable to discern any essential difference in the character or effect of the various forms of agreement of indemnity made by the respondent and advertised in its catalogue. Each constitutes an undertaking to indemnify against failure from any cause except fire or theft and therefore covers loss or damage resulting from any and every hazard of travel, not excepting negligence of the automobile driver or another. It is **260 substantially an unconditional promise of indemnity, and that is insurance....

第二节 保险合同

一、中国的保险合同

保险合同是投保人与保险人约定保险权利义务关系的协议。订立保险合同，应当协商一致，遵循公平原则确定各方的权利和义务。除法律、行政法规规定必须保险的外，保险合同由当事人自愿订立。

（一）保险合同的主体

保险合同中，通常会涉及如下几类主体：投保人，与保险人订立保险合同，并按照合同约定负有支付保险费义务的人。保险人，与投保人订立保险合同，并按照合同约定承担赔偿或者给付保险金责任的保险公司。被保险人，财产或者人身受保险合同保障，享有保险金请求权的人。投保人可以为被保险人。受益人，人身保险合同中由被保险人或者投保人指定的享有保险金请求权的人。投保人、被保险人可以为受益人。

（二）保险合同的客体

保险合同的客体即保险利益。保险利益是指投保人或者被保险人对保险标的具有的法律上承认的利益。保险利益并非保险人在保险合同中承保的具体财产或者被保险人的身体、生命，而是投保人或者被保险人与保险标的之间所存在的法律认可的经济利害关系。[①]人身保险的投保人在保险合同订立时，对被保险人应当具有保险利益。财产保险的被保险人在保险事故发生时，对保险标的应当具有保险利益。

（三）保险合同的形式与内容

投保人提出保险要求，经保险人同意承保，保险合同成立。保险人应当及时向投保人签发保险单或者其他保险凭证。保险单或者其他保险凭证应当载明当事人双方约定的合同内容。当事人也可以约定采用其他书面形式载明合同内容。保险合同应当包括下列事项：（1）保险人的名称和住所；（2）投保人、被保险人的姓名或者名称、住所，以及人身保险的受益人的姓名或者名称、住所；（3）保险标的；（4）保险责任和责任免除；（5）保险期间和保险责任开始时间；（6）保险金额；（7）保险费以及支付办法；（8）保险金赔偿或者给付办法；（9）违约责任和争议处理；等等。但采用保险人提供的格式条款订立的保险合同，不得具有免除保险人依法应承担的义务或者加重投保人、被保险人责任，排除投保人、被保险人或者受益人依法享有的权利的条款，否则该条款无效。投保人和保险人协商变更保险合同的，应当由保险人在保险单或者其他保险凭证上批注或者附贴批单，或者由投保人和保险人订立变更的书面协议。

（四）保险合同的解除

在中国，除法律另有规定或者保险合同另有约定外，保险合同成立后，投保人享有任意解除权，可以随时解除合同，但保险人不得随意解除合同。

除非保险合同另有约定，保险人有权解除合同的情形非常有限，主要限于投保人的虚假陈述。根据中国《保险法》的规定，订立保险合同，保险人就保险标的或者被保险人的有关情况提出询问的，投保人应当如实告知。投保人故意或者因重大过失未履行如实告知义务，足以影响保险人决定是否同意承保或者提高保险费率的，保险人有权解除

---

① 贾林青. 保险法. 北京：中国人民大学出版社，2009：89.

合同。但是，为了维护被保险人或受益人的利益，中国《保险法》又对保险人的这种解除权施加了一定的限制：这种解除权，自保险人知道有解除事由之日起，超过30日不行使而消灭；自合同成立之日起超过2年的，保险人不得解除合同；保险人在合同订立时已经知道投保人未如实告知的情况的，保险人不得解除合同。

（五）保险合同的格式条款

保险合同的订立，往往是采用保险人提供的格式条款。订立保险合同，采用保险人提供的格式条款的，保险人向投保人提供的投保单应当附格式条款，保险人应当向投保人说明合同的内容。

对保险合同中免除保险人责任的条款，保险人在订立合同时应当在投保单、保险单或者其他保险凭证上作出足以引起投保人注意的提示，并对该条款的内容以书面或者口头形式向投保人作出明确说明；未作提示或者明确说明的，该条款不产生效力。

二、美国的保险合同

在美国，保险合同是规范保险当事人权利义务的法律文件。保险合同，通常表现为保单（policy）等书面形式，但是在保单签署之时或之前作出的任何陈述（representation）或明示性担保（express warranty）往往也被视为保险合同的一部分，对保险合同当事人产生约束。

保险合同，主要涉及保险人和被保险人双方当事人。通常，除了要获得州保险监管部门颁发的经营许可之外，法律对保险人并无特殊的资格限制。任何有能力订立合同的人，均可成为保险人。对于被保险人，法律也几乎不作限制。例如，依据《加州保险法典》（California Insurance Code）的规定，除人民公敌（public enemy）之外的任何人均可以是被保险人。

在美国，当事人可以为范围广泛的事件或风险而订立保险合同，只要保险的对象对被保险人而言具有可保利益（insurable interest）。例如，依据《加州保险法典》的规定，除该法另有规定外，任何或有事件或未知事件，无论是过去的还是未来的事件，只要可能给一个享有可保利益的人造成损害或者使其承担责任，均可予以投保。如果被保险人没有可保利益，那么保险合同无效。

财产上的任何利益或与财产的任何联系或者关于财产的任何责任，均可成为可保利益，只要被保险人可能因之遭受损害。财产上的可保利益包括：现存的利益，在现存利益基础之上的尚未完全形成的利益以及与现存利益相关的一种预期。仅仅只是对某个物体的或有利益或预期利益，并非建立在对该物体的实际权利基础之上，也非基于对该物体的任何有效的合同，不可投保。对财产的可保利益的衡量，应以被保险人可能遭受的损失或损害程度为准，除非被保险人是作为承运人或保管人而持有该财产。任何物体的承运人或保管人对其所持有的该物体在该物体的价值范围内享有可保利益。对投保的财产的利益必须在保险发生效力时存在或在损失发生之时存在，对被保险人的生命或健康的利益必须在保险生效之时存在，但是并不要求在其后也存在或是在损失发生之时存在。

在美国，保险合同的订立，同其他一般性的商事合同一样，适用普通法关于合同订立的规则。普通法对于合同成立条件的要求包括：（1）要约和承诺；（2）对价；（3）具有相应的缔约能力；（4）合同形式合法；（5）合同目的合法。在美国，合同法里的这些要求也完全适用于保险交易中。

保单是保险人和被保险人之间的书面合同。在美国，保单通常分为开口保单（open policy）、定值保单（valued policy）和流动保单（running policy）。开口保单是指当事人并未对标的物的价值予以约定，在损失发生之时以实际发生的损失作为赔偿依据；定值保单是指保险合同双方就保险标的价值事先约定，当损失发生之时以约定的价值作为赔偿依据；流动保单事先约定承保物品的总价值，一旦总价值保尽，保单即告终止。保单通常都应当载明如下事项：订立合同的当事人；被保险的财产或生命；被保险人对投保财产的利益（如果其并非是该财产的完全所有人）；被保险的风险；保险持续的时间；保费的数额或计算方式。为保护消费者利益，美国许多州都立法强制规定保单中必须包括某些条款（如规定保险公司解除或不予续保财产和意外保险的条件）。人寿保险特别是意外和健康保险保单都有这种规定。

在保险合同的订立过程中，信息披露是非常重要的一个方面。美国各州的保险法律均规定，保险合同的任何一方当事人均有义务将其所知的信息告知给对方。以加州为例，根据《加州保险法典》第 332 条的规定，保险合同的任何一方均应将其所知的所有事实善意地告知另一方，只要该等事实对于保险而言是重大的或者其认为是重大的并且他并未对该事实作出担保同时另一方当事人无法对该等事实进行确认。但是，对于如下事项的信息，除非在对方问起时予以答复，保险合同的任何一方均无义务予以告知：（1）另一方已经知晓的事项；（2）另一方通过行使一般的注意义务应当知晓并且对方没有理由设想另一方当事人忽视了该等事项；（3）另一方放弃了获得通知的权利；（4）证明或可能证明被担保条款予以排除的风险的存在的事项且该等事项并非重大；（5）与保险合同已经排除的风险相关并且并非重大的事项。保险合同当事人所需要披露的信息，必须是重大的（material）。至于重大的标准，《加州保险法典》的规定是：重大性并非由事件本身决定，而仅仅是依据事实对应被告知的那一方当事人在作出对拟定的保险合同的缺点的预估或在作出对对方的询问时可能的及合理的影响来确定。[①]

---

① 原文是：Materiality is to be determined not by the event, but solely by the probable and reasonable influence of the facts upon the party to whom the communication is due, in forming his estimate of the disadvantages of the proposed contract, or in making his inquiries.

三、案例资料

保险合同，既可以由保险公司与投保人直接订立，也可以由保险代理人代保险公司与投保人订立，还可以由保险经纪人代投保人与保险公司订立。在许多情况下，保险合同是在保险公司与保险经纪人之间达成的：保险经纪人代投保人寻找相关保险服务的信息，并将之提供给投保人，同时给予投保人购买保险的建议，最后由保险经纪人代表投保人与保险公司签订保险合同。

为了招揽业务，保险公司经常对保险经纪人采取一些激励性措施，向给其带来业务的保险经纪人提供奖励金。那么，对于这类激励性安排，保险经纪人有无法定义务披露给投保人呢？下面的 People ex rel. Cuomo v. Wells Fargo Ins. Services, Inc. 案对此问题进行了分析。

该案中，被告 Wells Fargo 保险服务公司（一家保险经纪公司）参与了一项针对保险经纪人的激励性安排。根据该安排，保险公司承诺根据保险经纪人为他们带来的业务数量向保险经纪人支付现金奖励。但是，Wells Fargo 并未将其参与这一安排的事实向其客户（投保人）披露。纽约州总检察长认为，Wells Fargo 违反了其对客户的信义义务（fiduciary duties），对 Wells Fargo 提起诉讼，以请求法院宣布被告的行为违法。

纽约州检察长没有指控被告存在任何违反其忠实义务的行为（如向投保人推荐价高质次的保险），其仅要求法院判定，保险经纪人参与保险公司的激励安排并且未向投保人披露这一行为本身就违反了保险经纪人的信义义务。纽约州检察长的论点是：保险经纪人是投保人的代理人，而代理关系（a principal-agent relationship）本身在性质上就是一种信义义务关系（a fiduciary relationship）；在信义义务关系之下，受信人应当在特定的交易中向本人披露导致受信人的忠实职责分离的利益。

法院认为，尽管保险经纪人是投保人的代理人，但是其通常是为保险人而非被保险人招揽业务，而且其有时还扮演着保险人的代理人的角色——例如，替保险人收取保险费。因此，保险经纪人处于“双重代理的地位”（dual agency status）。在保险交易中，保险经纪人仅仅是中介商，其并不对交易的某一方负有完全的不可分离的忠实义务。基于保险经纪人的这种特殊角色，法院认为，其无须将其与保险公司之间的相关协议安排向投保人披露。

当然，法院承认，不披露可能是不好的做法。对此，纽约州的保险监管部门已经颁布禁止性的规章。但是，该规章颁布于被告行为之后，没有溯及力。法院认为，对待这种不披露的行为，最好还是由政府部门的规章去解决，而非让法院创制一项新的普通法规则。

People ex rel. Cuomo v. Wells Fargo Ins. Services, Inc.

16 N.Y.3d 166, 944 N.E.2d 1120, 919 N.Y.S.2d 481 (N.Y., 2011)

SMITH, J.

We hold that an insurance broker does not have a common-law fiduciary duty to disclose to its customers "incentive" arrangements that the broker has entered into with insurance companies.

I

The Attorney General brought this action against a large insurance brokerage firm now known as Wells Fargo Insurance Services, Inc. The complaint contains four causes of action, alleging that Wells Fargo engaged in "repeated fraudulent or illegal acts" in violation of Executive Law § 63(12), was unjustly enriched, committed common-law fraud and breached its fiduciary duties.

The complaint alleges the following facts: Insurance brokers, including Wells Fargo, act as agents for organizations and individuals seeking to purchase insurance. Wells Fargo deals with insurance companies on those customers' behalf, obtains quotes from the insurers, and presents them to the customers; and it also offers the customers recommendations about what coverage will best suit their needs. Wells Fargo "often has advised its customers in complex insurance placements where all things are rarely equal, and where subjective decisions must be made among competitors with varying coverages, financial stability, and price." Customers rely on Wells Fargo "to make its recommendations strictly based on the customer's best interest."

The complaint also alleges that Wells Fargo entered into a number of "incentive" arrangements with insurance companies, in which the insurance companies rewarded Wells Fargo for bringing them business. The complaint focuses especially on Wells Fargo's "Millennium Partners Program," in which participating insurers agreed to pay cash compensation to Wells Fargo based on the volume of business that the broker brought to them. It alleges that, as a result of the incentive programs, Wells Fargo "steered" its customers to particular insurance *170 companies and away from others that did not participate in the programs.

The complaint alleges that the incentive payments were not disclosed to Wells Fargo's customers. It does not allege, however, that Wells Fargo made any affirmative misrepresentations or that any customer suffered demonstrable harm from the incentive arrangements. There is no allegation that any customer was persuaded to buy inferior, or overpriced, insurance in order to help Wells Fargo earn its incentives.

Supreme Court dismissed the complaint with leave to replead (18 Misc.3d 1117[A], 2008 N.Y. Slip Op. 50114[U], 2008 WL 162147). The Attorney General chose not to replead, but appealed to the Appellate Division, which affirmed the dismissal (People v. Wells Fargo Ins. Servs., Inc., 62 A.D.3d 404, 879 N.Y.S.2d 398 [2009]). We granted leave to appeal (13 N.Y.3d 717, 895 N.Y.S.2d 317, 922 N.E.2d 906 [2010]), and now affirm.

II

Though the complaint relies on various legal theories, they can all be boiled down to a claim for breach of fiduciary duty. In **1122 ***483 the absence of an allegation that Wells Fargo misrepresented any fact to its customers, or that it did anything to cause actual injury to the customers' interests, the case rests on the rule that one acting as a fiduciary in a particular transaction may not receive, in connection with that transaction, undisclosed compensation from persons with whom the principal's interests may be in conflict (see generally EBC I, Inc. v. Goldman, Sachs & Co., 5 N.Y.3d 11, 19-22, 799 N.Y.S.2d 170, 832 N.E.2d 26 [2005]). The rule is a sound one in general, but we conclude that it does not apply here.

Wells Fargo, relying on Murphy v. Kuhn, 90 N.Y.2d 266, 660 N.Y.S.2d 371, 682 N.E.2d 972 (1997), asserts that we have already decided the fiduciary duty issue in its favor. We said in Murphy:

"Generally, the law is reasonably settled on initial principles that insurance agents have a common-law duty to obtain requested coverage for their clients within a reasonable time or inform the client of the inability to do so; however, they have no continuing duty to advise, guide or direct a client to obtain additional coverage" (id. at 270, 660 N.Y.S.2d 371, 682 N.E.2d 972).

We agree with the Attorney General that Wells Fargo reads Murphy too broadly. Murphy did not imply that insurance brokers are exempt from the general rule that an agent owes a duty of loyalty to its principal. Even if it had no duty to give *171 advice, Wells Fargo clearly could not give advice in bad faith—it could not, for example, advise a customer to buy coverage that Wells Fargo knew to be inferior, in exchange for an under-the-table payment to

Wells Fargo from the insurer. But this complaint does not allege that Wells Fargo did anything of that kind. Indeed, the complaint alleges nothing that breached Wells Fargo's duty of loyalty, unless it was a breach of that duty to enter into undisclosed incentive arrangements with insurance companies.

In arguing that it was, the Attorney General relies on three propositions: that an insurance broker is the agent of the insured (see Security Mut. Ins. Co. of N.Y. v. Acker-Fitzsimons Corp., 31 N.Y.2d 436, 442 n. 3, 340 N.Y.S.2d 902, 293 N.E.2d 76 [1972]); that a principal-agent relationship is, by nature, a fiduciary relationship (see Sokoloff v. Harriman Estates Dev. Corp., 96 N.Y.2d 409, 416, 729 N.Y.S.2d 425, 754 N.E.2d 184 [2001]; Restatement [Third] of Agency § 1.01); and that a fiduciary must disclose to its principal any interest in a particular transaction that causes the fiduciary's loyalties to be divided (Dubbs v. Stribling & Assoc., 96 N.Y.2d 337, 340-341, 728 N.Y.S.2d 413, 752 N.E.2d 850 [2001]). There is truth in all these propositions, but the relationship between an insurance broker and a purchaser of insurance is not as simple as the Attorney General suggests. A broker is the agent of the insured, but it customarily looks for compensation to the insurer, not the insured, and it is sometimes the insurer's agent also—for example, when collecting premiums. We have thus referred to the broker's "dual agency status" (Bohlinger v. Zanger, 306 N.Y. 228, 230, 117 N.E.2d 338 [1954]). Indeed, the word "broker" suggests an intermediary—not someone with undivided loyalty to one or the other side of the transaction.

Recognizing the complexity of an insurance broker's role, several Appellate Division cases hold that such a broker need not disclose to its customers contractual arrangements it has made with insurance companies (People v. Liberty Mut. Ins. Co., 52 A.D.3d 378, 861 N.Y.S.2d 294 [1st Dept. 2008]; Hersch v. DeWitt Stern Group, Inc., 43 A.D.3d 644, 645, 841 N.Y.S.2d 516 [1st Dept. 2007]; **1123 ***484 Wender v. Gilberg Agency, 304 A.D.2d 311, 757 N.Y.S.2d 286 [1st Dept. 2003]). We agree that such disclosure is not normally required—and if there are exceptions to that rule, this case does not present one. The complaint does not allege that anything Wells Fargo did was contrary to industry custom; indeed, the parties seem to agree that arrangements like those the Attorney General complains of have been commonplace, and have not generally been disclosed.

This nondisclosure may be a bad practice. Indeed, it is prohibited by a recently adopted regulation of the Insurance *172 Department, but that regulation did not exist at the time of the conduct at issue here (see 11 NYCRR 30.3[a][2] [eff. Jan. 1, 2011] [requiring disclosure to a purchaser of insurance if a broker "will receive compensation from the selling insurer... based in whole or in part on the insurance contract" that the broker sells]). A regulation, prospective in effect, is a much better way of ending a questionable but common practice than what the Attorney General asks us to do here: in substance to outlaw the practice retroactively by creating a new common-law rule.

Accordingly, the order of the Appellate Division should be affirmed, with costs.

第三节 保险机构

一、中国的保险机构

根据中国《保险法》的规定，中国的保险机构主要包括两类：一类是直接提供保险服务的保险公司；另一类是保险中介机构，包括保险代理人、保险经纪人以及保险公估机构。

（一）保险公司

在中国，设立保险公司应当符合一定的条件并经中国保监会批准。中国保监会在审查保险公司的设立申请时，应当考虑保险业的发展和公平竞争的需要。

保险公司应当在中国保监会依法批准的业务范围内从事保险经营活动，包括人身保险业务和财产保险业务（但不得兼营二者）。除此之外，经中国保监会批准，保险公司还可以经营再保险业务，包括分出保险和分入保险。

除了从事保险经营活动外，保险公司还可以通过多方式运用保险资金，从事其他经营活动。当然，为了保障保险公司的偿付能力，保险公司的资金运用必须稳健，遵循安全性原则。保险公司的资金运用限于下列形式：（1）银行存款；（2）买卖债券、股票、证券投资基金份额等有价证券；（3）投资不动产；（4）国务院规定的其他资金运用形式。经中国保监会会同中国证监会批准，保险公司还可以设立保险资产管理公司，保险资产管理公司可根据中国《证券法》的规定从事证券投资活动。

由于保险公司的经营，牵涉到诸多被保险人或受益人的利益，因此，中国对保险公司的经营设定了多项有别于一般公司的要求：（1）最低偿付能力的维持。保险公司应当具有与其业务规模和风险程度相适应的最低偿付能力。保险公司的认可资产减去认可负债的差额不得低于中国保监会规定的数额；低于规定数额的，应当按照中国保监会的要求采取相应措施达到规定的数额。（2）保证金。保险公司应当按照其注册资本总额的一定比例提取保证金，存入中国保监会指定的银行，除公司清算时用于清偿债务外，不得动用。（3）保险公积金。保险公司应当依法提取公积金。（4）保险准备金。保险公司应当根据保障被保险人利益、保证偿付能力的原则，提取各项责任准备金。（5）保险保障基金。保险公司应当缴纳保险保障基金。

中国《保险法》还对保险公司的风险管理进行了规定：（1）自留保险费。经营财产保险业务的保险公司当年自留保险费，不得超过其实有资本金加公积金总和的四倍。（2）承包责任的限制。保险公司对每一危险单位，即对一次保险事故可能造成的最大损失范围所承担的责任，不得超过其实有资本金加公积金总和的 10%；超过的部分应当办理再保险。（3）再保险。保险公司应当按照中国保监会的规定办理再保险，并审慎选择再保险接受人。

（二）保险中介机构

保险中介机构是在保险经营机构之间以及保险金融机构与投保人之间，专门从事保险业务咨询与销售、风险管理与安排、价值衡量与评估、损失鉴定与理算等中介服务活动的单位或个人，其主要包括保险代理机构、保险经纪人以及保险公估机构等。

保险代理机构是根据保险人的委托，向保险人收取佣金，并在保险人授权的范围内代为办理保险业务的机构。保险代理机构包括专门从事保险代理业务的保险专业代理机构和兼营保险代理业务的保险兼业代理机构。其中，保险专业代理机构应当采取有限责任公司或股份有限公司的组织形式，其经营范围包括：代理销售保险产品；代理收取保险费用；代理相关保险业务的损失勘查和理赔以及中国保监会批准的其他业务。

保险经纪人是基于投保人的利益，为投保人与保险人订立保险合同提供中介服务，并依法收取佣金的有限责任公司。再保险经纪人是指基于原保险人利益，为原保险人与再保险人安排分出、分入业务提供中介服务，并依法收取佣金的有限责任公司。保险经纪人经营保险中介业务，需要得到中国人民银行批准。经批准的，保险经纪人可以经营如下业务：（1）以订立保险合同为目的，为投保人提供防灾、防损或风险评估、风险管理咨询服务；（2）以订立保险合同为目的，为投保人拟定投保方案、办理投保手续；（3）为被保险人或受益人代办检验、索赔；（4）为被保险人或受益人向保险人索赔；（5）安排国内分入、分出业务；（6）安排国际分出、分入业务等。

保险公估机构是指接受委托，专门从事保险标的或者保险事故评估、勘验、鉴定、估损理算等业务，并按约定收取报酬的机构。在中国，保险公估机构应采取有限责任公司、股份有限公司或者合伙企业的组织形式，其经营业务包括：保险标的承保前后的检验、股价及风险评估；保险标的出险后的查勘、检验、估损理算及出险保险标的残值处理；风险管理咨询以及中国保监会批准的其他业务等。

二、美国的保险机构

（一）保险公司

在美国，经营保险业务的保险人主要是各式各样的保险公司。设立保险公司，必须向所在州的保险监管部门提出申请并获得其批准。州保险监管部门对申请人提交的文件进行审查，认为符合要求的将签发经营许可证书。美国的保险公司可以跨州设立分支公司，但分支机构须获得所在州的许可证方能开展业务。获得许可后，保险公司可以在该州经营法律规定的广泛的保险业务。

美国各州对保险公司往往有着严格的限制：第一，在保险公司形式方面，美国保险人的标准组织形式是股份公司和互助保险公司；第二，在保险公司所有权控制上，半数以上的州规定不能批准由外国政府拥有或控制保险人，或任何外国或本州外地保险人控制保险人；第三，美国对保险人有着严格的资金来源要求，各州均要求在本州新成立的保险公司，必须具有一定的最低数额的资本流入额，或者在互助公司的情况下，要满足最低数额的盈余（surplus），它们必须一直保持法律所要求的水平；第四，美国几乎所有的州都有报复性规定，它一般针对州外的或外国的保险公司，除了每个公司都要符合的条件和要求外，如果州外和外国保险公司所属地方的法律对保险公司有额外的要求、收费或税收，那么州外和外国的保险公司在本州也要受这些额外要求的规范。除此之外，美国各州的保险规范还对州外保险人（foreign insurers）和外国保险人（alien insurers）都设立了相应的特别准则。

保险公司获准在州内经营后，其经营行为受到该州保险监管部门的持续监管。监管部门采取的监管方式主要是报告和检查。每个保险公司都必须向其开展业务的州保险监管部门呈递年度报告，报告内容包括详细的财务状况，如资产、负债、储备、投资、赔付等。州保险监管部门还定期对保险公司进行现场检查。如果州保险监管部门认为有必要，还可以随时对辖区内的任何一家保险公司进行检查。

在美国，保险公司由各州自行监管，包括保险公司的破产，亦是如此。关于保险公司重组和清算的条款已成为州保险法标准组成部分。在保险公司破产时，为了确保被保险人能得到合理的偿付，各州纷纷采用保险人破产保证基金制度，由相关基金会替破产的保险人对保险索赔进行赔付。最后的赤字由其他所有获得许可经营的保险人，以特别股价的形式或以预先基金捐款的方式承担。大多数州对寿险和非寿险分别设立了基金，有的州还有为人工赔偿和车险设立的特别破产基金。①

（二）保险中介

美国的保险中介机构主要为保险代理人和保险经纪人，还包括其他的保险中介。

保险代理人是美国保险中介市场的中心角色，根据保险公司的授权，代理保险公司推销保单和收取保费，在某些情况下还享有签发保险单的权力，有时甚至可以修改保险合同的条款（特别是在财产保险和责任保险领域）。

---

① 哈威尔·E·杰克逊，小爱德华·L·西蒙斯. 金融监管. 吴志攀，等，译. 北京：中国政法大学出版社，2003：429.

在美国，保险代理人必须通过相应的考试以获取专业资格。获得专业资格后，经申请获得执照，方可在该州执业。按保险代理人代表保险公司数量的多寡，美国有专业代理人与独立代理人之分。独立代理人具有独立的地位，可同时为几家保险公司代理业务而不受利益冲突的限制；专业代理人则只能为一家保险公司或某一保险集团代理业务。保险人必须承担代理人在授权范围内的行为所带来的责任，因此保险人会发出各种通告来使代理人全面了解其权力和责任，同时通过代理合同来加强对保险代理人的管理。

同保险代理人一样，保险经纪人也是从保险公司处获取佣金，但是保险经纪人是作为投保人（或者是被保险人）的代表促成保险合同的订立，这是保险经纪人区别于保险代理人的主要之处。在美国，大多数州的法律要求保险经纪人要通过规定的资格考试，并申请执照方可在该州执业。保险经纪人主要活跃于财产险领域，介入寿险领域较少，在一些州（如纽约州）有规定，保险经纪人不得办理人寿保险和年金保险业务。

除此之外，在美国，保险中介还包括诸如保险公估人、保险事故调查机构和保险律师等。但其中较有特色的还属保险评级机构。保险评级机构在为保险客户和保险公司提供信息服务以及完善保险市场和监管、促进保险业的公平竞争等方面都发挥着重大作用。在美国，保险评级机构的主要功能在于，通过对保险公司的财务信息进行审查，给各个保险公司评定等级，等级越高，该保险公司的安全性越高。保险评级机构的工作，一方面为消费者购买保险提供了选择依据和便利；另一方面也为保险公司的市场营销提供了广告效应，同时还能督促一些评级不高的保险公司改善经营。

三、案例资料

在美国，除了提供保险服务的保险公司（insurer/underwriter）之外，保险机构还包括被称为保险销售人（producer）的机构。保险销售人是行业术语，是指代保险代理人（insurance agent）和保险经纪人（insurance broker）。保险代理人和保险经纪人，虽然都从事保险销售活动，但是二者的法律地位有很大的差异：保险代理人作为保险人的代理人以保险人的名义行事，而保险经纪人则代表被保险人为其与保险人订立保险合同提供中介服务。

在下面的 In the Matter of American Reliable Insurance Company 案中，American Reliable 是一家保险公司，Cabrillo 为其保险总代理商，而 Superior Access 则是其保险分销商（sub-producer）。

加州保险监理官通过分析 Superior Access 的相关行为及其与 American Reliable 之间的关系，认定 Superior Access 是 American Reliable 的保险代理人而非保险经纪人。因此，Superior Access 的行为将被视为 American Reliable 的行为。由于 Superior Access 违规收取了除核准的保险费之外的额外费用，American Reliable 应对 Superior Access 的违规行

为承担责任。因此，加州保险监理官对 American Reliable 作出相应的处罚，责令 American Reliable 改正违规行为，并对其处以罚金。

该案中，Superior Access 的身份是关键因素。如果加州保险监理官认定 Superior Access 是 American Reliable 的保险经纪人而非保险代理人，那么案件的结果就完全不一样了。

In the Matter of American Reliable Insurance Company

DECISION AND ORDER File No.: DISP 06091926

BEFORE THE INSURANCE COMMISSIONER OF THE STATE OF CALIFORNIA.

This matter came before the Commissioner pursuant to a Notice of Noncompliance and Order to Show Cause ("Pleading") served on Respondent by the Department of Insurance on May 9, 2006. The parties executed a Special Notice of Defense, pursuant to which the Commissioner hereby makes the following findings of fact and conclusions of law, and issues this Decision and Order.

Respondent American Reliable at all relevant times has been an insurer licensed by the Department to transact insurance in this state.

Cabrillo General Insurance Agency, Inc. at all relevant times has been a general agent of American Reliable, authorized to accept insurance applications on American Reliable's behalf, and to enter into agreements with subproducers to write insurance with American Reliable.

Superior Access Insurance Services is a California licensed fire and casualty broker-agent and "producer" of insurance. The word "producer" is an industry term of art that refers to both insurance agents and insurance brokers. Insurance agents and insurance brokers both transact insurance by soliciting, negotiating, and/or executing insurance contracts. However, insurance agents (as defined in sections 31 and 1621)[1] differ from insurance brokers (as defined in sections 33 and 1623).[2] A producer acts as an insurance agent if it transacts insurance on behalf of an insurer, even if it also transacts on behalf of an insured. A producer acts as an insurance broker if it transacts insurance on behalf of the insured but not on behalf of the insurance company.[3] Whether a producer is an agent or a broker depends on the nature of the producer's relationship with the insurance company with which the producer places a particular client.

Under section 1731[4], a producer acts as an insurance agent in a particular transaction when it is appointed as an agent of an insurer pursuant to section 1704.[5] A producer also acts as an insurance agent in a particular transaction when it should be appointed as an agent, even if it is not appointed. A producer should be appointed as an agent of an insurer if the producer would be deemed an agent of that insurer under common law, i.e., if the producer represents or acts on behalf of the insurer. A producer represents or acts on behalf of an insurer, inter alia, whenever: the insurer has given the producer discretion to issue insurance binders; the insurer has obtained the producer's express or tacit agreement to apply specific underwriting or rating factors before submitting applications to the insurer; the insurer has directed or controlled the producer in any respect or reserved the right to do so; the insurer has permitted the producer to display the insurer's name or logo on the producer's signage, stationery or business cards in a manner that implies ostensible agency; the insurer refers potential or existing insureds to the producer; the insurer refers the producer to potential or existing insureds; the insurer attempts to control the licensee's conduct by disciplining the licensee (other than by terminating), or maintaining the right to discipline him, for failing to follow the insurer's rules or for failing to meet production standards; the insurer provides the same or substantially similar training to supposed brokers as to any appointed agents; the relationship between the producer and the insurer is functionally indistinguishable from the relationship between the insurer and its appointed agents; the producer has placed the insurer's interests above that of the insured and the insurer has accepted the benefits thereof; the insurer has incentivized the producer to act on the insurer's behalf by promising to provide compensation contingent upon the producer meeting a premium volume threshold, loss ratio or level of profitability. Superior Access has transacted insurance with American Reliable as American Reliable's agent.

Superior Access arguably had written binding authority from American Reliable. Binding authority is a dispositive indicium of an agency relationship.

The underwriting of insurance applications is a function that is always performed by insurers or agents of insurers. For obvious reasons, an insurer does not want, and no insurer has ever allowed, applicants for insurance to underwrite themselves.

When an insurer provides its underwriting criteria or guidelines to a producer, solicits or instructs the producer to apply that criteria to applications, and expressly or implicitly asks or incentivizes the producer to submit compliant applications to it (or not to submit noncompliant applications to it), the insurer thereby asks the producer to perform an insurer function, and thus to act on behalf of the insurer. When a producer acts on behalf of an insurer in a transaction, the producer acts as an agent of the insurer pursuant to sections 31 and 1631 and general agency law.

American Reliable, via Cabrillo, provided its underwriting guidelines to Superior Access, instructed Superior Access to apply those criteria to applications, and directed and incentivized Superior Access to submit compliant applications to it and not to submit noncompliant applications to it. American Reliable, via Cabrillo, thereby asked Superior Access to perform an insurer function, and thus to act on behalf of American Reliable. Consequently, Superior Access was American Reliable's agent.

In any transaction involving three parties, an intermediary between the other two parties is deemed to be the agent of any party that directs or controls the intermediary. If the intermediary is subject to the direction and control of both other parties, the intermediary is a dual agent. Pursuant to sections 31 and 1631, a dual agent is deemed to be an insurance agent, not an insurance broker. American Reliable, via Cabrillo, directed and controlled Superior Access with respect transactions of insurance by Superior Access with American Reliable. Superior Access therefore acted as an agent of American Reliable.

One factor that can establish agency is the frequency and regularity of the relationship between the producer and the insurer.

> A broker is, in essence, employed in each instance as a special agent for a single purpose, while the very definition of agent indicates an ongoing and continuous relationship.... [B]rokers and insureds are ordinarily involved in what can be viewed as a series of discrete transactions, while agents and insurers tend to be under some duty to each other during the entire length of the relationship. 3 Couch on Insurance (3d ed. 1997) § 45:1, pp. 45-3 to 45-4, fns. omitted.

Superior Access had an ongoing and continuous relationship with American Reliable via Cabrillo, and was thus an agent of American Reliable, rather than a broker for the insured.

A producer may not charge or collect a fee in addition to the premium for placing insurance with an insurer for which the producer is acting as an insurance agent. This prohibition derives from several legal principles:

(a) Under California case law, all money received by an insurance agent for a transaction of insurance is deemed constructively received by the insurer, i.e., the money is considered premium.

(b) Property and casualty premium rates must be approved by the Department, per section 1861.01 (c) (sections 11735 (a) and (c) for workers' compensation policies). When a fee that is in addition to the premium (i.e., which fee has not been approved by the Department as part of an insurer's rate filing) is received by an agent and imputed to the insurer, the insurer effectively will have charged and collected more premium than permitted under its approved rate.

(c) Property and casualty premium rates may not be unfairly discriminatory, per section 1861.05 (a). When one agent charges and collects a fee, and another agent of the same insurer selling the same type of policy either charges and collects no fee or a different fee, the insurer effectively will have charged unfairly discriminatory rates.

(d) Insurance premium is taxable by the State. When an agent collects a fee, and that fee is not reported as premium by the insurer for which the agent was acting, the insurer will fail to pay its proper premium tax.

From at least September 2003, American Reliable permitted Superior Access, while acting as American Reliable's agent, to collect fees from American Reliable policyholders. These fees were in addition to the premium American Reliable was entitled to charge based on its approved rates. American Reliable constructively received the fees, which fees are therefore premium. American Reliable did not receive the Department's prior approval to collect or have Superior Access collect these fees.

By permitting Superior Access to charge and collect fees, American Reliable constructively charged and collected premium in excess of the premium permitted under the rate filings approved for it by the Department, in violation of section 1861.01 (c).

Because Superior Access charged fees while other American Reliable agents did not, for policies subject to the same rate, rating plan or rating system, American Reliable insureds were subjected to unfair rate discrimination, in violation of section 1861.05 (a). American Reliable willfully or negligently permitted the rate discrimination to occur.

The above findings establish that American Reliable used a rate, rating plan or rating system in violation of Chapter 9 of Part 2 of Division 1 of the Insurance Code, and provide grounds for a fine of $5 000 for each policy in which Respondents permitted a fee to be charged by Superior Access, pursuant to section 1858.07 (a).

The above findings establish that American Reliable has conducted its business and affairs in a manner that is hazardous to policyholders and the public, and constitute grounds for the Commissioner to issue an Order, pursuant to sections 1065.1 and/or 1065.3, requiring Respondents to:

a. Exercise due diligence to prevent its agents from charging a fee for a transaction of insurance;
b. Reimburse the Department $5 000 for its costs in investigating and prosecuting this matter;
c. Refund all fees illegally collected by Superior Access and constructively received by American Reliable;

ORDER

Respondent is ordered to:

a. Use due diligence to assure that none of its agents charges a fee for a transaction of insurance;
b. Pay the Department $5 000 to reimburse it for its costs in investigating and prosecuting this matter, pursuant to the Special Notice of Defense;
c. Pay the Department $10 000 as a monetary penalty, pursuant to the Special Notice of Defense;
d. Refund all fees collected by Superior Access associated with the placement of a policy with Respondent, in accordance with the agreement contained in Special Notice of Defense;
e. Otherwise comply with the Special Notice of Defense.

(Footnote omitted)

第四节 保险业务

一、中国的保险业务

在中国，保险业属于特许行业。依据中国《保险法》的规定，保险业务由依法设立的保险公司以及法律、行政法规规定的其他保险组织经营，其他单位和个人不得经营保险业务。

在中国，保险业务主要包括人身保险业务（包括人寿保险、健康保险、意外伤害保险等保险业务）、财产保险业务（包括财产损失保险、责任保险、信用保险、保证保险等保险业务）。中国《保险法》规定，保险人不得兼营人身保险业务和财产保险业务。但是，经营财产保险业务的保险公司经中国保监会批准，可以经营短期健康保险业务和意外伤害保险业务。

保险公司开展业务，应当遵循公平竞争的原则，不得从事不正当竞争。中国《保险法》明令禁止保险公司及其工作人员在保险业务活动中从事下列行为：（1）欺骗投保人、被保险人或者受益人；（2）对投保人隐瞒与保险合同有关的重要情况；（3）阻碍投保人履行本法规定的如实告知义务，或者诱导其不履行本法规定的如实告知义务；（4）给予或者承诺给予投保人、被保险人、受益人保险合同约定以外的保险费回扣或者其他利益；（5）拒不依法履行保险合同约定的赔偿或者给付保险金义务；（6）故意编造未曾发生的保险事故、虚构保险合同或者故意夸大已经发生的保险事故的损失程度进行虚假理赔，骗取保险金或者牟取其他不正当利益；（7）挪用、截留、侵占保险费；（8）委托未取得合法资格的机构或者个人从事保险销售活动；（9）利用开展保险业务为其他机构或者个人牟取不正当利益；（10）利用保险代理人、保险经纪人或者保险评估机构，从事以虚构保险中介业务或者编造退保等方式套取费用等违法活动；（11）以捏造、散布虚假事实等方式损害竞争对手的商业信誉，或者以其他不正当竞争行为扰乱保险市场秩序；（12）泄露在业务活动中知悉的投保人、被保险人的商业秘密；（13）违反法律、行政法规和中国保监会规定的其他行为。

二、美国的保险业务

美国的保险业务分人寿与健康（包括人身事故）保险、财产与灾害保险两大类。针对个人和家庭的主要险种有：人寿、退休金、健康、汽车和住房。针对团体的主要险种有：火灾、员工工伤、产品责任、员工家庭成员健康、退休金。理论上，只要不违反公共政策的限制，任何与合法行为相关的风险，保险人都选择进行评估并给予保险。

美国保险业实行分业经营体制，这包括两方面的内容：一是保险业与其他金融行业的分业经营，二是寿险业与非寿险业的分业经营。首先，受制于 1933 年《格拉斯—斯蒂格尔法案》的限制，保险业不得进入其他金融领域，这一限制一直体现在各州的保险立法中。尽管《1999 年金融服务现代化法》提到了金融控股公司的概念，规定金融控股公司可以从事在性质上属于金融活动或辅助性金融活动以及补充性金融活动的业务（具体包括存贷款、保险、金融咨询服务以及证券业务等），也可收购并持有从事这些业务的公司的股份，但该法继续确认保险业务仍然由各州法律规范的体制。因此，保险公司进入其他金融领域，还是存在各种障碍。其次，就美国各州的保险法律来看，大部分法律都规定，寿险公司不得经营财产和责任保险业务，非寿险公司不得经营寿险业务，但都可兼营意外伤害和健康险业务。

在美国，跨州的商业活动一般由联邦政府管理，但保险业却是个例外。保险业在美国是由各州自行管理的，美国各州立法机关均制定保险法律，以规范保险公司、保险中介人等的保险经营活动，保障被保险人的合法权益，维持保险市场的健康、有序发展。在保险业务的开展过程中，保险公司及保险中介机构必须遵守所在州的保险法律及监管部门的监管要求。这些保险法律和监管要求通常都会规定如下的内容：保险公司或保险代理机构和保险经纪机构必须获得保险监管部门的批准和许可证之后方可在该州开展业务；保单销售过程中不得作误导性或欺骗性的陈述，不得用误导的手段引诱投保人放弃已经从其他公司购买到的保单而购买其推销的保单；禁止保险公司或保险中介机构向客户支付保单规定之外的回扣或其他好处；保险公司必须在时限之内对被保险人或第三方索赔人的索赔作出答复；等等。

除了各种市场行为受到州监管部门的监管之外，在保险价格的确定方面，保险公司同样要遵守州监管部门的监管要求。美国各州对保险价格进行监管，以维持保险价格处于适当的水平，即，既不能过低以免导致保险人破产，也不能过高而导致保险的可得性（availability）降低及被保险人利益损失。此外，在确定保险价格时，不得进行歧视，即相似的风险应有接近的价格，不得因肤色、种族、国籍和信仰等因素而给予歧视性的不同对待。为此，美国各州监管部门一般采取如下两种价格管理方式：（1）事先批准制，要求保险公司在使用某险种费率前应得到州监管部门的批准；（2）开放费率制，允许保险公司使用自己选择的费率，但使用后必须将费率在州监管部门备案，并允许监管部门随时废除任何正在使用的费率，这种方式既保留了保险公司享有的自由使用费率的权利，又保留了州监管部门的监管权利。

三、案例资料

政府对保险业务进行管理，是各国通行的做法。但是，政府对保险业务的管理与保险公司的经营之间往往存在冲突。如何平衡政府管理权限和保险公司经营权利，成为难题。在美国，这一问题可诉诸宪法予以解决。下面的 Calfarm Ins. Co. v. Deukmejian 案涉及政府对保险业务中保险费率等问题的干预所引发的争议。

在该案中，加利福尼亚州通过了一项法案，要求所有保险公司进行为期一年的不少于 20%的保险费率减免，禁止保险公司基于未缴纳保费、欺诈、危险显著增加以外的原因拒绝更新保单，同时要求保险公司告知其客户有权加入一个旨在保护被保险人利益的公益组织等。对此法案，保险公司请求法院判令其内容违反宪法。

法院经过分析比较，作出了如下三点判断：

首先，法案中关于保险监理官仅在保险公司面临破产危险的情况下才能批准提升保险费率的规定违反了宪法，因为保险公司无法在保险费率可能是惩罚性质的情形下寻求救济。同时，这种对于权利的限制也不属于临时措施，因为高昂的保险费用是日积月累而形成的，这个问题是通过强迫保险公司进行一年的利润返还无法解决的。但是，法案中关于保险费率减免的其他条款并不违反宪法，因为法案授予了保险监理官足够的权力，能够及时对保险公司提供救济。

其次，法案中关于对保险公司更新保单进行的限制并不违反宪法对合同义务的保护。因为保险公司仍然可以基于未缴纳保费、欺诈、危险显著增加的原因拒绝更新保单，与此同时，广大被保险人在新法案背景下所能获得的利益得到了有力保障，因此所实现的公共利益远大于对合同义务的损害。

最后，法案中要求保险公司向客户提供有权加入消费者组织的通知的规定违宪，因为州宪法禁止通过此类法案授予私人组织公共权力。

Calfarm Ins. Co. v. Deukmejian

48 Cal. 3d 805 (1989)

BROUSSARD, J.

In this case we consider various challenges to Proposition 103, an initiative measure enacted November 8, 1988, making numerous fundamental changes in the regulation of automobile and other types of insurance….

The initiative begins with a statement of findings and purpose, asserting that "[e]normous increases in the cost of insurance have made it both *813 unaffordable and **1250 unavailable to millions of Californians," and that "the existing laws inadequately protect consumers and allow insurance companies to charge excessive, unjustified and arbitrary rates." The initiative's stated purpose is to ensure that "insurance is fair, available, and affordable for all Californians."

Insurance rates are to be immediately reduced to "at least 20 percent less" than those in effect on November 8, 1987 (approximately the date when the initiative was proposed, and one year prior to its enactment). (§ 1861.01, subd. (a); all statutory references are to the Insurance Code, unless otherwise stated.) All rate increases require the approval of the Insurance Commissioner, who may not approve rates which are "excessive, inadequate, unfairly discriminatory or otherwise in violation of [the initiative]." (§ 1861.05.) Prior to November 8, 1989, however, rates may be increased only if the commissioner finds "that an insurer is substantially threatened with insolvency." (§ 1861.01, subd. (b).) Certain procedures are specified for hearing applications for rate approvals. (§§ 1861.04-1861.10.)

The initiative prohibits an insurer from declining to renew a policy except for nonpayment of premium, fraud, or significant increase in the hazard insured against. (§ 1861.03, subd. (c).) Insurers are required to mail notices to policy holders informing them they may join a nonprofit corporation to be formed to represent their interests by persons appointed for this purpose by the Insurance Commissioner. (§ 1861.10.)....

1. Provisions relating to the reduction and subsequent adjustment of insurance rates.

The constitutional test for the validity of state price controls was established in Nebbia v. New York (1934) 291 U.S. 502, 539, 54 S.Ct. 505, 517, 78 L.Ed. 940: "Price control, like any other form of regulation, is unconstitutional only if arbitrary, discriminatory, or demonstrably irrelevant to the policy the legislature is free to adopt, and hence an unnecessary and unwarranted interference with individual liberty." The United States Supreme Court reaffirmed this test in Pennell v. City of San Jose (1988) 485 U.S. 1, __, 108 S.Ct. 849, 857, 99 L.Ed.2d 1. We followed it in Birkenfeld v. City of Berkeley (1976) 17 Cal.3d 129, 130 Cal. Rptr. 465, 550 P.2d 1001, a rent control case, and went on to explain that "[t]he provisions are within the police power if they are reasonably calculated to eliminate excessive rents and at the same time provide landlords with a just and reasonable return on their property." (P. 165, 130 Cal. Rptr. 465, 550 P.2d 1001.)

The state and federal Constitutions are concerned not so much with the way in which the initial rates are set as with whether the rates as finally set are confiscatory. "[I]t is the result reached not the method employed which is controlling." (Power Comm'n v. Hope Gas Co. (1944) 320 U.S. 591, 602, 64 S.Ct. 281, 287, 88 L.Ed. 333; see Duquesne Light Co. v. Barasch (1989) 488 U.S. 299, 109 S.Ct. 609, 617, 102 L.Ed.2d 646.) In Fisher v. City of Berkeley (1984) 37 Cal.3d 644, 683, 209 Cal. Rptr. 682, 693 P.2d 261, we reaffirmed the rule that "whether a regulation produces a return that is confiscatory or fair depends ultimately on the result, and... we will invalidate an ordinance on its face only if its terms preclude avoidance of confiscatory results." Petitioners must show that the law is "so restrictive as to facially preclude any possibility of a just and reasonable return" (Hutton, supra, 350 A.2d 1, 16); that "its terms will not permit those who administer it to avoid confiscatory results" (Birkenfeld v. City of Berkeley, supra, 17 Cal.3d 129, 165, 130 Cal. Rptr. 465, 550 P.2d 1001).

Consequently, we focus less on the rate specified in the statute than on the ability of the seller to obtain relief if that rate proves confiscatory. The face of a statute rarely reveals whether the rates it specifies are confiscatory *817 or arbitrary, but necessarily ***167 **1253 discloses its provisions, if any, for rate adjustment....

[1] We therefore begin our discussion by considering the provisions in Proposition 103 which would permit an insurer to seek relief from any rate it considers confiscatory. Section 1861.05 provides that "[e]very insurer which desires to change any rate shall file a complete rate application with the commissioner." Subdivision (a) states that the commissioner may not approve or permit any rate "which is excessive, inadequate, unfairly discriminatory or otherwise in violation of this chapter"—language which makes it clear that the commissioner can grant relief from confiscatory rates. Section 1861.01, subdivision (b), however, qualifies section 1861.05 by limiting rate adjustments prior to November 1989 to insurers substantially threatened with insolvency. Petitioners attack the constitutionality of this limitation.

*818 Section 1861.01, subdivision (b), provides that "[b]etween November 8, 1988, and November 8, 1989, rates and premiums reduced pursuant to subdivision (a) may be only increased if the commissioner finds, after a hearing, that an insurer is substantially threatened with insolvency." "Insolvency" has various meanings, but none will allow us to construe subdivision (b) to conform to the constitutional standard of a fair and reasonable return. A company may be insolvent because it has more liabilities than assets, or because it is unable to pay its obligations as they fall due....

The insolvency standard of subdivision (b) refers to the financial position of the company as a whole, not merely to the regulated lines of insurance. Many insurers do substantial business outside of California, *819 or in lines of insurance within this state which are not regulated by Proposition 103. If an insurer had substantial net worth, or significant income from sources unregulated by Proposition 103, it might be able to sustain substantial and continuing losses on regulated insurance without danger of insolvency. In such a case the continued solvency of the insurer could not suffice to demonstrate that the regulated rate constitutes a fair return.

The effect of section 1861.01, subdivision (b), is thus to bar safely solvent insurers from obtaining relief from "inadequate" rates until November 1989. Temporary rates which might be below a fair and reasonable level might compel insurers to return to their customers surpluses exacted through allegedly excessive past rates. But the concept that rates may be set at less than a fair rate of return in order to compel the return of past surpluses is not one supported by precedent. "The just compensation safeguarded to the utility by the Fourteenth Amendment is a reasonable return on the value of the property used at the time that it is being used for the public service.... [T]he law does not require the company to give up for the benefit of future subscribers any part of its accumulations from past operations. Profits of the past cannot be used to sustain confiscatory rates for the future." (Board of Comm'rs v. N.Y. Tel. Co., supra, 271 U.S. 23, 31-32, 46 S.Ct. 363, 366, 70 L.Ed. 808; accord, American Toll Bridge Co. v. Railroad Com. (1938) 12 Cal.2d 184, 203, 83 P.2d 1.) Hutton, supra, said that if past rents were excessive an ordinance could refuse to give landlords credit for current cost increases if the diminished rate of return was still just and reasonable. (350 A.2d at p. 16.) But no case supports an unreasonably low rate of return on the ground that past profits were excessive.

Proponents urge that the insolvency standard can be sustained as a temporary or emergency measure. They point out that temporary freezes while administrative machinery is set up are commonly approved, even if they lack any method whereby a seller can get relief. (See, e.g., Trans Alaska Pipeline Rate Cases (1978) 436 U.S. 631, 98 S.Ct. 2053, 56 L.Ed.2d 591; United States v. SCRAP (1973) 412 U.S. 669, 93 S.Ct. 2405, 37 L.Ed.2d 254; Western States Meat Packers Assn., Inc. v. Dunlop (T.E.C.A.1973) 482 F.2d 1401.) Most freezes are for periods of much less than one year, but courts have sustained freezes of a year or longer. (See, e.g., ***169 Mass. Med. Society v. Comm'r of Ins. (1988) 402 Mass. 44, 520 N.E.2d 1288 [two-year freeze on medical malpractice insurance rates].) The cases, however, proceed *820 on the assumption that the frozen prices were those set by a seller in a competitive market, and thus were fair rates, so that **1255 the only concern is increased costs during the freeze. (See discussion in Birkenfeld v. City of Berkeley, supra, 17 Cal.3d 129, 166, 130 Cal. Rptr. 465, 550 P.2d 1001.) Here we have a law which mandates not maintenance of a rate set by the seller, but a reduction to at least 20 percent less than former rates. The risk that the rate set by the statute is confiscatory as to some insurers from its inception is high enough to require an adequate method for obtaining individualized relief.

Proponents further argue that the insolvency standard in Proposition 103 was inserted to combat an emergency created by unavailable and unaffordable insurance. They assert that between 1983 and 1986 automobile insurance rates doubled, while commercial rates increased over 200 percent. They observe also that in 1984 the Legislature enacted the Robins-McAlister Financial Responsibility Act (Stats.1984, ch. 1322), requiring all motorists to purchase liability insurance and carry proof of financial responsibility.

We recognize that emergency situations may require emergency measures. As the court explained in Hutton, a rent control case, "[t]he term 'confiscatory' must be understood in light of the surrounding circumstances. There are undoubtedly times of great public exigency during which landlords may temporarily be required to rent their property at rates which do not permit them to obtain what would ordinarily be considered a fair return." (350 A.2d at p. 13.) Numerous cases confirm that measures enacted to combat an emergency of limited duration may be valid even though they do not guarantee a fair rate of return....

To justify a measure which deprives persons of a fair return, however, "an emergency would have to be a temporary situation of such enormity *821 that all individuals might reasonably be required to make sacrifices for the common weal." (Hutton, 350 A.2d 1, 14.) We do not believe that the circumstances which inspired Proposition 103 meet this requirement. Our concern is not with the magnitude of the problem, but with its character. The asserted rise in insurance rates, rendering insurance unavailable or unaffordable to many, is not a temporary problem; it is a long term, chronic situation which will not be solved by compelling insurers to sell at less than a fair return for a year. Over the long term the state must permit insurers a fair return; we do not perceive any short term conditions that would require depriving them of a fair return. We therefore conclude that subdivision (b) cannot be sustained ***170 as a emergency measure fashioned to meet a temporary exigency.

Having determined that section 1861.01, subdivision (b), precludes adjustments necessary to achieve the constitutional standard of fair and reasonable rates, and that the subdivision cannot be sustained as a temporary or emergency measure, we hold **1256 it invalid under the due process clauses of the state and federal Constitutions....

The invalidation of this subdivision leaves untouched the general standard for rate adjustment set out in section 1861.05, subdivision (a). That provision states that "[n]o rate shall be approved or remain in effect which is excessive, inadequate, unfairly discriminatory, or otherwise in violation of this chapter. In considering whether a rate is excessive, inadequate or unfairly discriminatory no consideration shall be given to the degree of competition and the commissioner shall consider whether the rate mathematically reflects the insurance company's investment income."

Petitioners raise no question of the constitutionality of rates set pursuant to that section. Its prohibition on excessive or inadequate rates echoes similar language in the laws of most states, as well as former ***171 section 1852 which it replaces. Since a confiscatory rate is necessarily an "inadequate" rate under the statutory language, section 1861.05 requires rates **1257 within *823 that range which can be described as fair and reasonable and prohibits approval or maintenance of confiscatory rates....

[5] Petitioners argue, however, that even if section 1861.05 provides a constitutionally valid standard for rate adjustment, insurers will be compelled to charge confiscatory rates pending administrative relief. They compare the procedures established by Proposition 103 with those in Birkenfeld v. City of Berkeley, supra, 17 Cal.3d 129, 130 Cal. Rptr. 465, 550 P.2d 1001, where we invalidated a rent control ordinance because "the inexcusably cumbersome rent adjustment procedure" was "not reasonably related to [its] stated purpose of preventing excessive rents." (P. 173, 130 Cal. Rptr. 465, 550 P.2d 1001.)

The city ordinance at issue in Birkenfeld governed rents for about 22 000 units. (17 Cal.3d at p. 169, 130 Cal. Rptr. 465, 550 P.2d 1001.) No landlord could apply for a rent increase for *824 any unit until he had obtained a certificate of compliance from the city building inspector. (P. 170, 130 Cal. Rptr. 465, 550 P.2d 1001.) Every application required a hearing, regardless of the size of the increase, the reason for the request, or the consent of the tenant. (P. 171, 130 Cal. Rptr. 465, 550 P.2d 1001.) The rent control board was required to hear each application personally; it could not consolidate applications or delegate the task to a hearing officer. (Ibid.) "In short, [the board was] denied the means of reducing its job to manageable proportions through the formulation and application of general rules, the appropriate delegation of responsibility, and the focusing of the adjudicative ***172 process upon issues which cannot fairly be resolved in any other way." (Ibid.)

We find no similar barriers to efficient decision making in Proposition 103. It does not establish a detailed method of processing and deciding rate applications....

Moreover, the commissioner has the power to grant interim relief from plainly invalid rates. Her powers are not limited to those expressly conferred by statute;....

In short, any insurer who believes the rates set by section 1861.01, subdivision (a), are confiscatory may file an application with the Insurance Commissioner for approval of a higher rate. If that application is filed before November 8, 1989, the insurer may immediately begin charging that higher rate pending approval from the commissioner. After that date insurance rates subject to Proposition 103 must be approved by the commissioner prior to their use, but, as we have explained, the commissioner can approve an interim rate pending her final decision. If the commissioner ***173 finds the initiative's rate, or some other rate less than the insurer charged, is fair and reasonable, the insurer must refund excess premiums collected with interest. No insurer, however, will be compelled to charge the rates set by the initiative unless it either acquiesces in that rate or is unable to prove that a higher rate is **1259 constitutionally required. In view of these safeguards we conclude that the initiative provision requiring a reduction in rate to at least 20 percent below 1987 rates does not, on its face, violate the due process rights of insurers.

In summary, we have concluded (a) that section 1861.01, subdivision (b), limiting first-year-rate adjustments to insurers substantially threatened with insolvency, is facially invalid…; (b) that the procedures for adjustment of *826 insurance rates—including application to the commissioner, the opportunity to seek interim relief, a hearing in accordance with the Administrative Procedure Act, and judicial review—meet constitutional standards; and (c) that in view of the safeguards described in this opinion, the rate rollback and reduction of Proposition 103 is not invalid on its face, but the rates thereby established are necessarily subject to the right of an insurer to demonstrate that a particular rate is, as applied to it, a confiscatory rate.

2. Restrictions upon the insurers' right to refuse to renew policies.

Proposition 103, in section 1861.03, subdivision (c) [hereafter non-renewal provision], provides: "Notwithstanding any other provision of law, a notice of cancellation or non-renewal of a policy for automobile insurance shall be effective only if it is based on one or more of the following reasons: (1) nonpayment of premiums; (2) fraud or material misrepresentation affected the policy or insured; (3) a substantial increase in the hazard insured against." Before enactment of Proposition 103 insurers had an unfettered right to refuse to renew policies (see Greene v. Safeco Ins. Co. (1983) 140 Cal. App.3d 535, 538, 189 Cal. Rptr. 616).

Respondent Attorney General and proponents contend that the non-renewal provision applies to policies issued before enactment of Proposition 103. Petitioners agree that the provision was intended to apply to policies in force when Proposition 103 was enacted but maintain that the application of this provision to such policies would in effect alter their terms, and thereby violate the constitutional prohibition against a "law impairing the obligation of contracts." (U.S. Const., art. I, § 10; see Cal. Const., art. I, § 9.)

…

We begin by assessing the severity of the impairment, since that assessment "measures the height of the hurdle the state legislation must clear" (Allied Structural Steel v. Spannaus, supra, 438 U.S. 234, 245, 98 S.Ct. 2716, 2723), then examine the public interest advanced to justify the impairment.

[7] In the present case the impairment, while not so low as to escape constitutional scrutiny, is relatively moderate and restrained, and the hurdle correspondingly low. The insurer

may still refuse to renew policies for nonpayment of premium, fraud or misrepresentation, or substantial increase in the hazard insured against. And when it renews pursuant to Proposition 103 it is guaranteed fair and reasonable rates.

Insurance, moreover, is a highly regulated industry, and one in which further regulation can reasonably be anticipated. As we said in Carpenter v. Pacific Mut. Life Ins. Co. (1937) 10 Cal.2d 307, 74 P.2d 761: "It is no longer open to question that the business of insurance is affected with a public interest.... Neither the company nor a policyholder has the inviolate rights that characterize private contracts. The contract of the policyholder is subject to the reasonable exercise of the state's police power." (P. 329, 74 P.2d 761; see *831 People v. United National Life Ins. Co. (1967) 66 Cal.2d 577, 595, 58 Cal. Rptr. 599, 427 P.2d 199 and cases there cited.) Indeed it is clear that during the year prior to November 8, 1988—a year during which almost all automobile insurance policies in effect on that date were issued or renewed—insurers were well aware of the possibility that initiatives or ordinary legislation might be enacted that would affect existing policies.

Finally, Proposition 103 does not prevent an insurer from discontinuing its California business. Sections 1070 through 1076 spell out the procedure by which an insurer may withdraw from California by surrendering its certificate of authority. The initiative did not repeal those sections, and indeed recognizes the possibility that insurers may withdraw from some insurance markets by ***177 authorizing the commissioner to establish a joint underwriting authority to serve such markets. (§ 1861.11, quoted in fn. 21, ante.)

We turn now to examine the public interest to determine whether it justifies the impairment. As we noted earlier, the drafters and the voters were evidently concerned that the enactment of Proposition **1263 103 might cause some insurers not to renew some or all of their existing policies, an action which would undermine Proposition 103's goal of making insurance "available" for all Californians. Indeed if many insurers refused to renew the state could face a crisis in which many of its residents would be unable to obtain insurance and thus could not legally drive, and others would be forced to accept inadequate protection. We conclude that the public interest in averting this danger, when measured against the relatively low degree of impairment of contract rights involved, is sufficient to justify Proposition 103's non-renewal provision, and accordingly that this provision can be applied to existing policies without violating the state or federal Constitutions.

3. Notice of formation of a consumer-advocacy corporation.

Section 1861.10, subdivision (c), provides for the creation of a consumer-advocacy corporation, and notice to all California policyholders of their opportunity to become members of the corporation. It reads in full as follows: "(1) The commissioner shall require every insurer to enclose notices in every policy or renewal premium bill informing policyholders of the opportunity to join an independent, non-profit corporation which shall advocate the interests of insurance consumers in any forum. This organization shall be established by an interim board of public members designated by the commissioner and operated by individuals who are democratically elected from its membership. The corporation shall proportionately reimburse insurers for any additional costs incurred by insertion of the enclosure, *832 except no postage shall be charged for any enclosure weighing less than 1/3 of an ounce. (2) The commissioner shall by regulation determine the content of the enclosures and other procedures necessary for implementation of this provision. The legislature shall make no appropriation for this subdivision."

Petitioners contend that the foregoing provision violates article II, section 12 of the California Constitution, which states: "No amendment to the Constitution, and no statute proposed to the electors by the Legislature or by initiative, that names an individual to hold any office, or names or identifies any private corporation to perform any function or to have any power or duty, may be submitted to the electors or have any effect." Petitioners further argue that since the constitutional provision says that no statute which violates it "may... have any effect," the invalid language is non-severable and invalidates the whole of Proposition 103. We hold that the consumer-advocacy provision of Proposition 103 does violate article II, section 12, but is severable and does not affect the balance of the initiative….

We hold that the insolvency standard, section 1861.01, subdivision (b), on its face violates the due process clauses of both state and federal Constitutions. The consumer advocacy provision, section 1861.10, subdivision (c), violates article II, section 12, of the California Constitution….

第五节　保险业的监管

一、中国对保险业的监管

依据中国《保险法》的规定，中国保监会依法对保险业实施监督管理。中国保监会于 1998 年 11 月 18 日成立，其依照保险法律、法规和国务院规定的职责，对保险业实施监督管理，维护保险市场秩序，保护投保人、被保险人和受益人的合法权益。中国保监会根据履行职责的需要设立派出机构，派出机构按照中国保监会的授权履行监督管理职责。除此之外，中国保险行业的自律性组织（如 2001 年成立的中国保险行业协会）在保险业监管的过程中也发挥着重要的作用。

中国保险监管立足国情和行业实际，在消化吸收国际经验的基础上进行再创新，在监管框架、法律法规、制度规则等方面建立了既符合中国实际又与国际标准趋同的监管体系。

从中国保监会的监管角度来看，根据中国《保险法》的相关规定，中国保监会主要从以下几个方面对中国保险业进行监管：

市场准入的监管。在中国，设立保险机构、从事保险业务，需经中国保监会批准。中国保监会审核的内容包括：有符合法律规定的公司章程，达到符合规定的注册资本最低限额，有具备任职资格的高级管理人员，有健全的组织机构和管理制度，有符合要求的营业场所。其中，资本金、高级管理人员任职资格和保险公司业务范围是核心内容。未经批准擅自设立保险公司或者非法从事保险业务活动的，由中国保监会予以取缔。

保险公司运营的监管。在中国，保险公司的经营必须符合一定的要求，中国保监会对此进行持续性监管。首先是对保险公司的偿付能力实施监控。对偿付能力不足的保险公司，中国保监会可将其列为重点监管对象，并可以根据具体情况采取下列措施：（1）责令增加资本金、办理再保险；（2）限制业务范围；（3）限制向股东分红；（4）限制固定资产购置或者经营费用规模；（5）限制资金运用的形式、比例；（6）限制增设分支机构；（7）责令拍卖不良资产、转让保险业务；（8）限制董事、监事、高级管理人员的薪酬水平；（9）限制商业性广告；（10）责令停止接受新业务。如果保险公司的偿付能力严重不足的，中国保监会甚至可以对其实行接管。其次是责任准备金、再保险及保险资金运用的监管。保险公司未依照法律规定提取或者结转各项责任准备金，或者未依照法律规定办理再保险，或者严重违反本法关于资金运用的规定的，由中国保监会责令限期改正，保险公司逾期未改正的，中国保监会可以决定选派保险专业人员和指定该保险公司的有关人员组成整顿组，对公司进行整顿。

保险业市场的监管。为维护保险市场秩序，培育和发展保险市场，完善保险市场体系，促进保险企业公平竞争，中国保监会拟定了相关的保险业市场规则及规章制度，并检查和规范保险中介机构的市场行为，查处违法、违规行为。此外，对保险公司使用的保险条款和保险费率进行监管，也是很重要的一方面。依照中国《保险法》的规定，关系社会公众利益的保险险种、依法实行强制保险的险种和新开发的人寿保险险种等的保险条款和保险费率，应当报中国保监会批准。中国保监会审批时，应当遵循保护社会公众利益和防止不正当竞争的原则。其他保险险种的保险条款和保险费率，应当报中国保监会备案。保险公司使用的保险条款和保险费率违反法律、行政法规或者中国保监会的有关规定的，由中国保监会责令停止使用，限期修改；情节严重的，可以在一定期限内禁止申报新的保险条款和保险费率。

为履行其监管职责，中国保监会有权采取下列措施：（1）对保险公司、保险代理人、保险经纪人、保险资产管理公司、外国保险机构的代表机构进行现场检查；（2）进入涉嫌违法行为发生场所调查取证；（3）询问当事人及与被调查事件有关的单位和个人，要求其对与被调查事件有关的事项作出说明；（4）查阅、复制与被调查事件有关的财产权登记等资料；（5）查阅、复制保险公司、保险代理人、保险经纪人、保险资产管理公司、外国保险机构的代表机构以及与被调查事件有关的单位和个人的财务会计资料及其他相关文件和资料；对可能被转移、隐匿或者毁损的文件和资料予以封存；（6）查询涉嫌违法经营的保险公司、保险代理人、保险经纪人、保险资产管理公司、外国保险机构的代表机构以及与涉嫌违法事项有关的单位和个人的银行账户；（7）对有证据证明已经或者可能转移、隐匿违法资金等涉案财产或者隐匿、伪造、毁损重要证据的，经保险监督管理机构主要负责人批准，申请人民法院予以冻结或者查封。

二、美国对保险业的监管

美国保险监管体系的确立是一个各方利益长期博弈的过程。早期，美国的保险业经营相对自由，保险业的监管由各个州自行负责，不受联邦政府的干预。但是，这种分散的监管体制给保险公司的跨州经营造成诸多不便。一些保险公司力图促使联邦统一对保险业进行监管，但是这涉及美国宪法中联邦与各州权力的划分，因此他们试图通过法院在个案中对美国宪法予以解释，来确定联邦是否有权对保险业进行监管。

在 1869 年的 Paul v. Virginia①案中，关于联邦对保险业监管的问题被摆在了美国联邦最高法院面前。但是，推动联邦统一监管的努力最终破灭了，因为美国联邦最高法院宣告：保险保单的签发不是一种商业交易行为，因此联邦政府无权根据《美国宪法》中的贸易条款（Commerce Clause）②对保险业进行监管。在 Paul v. Virginia 案判决之后的很长一段时间里，美国一直维持着各州分别监管保险业的格局。为了协调各州监管机构对跨州经营保险业务的监管，统一监管标准，1871 年各州自愿成立美国保险监理官协会（NAIC）。

但是，1944 年，美国联邦最高法院在 United States v. South-Eastern Underwriter

① Paul v. Virginia, 75 U. S. 168 (1869).

② 贸易条款是指《美国宪法》中第 1 条第 8 款第 3 段的规定，即国会有权对与外国的贸易、各州之间的贸易以及与印第安部落之间的贸易进行管理（[The Congress shall have Power] To regulate Commerce with foreign Nations, and among the several States, and with the Indian tribes）。

Association[①]案中推翻了 1869 年 Paul v. Virginia 案的判决。美国联邦最高法院判定，保险业属于州际商业，属于《美国宪法》“贸易条款”项下的贸易，受到联邦监管。该案的判决不仅强调联邦有权监管保险业，还表明所有规制跨州贸易的联邦法律（包括反垄断法）都适用于保险人。这一判决，彻底将监管保险业的权力从各州收归联邦政府。

但是，保险行业、各州的保险监管者以及 NAIC 纷纷行动起来，力促国会通过法律，维持由各州监管保险业的现状。最终，1945 年美国国会通过了《麦卡伦—弗格森法案》（McCarran-Ferguson Act of 1945）。该法重申了国会承认各州对保险业监管的现行体制和法律，并规定只有在州政府没有对保险业进行规制时，联邦层面的谢尔曼法、克莱顿法和联邦贸易委员会法等才适用于保险行业。自此，美国保险业以州监管为主的格局最终得以确立。目前，美国各州都设一名保险监理官，具体负责对州内经营的保险公司的偿付能力、费率和市场行为等进行监管。根据美国法律的规定，所有美国保险公司和再保险公司必须在至少一个州登记注册，并接受所在州和有营销业务的州的监管。

美国这种分散的监管体制，给欲跨州经营的保险公司带来麻烦。保险公司需要同时符合不同州的监管要求，而大部分保险公司发现要同时符合各个州不同的监管要求是非常困难的。为了弥补这种缺陷，NAIC 发挥着重要作用。NAIC 是一个非营利性组织，由美国 50 个州、哥伦比亚特区以及 4 个美国属地的保险监理官组成。NAIC 主要任务是向各州保险监理官提出富有建设性的建议，定期相互交流保险监管的信息与观点，拟定样板法律和条例供各州保险立法参考。在 NAIC 的努力下，美国各州保险法内容的差异在逐渐减小，监管标准趋于一致。

但是，美国这种各州独立进行监管、自愿参与跨州协调的保险监管制度，仍旧存在着弊端：一是各州独立的监管制度缺乏联邦层面的监管联动性，不利于对全国系统性风险进行防范和管理；二是由于各州保险监管政策和法规不一致，在参与国际规则的商讨和制定中难以达成共识，不利于在国家间博弈时争取更有利政策；三是对市场有效竞争和主体发展存在一定的消极影响。[②]2008 年金融危机的爆发，凸显了这种保险监管体制的弊端。

2010 年 7 月，美国国会通过了《多德—弗兰克华尔街改革和消费者保护法案》，该法第四部分（《联邦保险办公室法》）涉及美国保险业的监管改革。针对此前保险业没有联邦监管机构的制度空白，该法案决定在财政部内部新设联邦保险办公室。联邦保险办公室对保险业进行监控，就保险领域的系统风险向金融稳定监管委员会提供咨询，并与各州保险监管机构协商国家层面保险问题。该法案还要求联邦保险办公室向国会提交改善保险业

① United States v. South-Eastern Underwriter Association, 322 U.S. 533, 64 S.Ct. 1162, 88 L.Ed. 1440 (1944).

② 上海保监局. 透视美国保险监管制度改革. 中国保险报，2010-04-07（06）

监管规定的意见和建议，就推进保险业监管现代化的途径向国会提交报告。这一改革，加强了联邦对保险业的干预，但是美国以州监管为主的监管体系并未因此而改变。

三、案例资料

在美国保险业监管的历史上，两个联邦最高法院的判例和两部国会通过的法律对美国当前保险监管体制的形成起着至关重要的作用：1869 年的 Paul v. Virginia 案和 1944 年的 United States v. South-Eastern Underwriter Association 案先后肯定和否定了各州对保险业的监管权力。1945 年的《麦卡伦—弗格森法案》以成文法律的形式确立了各州的监管权力，而 2010 年的《联邦保险办公室法》则又强化了联邦对保险业的监管和干预。

（一）McCarran-Ferguson Act of 1945

该法是为应对美国联邦最高法院 1944 年判决的 United States v. South-Eastern Underwriter Association 案而制定的。该法规定，美国国会承认，由各州对保险业继续监管和征税，符合公共利益，国会对此问题的沉默不应被理解为对各州的监管和征税设置了任何障碍；保险业以及从事保险业经营的任何人，都应受到各州与保险业的监管与征税相关的法律的规制；国会的任何法律均不应被理解为撤销、减损或取代任何由各州制定的有关保险业监管及征税的法律。

该法同时规定，各州政府的保险监管是有条件的：第一，如果一个州没有自己的保险监管法律，联邦法律就适用于该州的保险业务；第二，如果国会通过了专门适用于保险的、而不是一般商业行为的法律，那么在此法律范围内联邦法律具有优于各州保险监管的权利。

最后，该法还规定了联邦反垄断法针对保险业豁免的条件，事实上这是该法通过的最主要原因。该法规定保险公司的行为符合以下三个条件才能享有豁免：（1）属于“保险业务”；（2）有“州法监管”；（3）不能构成联合抵制(boycotts)。

Public Law 79-15
McCarran-Ferguson Act
by the 79th Congress of the United States

An Act

To express the intent of the Congress with reference to the regulation of the business of insurance.

Be it enacted by the Senate and House of Representatives of the United States of America in Congress assembled.

That the Congress hereby declares that the continued regulation and taxation by the several States of the business of insurance is in the public interest, and that silence on the part of the Congress shall not be construed to impose any barrier to the regulation or taxation of such business by the several States.

Sec. 2. (a) The business of insurance, and every person engaged therein, shall be subject to the laws of the several States which relate to the regulation or taxation of such business.

(b) No Act of Congress shall be construed to invalidate, impair, or supersede any law enacted by any State for the purpose of regulating the business of insurance, or which imposes a fee or tax upon such business, unless such Act specifically relates to the business of insurance:

> Provided, That after January 1, 1948, the Act of July 2, 1890, as amended, known as the Sherman Act, and the Act of October 15, 1914, as amended, known as the Clayton Act, and the Act of September 26, 1914, known as the Federal Trade Commission Act, as amended, shall be applicable to the business of insurance to the extent that such business is not regulated by State law.

Sec. 3. (a) Until January 1, 1948, the Act of July 2, 1890, as amended, known as the Sherman Act, and the Act of October 15, 1914, as amended, known as the Clayton Act, and the Act of September 26, 1914, known as the Federal Trade Commission Act, as amended, and the Act of June 19, 1936, known as the Robinson-Patman Anti-discrimination Act, shall not apply to the business of insurance or to acts in the conduct thereof.

(b) Nothing contained in this Act shall render the said Sherman Act inapplicable to any agreement to boycott, coerce, or intimidate, or act of boycott, coercion, or intimidation.

Sec. 4.Nothing contained in this Act shall be construed to affect in any manner the application to the business of insurance of the Act of July 5, 1935, as amended, known as the National Labor Relations Act, or the Act of June 25, 1938, as amended, known as the Fair Labor Standards Act of 1938, or the Act of June 5, 1920, known as the Merchant Marine Act, 1920.

Sec. 5.As used in this Act, the term "State" includes the several States, Alaska, Hawaii, Puerto Rico, and the District of Columbia.

Sec. 6.If any provision of this Act, or the application of such provision to any person or circumstances, shall be held invalid, the remainder of the Act, and the application of such provision to persons or circumstances other than those as to which it is held invalid, shall not be affected.

Approved March 9, 1945.

（二）Federal Insurance Office Act of 2010

在对2008年发生于美国的金融危机进行全面反思总结的基础之上，美国国会于2010年通过《多德—弗兰克华尔街改革和消费者保护法案》，对美国金融监管体制进行全面改革。其中，《联邦保险办公室法》为其中涉及保险业监管改革部分的一部法律。

针对之前保险业分散监管的弊端，《联邦保险办公室法》提出了一条重大的改革措施：设立联邦保险办公室。联邦保险办公室的职责和权力包括信息监测与收集、咨询建议以及协调各州的监管政策等。

联邦保险办公室并不具有直接监管保险业务的权力，具体业务监管仍然由各州监管机构负责。但是，联邦政府将能通过联邦保险办公室进一步完善保险监管体系。

DODD-FRANK WALL STREET REFORM AND CONSUMER PROTECTION ACT

Public Law 111-203

111th Congress

TITLE V—INSURANCE

…

SEC. 502. FEDERAL INSURANCE OFFICE.

(a) Establishment of Office. —Subchapter I of chapter 3 of subtitle I of title 31, United States Code, is amended—

(1) by redesignating section 312 as section 315;

(2) by redesignating section 313 as section 312; and

(3) by inserting after section 312 (as so redesignated) the following new sections:

SEC. 313. FEDERAL INSURANCE OFFICE.

(a) Establishment. —There is established within the Department of the Treasury the

Federal Insurance Office.

(b) Leadership. —The Office shall be headed by a Director, who shall be appointed by the Secretary of the Treasury. The position of Director shall be a career reserved position in the Senior Executive Service, as that position is defined under section 3132 of title 5, United States Code.

(c) Functions. —

(1) Authority pursuant to direction of secretary. —The Office, pursuant to the direction of the Secretary, shall have the authority—

(A) to monitor all aspects of the insurance industry, including identifying issues or gaps in the regulation of insurers that could contribute to a systemic crisis in the insurance industry or the United States financial system;

(B) to monitor the extent to which traditionally underserved communities and consumers, minorities (as such term is defined in section 1204 (c) of the Financial Institutions Reform, Recovery, and Enforcement Act of 1989 (12 U.S.C. 1811 note)), and low—and moderate-income persons have access to affordable insurance products regarding all lines of insurance, except health insurance;

(C) to recommend to the Financial Stability Oversight Council that it designate an insurer, including the affiliates of such insurer, as an entity subject to regulation as a nonbank financial company supervised by the Board of Governors pursuant to title I of the Dodd-Frank Wall Street Reform and Consumer Protection Act;

(D) to assist the Secretary in administering the Terrorism Insurance Program established in the Department of the Treasury under the Terrorism Risk Insurance Act of 2002 (15 U.S.C. 6701 note);

(E) to coordinate Federal efforts and develop Federal policy on prudential aspects of international insurance matters, including representing the United States, as appropriate, in the International Association of Insurance Supervisors (or a successor entity) and assisting the Secretary in negotiating covered agreements (as such term is defined in subsection (r));

(F) to determine, in accordance with subsection (f), whether State insurance measures are preempted by covered agreements;

(G) to consult with the States (including State insurance regulators) regarding insurance matters of national importance and prudential insurance matters of international importance; and

(H) to perform such other related duties and authorities as may be assigned to the Office by the Secretary.

(2) Advisory functions. —The Office shall advise the Secretary on major domestic and prudential international insurance policy issues.

(3) Advisory capacity on council. —The Director shall serve in an advisory capacity on the Financial Stability Oversight Council established under the Financial Stability Act of 2010.

(d) Scope. —The authority of the Office shall extend to all lines of insurance except—

(1) health insurance, as determined by the Secretary in coordination with the Secretary of Health and Human Services based on section 2791 of the Public Health Service Act (42 U.S.C. 300gg-91);

(2) long-term care insurance, except long-term care insurance that is included with life or annuity insurance components, as determined by the Secretary in coordination with the Secretary of Health and Human Services, and in the case of long-term care insurance that is included with such components, the Secretary shall coordinate with the Secretary of Health and Human Services in performing the functions of the Office; and

(3) crop insurance, as established by the Federal Crop Insurance Act (7 U.S.C. 1501 et seq.).

(e) Gathering of Information. —

(1) In general. —In carrying out the functions required under subsection (c), the Office may—

(A) receive and collect data and information on and from the insurance industry and insurers;

(B) enter into information-sharing agreements;

(C) analyze and disseminate data and information; and

(D) issue reports regarding all lines of insurance except health insurance.

(2) Collection of information from insurers and affiliates. —

(A) In general. —Except as provided in paragraph (3), the Office may require an insurer, or any affiliate of an insurer, to submit such data or information as the Office may reasonably require in carrying out the functions described under subsection (c).

(B) Rule of construction. —Notwithstanding any other provision of this section, for purposes of subparagraph (A), the term "insurer" means any entity that writes insurance or reinsures risks and issues contracts or policies in 1 or more States.

(3) Exception for small insurers. —Paragraph (2) shall not apply with respect to any insurer or affiliate thereof that meets a minimum size threshold that the Office may establish, whether by order or rule.

(4) Advance coordination. —Before collecting any data or information under paragraph (2) from an insurer, or affiliate of an insurer, the Office shall coordinate with each relevant Federal agency and State insurance regulator (or other relevant Federal or State regulatory agency, if any, in the case of an affiliate of an insurer) and any publicly available sources to determine if the information to be collected is available from, and may be obtained in a timely manner by, such Federal agency or State insurance regulator, individually or collectively, other regulatory agency, or publicly available sources. If the Director determines that such data or information is available, and may be obtained in a timely manner, from such an agency, regulator, regulatory agency, or source, the Director shall obtain the data or information from such agency, regulator, regulatory agency, or source. If the Director determines that such data or information is not so available, the Director may collect such data or information from an insurer (or affiliate) only if the Director complies with the requirements of subchapter I of chapter 35 of title 44, United States Code (relating to Federal information policy; commonly known as the Paperwork Reduction Act), in collecting such data or information. Notwithstanding any other provision of law, each such relevant Federal agency and State insurance regulator or other Federal or State regulatory agency is authorized to provide to the Office such data or information.

(5) Confidentiality. —

(A) Retention of privilege. —The submission of any nonpublicly available data and information to the Office under this subsection shall not constitute a waiver of, or otherwise affect, any privilege arising under Federal or State law (including the rules of any Federal or State court) to which the data or information is otherwise subject.

(B) Continued application of prior confidentiality agreements. —Any requirement under Federal or State law to the extent otherwise applicable, or any requirement pursuant to a written agreement in effect between the original source of any nonpublicly available data or information and the source of such data or information to the Office, regarding the privacy or confidentiality of any data or information in the possession of the source to the Office, shall continue to apply to such data or information after the data or information has been provided pursuant to this subsection to the Office.

(C) Information-sharing agreement. —Any data or information obtained by the Office may be made available to State insurance regulators, individually or collectively, through an information-sharing agreement that—

(i) shall comply with applicable Federal law; and

(ii) shall not constitute a waiver of, or otherwise affect, any privilege under Federal or State law (including the rules of any Federal or State court) to which the data or information is otherwise subject.

(D) Agency disclosure requirements. —Section 552 of title 5, United States Code, shall apply to any data or information submitted to the Office by an insurer or an affiliate of an insurer.

(6) Subpoenas and enforcement. —The Director shall have the power to require by subpoena the production of the data or information requested under paragraph (2), but only upon a written finding by the Director that such data or information is required to carry out the functions described under subsection (c) and that the Office has coordinated with such regulator or agency as required under paragraph (4). Subpoenas shall bear the signature of the Director and shall be served by any person or class of persons designated by the Director for that purpose. In the case of contumacy or failure to obey a subpoena, the subpoena shall be enforceable by order of any appropriate district court of the United States. Any failure to obey the

order of the court may be punished by the court as a contempt of court.

(f) Preemption of State Insurance Measures. —

(1) Standard. —A State insurance measure shall be preempted pursuant to this section or section 314 if, and only to the extent that the Director determines, in accordance with this subsection, that the measure—

(A) results in less favorable treatment of a non—United States insurer domiciled in a foreign jurisdiction that is subject to a covered agreement than a United States insurer domiciled, licensed, or otherwise admitted in that State; and

(B) is inconsistent with a covered agreement.

(2) Determination. —

(A) Notice of potential inconsistency. —Before making any determination under paragraph (1), the Director shall—

(i) notify and consult with the appropriate State regarding any potential inconsistency or preemption;

(ii) notify and consult with the United States Trade Representative regarding any potential inconsistency or preemption;

(iii) <<NOTE: Federal Register, publication.>> cause to be published in the Federal Register notice of the issue regarding the potential inconsistency or preemption, including a description of each State insurance measure at issue and any applicable covered agreement;

(iv) <<NOTE: Comments.>> provide interested parties a reasonable opportunity to submit written comments to the Office; and

(v) consider any comments received.

(B) Scope of review. —For purposes of this subsection, any determination of the Director regarding State insurance measures, and any preemption under paragraph (1) as a result of such determination, shall be limited to the subject matter contained within the covered agreement involved and shall achieve a level of protection for insurance or reinsurance consumers that is substantially equivalent to the level of protection achieved under State insurance or reinsurance regulation.

(C) Notice of determination of inconsistency. —Upon making any determination under paragraph (1), the Director shall—

(i) notify the appropriate State of the determination and the extent of the inconsistency;

(ii) establish a reasonable period of time, which shall not be less than 30 days, before the determination shall become effective; and

(iii) notify the Committees on Financial Services and Ways and Means of the House of Representatives and the Committees on Banking, Housing, and Urban Affairs and Finance of the Senate.

(3) Notice of effectiveness. —Upon the conclusion of the period referred to in paragraph (2) (C) (ii), if the basis for such determination still exists, the determination shall become effective and the Director shall—

(A) cause to be published a notice in the Federal Register that the preemption has become effective, as well as the effective date; and

(B) notify the appropriate State.

(4) Limitation. —No State may enforce a State insurance measure to the extent that such measure has been preempted under this subsection.

(g) Applicability of Administrative Procedures Act. —Determinations of inconsistency made pursuant to subsection (f) (2) shall be subject to the applicable provisions of subchapter II of chapter 5 of title 5, United States Code (relating to administrative procedure), and chapter 7 of such title (relating to judicial review), except that in any action for judicial review of a determination of inconsistency, the court shall determine the matter de novo.

(h) Regulations, Policies, and Procedures. —The Secretary may issue orders, regulations, policies, and procedures to implement this section.

(i) Consultation. —The Director shall consult with State insurance regulators, individually or collectively, to the extent the Director determines appropriate, in carrying out the functions of the Office.

(j) Savings Provisions. —Nothing in this section shall—

(1) preempt—

(A) any State insurance measure that governs any insurer's rates, premiums, underwriting, or sales practices;

(B) any State coverage requirements for insurance;

(C) the application of the antitrust laws of any State to the business of insurance; or

(D) any State insurance measure governing the capital or solvency of an insurer, except to the extent that such State insurance measure results in less favorable treatment of a non-United State insurer than a United States insurer;

(2) be construed to alter, amend, or limit any provision of the Consumer Financial Protection Agency Act of 2010; or

(3) affect the preemption of any State insurance measure otherwise inconsistent with and preempted by Federal law.

(k) Retention of Existing State Regulatory Authority. —Nothing in this section or section 314 shall be construed to establish or provide the Office or the Department of the Treasury with general supervisory or regulatory authority over the business of insurance.

(l) Retention of Authority of Federal Financial Regulatory Agencies. —Nothing in this section or section 314 shall be construed to limit the authority of any Federal financial regulatory agency, including the authority to develop and coordinate policy, negotiate, and enter into agreements with foreign governments, authorities, regulators, and multinational regulatory committees and to preempt State measures to affect uniformity with international regulatory agreements.

(m) Retention of Authority of United States Trade Representative. —Nothing in this section or section 314 shall be construed to affect the authority of the Office of the United States Trade Representative pursuant to section 141 of the Trade Act of 1974 (19 U.S.C. 2171) or any other provision of law, including authority over the development and coordination of United States international trade policy and the administration of the United States trade agreements program.

(n) Annual Reports to Congress. —

(1) Section 313 (f) reports. —Beginning September 30, 2011, the Director shall submit a report on or before September 30 of each calendar year to the President and to the Committees on Financial Services and Ways and Means of the House of Representatives and the Committees on Banking, Housing, and Urban Affairs and Finance of the Senate on any actions taken by the Office pursuant to subsection (f) (regarding preemption of inconsistent State insurance measures).

(2) Insurance industry. —Beginning September 30, 2011, the Director shall submit a report on or before September 30 of each calendar year to the President and to the Committee on Financial Services of the House of Representatives and the

Committee on Banking, Housing, and Urban Affairs of the Senate on the insurance industry and any other information as deemed relevant by the Director or requested by such Committees.

(o) Reports on U.S. and Global Reinsurance Market. —The Director shall submit to the Committee on Financial Services of the House of Representatives and the Committee on Banking, Housing, and Urban Affairs of the Senate—

(1) a report received not later than September 30, 2012, describing the breadth and scope of the global reinsurance market and the critical role such market plays in supporting insurance in the United States; and
(2) a report received not later than January 1, 2013, and updated not later than January 1, 2015, describing the impact of part II of the Nonadmitted and Reinsurance Reform Act of 2010 on the ability of State regulators to access reinsurance information for regulated companies in their jurisdictions.

…

第八章

金融衍生产品法律制度

第一节　金融衍生产品简述

金融衍生产品（Derivative）是与金融相关的派生物，通常是指其价值依赖于基础资产（underlying assets）价值变动的合约（contracts），主要包括远期、期货、互换、期权以及它们与其他金融工具经分解组合形成的混合金融产品。

远期是一种较为简单的衍生工具，是一种在确定的将来时间按确定的价格购买或出售某种资产的协议；期货是两个交易对手之间签订的一种在确定的未来时间按确定的价格购买或出售某项资产的协议；互换也称掉期，是指合约双方在未来按照事先约定的规则互换现金流的一种协议，它可以把资产或负债相关的现金流转化为公司所需要的形态；期权是一种选择权，期权的买方向卖方支付一定数额的权利金后，就获得这种权利，即拥有在一定时间内以一定的价格（执行价格）出售或购买一定数量的标的物（实物商品、证券或期货合约）的权利。

金融衍生产品的交易可分为场内交易和场外交易。场内交易，又称交易所交易，指所有的供求方集中在交易所进行竞价交易的交易方式。在这种交易模式之下，交易所事先设计出标准化的金融合同，由投资者选择与自身需求最接近的合同和数量进行交易。期货交易和部分标准化期权合同交易都属于这种交易方式。场外交易，又称柜台交易（over the counter, OTC），指交易双方直接成为交易对手的交易方式。在这种交易模式之下，每个交易的清算是由交易双方相互负责进行的，交易参与者限于信用程度高的客户（通常为大型的金融机构或企业）。掉期交易和远期交易是具有代表性的柜台交易的衍生产品。

金融衍生产品是全球金融创新的浪潮中涌现出的高科技产品，是金融创新工具的重要组成部分。目前在金融市场上，金融衍生产品越来越多地被用于规避和对冲风险、增加金融市场的流通性、促进国际资金的交易、提高投资效率、优化资金配置等方面。

一、中国的金融衍生产品

依据中国银监会颁布的《银行业金融机构衍生产品交易业务管理办法》（2011 年修正）中的定义，在中国，衍生产品是一种金融合约，其价值取决于一种或多种基础资产或指数，合约的基本种类包括远期、期货、掉期（互换）和期权，还包括具有远期、期货、掉期（互换）和期权中一种或多种特征的混合金融工具。

中国国内的金融衍生产品市场起步较晚，但是发展迅速，衍生产品交易的品种在不断增加，规模也在不断地扩大。金融衍生产品在中国已变成规避风险、交易获利、代客服务、做市流通的一种有效工具。

早在 1992 年，中国国内就出现了相关金融衍生产品——国债期货和金融期权（表现形式为配股权证），但不久即因为过度投机而被相关监管部门终止。随着金融开放和金融深化程度的不断提高，中国又逐渐放开了金融衍生产品交易。目前，无论在场内市场还是在场外市场，中国金融衍生产品均不断丰富，推陈出新。

在场内市场方面，2005 年 8 月，宝钢权证在中国上海证券交易所挂牌上市，标志着中国金融衍生产品市场的大幕已经拉开，中国金融衍生产品市场正式开市。目前，中国已经设立有郑州商品交易所、大连商品交易所和上海期货交易所开展期货产品的交易，相关的期货上市品种涵盖了强麦、硬麦、棉花、白糖、PTA、菜籽油、早籼稻和甲醇（郑州商品交易所），玉米、黄大豆 1 号、黄大豆 2 号、豆粕、豆油、棕榈油、聚乙烯、聚氯乙烯和焦炭（大连商品交易所）以及铜、铝、锌、铅、黄金、螺纹钢、线材、燃料油、天然橡胶和 ISIN 编码（上海期货交易所）。[①]2006 年 9 月 8 日，中国金融期货交易所在上海成立，该交易所负责组织安排金融期货等金融衍生品上市交易、结算和交割，是中国金融衍生品交易发展的另一重要里程碑。2010 年 3 月 24 日，中国证监会正式作出批复，同意中国金融期货交易所上市沪深 300 股票指数期货合约，股指期货于 2010 年 4 月 16 日起正式在中国挂牌交易，进一步丰富了中国场内的金融衍生产品。

相对而言，中国场内交易的金融衍生产品品种仍显单一，且交易受到种种限制。在场外交易方面，中国对金融衍生产品交易的限制则要小得多，衍生产品的品种也更为丰富。近年来，中国人民银行相继推出了债券远期、人民币利率互换、远期利率协议、外汇远期、外汇掉期等金融衍生产品，兼有本币和外币的衍生品。尤其值得一提的是，2007 年 10 月，中国银行间市场交易商协会根据中国人民银行的授权公布了《中国银行间市场

---

① 参见郑州商品交易所（http://www.czce.com.cn/portal/index.htm）、大连商品交易所（http://www.dce.com.cn/portal/template/index.html）和上海期货交易所（http://www.shfe.com.cn/），访问日期 2011/12/15。

金融衍生产品交易主协议（2007年版）》（随后又颁布了2009年版）。该协议的推出为场外金融衍生产品交易提供了标准参照，对于提高衍生产品交易的效率，促进衍生产品市场健康发展起到了积极的作用。中国场外金融衍生产品市场呈现出稳步发展的局面。

尽管中国场内、场外金融衍生产品市场均已取得了一定的发展，但与发达国家相比仍处于初级阶段，尚不能完全满足金融市场参与者风险防范和投资需求，也落后于中国经济发展的节奏。因此，在借鉴国际场外金融衍生产品市场发展的经验和教训基础上，中国仍需坚持推动金融衍生产品市场的规范发展。

二、美国的金融衍生产品

美国没有专门法律对衍生产品予以定义，但却有一些对衍生产品非立法性的定义。其中，较有代表性的是以下两种：美国联邦储备委员会将其定义为“一种金融合约，而不是借贷资金，其主要目的在于转移由于资产价值波动所带来的神秘感”。[①]美国著名的银行业研究机构“华盛顿30人小组”在1993年7月发布的《衍生产品：惯例与准则》报告中指出：“衍生产品，正如其名称一样，是价值衍生于基础资产或基础参考比率或指数的一种双边合约或支付协议。”[②]

金融衍生产品交易是依赖于基础资产但却又脱离基础资产的交易，被视为金融创新的代表。美国在金融创新方面走在世界前列，所生产的金融衍生产品也层出不穷。作为金融衍生产品的发源地以及当今世界上规模最大、创新最为活跃的衍生品市场，美国引领着世界各地衍生品的发展趋势。

最早的严格意义上的金融衍生品产生于1972年的美国。当时，以固定汇率为主要内容的布雷顿森林体系崩溃，导致汇率变得波动不稳定。出于规避汇率风险的需要，在芝加哥商品交易所（CME）诞生了首份外汇期货合约。此后，至20世纪90年代，在美国先后出现了外汇期货、股票期货、抵押债券期货、国库券期货、长期政府债券期货、场外货币期权、货币互换、股票指数期货、外汇期货期权、股票指数期货期权、欧洲美元期权、互换期权平均期权、复合期权、利率互换期货、股票指数互换、证券组合互换以及特种互换等金融衍生品。时至今日，美国拥有世界上品种最多、结构最为复杂的金融衍生产品。

金融衍生产品在美国大行其道，金融机构只要选定资产、信用进行包装设计，就可形成一款金融衍生产品推向市场，这在为美国的金融机构牟取巨额利益的同时，也使得金融机构暴露在巨大的风险之中。2008年美国金融危机的爆发，就与金融衍生产品密切

---

① 贾炜莹. 中国上市公司衍生工具运用研究. 北京：对外经济贸易大学出版社，2010：16.

② Global Derivatives Study Group. Derivatives: Practices and Principles (Group of Thirty Report). Washington, DC, July 1993: 28.

相关。美国华尔街的金融精英们将企业贷款、物业贷款、个人信用贷款和垃圾级贷款等包装成金融衍生产品，从衍生产品再制造衍生产品，再由评级公司加以评估，评为优质债券，如债务抵押凭证，被美国金融界称之为 CDO（collateralized debt obligation），证券交易商将有些 CDO，由保险公司担保后，称它为 CDS（credit default swap，信用违约互换），证券交易商把它推销给全球投资机构和投资者。最终，CDS 出现大规模违约，引发了席卷全美乃至全球的金融危机。

三、案例资料

期货，是最早发展起来的金融衍生产品，也是最重要且最基础的金融衍生产品。对于期货交易而言，由于其本身存在的巨大风险性，因此需要交易的当事方具备相当程度的技能。在此条件下，交易的风险很大程度上是由交易当事人自担的。如果交易的一方因为交易对方的违法行为而遭受了损失，但法律并未明文规定其可以起诉对方要求赔偿，那么其能否就此向法院提起赔偿诉讼？下面的 Merrill Lynch, Pierce Fenner & Smith Inc. v. Curran 案对上述问题作出了回答。

该案涉及美国期货交易相关的法律与现实中投资者诉求的冲突问题。

在美国，早期是由《商品交易法》即 CEA 规制商品期货交易的。1974 年通过的《商品期货交易委员会法》对 CEA 的规定有了重大的修改，同时商品期货交易委员会也据此设立，以承担期货监管职责。商品期货交易委员会的权限包括对任何因期货经纪商、商品交易咨询商违反 CEA 或该委员会发布的执行规章的行为而遭受损失的个人采取救济赔偿措施。但问题是，CEA、《商品期货交易委员会法》以及之后的其他相关法律均未对个人因他人违反 CEA 而遭受损失能否提起私人救济的诉讼作出明确规定。

在法律没有明确规定的前提下，受损害的个人能否直接对期货经纪商提供私人赔偿的诉讼？最终，美国联邦最高法院对此予以了回答。

首先，最高法院从美国期货市场的产生以及发展过程出发，总结出期货市场交易会对三类人产生直接的经济影响：（1）套期保值者；（2）投机者或投资者；（3）期货经纪公司、经纪人以及期货市场经营者。而该案中涉及双方当事人分属第二类和第三类人。

接着，最高法院围绕 CEA 的起草以及修订过程论述了国会对期货市场的认识以及监管理念，并指出：无论是该法案或者是其后的修正案，都并未对“作为私人投资者是否可以对期货交易经纪人（或期货交易经纪公司）违反《商品交易法》的行为所导致的损害向法院提起赔偿诉讼”这一问题作出明确规定。

最后，最高法院根据当时期货市场立法监管的背景环境以及国会的立法目的进一步得出结论：国会在法案的起草以及修订过程中并非排除这一诉因，而是暗含了这一内容的。最高法院从两个方面展开分析：第一，当时的立法环境，即整个期货市场的监管趋势是加强监管力度；第二，法案的立法目的，应该包括了对作为期货市场交易中直接受到经济影响的对象之一的投资者或投机者的保护。

Merrill Lynch, Pierce Fenner & Smith Inc. v. Curran

456 U.S. 353 (1982)

JUSTICE STEVENS delivered the opinion of the Court.

The Commodity Exchange Act (CEA), 7 U.S.C. 1 et seq. (1976 ed. and Supp. IV), has been aptly characterized as "a comprehensive regulatory structure to oversee the volatile and esoteric futures trading complex." The central question presented by these cases is whether a private party may maintain an action for damages caused by a violation of the CEA. The United States Court of Appeals for the Sixth Circuit answered that question affirmatively, holding that an investor may maintain an action against his broker for violation of an antifraud provision of the CEA. The Court of Appeals for the Second Circuit gave the same answer to the question in actions brought by investors claiming damages resulting from unlawful price manipulation that allegedly could have been prevented by the New York Mercantile Exchange's enforcement of its own rules.

We granted certiorari to resolve a conflict between these decisions and a subsequent decision of the Court of Appeals for the Fifth Circuit, and we now affirm. Prefatorily, we describe some aspects of the futures trading business, summarize the statutory scheme, and outline the essential facts of the separate cases.

I

Prior to the advent of futures trading, agricultural products generally were sold at central markets. When an entire crop was harvested and marketed within a short time span, dramatic price fluctuations sometimes created severe hardship for farmers or for processors. Some of these risks were alleviated by the adoption of quality standards, improvements in storage and transportation facilities, and the practice of "forward contracting"—the use of executory contracts fixing the terms of sale in advance of the time of delivery.

…

Thus, in a broad sense, futures trading has a direct financial impact on three classes of persons. Those who actually are interested in selling or buying the commodity are described as "hedgers;" their primary financial interest is in the profit to be earned from the production or processing of the commodity. Those who seek financial gain by taking positions in the futures market generally are called "speculators" or "investors;" without their participation, futures markets "simply would not exist." Finally, there are the futures commission merchants, the floor brokers, and the persons who manage the market; they also are essential participants, and they have an interest in maximizing the activity on the exchange. The petitioners in these cases are members of this third class whereas their adversaries, the respondents, are speculators or investors.

II

Because Congress has recognized the potential hazards as well as the benefits of futures trading, it has authorized the regulation of commodity futures exchanges for over 60 years. In 1921 it enacted the Future Trading Act, 42 Stat. 187, which imposed a prohibitive tax on grain futures transactions that were not consummated on an exchange designated as a "contract market" by the Secretary of Agriculture. The 1921 statute was held unconstitutional as an improper exercise of the taxing power in Hill v. Wallace, 259 U.S. 44 (1922), but its regulatory provisions were promptly reenacted in the Grain Futures Act, 42 Stat. 998, and upheld under the commerce power in Chicago Board of Trade v. Olsen, 262 U.S. 1 (1923). Under the original legislation, the principal function of the Secretary was to require the governors of a privately organized exchange to supervise the operation of the market. Two of the conditions for designation were that the governing board of the contract market prevent its members from disseminating misleading market information and prevent the "manipulation of prices or the cornering of any grain by the dealers or operators upon such board." The requirement that designated contract markets police themselves and the prohibitions against disseminating misleading information and manipulating prices have been part of our law ever since.

In 1936 Congress changed the name of the statute to the Commodity Exchange Act, enlarged its coverage to include other agricultural commodities, and added detailed provisions regulating trading in futures contracts. Commodity Exchange Act, ch. 545, 49 Stat. 1491. Among the significant new provisions was 4b, prohibiting any member of a contract market from defrauding any person in connection with the making of a futures contract, and 4a, authorizing a commission composed of the Secretary of Agriculture, the Secretary of Commerce, and the Attorney General to fix limits on the amount of permissible speculative trading in a futures contract. The legislation also required registration of futures commission merchants and floor brokers.

In 1968 the CEA again was amended to enlarge its coverage and to give the Secretary additional enforcement authority. Act of Feb. 19, 1968, 82 Stat. 26. The Secretary was authorized to disapprove exchange rules that were inconsistent with the statute, and the contract markets were required to enforce their rules; the Secretary was authorized to suspend a contract market or to issue a cease-and-desist order upon a showing that the contract market's rules were not being enforced. In addition, the criminal sanctions for price manipulation were increased significantly, and any person engaged in price manipulation was subjected to the Secretary's authority to issue cease-and-desist orders for violations of the CEA and implementing regulations.

In 1974, after extensive hearings and deliberation, Congress enacted the Commodity Futures Trading Commission Act of 1974. 88 Stat. 1389. Like the 1936 and the 1968 legislation, the 1974 enactment was an amendment to the existing statute that broadened its coverage and increased the penalties for violation of its provisions. The Commission was authorized to seek injunctive relief, to alter or supplement a contract market's rules, and to direct a contract market to take whatever action deemed necessary by the Commission in an emergency. The 1974 legislation retained the basic statutory prohibitions against fraudulent practices and price manipulation, as well as the authority to prescribe trading limits. The 1974 amendments, however, did make substantial changes in the statutory scheme; Congress authorized a newly created Commodities Futures Trading Commission to assume the powers previously exercised by the Secretary of Agriculture, as well as certain additional powers. The enactment also added two new remedial provisions for the protection of individual traders. The newly enacted 5a (11) required every contract market to provide an arbitration procedure for the settlement of traders' claims of no more than \$15 000. And the newly enacted 14 authorized the Commission to grant reparations to any person complaining of any violation of the CEA, or its implementing regulations, committed by any futures commission merchant or any associate thereof, floor broker, commodity trading adviser, or commodity pool operator. This section authorized the Commission to investigate complaints and, "if in its opinion the facts warrant such action," to afford a hearing before an administrative law judge. Reparations orders entered by the Commission are subject to judicial review.

The latest amendments to the CEA, the Futures Trading Act of 1978, 92 Stat. 865, again increased the penalties for violations of the statute. The enactment also authorized the States to bring parens patriae actions, seeking injunctive or monetary relief for certain violations of the

CEA, implementing regulations, or Commission orders.

Like the previous enactments, as well as the 1978 amendments, the Commodity Futures Trading Commission Act of 1974 is silent on the subject of private judicial remedies for persons injured by a violation of the CEA.

III

"When Congress intends private litigants to have a cause of action to support their statutory rights, the far better course is for it to specify as much when it creates those rights. But the Court has long recognized that under certain limited circumstances the failure of Congress to do so is not inconsistent with an intent on its part to have such a remedy available to the persons benefited by its legislation." Cannon v. University of Chicago, 441 U.S. 677, 717 (1979).

Our approach to the task of determining whether Congress intended to authorize a private cause of action has changed significantly, much as the quality and quantity of federal legislation has undergone significant change. When federal statutes were less comprehensive, the Court applied a relatively simple test to determine the availability of an implied private remedy. If a statute was enacted for the benefit of a special class, the judiciary normally recognized a remedy for members of that class. Texas & Pacific R. Co. v. Rigsby, 241 U.S. 33 (1916). Under this approach, federal courts, following a common-law tradition, regarded the denial of a remedy as the exception rather than the rule.

Because the Rigsby approach prevailed throughout most of our history, there is no merit to the argument advanced by petitioners that the judicial recognition of an implied private remedy violates the separation-of-powers doctrine. As Justice Frankfurter explained:

"Courts... are organs with historic antecedents which bring with them well-defined powers. They do not require explicit statutory authorization for familiar remedies to enforce statutory obligations. A duty declared by Congress does not evaporate for want of a formulated sanction. When Congress has 'left the matter at large for judicial determination,' our function is to decide what remedies are appropriate in the light of the statutory language and purpose and of the traditional modes by which courts compel performance of legal obligations. If civil liability is appropriate to effectuate the purposes of a statute, courts are not denied this traditional remedy because it is not specifically authorized."

During the years prior to 1975, the Court occasionally refused to recognize an implied remedy, either because the statute in question was a general regulatory prohibition enacted for the benefit of the public at large, or because there was evidence that Congress intended an express remedy to provide the exclusive method of enforcement. While the Rigsby approach prevailed, however, congressional silence or ambiguity was an insufficient reason for the denial of a remedy for a member of the class a statute was enacted to protect.

In 1975 the court unanimously decided to modify its approach to the question whether a federal statute includes a private right of action. In Cort v. Ash, 422 U.S. 66 (1975), the Court confronted a claim that a private litigant could recover damages for violation of a criminal statute that had never before been thought to include a private remedy. In rejecting that claim the Court outlined criteria that primarily focused on the intent of Congress in enacting the statute under review. The increased complexity of federal legislation and the increased volume of federal litigation strongly supported the desirability of a more careful scrutiny of legislative intent than Rigsby had required. Our cases subsequent to Cort v. Ash have plainly stated that our focus must be on "the intent of Congress."

IV

In determining whether a private cause of action is implicit in a federal statutory scheme when the statute by its terms is silent on that issue, the initial focus must be on the state of the law at the time the legislation was enacted. More precisely, we must examine Congress' perception of the law that it was shaping or reshaping. When Congress enacts new legislation, the question is whether Congress intended to create a private remedy as a supplement to the express enforcement provisions of the statute. When Congress acts in a statutory context in which an implied private remedy has already been recognized by the courts, however, the inquiry logically is different. Congress need not have intended to create a new remedy, since one already existed; the question is whether Congress intended to preserve the pre-existing remedy.

Prior to the comprehensive amendments to the CEA enacted in 1974, the federal courts routinely and consistently had recognized an implied private cause of action on behalf of plaintiffs seeking to enforce and to collect damages for violation of provisions of the CEA or rules and regulations promulgated pursuant to the statute.

Although the consensus of opinion concerning the existence of a private cause of action under the CEA was neither as old nor as overwhelming as the consensus concerning Rule 10b-5, it was equally uniform and well understood. This Court, as did other federal courts and federal practitioners, simply assumed that the remedy was available.

In view of the absence of any dispute about the proposition prior to the decision of Cort v. Ash in 1975, it is abundantly clear that an implied cause of action under the CEA was a part of the "contemporary legal context" in which Congress legislated in 1974. Cf. Cannon v. University of Chicago, 441 U.S., at 698-699. In that context, the fact that a comprehensive reexamination and significant amendment of the CEA left intact the statutory provisions under which the federal courts had implied a cause of action is itself evidence that Congress affirmatively intended to preserve that remedy. A review of the legislative history of the statute persuasively indicates that preservation of the remedy was indeed what Congress actually intended.

V

Congress was, of course, familiar not only with the implied private remedy but also with the long history of federal regulation of commodity futures trading. From the enactment of the original federal legislation, Congress primarily has relied upon the exchanges to regulate the contract markets. The 1922 legislation required for designation as a contract market that an exchange "provide for" the making and filing of reports and records, the prevention of dissemination of false or misleading reports, the prevention of price manipulation and market cornering, and the enforcement of Commission orders. To fulfill these conditions, the exchanges promulgated rules and regulations, but they did not always enforce them. In 1968, Congress attempted to correct this flaw in the self-regulation concept by enacting 5a(8), 7 U.S.C. 7a(8), which requires the exchanges to enforce their own rules.

The enactment of 5a(8), coupled with the recognition by the federal courts of an implied private remedy for violations of the CEA, gave rise to a new problem. As representatives of the exchanges complained during the hearing preceding the 1974 amendments, the exchanges were being sued for not enforcing their rules. The complaint was taken seriously because it implicated the self-regulation premise of the CEA:

"In the few years [5a(8)] has been in the present Commodity Exchange Act, there is growing evidence to indicate that, as opposed to strengthening the self-regulatory concept in present law, such a provision, coupled with only limited federal authority to require the exchanges to make and issue rules appropriate to enforcement of the Act—may actually have worked to weaken it. With inadequate enforcement personnel the Committee was informed that attorneys to several boards of trade have been advising the boards to reduce—not expand exchange regulations designed to insure fair trading, since there is a growing body of opinion that failure to enforce the exchange rules is a violation of the Act which will support suits by private litigants." House Report, at 46 (emphasis in original).

Congress could have removed this impediment to exchange rulemaking by eliminating the implied private remedy, but it did not follow that course. Rather, it solved the problem by authorizing the new Commodity Futures Trading Commission to supplement exchange rules. Congress thereby corrected the legal mechanism of self-regulation while preserving a significant incentive for the exchanges to obey the law. Only this course was consistent with the expressed purpose of the 1974 legislation, which was to "amend the Commodity Exchange Act to strengthen the regulation of futures trading."

Congress in 1974 created new procedures through which traders might seek relief for violations of the CEA, but the legislative evidence indicates that these informal procedures were intended to supplement rather than supplant the implied judicial remedy. These procedures do not substitute for the private remedy either as a means of compensating injured traders or as a means of enforcing compliance with the statute.

The late addition of a saving clause in 2 (a) (1) provides direct evidence of legislative intent to preserve the implied private remedy federal courts had recognized under the CEA. Along with an increase in powers, the Commission was given exclusive jurisdiction over commodity futures trading. The purpose of the exclusive-jurisdiction provision in the bill passed by the House was to separate the functions of the Commission from those of the Securities and Exchange Commission and other regulatory agencies. But the provision raised concerns that the jurisdiction of state and federal courts might be affected. Referring to the treble damages action provided in another bill that he and Senator McGovern had introduced, Senator Clark pointed out: "[T]he House bill not only does not authorize them, but section 201 of that bill may prohibit all court actions. The staff of the House Agriculture Committee has said that this was done inadvertently and they hope it can be corrected in the Senate." It was. The Senate added a saving clause to the exclusive-jurisdiction provision, providing that "[n]othing in this section shall supersede or limit the jurisdiction conferred on courts of the United States or any State." The Conference accepted the Senate amendment.

The inference that Congress intended to preserve the pre-existing remedy is compelling. As the Solicitor General argues on behalf of the Commission as amicus curiae, the private cause of action enhances the enforcement mechanism fostered by Congress over the course of 60 years. In an enactment purporting to strengthen the regulation of commodity futures trading, Congress evidenced an affirmative intent to preserve this enforcement tool. It removed an impediment to exchange rulemaking caused in part by the implied private remedy not by disapproving that remedy but rather by giving the Commission the extraordinary power to supplement exchange rules. And when several Members of Congress expressed a concern that the exclusive-jurisdiction provision, which was intended only to consolidate federal regulation of commodity futures trading in the Commission, might be construed to affect the implied cause of action as well as other court actions, Congress acted swiftly to dispel any such notion. Congress could have made its intent clearer only by expressly providing for a private cause of action in the statute. In the legal context in which Congress acted, this was unnecessary.

In view of our construction of the intent of the Legislature there is no need for us to "trudge through all four of the factors when the dispositive question of legislative intent has been resolved." See California v. Sierra Club, 451 U.S., at 302 (REHNQUIST, J., concurring in judgment). We hold that the private cause of action under the CEA that was previously available to investors survived the 1974 amendments.

…

第二节　对金融衍生产品的监管

对金融衍生产品的监管，中国和美国有类似之处：二者均未成立专门的统一的监管机构，而是由多个部门和组织，在不同层次上对金融衍生产品实施多头监管。最终，形成多个政府监管部门和相关行业协会以及交易所合作监管的体系。

多头监管的优势在于，监管更具针对性。多个监管部门对金融机构和产品之间的差异能够给予足够的认识和区分，区别对待从而实现更好的监管效果。但是其缺点也是显而易见的。在各个监管机构权限划分不够清晰以及新生事物监管无明确的情况下，就会造成重复监管或无人监管的局面，使得监管达不到预期效果，造成市场混乱。

一、中国对金融衍生产品的监管

在中国，最重要的金融衍生产品交易监管主体是中国银监会和中国证监会。

中国银监会实施机构监管，负责监管从事金融衍生产品交易业务的银行业金融机构。早在 2004 年，中国银监会就发布了《金融机构衍生产品交易业务管理暂行办法》（下称《暂行办法》，于 2007 年和 2011 年经过修订），对中国境内的银行业金融机构从事金融衍生产品进行系统性地规定。按照《暂行办法》的规定，中国境内的银行业金融机构（包括依法设立的商业银行、城市信用合作社、农村信用合作社等吸收公众存款的金融机构以及政策性银行与依法设立的金融资产管理公司、信托公司、企业集团财务公司、金融租赁公司，以及经中国银监会批准设立的其他银行业金融机构）从事衍生产品业务应当经过中国银监会批准，同时接受中国银监会的监督和检查。

中国证监会同时实施机构监管和行为监管。按照中国2007年颁布的《期货交易管理条例》的规定，国务院期货监督管理机构对期货市场实行集中统一的监督管理，其中的“国务院期货监督管理机构”实际上是中国证监会。中国证监会依法对证券机构、期货交易所、结算机构以及期货市场中介实施监管，同时还对期货市场上的违法、违规行为进行监管。此外，对于资本市场上流通的其他类型的金融衍生产品（如权证），中国证监会亦有完全的监管权利。

中国银监会重点监管银行业金融机构所实施的衍生品交易，包括场内和场外；而中国证监会的监管，则主要是针对场内衍生品交易。就场外衍生品交易而言，中国国家外汇管理局、中国人民银行等是非常重要的监管主体，它们实施行为监管。

自2005年6月15日银行间债券市场正式推出债券远期交易以来，中国人民银行先后推出了人民币外汇远期、人民币利率互换、人民币外汇掉期、远期利率协议等场外衍生品业务。为加强对该等场外衍生品交易的监管，中国人民银行与国家外汇管理局针对不同场外金融衍生产品制定了不同的管理规定，如《远期利率协议业务管理规定》、《全国银行间债券市场债券远期交易管理规定》、《关于在银行间外汇市场开办人民币外汇货币掉期业务有关问题的通知》等，从市场准入、交易结算安排、交易信息备案、市场监测等方面对市场加以制度性规范。

除了政府监管机构之外，中国还设立有相关的行业自律性组织，它们对金融衍生产品的交易也进行着一定的监管。这种行业自律性组织包括两类：一类是相关的行业协会，中国已经先后成立了中国证券业协会、中国期货业协会以及中国国债协会等；另一类是相关的交易平台机构，中国已成立了上海和深圳两个证券交易所、大连和郑州两个商品交易所以及上海期货交易所和中国金融期货交易所等。这些行业自律性组织制定、发布和实施相关自律性监管规则，对于金融衍生产品交易的监管起到了积极的补充作用。

二、美国对金融衍生产品的监管

美国是金融衍生产品交易最发达的国家，其对金融衍生品监管的法律制度也较为健全。早在1922年，美国国会即通过了《谷物期货法》，开始对商品期货予以监管。在随后陆续发布的《商品交易法》、《商品期货交易委员会法》、《2000年商品期货现代化法》以及诸多修正案中，美国对金融衍生品监管的法律制度日渐成熟。

随着监管法律制度的不断完善，美国已经形成以商品期货交易委员会（CFTC）和证券交易委员会（SEC）为核心的监管体系。目前，CFTC负责监管大部分场内交易的商品、金融期货和期货期权，以及零售客户的场外交易；而SEC则负责监管场内交易的证券类衍生品，包括股票及股票指数期权和在证券交易所上市的外汇期权等。CFTC 和 SEC 在长期的监管实践之中，形成了体系完善的监管架构与机制。

在美国，行业自律性组织在衍生品监管方面也发挥着非常重要的作用。例如，期货经纪商、商品基金、从业人员等必须加入全国期货业协会（NFA）成为会员，NFA 根据 CFTC 的授权进行会员管理；而交易所则对衍生品市场进行一线监管。

但是，传统上，美国对金融衍生产品的监管主要集中于场内交易上，场外衍生品市场监管几乎是空白。这是因为，《商品期货现代化法》确定了“合格的合约交易者”（Eligible Contract Participant, ECPs）制度，规定对于大型银行、券商、基金等金融机构之间的场外衍生品交易，不受 CFTC 和 SEC 的监管，法律让其风险自担。ECPs 没有受到监管机构太多的束缚，只被要求符合银行或券商业务的基本监管要求。

场外衍生品的交易，主要就是在 ECPs 之间展开的。对场外金融衍生品缺乏监管，成为美国 2008 年金融危机的导火索。一款名为信用违约互换的场外衍生品出现大规模违约，引发金融危机。危机过后，美国国会开始对金融市场进行大规模改革，其中很重要的一个方面就是对金融衍生产品尤其是场外衍生品交易加强监管。

2010 年 7 月，美国国会通过《多德—弗兰克华尔街改革和消费者保护法案》。该法案特别加强了对场外交易的衍生产品和资产支持证券等产品的监管，重要内容包括：修正了场外衍生品的豁免原则，将场外衍生品主要是互换纳入到衍生品监管当局的监管范围，由 CFTC 和 SEC 进行监管；将大部分场外金融衍生产品移入交易所和清算中心；要求银行剥离信用违约互换、农产品、未明确大宗商品、能源及多数金属的掉期交易业务等风险最高的衍生品交易业务，或将其转至非银行分支机构；加强了互换交易商（Swap Dealers）与大型互换参与人（Major Swap Participants, MSP）等场外衍生品市场主体的注册与行为监管，对其实施特别的资本比例、保证金、交易记录和职业操守等监管要求；还对衍生品市场的透明度提出了相应的要求。

三、案例资料

美国对金融衍生产品的监管，是一种多头交叉监管的体制。其中，对银行从事衍生品交易，银行的监管部门也有权监管（机构监管）。但是，对银行的监管有些特殊：银行被认为是“合格的合约交易者”，因而只需要满足“安全与稳健”（Safety and Soundness）原则，按规定的方法计提风险资本，满足资本充足率要求即可，而并非像其他的市场参与者那样受到严厉监管。但是，基于天然的逐利性，银行往往突破了“安全与稳健”原则的要求。

在下面的案例中，一家银行因违背了银行业的监管部门——联邦存款保险公司（FDIC）发布的一项备忘录（该备忘录要求银行制作为处理利率风险敞口以及规范基于减小利率风险使用期货的书面凭据；还要求银行每次为降低利率风险而使用期货之时，均应提供详细的理由），因而 FDIC 发布了“停止与禁止令”（Cease and Desist Order），要求该银行纠正其违规行为，遵守 FDIC 发布的备忘录及政策声明。银行对此不服，提起诉讼。

依据美国《联邦存款保险法》的相关规定，除非能够证明 FDIC 采取的措施是武断恣意的或者违法的，否则法院不得撤销 FDIC 采取的措施。在该案中，考虑到期货交易的高风险性，FDIC 认为，原告银行不遵守备忘录的行为，是不安全且不稳健的。至于判断标准，依据美国《联邦存款保险法》的相关规定，如果某一行为被认为与公认的银行业经营准则相违背，从而可能会给该银行或其股东带来异常的风险或损失，那么该行为就会被认为是不安全或不稳健的。该案的审理法院最终支持了 FDIC 的裁决。

Greene County Bank v. Federal Deposit Insurance Corp.

92 F.3d 633 (C.A.8, 1996)

JACKSON, District Judge.

The Greene County Bank appeals a cease and desist order issued by the Board of Directors of the Federal Deposit Insurance Corporation (“FDIC”). The order requires the Bank to comply with a February 12, 1992 Memorandum of Understanding (“MOU”) regarding certain activities in the futures and securities markets, and was prompted by the alleged failure of the Bank to comply with the MOU. The Bank attacks the order as not *635 supported by substantial evidence and as arbitrary and capricious. The Bank also argues that the FDIC applied an incorrect standard in determining that the Bank engaged in unsafe and unsound practices. We uphold the cease and desist order.

I. BACKGROUND

The FDIC initiated an administrative action against the Bank pursuant to 12 U.S.C. s 1818 (b) on July 26, 1993 by issuing a Notice of Charges and Hearing. Following a three-day hearing, an Administrative Law Judge (“ALJ”) recommended against the issuance of a cease and desist order. Upon review of the ALJ’s decision, the FDIC Board found failures of compliance that constituted violations of the MOU and the FDIC Policy Statement as well as unsafe and unsound practices. As a result, the FDIC issued a cease and desist order requiring the Bank to comply with the MOU and FDIC Policy Statement.

II. DISCUSSION

[1][2] In considering the Bank’s challenge to the sufficiency of the evidence to support

the cease and desist order, our review is limited to a determination of whether the agency decision is supported by substantial evidence on the record as a whole. Northwest National Bank v. United States Dept. of the Treasury, 917 F.2d 1111 (8th Cir. 1990); First Nat'l Bank of Eden v. Dept. of the Treasury, 568 F.2d 610, 611 (8th Cir. 1978). Substantial evidence "is such relevant evidence as a reasonable mind might accept as adequate to support a conclusion." Culbertson v. Shalala, 30 F.3d 934, 939 (8th Cir. 1994). In reviewing the agency decision, we consider the entire record, including the ALJ's recommendation. Simon v. Simmons Foods, Inc., 49 F.3d 386, 389 (8th Cir. 1995). If the agency departs from the findings of the ALJ, it must show that it gave "attentive consideration" to the ALJ's conclusions. Id. at 390.

[3] At issue in this case is whether the process by which the Bank engaged in futures and securities market activities complied with the procedures set forth in the MOU. The MOU requires the Bank to (1) develop written policies for addressing interest rate risk exposure and governing the use of futures to reduce interest rate risk and (2) provide detailed justification each time the Bank uses futures to reduce interest rate risk. The MOU also incorporates the FDIC Policy Statement which, in part, requires the Bank's board of directors to approve any plan to engage in futures market activities. In his recommended decision, the ALJ concluded that the Bank had complied with the MOU in material respects but had not adopted an investment policy in compliance with Section 1 (c). The ALJ, however, did not recommend the issuance of a cease and desist order. In its reversal of the ALJ decision, the FDIC found that the Bank had in fact failed to adhere to the MOU requirements by engaging in futures and securities market transactions without prior approval by the Bank's board of directors and without proper analysis and documentation. The FDIC concluded that in light of the risks involved in these types of transactions, complete compliance with the MOU was required, and the cease and desist order was necessary to ensure such compliance.

The record shows that the Bank failed to comply with the terms of the MOU and the FDIC Policy Statement when it did not properly document and obtain approval of the acquisition of a number of spread positions. The Bank began acquiring these positions in the Fall of 1992. However, these investments were not formally approved by the Board until March 29, 1993, months after they were made. The only document in the record which contained the Bank's explanation of its strategy for this type of investment *636 was undated. The FDIC concluded that to the extent that any documents contained language that could be construed as authorizing the acquisition of these spread positions, such language was too vague to comply with the requirements of the FDIC Policy Statement. The testimony of the

FDIC examiner in charge supports this conclusion.

The FDIC's decision was also based on substantial evidence of deficiencies regarding the Bank's calculation and analysis of interest rate risk exposure. The evidence revealed that the Bank did not calculate and analyze its interest rate risk exposure on a regular basis as the MOU required. Although the ALJ believed that this deficiency could be excused because the Bank was receiving gap analyses measuring the exposure from the FDIC and other examiners, clearly the terms of the MOU required regular monitoring by the Bank.

After reviewing the record as a whole, we find that the FDIC's determination that the Bank failed to fully comply with the conditions of the MOU is supported by substantial evidence.

[4][5] The Bank also attacks as arbitrary and capricious the FDIC's decision to issue a cease and desist order. Our review of the remedy imposed by the FDIC to address unsafe and unsound banking practices is limited. The remedy may not be set aside unless it is "arbitrary, capricious, or otherwise contrary to law." Currie State Bank v. FDIC, 878 F.2d 215, 218 (8th Cir. 1989). Pursuant to 12 U.S.C. s 1818 (b) (1), the FDIC may issue a cease and desist order to prevent a bank from engaging in unsafe or unsound practices. Proof of misconduct alone entitles the FDIC to invoke its broad cease and desist enforcement powers. Oberstar v. FDIC, 987 F.2d 494, 502 (8th Cir. 1993).

[6] In this case, the FDIC concluded that the Bank's failure to comply with the MOU constituted an unsafe and unsound banking practice, justifying the issuance of a cease and desist order. As discussed above, the record contains substantial evidence to support the agency's decision. Upon finding an unsafe and unsound banking practice, the FDIC may require a bank to "take affirmative action to correct the conditions resulting from any such... practice." 12 U.S.C. s 1818 (b) (1). The requirements imposed by the cease and desist order constitute the type of affirmative action that is authorized by the statute. See Eden, 568 F.2d at 611 n. 1 (upholding cease and desist order to address the failure to implement internal controls and auditing procedures). Based on the foregoing, we conclude that the choice of remedy by thc FDIC in this case was not arbitrary and capricious.

[7] Finally, the Bank argues that the FDIC applied the wrong standard in determining that the Bank's failure to comply with the MOU constituted an unsafe and unsound practice. The Bank argues that application of the "unsafe and unsound practice" standard is limited to practices having a reasonably direct effect on the Bank's financial soundness, a situation not present in this case. See Matter of Seidman, 37 F.3d 911 (3rd Cir. 1994); Hoffman v. FDIC,

912 F.2d 1172 (9th Cir. 1990); Gulf Federal Savings & Loan v. FHLBB, 651 F.2d 259 (5th Cir. 1981), cert. denied, 458 U.S. 1121, 102 S.Ct. 3509, 73 L.Ed.2d 1383 (1982). It is well-settled in this Circuit, however, that an "unsafe or unsound practice" exists where the conduct is "deemed contrary to accepted standards of banking operations which might result in abnormal risk or loss to a banking institution or shareholder." Eden, 568 F.2d at 611 n. 2. See also Oberstar, 987 F.2d at 502. We conclude that the FDIC in this case applied the appropriate standard to determine whether the challenged action constituted an "unsafe or unsound practice."

The August 1, 1995 Decision and Order of the FDIC Board of Directors is affirmed.

9 第九章 国际金融法律制度

第一节 国际金融市场的准入

国际金融市场的准入，是国际金融法首先要解决的问题。自由开放的金融市场准入，是国际金融交易繁荣发展的前提。目前，国际金融市场的准入制度，体现在四个层面：全球多边准入体系、区域性准入体系、双边准入体系以及一国国内的准入制度。其中，区域性和双边的准入体系，以各国之间达成的区域经济一体化协议及双边协定为基础，这些协议/协定之中有关金融服务的制度，包含了金融市场准入的内容。全球多边准入体系，目前主要是由以 WTO 体系下的《服务贸易总协定》（下称 GATS）及有关金融服务的《第五议定书》为基础建立起来的。

一、WTO 体系下的金融市场准入

GATS 对服务贸易提供的四种方式进行了全面的界定，包括跨境提供（cross-border supply）、境外消费（consumption abroad）、商业存在（commercial establishment）以及自然人移动（movement of natural persons）。根据 GATS 的相关规定，WTO 成员方影响通过以上四种服务提供方式所发生的金融服务的所有措施，均受 WTO 规则的约束。WTO 所建立起来的多边金融市场准入制度，主要体现在 GATS 第三部分（对成员方就市场准入、国民待遇以及附加承诺的规定）和与之相联系的金融服务承诺表中，同时受 GATS 其他部分和金融服务附件（Annex on Financial Service）规定的约束。

在 WTO 体系下，就市场准入而言，与货物贸易不同，服务贸易领域各成员方有着更大的自由裁量权。在服务贸易领域，由于各国发展水平差距较大，市场准入和国民待遇并不构成各成员方普遍性、一般性义务，不能自动在所有成员方的各个服务部门适用，

而需由各成员方具体作出承诺。在金融服务部门，选择何种金融服务的市场准入和国民待遇承诺，GATS 允许各成员方自由决定。

WTO 关于金融市场准入的规定，由三个部分构成：GATS、金融服务附件以及金融服务承诺表。其中，GATS 是关于服务贸易的一般性规定，由于金融服务贸易属于服务贸易的组成部分，因此 GATS 的规定适用于金融服务；金融服务附件是针对金融业的特点和需要而制定的，其将 GATS 的有关规定具体化而适用于金融服务领域；金融服务承诺表则记载 WTO 各成员方在金融服务贸易方面对市场准入和国民待遇的承诺以及附加承诺。[①]

二、中国金融市场对外准入制度

中国在 2001 年加入 WTO 时，就其银行业（包括一般银行服务、非银行金融机构从事的汽车消费信贷以及其他金融服务）、证券业以及保险业等作出了相关的开放承诺。为履行在 WTO 下的承诺，中国对国内的相关法律、法规进行了修改，逐步放开了相关金融服务市场，建立起了与 WTO 承诺相符的对外准入法律制度。

根据中国入世所作的承诺，中国的金融市场对外准入制度，主要体现在金融服务提供的四种方式下的市场准入限制和国民待遇限制方面。以证券业为例，对于跨境提供方式下的证券服务的市场准入，除承诺外国证券机构可直接从事 B 股交易外，中国没有作出承诺，对准入的证券服务中国没有国民待遇限制；对于境外消费方式下的市场准入和国民待遇，中国都没有限制；对于商业存在方式下的证券服务的市场准入，中国存在一些市场准入方面的限制（如投资方式、股权比例），并未完全放开，但是对准入的证券服务没有国民待遇限制；对自然人流动方式下的市场准入和国民待遇，中国则除水平承诺的内容外没有进行承诺。

当然，中国在 WTO 下的承诺，仅是对中国最低限度的要求。在实践中，中国的一些举措甚至超出其承诺的水平。例如，中国于 2002 年制定《合格境外机构投资者境内证券投资管理暂行办法》，实施了 QFII（Qualified Foreign Institutional Investor）制度。在人民币资本项下未完全实现自由兑换的情况下，QFII 制度允许境外资金通过 QFII 投资 A 股市场，这是中国在证券业的承诺表中所没有的。

三、案例资料

2010 年 6 月，全球最大的支付公司 Visa 与中国银联之间爆发争端。Visa 由于无法打开中国国内市场，同时又面临中国银联不断拓展海外市场所带来的冲击，于是向其合作银行发函，要求在境外“封杀”中国银联。中国银联随后展开了一系列反击措施。争

① 韩龙. 国际金融法前沿问题. 北京：清华大学出版社，2010：154.

端不断升级，最终引发美国就“中国电子支付服务措施案”向WTO提出申诉。

2010年9月15日，就“中国对有关支付卡交易的电子支付服务及其提供商实施的限制和要求”问题，美国要求与中国展开磋商。美国声称，中国自2001年以来发布了多项限制措施，使人民币支付卡交易由中国银联垄断，对外国服务提供商造成歧视，违反了中国开放金融服务业市场的相关承诺。磋商失败后，2011年2月11日，美国要求设立专家组。WTO的争端解决机构（DSB）在其2011年3月25日的会议上设立了专家组，专家组的成员于2011年7月4日确定。目前，此案尚未作出最终裁决。

这是美国就金融服务业状告中国的首宗案件，也是美国试图打开整个中国服务业市场的一块“敲门砖”。案件的核心在于，中国对相关金融市场的准入制度是否违反了WTO承诺。在服务贸易领域，成员方只对承诺表中已经承诺的服务项目履行义务，对没有承诺的项目没有履行义务。因此，本案争议的焦点，将是人民币支付卡业务是否属于中国列举于承诺表中的开放项目，对此中美有不同的理解。最终的结果，有待专家组或上诉机构的裁决。以下是美国提交给WTO的起诉书，我们可以看看美国对中国的指责，是否有道理。

China—Certain Measures Affecting Electronic Payment Services

<u>Request for the Establishment of a Panel by the United States</u>

The following communication, dated 11 February 2011, from the delegation of the United States to the Chairman of the Dispute Settlement Body, is circulated pursuant to Article 6.2 of the DSU.

On 15 September 2010, the United States requested consultations with the Government of the People's Republic of China ("China") pursuant to Articles 1 and 4 of the *Understanding on Rules and Procedures Governing the Settlement of Disputes* ("DSU"), and Article XXII of the *General Agreement on Trade in Services* ("GATS") with respect to certain restrictions and requirements maintained by China affecting electronic payment services① for payment card transactions and the suppliers of those services ("electronic payment services suppliers"). The

① "Electronic payment services" involve the services through which transactions involving payment cards (as defined below) are processed and through which transfers of funds between institutions participating in the transactions are managed and facilitated. Suppliers of electronic payment services supply, directly or indirectly, a system that typically includes the following: the processing infrastructure, network, and rules and procedures that facilitate, manage, and enable transaction information and payment flows and which provide system integrity, stability and financial risk reduction; the process and coordination of approving or declining a transaction, with approval generally permitting a purchase to be finalized or cash to be disbursed or exchanged; the delivery of transaction information among participating entities; the calculation, determination, and reporting of the net financial position of relevant institutions for all transactions that have been authorized; and the facilitation, management and/or other participation in the transfer of net payments owed among participating institutions.

United States held consultations with China on 27-28 October 2010. Unfortunately, those consultations did not resolve the dispute.

In the financial services sector, as set out in China's GATS Schedule of Specific Commitments on Services (the "Schedule"), China undertook commitments under Articles XVI and XVII of the GATS with respect to:

- "Banking services as listed below: ... All payment and money transmission services, including credit, charge and debit cards, travellers cheques and bankers drafts (including import and export settlement)";
- "Other financial services as listed below: ... Provision and transfer of financial information, and financial data processing and related software by supplier of other financial services"; and
- "Advisory, intermediation and other auxiliary financial services on all activities listed in subparagraphs (a) through (k), including credit reference and analysis, investment and portfolio research and advice, advice on acquisitions and on corporate restructuring and strategy."

Despite those commitments, China imposes market access restrictions and requirements on service suppliers of other Members seeking to supply electronic payment services in China. Through these and other related and reinforcing requirements and restrictions China accords less favorable treatment to electronic payment services suppliers of other Members than to Chinese suppliers of these services.

China UnionPay ("CUP"), a Chinese entity, is the only entity that China permits to supply electronic payment services for payment card transactions denominated and paid in renminbi ("RMB") in China. China also requires the handling by CUP of all RMB transactions in Macao or Hong Kong using payment cards issued in Mainland China, as well as any RMB transactions in Mainland China using RMB payment cards issued in Hong Kong, China or Macao, China. The United States considers that these measures are inconsistent with China's obligations under GATS Article XVI:1 to accord services and services suppliers of any other Member treatment no less favorable that that provided for in China's Schedule and that China is maintaining or adopting measures set out in Article XVI:2 of the GATS. These measures also appear inconsistent with China's obligations under GATS Article XVII to accord to services and service suppliers of any other Member treatment no less favorable than that it accords to its own like services and service suppliers.

In addition, China requires all payment card processing devices at merchant locations, all automated teller machines ("ATMs"), and all point-of-sale ("POS") terminals in China to be compatible with CUP's system and capable of accepting CUP payment cards. China also requires that all acquiring institutions post the CUP logo and be capable of accepting all payment cards bearing the CUP logo. China further requires that all payment cards, including "dual currency" cards, issued in China capable of being used for transactions denominated and paid in RMB bear the CUP logo. This means that issuing banks must have access to the CUP system, and must pay CUP for that access. These measures do not impose similar requirements regarding non-CUP payment cards or to transactions using non-CUP payment cards. The United States considers that these measures are inconsistent with China's obligations under GATS Article XVI:1 to accord services and services suppliers of any other Member treatment no less favorable that that provided for in China's Schedule and that China is maintaining or adopting measures set out in Article XVI:2. The United States considers that these measures are inconsistent with China's obligations under GATS Article XVII to accord to services and service suppliers of any other Member treatment no less favorable than that it accords to its own like services and service suppliers.

China also requires that all cross-bank or inter-bank transactions involving payment cards be handled through CUP. China prohibits the use of non-CUP payment cards for cross-region or cross-bank or inter-bank transactions. The United States also considers that these measures are inconsistent with China's obligations under GATS Article XVI:1 to accord services and services suppliers of any other Member treatment no less favorable that that provided for in China's Schedule and that China is maintaining or adopting measures set out in Article XVI:2. The United States also considers that these measures are inconsistent with China's obligations under GATS Article XVII to accord to services and service suppliers of any other Member treatment no less favorable than that it accords to its own like services and service suppliers.

The United States understands that the instruments through which China maintains these measures include….

The United States considers that these measures are inconsistent with China's obligations under Articles XVI, including XVI:1 and XVI: 2 (a), and XVII of the GATS. These measures also appear to nullify or impair the benefits accruing to the United States directly or indirectly under the cited agreements.

Accordingly, the United States respectfully requests that, pursuant to Article 6 of the DSU, the Dispute Settlement Body establish a panel to examine the matter, with the standard terms of reference as set out in Article 7.1 of the DSU.

资料来源：世界贸易组织网站：WT/DS413/2 (14 February 2011), available at http://docsonline.wto.org/imrd/directdoc.asp?DDFDocuments/t/WT/DS/413-2.doc.

第二节 国际银行业监管

20 世纪 70 年代以来，银行业国际化和金融市场全球化、一体化深入发展，银行等金融企业不断跨越国界设立机构从事经营。各国的银行监管机构都要负责对本国银行的境外分支机构和境内外资银行实施监管，即要同时充当母国监管机构和东道国监管机构的角色，这对各国监管机构实施有效监管提出了更高的要求。因此，各国银行监管机构越来越关注监管的国际合作问题。

要确保跨境银行业务得到有效监管，避免因各国监管机构的各自为政所导致的监管遗漏或重叠，就必须建立一种行之有效的国际协调和国际合作机制。对跨境银行业务，母国监管机构需实施全球并表监管，对银行在世界各地的业务，特别是其外国分行、附属机构的各项业务，进行充分有效的监管；同时，东道国监管机构也需对境内的外国银行机构实施有效监管。由此，母国与东道国监管机构建立监管合作机制就显得非常重要。有了这样的监管合作机制，就能确保监管的充分有效性，维护银行业的安全与稳定。

一、巴塞尔委员会

巴塞尔委员会全称为“巴塞尔银行监管委员会”（The Basle Committee On Banking Supervision），成立于 1974 年，是顺应加强银行监管的国际协调合作这一需要而设立的，是国际银行监管领域最重要且最有影响力的一个组织。多年以来，该委员会以其卓越的工作，极大地推动了国际银行监管的完善。

作为国际清算银行的一个正式机构，巴塞尔委员会以各国中央银行官员和银行监管当局为代表。委员会每年定期集会 4 次，并拥有近 30 个技术机构，执行每年集会所订目标或计划。

该委员会的一项重要任务是堵塞国际监管中的漏洞，它遵循着两项基本原则：没有任何境外银行机构可以逃避监管；监管应当是充分的（no foreign banking establishment should escape supervision; and that supervision should be adequate）。为此，委员会采取了一系列措施：交换各国的监管安排方面的信息、提高国际银行业务监管技术的有效性、确立最低限度的监管标准。

巴塞尔委员会制定了许多监管标准和指导原则，提倡最佳监管做法，期望各国采取措施，根据本国的情况，通过具体的立法或其他安排予以实施。委员会鼓励采用共同的方法和共同的标准，但并不强求成员国在监管技术上一致。委员会制定和发布的诸多规则已经成为国际银行监管的范本，为诸多国家所吸纳和借鉴。值得说明的是，巴塞尔委员会并非一个超国家组织，其并不具备任何凌驾于国家之上的正式监管特权，其文件从不具备亦从未试图具备任何法律效力，而是仅供各国参考。

二、中国的监管

中国《银行业监督管理法》规定，“国务院银行业监督管理机构可以和其他国家或者地区的银行业监督管理机构建立监督管理合作机制，实施跨境监督管理”。中国银监会作为“国务院银行业监督管理机构”，获得立法授权，可以直接同境外的银行业监管机构展开合作。

随着中国金融体系的逐步对外开放，越来越多的外国银行涌入中国；同时，中国的银行业金融机构为提高国际竞争力，也纷纷走出国门，走国际化发展的道路。这就要求中国的银行业监管不断提高国际化水平，加强跨境监管。无论是作为东道国监管机构还是母国监管机构，都需要中国银行监管机构与境外监管机构展开合作，提高跨境监管能力，提升整体的银行监管水平。

中国银监会自成立以来，积极开展银行业监管的国际合作，有力地提升了监管技术水平和监管实效。截止 2011 年 6 月底，中国已经与 44 个国家和地区的银行监管当局签署了双边监管谅解备忘录或合作协议。此外，中国还加入了巴塞尔委员会，并通过发布指引的方式，有步骤地实施巴塞尔协议，使中国的监管与国际标准接轨。

三、案例资料

随着全球化的不断深入，银行业早已经进入跨国经营时代。在当前的形势之下，要真正实现对银行业的有效监管，离不开各国监管机构之间的合作。中美两国很早就展开了在银行业监管方面的合作。2002 年 1 月 18 日，因调查发现中国银行纽约分行存在严重违规行为，美国财政部货币监理署与中国人民银行联合发布消息，对中国银行纽约分行的违规行为作出严厉处罚。

在这一事件中，中美两国的银行业监管机构展开了良好的合作。在相对复杂的美国金融监管体系中，货币监理署负责美国全国性银行以及外国银行在美分行的现场检查。该机构的使命是“确保支持着美国公民、社区和经济的全国银行体系安全可靠并具有竞争力”。中国人民银行当时作为中国银行业监督管理部门（中国银监会当时尚未成立），履行对中国境内的中资银行和设立的外资银行的监管职责。由于事件涉及中国银行在美分支机构，经过中美两国银行业监管机构的联合调查，发现中国银行纽约分行存在一系列违规行为。随后，中美两国的监管机构共同发布了处罚声明：中行纽约分行将向美国货币监理署交纳 1 000 万美元罚款，其母公司中国银行则向中国人民银行交纳相当于

1 000 万美元的人民币罚款。

按照中国人民银行新闻发言人的说法，这一事件充分“体现了金融监管的严肃性以及两国金融监管机构的密切合作，也是对其他银行的警示，将有利于促进银行业的审慎经营和健康发展”。①

OCC and People's Bank of China Assess Money Penalties against Bank of China

January 18, 2002

WASHINGTON—The Office of the Comptroller of the Currency and the People's Bank of China announced today they have entered into separate actions against Bank of China and its U.S.-based federal branches for misconduct engaged in by prior management. The bank's New York branch will pay a $10 million penalty to the OCC and the parent bank, which is based in Beijing, will pay an equivalent amount in local currency to the People's Bank of China, for a total of $20 million. The bank and its U.S. branches have begun to implement measures to prevent future misconduct.

In reaching this settlement, the OCC noted that the bank's current management cooperated with the investigations conducted by the OCC and the People's Bank of China. The actions taken by the new management of the bank include removing officers suspected of misconduct, uncovering and reporting acts of misconduct to the two regulatory agencies, and requiring the U.S. branches to implement several action plans over the past 18 months to correct misconduct of prior management.

The OCC supervises Bank of China's three U.S.-based federal branches—two in New York and one in Los Angeles. The OCC's monetary penalties were levied against one of the New York branches, where the misconduct was uncovered, but the remedial measures cover all three branches. The People's Bank of China is the home-country regulator of Bank of China.

The misconduct, which resulted in significant losses to the New York Branch, included showing preferential treatment to certain customers of the New York branch who had personal relationships with some members of the New York branch's prior management.

The OCC had a number of other concerns about the Bank of China's U.S. branches under the former bank management, including large exposures to a single borrower, the facilitation

① 参见新华网：[2011-10-20]. http://news.xinhuanet.com/newscenter/2002-01/21/content_247532.htm.

of a fraudulent letter of credit scheme, the facilitation of a loan fraud scheme, the unauthorized release of collateral and the concealment of that action, and other suspicious activity and potential fraud.

In its consent order, the OCC required Bank of China's federal branches to: develop procedures to guard against fraud; provide for adequate customer due diligence, using an independent third party to verify compliance; and cease doing business with 34 specific individuals and companies, and affiliated entities. The consent order also requires Bank of China's federal branches to:

- Strengthen their Risk Management Division, ensuring that it has unrestricted access to documents, files and personnel of the federal branches, and authority to terminate customer relationships, deny loans and conduct investigations.
- Develop new policies and procedures to guard against fraud in trade settlement transactions, including direct verifications of documents submitted by customers.
- Adopt new policies and procedures to prevent loan fraud, including analysis of related accounts, requirements for audited financial statements and additional due diligence on large customers and those who conduct business with the large customers.
- Hire an independent third-party to conduct a portion of the direct verifications of trade settlement documents and conduct due diligence on large customers and their business relationships.
- Implement new procedures to identify account owners and beneficial owners. In the case of business accounts, officers, directors and major shareholders must be identified and, in some cases, credit reports are required for account owners, beneficial owners, shareholders and other parties.

Bank of China's U.S. branches have already begun to implement the remedial measures required in the consent order. In taking the enforcement action, both the OCC and the People's Bank of China recognized the bank's willingness to rectify past problems and the substantial progress that it has made. The two agencies believe that the bank's reorganization of the branches will better ensure compliance with applicable federal law and safe and sound banking practices.

The enforcement action stems from a lengthy investigation by the OCC and a separate inquiry by the People's Bank of China.

资料来源：美国货币监理署网站 *http://www.occ.gov/static/news-issuances/news-releases/002/nr-occ-2002-7.pdf,* 访问日期 2011/11/12.

第三节　国际证券业监管

证券监管是随着证券市场的发展而不断成熟起来的，其产生与发展都与证券市场息息相关。随着证券市场的全球化、一体化、混业化和电子化，全球证券市场已经联结成一个整体。在这一背景之下，各国证券监管机构面临着更多、更大的挑战。要有效应对当前监管的各种挑战，需各国政府通过相互协调与合作，共同对国际证券市场进行监管。加强证券市场国际监管的合作与协调，已成为各国的共同要求。

从目前各国的实际做法来看，国际证券监管合作的方式与途径主要包括：（1）采用双边监管合作的方式，即两国的证券主管机关之间为证券市场管理的一些法律性、技术性问题而开展交流和协作；（2）采用多边监管合作的方式，包括区域性多边合作和全球性多边合作两类。双边监管合作是最基本、最常见的形式，一般通过签订双边协定来实现，主要形式为“司法互助协定”和“谅解备忘录”。多边监管合作，则通过签订多边性监管合作协议来实现。

一、国际证监会组织

国际证监会组织（International Organization of Securities Commissions，IOSCO）是证券监管领域最重要的国际组织。IOSCO 成立于 1983 年，总部设在西班牙马德里。同巴塞尔委员会一样，IOSCO 为非政府国际组织，且不具备任何凌驾于国家之上的正式监管特权。IOSCO 通过其下设的多个委员会在推进证券监管的全球性多边合作与协调方面发挥了重要的作用。

根据 IOSCO 章程的规定，该组织的宗旨是：证券监管机构共同合作，确保从国内市场和国际层次更好地监管市场，以保持公正和有效的市场；根据各自的经验交换信息，以促进国内市场的发展；共同努力设定标准和建立对国际证券交易的有效监管；相互间提供协助，通过有力地执行各项标准和对违规的有效监管来确保市场的完善。

自成立以来，IOSCO 采取了一系列卓有成效的措施来推进国际证券监管的合作与协调，从而实现其宗旨。首先，IOSCO 及其各个委员会通过、制定、发布了一系列有关国际证券监管的决议、标准、准则、原则、建议、指南和报告等，为国际证券市场提供了统一的监管标准、原则与方法；其次，ISOCO 为打击国际证券与期货领域的各种违法犯罪行为制定了有关准则和指南，并推动各国和地区联合打击这些违法犯罪行为，对抑制和惩治证券期货欺诈违法犯罪活动的国际合作起到了巨大的推动促进作用；最后，ISOCO 通过进行发放调查问卷、制定供各会员进行自我评估而使用的评估标准等措施，监督其会员执行 IOSCO 的决议、标准、准则等；同时，对不执行上述决议、准则、标准等的会员进行道义上的劝导（moral suasion），敦促其予以执行。[①]

二、中国的监管

中国《证券法》规定，“国务院证券监督管理机构可以和其他国家或地区的证券监管机构建立监督管理合作机制，实施跨境监督管理”。在这一立法授权之下，中国证监会采用多种途径和方式，对外开展证券监管的国际合作。

从双边跨境合作来看，中国证监会自1992年成立以来，便积极开展与境外的证券监管机构之间的交流与合作。迄今为止，中国证监会已与美国、日本、英国、法国、德国等多个国家和地区的证券监管机构签署了证券监管合作谅解备忘录。

从多边国际监管合作来看，中国既开展了证券监管的区域性合作，如参加亚太经济合作组织，同时在全球性多边合作方面也有重大举措，如参加了IOSCO。尤其是，中国已加入IOSCO《关于磋商、合作和信息交流多边谅解备忘录》，这即意味着中国与所有多边谅解备忘录的成员同时签订了多个高标准的双边监管合作谅解备忘录。

三、案例资料

2009年12月24日，大公国际资信评估有限公司（下称大公）向美国证券交易委员会即SEC提交了注册成为“国家认可的统计评级组织”（NRSRO）[②]的申请。2010年9月22日，SEC发布裁定书，以“大公目前似乎无法遵守联邦证券法关于记录保留、文件制作以及检查的要求”为由，拒绝了大公的申请。

SEC拒绝大公注册申请的主要理由在于，SEC认为，大公能否遵守SEC的相关规定在一定程度上受限于其必须遵守中国国内法律和规定的义务，因此大公不能完全按照SEC的要求提供相关文件以供检查，SEC对大公履行监管职责存在障碍。

大公在申请中提出，采取监管互助形式能够解决SEC提出的监管问题，即由SEC首先将文件需求清单提交给中国证监会，然后中国证监会将代表SEC收集所需文件。

对于大公的提议，SEC指出，尽管其承认与非美国金融监管者合作进行跨境监管和证券法执行的重要性，但是中美之间关于证券监管合作的相关协议均没有涉及对受监管机构的跨境监管和检查的合作问题。尤其是这些协议并未考虑允许接触境外非公开监管信息或就境外的受监管机构进行现场检查的合作问题，而是关注于培训和技术协助、疑似违反法律情况的资料共享以及有关共同监管问题的解决方法的讨论。无论如何，目前

---

① 邱永红. 国际证监会组织（IOSCO）若干法律问题研究. 经济法学评论，2006，6.

② 国家认可的统计评级组织，英文全称“Nationally Recognized Statistical Rating Organizations”，是指经美国证券交易委员会批准注册的信用评级机构，美国证券交易委员会允许其他金融企业将其发布的信用评级用于特定的监管目的。截至目前，仅有10家信用评级机构获此资格。

的协议无法授权一国监管者代表另一国监管者履行监管职责。

对 SEC 的决定，大公难以接受。大公发布声明，指出：“跨境监管”事关国家主权，可以通过国家间监管部门协商或国际通行的“监管互助”解决，大公申请美国评级资质完全是一种市场行为，美证交会不应该把两者挂钩并以此为由拒绝大公的申请。[①]SEC 对此的回应是，SEC 承认不同公司可能会受到不同国家多个监管部门的监管。正因为如此，SEC 有相关的协议安排，来促进 SEC 与外国对等监管部门之间的监管信息交流，并允许外国注册公司的每一个监管部门能够实施跨境考察。每一个协议安排都承认保护监管机构的利益，包括保持其监管市场的完整性，并监管该市场中的参与者。对于大公而言，在现有条件下 SEC 无法完全实现对其监管检查。[②]

对监管对象实施跨境监管，是国际证券监管中的一项重要议题。由于涉及国家主权问题，在没有相关协议安排的情况下，一国的证券监管机构无权对监管对象进行跨境监管。要实现跨境监管，需要两国政府通过谈判达成相关监管合作的协议。在监管合作机制缺乏的情况下，一国的证券从业机构要进入他国的市场，将会遇到重重障碍。

Order Denying Application for Registration as a Nationally Recognized Statistical Rating Organization

Rel. No. 62968 / September 22, 2010

Admin. Proc. File No. 3-13860

I

Section 15E of the Securities Exchange Act of 1934 and related rules prescribe the process by which credit rating agencies may apply to the Commission for registration as Nationally Recognized Statistical Rating Organizations (“NRSROs”) and the requirements to which NRSROs must adhere if they become so registered. On December 24, 2009, Dagong Global Credit Rating Co., Ltd. (“Dagong”), a credit rating agency located in the People’s Republic of China (“China”), submitted an application for registration as an NRSRO. Exchange Act Section 15E(a) (2) (A) requires the Commission, not later than ninety days after a rating agency furnishes its application for NRSRO registration, to either grant that application or institute proceedings to determine whether the request should be denied.

---

① 声明全文可见大公国际资信评估有限公司网站.［2011-11-12］. http://www.dagongcredit.com/dagongweb/zx/show.php?id=1617&table=web_zxzx.

② 吴晓鹏. 大公国际在美申请评级遭拒，将针对美证交会发起法律反击. 21 世纪经济报道，2010-10-01（01）.

On April 14, 2010, we issued an order instituting proceedings to determine whether Dagong's application should be denied. In that order, we directed the parties to submit briefs addressing issues of law or fact in dispute and noted that the possible grounds for denial included: (1) whether Dagong has sufficient connection with U.S. interstate commerce to register as an NRSRO and invoke our regulatory and oversight authority; and (2) whether Dagong, if registered as an NRSRO, would be unable to comply with those provisions of the federal securities laws and rules that require registrants to create and maintain certain records that are subject at any time to Commission examination and that must be furnished to the Commission upon request. Dagong and the Commission's Division of Trading and Markets (the "Division") have submitted briefs in response to that order, and each attached several documents in support of its position. Neither party objected to any documents submitted by the other. Having considered all these submissions, we find that we must deny Dagong's application because, irrespective of the jurisdictional question, it does not appear possible at this time for Dagong to comply with the recordkeeping, production, and examination requirements of the federal securities laws.

II

A. Dagong's application for NRSRO status

Dagong was formed in 1994 and is the largest credit rating agency in China. Dagong is headquartered in Beijing and has more than two dozen branch offices throughout China, but it currently has no office in the United States. Dagong is licensed to operate as a credit rating institution by the China Securities Regulatory Commission ("CSRC") and is subject to its oversight, rules, and regulations. Dagong represents that it rates the credit of several Chinese companies that are listed on stock exchanges in the United States and that several American companies have used Dagong's Web site to consult its ratings.

B. OIA's efforts to clarify the CSRC's position with respect to the Commission's ability to inspect Dagong's records

At the request of the Division, the Commission's Office of International Affairs ("OIA") exchanged several letters with the CSRC from March to May 2010, inquiring about Dagong's ability to comply with the federal securities laws and regulations applicable to NRSROs. First, on March 10, 2010, OIA wrote a letter to the CSRC explaining that NRSROs are required by applicable laws and regulations to (1) allow Commission staff to conduct on-site reviews of the firm's books and records; (2) produce to Commission staff copies of the firm's books and records; and (3) furnish such reports as Commission staff deems necessary. The letter asked the CSRC to confirm that, under domestic Chinese law, Dagong would be able to comply with these requirements.

By letter dated March 26, 2010, the CSRC responded that the issue of on-site visits for examination of an NRSRO would require an arrangement between the Commission and the CSRC after the CSRC resolved an issue regarding the inspection of Chinese accounting firms by the Public Company Accounting Oversight Board ("PCAOB"). The CSRC's response did not address OIA's questions about the production of documents and reports.

On April 14, 2010, OIA responded to the CSRC, pointing out that the CSRC's March 26 letter was silent on the issue of whether Dagong would be able to provide documents to the Commission in response to requests. OIA also noted that it had informed the Division that the CSRC had been unable to confirm that Dagong would, under Chinese law, be able to produce directly to the Commission information it required as part of its ongoing supervision and regulation of an NRSRO. The CSRC responded by letter on May 10, 2010, stating that, because Dagong did not conduct any significant business in the United States, the CSRC "[did] not see any short-term necessity" for the Commission to conduet on-site inspections or review Dagong's "working papers." The CSRC reiterated its position that the resolution of issues arising from Dagong's NRSRO application were contingent upon resolving its concerns with the PCAOB about the inspection of Chinese accounting firms.

C. Dagong's view of its ability to comply with applicable law

At the request of Division staff during its consideration of Dagong's application, Dagong submitted a letter on March 10, 2010, expressing its intention to comply with the rules and regulations applicable to an NRSRO if it were to be so designated. In that letter, Dagong's president acknowledged that Dagong, as an NRSRO, would be subject to the document production provisions of Exchange Act Section 17 (b) and related rules. The letter explained that Dagong would make a "good-faith effort" to comply with those rules, subject to the requirements of Chinese law:

> Dagong intends to make a good-faith effort to comply with such rules and to produce such documents for examination and inspections as may be requested by the Commission, subject, however, to Dagong's compliance with the laws, rules and regulations of the People's Republic of China and the [CSRC] or such other appropriate Chinese regulatory authority.

In its opening brief, Dagong explained how the Commission would have access to Dagong's records in practice: "The Commission shall send the required document list first to the CSRC, and then the CSRC will collect the documents on behalf of the Commission." The documents would then be translated, Dagong noted. Dagong further explained that the document production would be subject to provisions in Chinese law that prohibit the disclosure of documents containing "state secrets or [information of] vital interest to relevant securities companies" without approval from the CSRC, China's State Archives Administration, the Administration for the Protection of State Secrets, or "other relevant authorities."

III

A. Applicable law

Exchange Act Sections 15E(a) (2) (C) (ii) (II), 15E(d), and 15 (b) (4) (D) provide that we must deny a credit rating agency's application for NRSRO status if the applicant would be subject to having its registration suspended or revoked because it is "unable to comply" with any provision of the securities laws and related rules. Among other things, Dagong must be able to comply with provisions in the Exchange Act and related rules that pertain to the Commission's examination of Dagong's records and Dagong's obligation to produce information to the Commission.

Exchange Act Section 17 (b) (1) provides, in relevant part, that "all records" of NRSROs (as well as national securities exchanges, broker-dealers, and certain other regulated entities) are subject at any time, or from time to time, to such reasonable periodic, special, or other examinations by representatives of the Commission... as the Commission... deems necessary or appropriate in the public interest, for the protection of investors, or otherwise in furtherance of the purposes of [the Exchange Act].

In addition, Exchange Act Rule 17g-2 requires NRSROs to create and retain certain records, including, for example, records regarding the identities of credit analysts who participate in ratings; the identities of persons paying for the ratings; compliance reports; internal audit plans and reports and supporting documentation; credit analysis reports ("including non-public information and work papers, used to form the basis for the opinions expressed in these reports"); and external and internal communications relating to the NRSRO's initiation, determination, maintenance, change, or withdrawal of a credit rating. The rule also provides that NRSROs "must promptly furnish the Commission or its representatives with legible, complete, and current copies, and, if specifically requested, English translations" of those records required by rule to be created and maintained.

B. Dagong's proposal for inspection and production of documents and reports is too restrictive to comply with securities laws and rules

Dagong's management represented that it "intends to make a good-faith effort" to comply with the recordkeeping and production requirements applicable to NRSROs but acknowledged that the extent of its compliance would be potentially limited by its concurrent obligation to comply with domestic laws and regulations. We credit Dagong's statement that it intends to make a sincere effort to comply with our oversight requirements. However, on the record before us, it appears that Dagong would not control what information would be produced to Commission staff. As an initial matter, we are unable to conclude that Dagong can comply with the recordkeeping, production, and inspection requirements of the Exchange Act because the CSRC has taken the position that it does not see "any short-term necessity" for the Commission to review Dagong's "working papers."

Moreover, we find that the process Dagong proposes for document production and inspection does not meet the requirements of Exchange Act Section 17 (b) and related rules. As Dagong explained in its brief, Commission staff must submit its document requests not to Dagong but to the CSRC, which would interpret the request, collect from Dagong those documents it deems responsive to the request, and remove any information that contains "state secrets" before sending them to the staff. However, under the Exchange Act and Rule 17g-2, the NRSRO must promptly provide complete documents to the Commission and permit our access to them. The nature of the review we must conduct—e.g., determining whether an NRSRO is following its disclosed policies for preventing misuse of material non-public information or for managing conflicts of interest—requires broad access to documents. The Exchange Act further requires the Commission to examine NRSRO records it deems necessary or appropriate in the public interest and in furtherance of the purposes of the Act.

The CSRC has stated that the Commission should "entrust" the CSRC to "implement" the Commission's oversight of Dagong, and Dagong notes that the two regulators have a common interest in overseeing Dagong's rating activities and share grounds for cooperation in that regard. It urges the Commission to permit the CSRC to administer its document production in accordance with the provisions of existing international arrangements. We recognize the critical importance of cooperation with non-U.S. financial regulators to achieve effective cross-border oversight and enforcement of securities laws. However, none of these arrangements is designed to cover cooperation in the supervision and oversight of cross-border regulated entities. In particular, the existing arrangements do not contemplate access to non-public supervisory information located abroad or cooperation in on-site inspections of regulated entities located abroad, instead focusing on training and technical assistance, information sharing in the context of a suspected violation of law, and the discussion of approaches to common regulatory issues. In any event, the existing arrangements do not authorize the delegation of oversight responsibilities from one regulator to another.

Dagong maintains that the CSRC's role "is not an impediment to the Commission's oversight obligations" because that oversight is focused generally on whether the NRSRO has accurately disclosed information regarding its procedures and methodologies in issuing credit ratings—topics that Dagong believes would not implicate those "issu[es] of national security, confidential[ity,] and state secrets" that would trigger the CSRC to withhold information. However, Dagong does not define "state secrets" in its briefs and suggests that domestic law permits withholding information of "vital interest" to "relevant securities companies." And Dagong does not explain what, if any, mechanism would exist to inform the Commission as to what information was withheld and the basis for withholding it. That potential information vacuum undermines the purposes of the NRSRO examination requirement.

Complicating matters further is the CSRC's position that it will permit no on-site inspections of Dagong until the CSRC resolves its disagreement with the PCAOB over an analogous issue. Dagong argues that Rule 17g-2 "is intended to provide for oversight without Commission staff going to do physical plant inspections." In support of its argument, Dagong cites to the final rule release for Rule 17g-2 in which we noted that the requirement for NRSROs to produce documents to the Commission "was designed to provide a mechanism for the Commission to inspect records maintained overseas without having to travel to the location." However, although document production by NRSROs is one tool with which we fulfill our oversight obligations, nothing in Exchange Act Rule 15E or Rule 17g-2 defines document production as the exclusive means of oversight. To the contrary, as noted previously, Exchange Act Section 17 (b) (1) provides that records of NRSROs are subject to such "other examinations... as the Commission... deems necessary" and does not distinguish between foreign or domestic NRSROs.

C. Dagong's further arguments

Dagong objects to what it perceives as the inappropriate conflation of its application for NRSRO registration with the PCAOB's ability to conduct on-site inspections of registered public accounting firms that are located in China. We recognize that the regulatory frameworks for NRSROs and PCAOB member firms are distinct. The discussions between the CSRC and PCAOB, however, raised concerns for Commission staff about whether the CSRC would take a similar position with respect to examinations of NRSROs. When the staff followed up on those concerns, the position of the CSRC with respect to Dagong—i.e., that the CSRC will not currently permit Commission staff to conduct on-site inspections of Dagong and sees no immediate need for the staff to examine its records—indicated that Dagong is unable to comply with the recordkeeping, examination, and production requirements applicable to NRSROs, as we discussed above.

Dagong argues that "many Chinese companies are registered with the Commission and that they in fact provide information to the Commission on a regular basis. There is no reason to believe that an NRSRO cannot do the same." However, the ability of Chinese companies registered under other provisions of the securities laws to discharge their disclosure and reporting obligations does not bear on Dagong's ability to comply with oversight requirements applicable to NRSROs.

Dagong also argues that the Commission "must assume" that Dagong, if granted NRSRO status, "will continue to comply with requests for information" in the same way that it has supplied information in support of its NRSRO application. However, the documents required to conduct an examination are not necessarily similar in kind or content to the documents Dagong has so far submitted in support of its application and, as noted above, under the proposed framework, Dagong's supervisory authority, and not Dagong, would manage the process of identifying, collecting, and producing documents for inspection. Therefore, Dagong's prior document submissions in this matter do not establish that it could comply with the inspection and production requirements of the Exchange Act and related rules.

Dagong also suggests that the Commission should grant its application because, in the event Dagong eventually fails to comply with the securities laws, "the Commission has the power and the authority to deregister [Dagong]" at a later time. However, Section 15E does not contemplate this kind of approach. To the contrary, Section 15E requires the Commission to reject a credit rating agency's application if the agency cannot comply with the federal securities laws at the time when the Commission considers its application for registration as an NRSRO.

We must, therefore, deny Dagong's application for NRSRO status. At this time, we cannot conclude that Dagong is able to comply with the Exchange Act's recordkeeping, production, and examination requirements. Because we find that Dagong is currently unable to comply with these requirements, we do not reach the issue of whether Dagong at this time has sufficient connection with U.S. interstate commerce to register as an NRSRO and invoke our regulatory and oversight authority.

Accordingly, IT IS ORDERED that the application for registration as a Nationally Recognized Statistical Rating Organization filed by Dagong Global Credit Rating Co., Ltd., on December 24, 2009 be, and it hereby is, DENIED.

资料来源：美国证券交易委员会网站 *http://www.sec.gov/litigation/admin/2010/34-62968.pdf,* 访问日期 2011/11/12. 为节省篇幅，省略了原文中的注释。

编后语：金融法比较研究

随着全球经济的迅猛发展，世界日益全球化。其中，以资本流动全球化、金融机构全球化以及金融市场全球化为表现的金融全球化，成为不可阻挡的趋势。在这一背景之下，金融法的比较研究显得愈加重要。通过对不同国家或地区的相关金融法律制度进行横向的比较研究，对认知外国金融法律制度进而反思、改革本国金融法律制度具有重要意义。

在当今世界，美国是金融业最发达的国家，也是金融法制最为完善的国家，其先进的立法水平和健全的金融法律体系，为其金融业的发展繁荣奠定了基础。中国要进一步改革和完善金融法制，有诸多可以参考借鉴美国金融法律制度的地方。

一、比较法基础理论

比较法，更确切的称呼为比较法研究，是指通过对不同国家的法律制度进行比较进而研究法律的方法。比较法，既包括本国法和外国法之间的比较，也包括不同外国法之间的比较，但最终的落脚点还是本国法：通过对不同法律制度的比较研究，最终为理解和改进本国法律制度服务。

比较法在形式上包括宏观比较和微观比较。宏观比较，即通过对不同的法律秩序的精神和样式及其通常使用的思想方法和操作方法相互比较；微观比较，比较的是各个具体的法律制度或者法律问题，比较那些在不同的法律秩序中用以解决某一具体问题或利益冲突的规则。通过横向的比较研究，能够非常生动明了地展示各种法律秩序已经发展出的关于具体问题的各种类型的解决办法，为批判性地观察这些解决办法及将本国的解决办法同它们进行比较衡量提供工具。

比较法研究，对于一国的法制发展，是非常有帮助的。通过比较法研究可以刺激本国法律秩序的不断批判，这种批判对本国法的发展所作的贡献比局限在本国国内进行的“教条式的议论”要大得多。比较法有几项特殊的实践功能：比较法的研究成果可以为立法者提供参考资料，立法者可以批判性地借鉴外国对于某一个问题的法律解决方法；比较法有助于增进对本国法律制度的了解，同时可用于辅助解释本国法律规范；最后，比较法作为实证主义、教条主义和狭隘民族主义的对立面，在法学教育层面，给法学界人士开阔视野从而更深入地认识和研究本国法律铺垫了基础。

比较法的研究，通常包括三个阶段：首先，搜集外国法的资料，深入了解外国相关法律制度；其次，利用搜集的资料与本国相关法律制度进行深入比较，寻找其中的异同；最后，对通过比较获得的结果进行批判性评价。尤其是批判性评价，显得尤为重要。如果只是简单了解外国相关法律制度的规定或者只是简单地把本国与外国的法律的共性和差异加以罗列，是不会有很多收获的。应对所有材料进行深入细致的比较，同时，不能仅限于对法律条文的比较，而应注意分析这些法律与社会、经济、政治、文化等各种因素的相互作用，最终作出恰当的分析和评价。

二、中美金融法的比较研究

金融业是现代经济的核心，在国民经济中处于牵一发而动全身的地位。因此，各国政府对发展本国金融业都非常重视。

金融业的繁荣发展，离不开健全的金融法律体系和完善的金融监管体制。中国现代金融业的发展不过三十多年的时间，尚处于金融业发展的初始阶段。目前，尽管中国已经初步建立了相对完备的金融法律体系及与金融业发展相适应的监管机制，但存在的问题也是不少的：首先，金融法律体系虽已初步形成但还存在空白领域，例如，存款保险制度仍然迟迟未能建立，金融机构市场退出制度仍未推出以及私募基金、产业基金还没有取得相应的法律地位等。其次，对投资者、金融消费者利益保护不足。再次，金融监管机构权限过大，对金融市场干预过多；此外，对金融机构的创新权利限制过严，抑制了金融业的进一步发展。最后，司法体制对金融业发展的保障作用尚未完全发挥。[①]总之，中国金融法制及监管体系还有很大的改革和完善的空间。对此，美国的一些成熟的做法和经验可供中国参考借鉴，因此进行中美金融法的比较研究，具有非常重要的实践意义。

本教材以中美金融法律制度的比较研究为切入点，在每个章节（第九章除外）均分别对中国和美国相关金融法律制度进行讲解，为读者进行中美金融法的比较研究提供素材。在阅读本教材之时，读者可以重点从以下三个方面展开比较研究：

第一，立法理念的比较，这属于宏观层面的比较。从整体上把握中美两国金融立法的指导理念、逻辑及哲学以及由此对相关金融法律制度产生的影响，深入发掘两国差异背后的原因，包括历史的、政治的、经济的以及文化的原因等。例如，美国是一个崇尚自由主义的国家，在金融领域也不例外，金融自由主义表现为政府对金融业的干预相对较少；而中国是一个强调政府管制的国家，政府对金融业的监管较严。因此，在金融法律制度安排上，美国多强调金融市场主体自身的作用，而中国多强调政府监管部门的监管。由此，中美在金融法律制度的构建方面有着相互借鉴的地方。此外，在经历 2008 年金融危机之后，美国对金融监管法律体系进行了全面的改革。美国的金融监管改革的

---

① 胡滨，全先银．法治视野下的中国金融发展——中国金融法治化进程、问题与展望．财贸经济，2009（5）．